Helping Children with Down Syndrome Communicate Better

Speech
and
Language Skills
for
Ages 6-14

Libby Kumin, Ph.D., CCC-SLP

Woodbine House ◆ 2008

Dedicated to

Dr. Herbert and Berniece Kumin, my parents,
who taught me that using knowledge
to make the world a better place
is a worthy goal

Dr. Jonathan Lazar, my son,
who infuses every day and every experience
with joy and sunshine

Published in the United States of America by Woodbine House, Inc., 6510 Bells Mill Rd., Bethesda, MD 20817. 800-843-7323. www.woodbinehouse.com

Library of Congress Cataloging-in-Publication Data

Kumin, Libby.
  Helping children with Down syndrome communicate better : speech and language skills for ages 6 - 14 / Libby Kumin. -- 1st ed.
     p. cm.
  Includes bibliographical references and index.
  ISBN 978-1-890627-54-6
  1. Children with mental disabilities--Education (Elementary) 2. Down syndrome. 3. Communicative competence in children. 4. Verbal ability in children. I. Title.
  LC4603.3.K86 2008
  371.92'8--dc22

                                                                                        2008026312

Manufactured in the United States of America

10 9 8 7 6 5 4 3 2 1

Table of Contents

Compliments of

**Northern
New England
Down Syndrome Congress**
P.O. Box 1234
Concord, NH 03302-1234
(603) 622-6904

Acknowledgements

Life is a journey. When I started working with infants and toddlers with Down syndrome and their families, my life changed for the better. This is my fifth publication with Woodbine House, beginning with the original 1994 book titled *Communication Skills in Children with Down Syndrome*.

I have learned so much and I have had the privilege of sharing my knowledge and experience with many families through books, conferences, and consultations. As your children grew, so did my quest for information, theories, and practical day-to-day suggestions that could also help older children, adolescents, and adults with Down syndrome and their families. I have seen many positive changes in the quality of life for people with Down syndrome and knowing that I have been a part of making those changes happen is deeply satisfying. There is still a great deal to be done to ensure that people with Down syndrome, at all ages, are able to communicate and live a fulfilling life, and I intend to continue to work for that goal. Currently, I am working on issues related to communication, speech intelligibility, technology, employment, and adult life.

Many people have helped me in my work. My parents, Dr. Herbert and Berniece Kumin, are and have always been people who use their knowledge to make the world a better place for all people. My son, Dr. Jonathan Lazar, is a source of great joy. His dedication to his family and friends, and his enthusiasm for his work and for living life is inspiring. Loyola College in Maryland (soon to become Loyola University) has been my professional home since 1976. From the early days of the Loyola University Columbia Speech and Language Center, I have worked side by side with Cheryl Mazaika Councill and Mina Silesky Goodman. Together, we have grown along with the families we have served, and developed ideas and practical strategies that are now used in clinical settings around the world. I value their knowledge, experience, hard work, and friendship.

My editor at Woodbine House, Susan Stokes, and I have worked together since 1993. Susan asks the questions that the readers want to know and ensures that my books are understandable and practical. She has keen intellect, and practical experience. I value her collaboration. Thanks also to Brenda Ruby, Fran Marinaccio, and Beth Binns at Woodbine House for their help at all stages of the publishing process.

There are many colleagues whose knowledge and commitment I value. I have been involved with colleagues and with families through national Down syndrome organizations and local and regional parent organizations. The parents and staff in these organizations work tirelessly, and the result has been a better world for all of us. The annual conferences of the National Down Syndrome Congress with the dances, concerts, and celebration of community are high points of the year for me. Thanks to Jessica Pearsall, for her friendship and for the many stories, IEP experiences, and insights we have shared as Alex and Austin grow. Thanks to Jay, Janis, and Melissa Silverman and Marilyn Miceli and Jason Kaufman, who have been there since the beginning of the Columbia Speech and Language Center.

There are many parents who have shared their experiences with me, and have been an important part of this journey. We talk together at conferences, at meetings, in restaurants, and in daily life as our paths cross. There are too many to name, but I want you to know that I value the time that we have spent together and intend to continue on the journey with you.

CHAPTER 1

Communication, Language, and Speech

In daily life, we send and receive messages in many different ways. When we are standing at the bakery counter in the supermarket, and the clerk asks, "Which bread do you want?" we can respond verbally or nonverbally. We can point to the bread, or we can say "I want the cinnamon raisin bread." Both are effective ways to communicate. When a car pulls up next to our car, and the driver asks which way to the expressway, we can point to the right or we can say "Go right." Both are effective ways of communicating.

But, in some situations, one type of communication works better. What if we want the bread to be sliced? We can't just point to the slicing machine unless it is right near us. Or what if we want a darker, more well-baked loaf? Telling the clerk

will be most effective. How about when we are at a picnic, and our friends are too far away to hear us? Speaking or even shouting may not be the best way to communicate. In that situation, we may want to use a gesture to communicate "come over here." How about when we are in a darkened movie theater, and we want to go out to get some popcorn? We will whisper in our friend's ear, because he would not be able to see us gesture in the dark. At school, whispering may be permissible in some situations but not in others. Speaking may only be allowed after a student raises his hand and is recognized by the teacher. Different situations call for different ways of communicating.

People use the terms *language, speech,* and *communication* all of the time. They often use the terms interchangeably. But, the words really have very distinct meanings. An individual may have far greater skills in one area than the other. For example, an actor who is deaf may eloquently and artistically use sign language, but may have great difficulty speaking. Also, one system may be more appropriate to the situation than other systems. For example, when you are listening to someone who is blind, it makes no sense to nod your head to let the speaker know that you are listening. You need to say "uh-huh" or use other verbal means of showing that you are listening. When you are listening to someone on the phone, you also need to say something to let the speaker know that you are listening. When you are listening to someone who is deaf speak, it makes more sense to nod your head to show that you are listening.

Some people are equally skilled in communication, language, and speech. When we watch a television news anchor or a talk show host, we see fairly equal skills in all three areas. The person delivering the news is an excellent communicator. He or she gets their message across clearly. They have good eye contact and gestures that support the words that they are saying. Their language is superb (after all, they have a staff of writers!) and eloquent. Their speech is clear, and everything they say can be easily understood. For the rest of us, skills may differ greatly among the three areas.

Having a clear grasp of the differences among communication, speech, and language is important for anyone who wants to understand the abilities of children with Down syndrome and the ways that a specific child with Down syndrome can best communicate with others. That is because children with Down syndrome do not progress at the same speed as they are developing skills in the three areas. Furthermore, once their skills are developed in adolescence or adulthood, they still usually do not have the same skill levels in the three areas.

By focusing on the differences among communication, language, and speech, you and the speech-language pathologist (SLP) can evaluate your child's skills in each area. Then, you can figure out how to help him improve his skills in the areas that are problematic for him.

What Is Communication?

Communication is the process by which one person formulates and sends a message to another person, who then receives and decodes the message. Communication is a large, all-encompassing term; it includes language and speech. Most hearing adults would say that they communicate primarily through speech, but they actually also use many gestures, facial expressions, body postures, and tones of voice to get their messages across. In fact, researchers have found that in most daily interactions, the nonverbal cues (such as a scowl or a smile) and vocal inflections (such as anger or fear in the voice) carry the meaning of the message more than the words themselves. So, if I say, "That's a great idea" with a scowl on my face and sarcasm in my voice, the listener will assume that I do not think the idea is a good one. The listener will trust my voice and facial expressions more than the words.

Communication is *holistic*. That is, it is more than the sum of its parts. To understand the meaning of a message, you need to pay attention not only to what is said, but also to how it is said. Communication is colored by factors such as how close I stand to you, whether I shrug my shoulders, whether I look confident or defeated, how my voice sounds, and whether I am smiling, smirking, or scowling.

There are many different forms of communication systems. We can communicate through sign language, facial expressions, gestures such as pointing, Morse code, and text message or instant message abbreviations such as SNF (so not fair) or CUL8R (see you later). The clothing that we choose to wear may communicate a message—for instance, a police uniform communicates authority. Different cultures may send different messages through their nonverbal and verbal communication. For example, all cultures have a facial expression such as smiling, but the situations when it is appropriate to use the expression may vary from one culture to another. In some cultures, it is appropriate to smile at a funeral. In other cultures, people look sad and do not smile.

What Is Language?

When people communicate, they usually use some kind of symbolic code or language. That is, they do not use the actual objects to relay a message. Instead, they use symbols to represent those objects. When they are talking about their pet dog, they do not hold up the dog; they use the word "dog." *Language* is a structured, arbitrary system of symbols used to communicate about the objects, relations, and events within a culture. It is a shared code that is understood by the members of a language

community, and that infants learn within their native language community. People learn language through social interaction, and we must *learn* language, because language is an arbitrary code. Through our experiences and the words that we hear, we learn to connect specific words with specific objects.

We see people with something on their head covering their hair, and if we are in an English speaking environment, we learn that the head covering is called a hat. If our environment is French speaking, we would learn to call it a chapeau. If we are in Mexico, we might learn the word sombrero. These words refer to the same object. There is no innate "hatness" in the object. Why do we call a telephone a telephone or phone? And how do we know the difference between a phone and a cellular phone? When I was growing up, every girl wanted a princess phone—an oval shaped table phone, often in pink. Girls growing up today probably would not be familiar with the term princess phone. Words are all arbitrary symbols. There is no intrinsic "telephone-ness." We call it a telephone because that is what we have been taught and because everyone in our language community understands what we mean when we say "telephone." We could call it a communication machine, but no one would know what we mean.

We use the words in our language in order to be understood. Once we know the meaning of a word and the concept that word represents, then we learn more specific terms that are within that concept. For example, once we know that a hat is an English word for head covering, then we begin to learn the differences between various types of hats such as baseball cap, helmet, and bonnet. And new words are constantly being added to language to describe new events, people, places, and things that occur. So, we now know what a *shuttle launch* means or what *to google* means.

Children learn many vocabulary words, but they also need to learn how to combine those words into phrases and sentences. They need to learn the rules of the language such as how to make a declarative sentence into a question ("It's light outside" and "Is it light outside?") or a positive into a negative ("I want to go" and "I don't want to go"). Children also learn how to modify word meanings using prefixes and suffixes and morphological markers—for example, we say "one shoe," but "two shoes" and "they played yesterday" but "they will play tomorrow." There are different rules in different languages for sequencing words to modify the meaning. For example, in Spanish, "Ana's bike" would be "la bicicleta de Ana." The word order would have the noun followed by the descriptor. "Pepe's green shirt" would be "la camisa verde de Pepe." In French, the word order is similar to Spanish, but different than English. In French, "le chapeau de Jean" would literally mean the hat of John, but would be equivalent to the English, "John's hat." Word endings and parts of words are called *morphology* and word order and sentence formulation are known as *syntax*. Usually the terms are combined, and the structure of language is known as *morphoyntax*.

RECEPTIVE VS. EXPRESSIVE LANGUAGE

Using language involves both receiving and understanding messages and formulating and sending messages. When we receive a language message and try to understand that message, we are *decoding* language. This is called **receptive language.** When we put messages together and send them, we are *encoding* language. This is called **expressive language.**

One of the ways of encoding and expressing language is through speech. Other ways of expressing language are through sign language, pointing to words or pictures on a communication board, writing, or formulating written messages on a computer. One of the ways we receive and understand a message is through listening, but other ways are through reading or through decoding sign language by watching the signer.

Different ways of receiving and sending messages are sometimes referred to as *channels,* so we may talk about the auditory channel or the visual channel. Children with Down syndrome usually learn more easily through the visual channel—that is, through reading and visual demonstrations—than through the auditory channel—that is, through listening and oral instructions. Children with Down syndrome are usually more advanced in receiving and understanding language messages than they are in encoding and producing language messages. In other words, their receptive language abilities are usually better than their expressive language abilities.

What Is Speech?

*S*peech is verbal language, or the process of producing voice and sounds and combining them into words to communicate. Speech makes it possible to be very specific when communicating. For hearing people, it is easier to know what someone wants when he uses speech. For instance, you understand what your child means more easily when he says "Let's go for pizza" or "Let's go to the mall" rather than when he points outside or points to the car. When he is able to order pepperoni pizza with a well-done crust, you know exactly what he wants. Speaking sends a more specific and easily decodable message than pointing does.

Speech is a difficult system to learn and use. Speech involves strength, coordination, and timing of precise muscle movements. Speaking also involves the coordination of many brain centers to formulate and then produce the spoken message. It is the most neurologically and physiologically complex of the communication systems. To be useful in daily living, speech must be easy to understand.

When we compare speech, language, and communication, speech is by far the most difficult for children with Down syndrome to use. Children with Down syndrome usually understand the concepts of communication and language very well and have the desire to communicate at an early age. Most children with Down syndrome are capable of communicating and using language many months—and sometimes even several years—before they are able to use speech.

By the early elementary school years, most children with Down syndrome are speaking. They may be using phrases, rather than long conversations. They are usually not using word markers or word endings, and have difficulty with grammar and making sentences. Their speech may be difficult to understand at this age. By late elementary school, children with Down syndrome are usually using longer sentences. Although they have articulation errors, they are usually easier to understand than they were at younger ages. They do well in social situations, but have greater difficulty with language in school, especially as it relates to following instructions and answering questions related to academic subjects.

Children with Down syndrome can have a wide variety of speech and language difficulties. Many children have extensive vocabularies but have difficulty combining words into grammatical sentences. Speech intelligibility ranges from excellent to unintelligible. The differences appear to be related to neurological function, and are especially dependent on whether the child has difficulty with combining and sequencing sounds into words, also known as childhood apraxia of speech. Some children also make extra sounds such as throat clearing or guttural noises that draw attention to themselves and interfere with communication.

By the teenage years, most adolescents with Down syndrome are using sentences and having conversations. Often, however, their conversations are short because they have difficulty knowing what to say related to a specific topics. Conversations may also seem rambling, which is related to the ability to stay on topic. Children who have had inclusion experiences, at school and/or in the community, appear to do better with language skills. Speech intelligibility often continues to be a problem, however. In the late elementary school and middle school years, fluency difficulties may add to the speech problems.

An important key to developing understandable speech is developing the *oral motor* (mouth movement) skills needed for speaking. As your child develops and matures, work on oral motor skills and speech will involve exercises and practice. Most of the work can be done at home, with the guidance and assistance of a speech-language pathologist. Most children with Down syndrome will need long-term speech-language pathology treatment during the early and later childhood years. As they improve their oral motor skills and speech planning and production skills, their speech intelligibility will improve. Research has shown that speech can continue to improve during later childhood and adolescence and adulthood. Research has also shown that even in adolescence and adulthood, treatment can be helpful and can result in improved speech.

Communication, Language, and Speech

COMMUNICATION

- Communication is holistic.
- Everyone communicates.
- Communication can have powerful effects on the environment.
- Communication may be unintentional or intentional.
- Communication includes verbal, vocal, and nonverbal messages

LANGUAGE

- Language is not innate; it is learned.
- Language is an arbitrary code that uses symbols to represent real objects and events.
- Language has rules that specify how to use the code.
- Language is used intentionally or purposefully.
- Language is a shared code.
- Children learn the language that is spoken in their community.
- Language is learned through social interaction.
- Language may include gestures, signs, pictures, and/or speech.

SPEECH

- Speech is verbal language.
- Speech uses the same systems in the body used for breathing, swallowing, and eating.
- Speech is a complex neuromotor skill.
- Speech involves muscle programming, movement, and coordination.
- Speech will develop later than language and communication.

Putting It All Together

The vast majority of children with Down syndrome eventually use all communication channels to communicate their messages. Usually from a young age, they point and gesture, use facial expressions, and pantomime. By the time they are three to four years old, they generally use at least some meaningful speech that family members can understand. By the time they are in their early teens, there will be a wide range of speaking abilities. Most adolescents speak well enough to get important messages across to familiar listeners. They use sentences and have short conversations. Some adolescents with Down syndrome speak fluently and intelligibly, and have long conversations. If the teen has other accompanying conditions such as autism and childhood apraxia of speech, these conditions will affect language and speech abilities. Language and speech skills continue to develop into adulthood for individuals with Down syndrome. Jobs, travel, hobbies, and relationships all contribute to improving language skills.

Our goal is for the child to develop language and to use speech as his primary communication system in daily living. As mentioned above, most children with Down syndrome understand and use language many months, or even years before they are able to use speech as their primary communication system. Although most will be using at least some speech by the time they enter kindergarten, many will still be struggling to make themselves understood. A small percentage of children and adolescents with Down syndrome will not develop speech that can be understood and that can support communication in school and in daily living. That is why we use sign language, communication boards, picture communication systems, and communication devices to enable the child who is having trouble getting his message across to continue to communicate with the people around them. We always use a Total Communication approach, providing speech models for the child, even when he is not yet able to use speech to answer. We want the child to continue to develop language.

Your child needs a usable communication system at every age and stage. Usually, that will be speech, but for some children at some stages, speech may need to be supplemented by assistive technology (augmentative/alternative communication AAC). For a discussion of the role of assistive technology, see Chapter 10.

While your child is developing speech, he can learn new words and concepts through language experiences. Your child can show through signs and pictures that he is understanding the language concepts. When he enters school, the language needs become more complex. Language is used for learning in all subjects, but language (language arts and reading) is also a subject that children need to learn. Language is the basis of testing in all subjects. Your child needs to use language to learn mathematics and science and social studies. Language is used to interact with many different people throughout a student's day—his parents and siblings, the school bus driver who picks him up, the children on the bus, the teacher, classroom aides, school nurse, office staff, and the administrators and the principal. Your child needs to communicate with the other children in his class and with other children at lunch and on the playground.

After school, your child might be involved in scouting or religious school, and interact with different children and adults. On vacations and family outings and community events, there is a larger community circle. Some of those people will talk with your child once; others will see your child regularly. Communication is important in many different situations each day, throughout the week, and through the seasons, holidays, and year.

The purpose of this book is to provide information and resources for parents and professionals of children aged about six to fourteen years. In children with Down syndrome in this age group, communication needs become more complex. Language needs to support the child's learning, as well as his relationships with others. He needs to be able to ask for help, and to offer help. His circle of friends and acquaintances has expanded, and he needs to be able to communicate with all of those people so that they can understand him. He needs to be able to understand what others are telling him and asking him to do. He needs to be able to evaluate what others are telling him, and to decide how to react. He needs to be able to give information, and to ask for information; to give directions, and to follow them.

In short, communication, language, and speech skills need to support your child's life. They need to help him do what he wants to do, and help him ask what he needs to ask. They need to support his life at home, in school, and in the community. This is an ambitious goal. To reach this goal, your child will need some help. The most effective help will come from your family, the people who spend the most time with your child.

If you have read *Early Communication Skills for Children with Down Syndrome*, worked with a speech-language pathologist, or attended workshops on communication skills, you probably have a good foundation for continuing to work on communication skills with your school-aged child. You realize that your child probably experiences fluctuating bouts of hearing loss, so may not always hear the words clearly. You have probably learned to emphasize certain words, and generally make the important language in the environment pop out at him. You have perhaps learned to do exercises to help strengthen his lips and tongue and jaw muscles. You may have used rehearsal and scripts to help him prepare for communication situations he will encounter. You have learned cueing systems, as needed. And you have probably learned to use your child's strong visual skills to help him learn.

Most likely, you already worked with one or more speech-language pathologists (SLPs) when your child was in early intervention or preschool special education. Most children with Down syndrome continue to need the services of an SLP in early elementary school, and many can benefit from seeing an SLP into their early teens and beyond. Your child's SLP can advise you, show you methods and activities to use at home, and coach you until you know how to help your child master a new language or speech skill. The SLP has knowledge and information regarding communication, language, and speech. She can share resources with you and translate complex concepts into understandable language.

Finding a Qualified Speech-Language Pathologist

Children with Down syndrome have risk factors that make speech and language more difficult for them. Speech and language therapy is essential for most children with Down syndrome to maximize their communication potential. Speech and language therapy (also known as speech-language pathology services) is the specialized evaluation and treatment of difficulties in communication, language, and speech. A good speech and language therapy program for a child with Down syndrome should:

1. be provided by a qualified speech-language pathologist (see the next section);
2. be individually designed for your child;
3. be comprehensive and address all areas of need;
4. use best practices—methods that have been used successfully with other children;
5. educate and include your family, so that practice is part of daily life and is not limited to therapy sessions.

WHAT MAKES A SPEECH-LANGUAGE PATHOLOGIST QUALIFIED?

Although everyone who provides speech-language therapy may be referred to as a "speech therapist," not all speech therapists are alike. There are many titles that are used, including speech therapist, language specialist, and speech teacher. Your child should receive speech therapy from someone who has earned the credentials of a "speech-language pathologist," although she may sometimes refer to herself as a "speech therapist," since that is the term the public is more familiar with.

The speech-language pathologist (SLP) should have the professional credentials Certificate of Clinical Competence in Speech-Language Pathology (CCC-SLP), awarded by the American Speech-Language-Hearing Association. To earn those credentials, SLPs must:

- complete an undergraduate and graduate level program that includes academic coursework as well as intensive supervised clinical practice with children and adults in the areas of speech, language, and hearing assessment and treatment;
- document evidence that they have mastered all required knowledge and skills in order to qualify for the speech-language pathologist credentials;
- earn a Master's degree from an accredited training program;
- pass a national certification examination, and complete a clinical fellowship training year (CFY) following graduation;
- document continuing education activities each year.

If the professional lists "CCC-SLP" following her name, you know that she has completed this rigorous professional process to attain her professional credentials, and is continuing to learn and develop as a professional.

Speech-language pathologists are generally licensed by each state and hold a state license, usually granted by the Department of Health. Three states (Colorado, Michigan, and South Dakota) do not currently have state licensure for SLPs. If you need to check whether a professional holds the CCC-SLP or the state license, you can call the professional licensing board in your state or call the American Speech-Language-Hearing Association. You can also check the ASHA website (www.asha.org) for contact information. (See the Resource Guide at the back of the book.)

Speech-language pathologists who work for a school system are required to hold the appropriate certificate from the state Department of Education, such as a license as a speech and hearing teacher, K-12. In some states, SLPs in the schools are required to hold the CCC-SLP, but in some states, they are not. Currently, twelve states require school-based SLPs to also be licensed within the state by the state regulatory board.

Some states do not require SLPs to maintain current certification by ASHA or a current state health department license. Since the dues and fees to maintain these two credentials are high, some professionals who work in schools choose not to apply for them or not to renew them and keep them current. Currently, all states in the United States except Colorado, South Carolina, and Michigan require newly hired SLPs to hold ASHA certification.

Most of the rulings requiring certification (rulings are known as universal licensure) are recent and do not apply to professionals already working in the school system. There are also rules that allow school systems to hire professionals on a temporary or emergency basis. And, some schools employ speech-language pathology assistants who help in therapy. So, you cannot be certain what credentials your child's "speech teacher" has unless you ask.

Of course, none of the credentials lets you know whether that professional has any experience in working with children with Down syndrome. All of the communication problems encountered by children with Down syndrome also occur in other children, but an inexperienced SLP may conclude that the speech problems she is observing are "part of Down syndrome" and may not realize that the difficulties are responsive to treatment. Children really benefit from the expertise of a SLP knowledgeable about the unique challenges that Down syndrome often poses. The national organization or state professional organizations do not offer information on specialty training, although the American Speech-Language-Hearing Association is beginning to develop recognition for specialties in fluency and language. You can ask the professional directly whether he or she has worked with many children with Down syndrome.

In the schools, SLPs are often assisted by an SLP-A, a speech pathology assistant or aide, also known as a communication aide. There are no national standards for SLP-A, although state licensure boards are beginning to establish guidelines for licensing credentials. As of 2008, thirty-five states regulate the use of SLP-A's. Twelve states require licensure, one state requires certification, and twenty-two states require registration. Requirements for SLP-A credentials are developed and regulated by the states. Currently, requirements range from a high school diploma and some additional experience to a bachelor's degree plus current enrollment in a Master's degree program.

The role of the SLP-A is generally to provide support for the SLP, developing materials for children in treatment and working directly on therapy exercises and activities. The SLP-A should be working under the guidance and supervision of the certified professional who is responsible for testing and planning the evaluation and treatment program. Twenty-two states define acceptable and unacceptable activities for SLP-A support personnel. Two states, Kentucky and Arkansas, restrict SLP-A's to working in school settings. The other states do not specify any restrictions and SLP-A's can work in any professional setting.

What is the best way to find an experienced professional? My feeling is that the most reliable source of information on qualified professionals experienced in working with children with Down syndrome is your local Down syndrome family support group. Parents have a strong resource network that can help you find professionals who have worked with other children with Down syndrome, who work with families, and who are well regarded by families in your community. For information on local support groups, contact the National Down Syndrome Congress, the National Down Syndrome Society, or search through websites that link to local family support groups (for instance, www.DS-health.com website has links to many local family support groups). See the Resource Guide.

HOW CAN YOUR FAMILY BE INCLUDED IN THE THERAPY PROGRAM?

The speech-language pathologist has the professional knowledge to help your child learn and improve his communication skills. However, your family (including siblings and extended family), classroom teachers, other educational specialists, occupational and physical therapists, friends, and community members also can contribute to your child's communication success. Language is part of daily living and needs to be practiced and reinforced as part of daily life. Although your child may need to learn a skill in a therapy session, communication practice must go on in the real world. That's what counts!

In our clinic, the Down Syndrome Speech and Language Center for Excellence at Loyola University in Maryland, families observe all sessions through a one-way mirror.

In some settings, parents are in the room with the child. We believe it is crucial for parents to observe or participate in sessions, since they are an important part of the communication team. They need ongoing information to help their child master language and speech skills, such as using plurals or elevating the tongue for the /t/ sound. Children (and even most teens) do not remember what they need to work on once they leave a therapy session, and therefore will not get the practice they need unless their parents and other adults in their daily lives are regularly informed about therapy goals and strategies.

Unfortunately, in most school settings, parents rarely, if ever, observe speech therapy sessions. They rely on reports from the speech-language pathologist, which may only occur as part of the IEP process at an annual meeting. When families are kept out of the loop like this, children and teens with Down syndrome receive little, if any, benefit from their speech-language therapy.

Communication needs to be two-way—school-to-home and home-to- school. Here's an example to illustrate why:

> *Ian, a ten-year-old boy with Down syndrome, had a therapy session in which the SLP worked with him on learning to sequence events and to then talk about those events in the order in which they occurred. The SLP did not talk with the family before this session. After the session, she sent home a note saying that Ian had great difficulty with the activity she had chosen to work on sequencing—namely, making a tuna fish sandwich. Ian's mother responded that they never ate tuna fish and that her son was therefore unfamiliar with making a tuna salad sandwich. She suggested more familiar activities, such as making pizza in the microwave or Ian's morning grooming activities. Clearly, if the SLP had sent a brief note home before the session, it would have resulted in a more useful and successful activity for Ian.*

Both SLPs and parents need ongoing information to help children learn speech and language skills, practice those skills, and generalize the skills mastered so that children will actually use those skills in daily life. In Chapters 5 and 6, we will discuss how families can participate in speech and language treatment for older children.

Conclusion

Communication, speech, and language are complex. As children with Down syndrome enter elementary school and progress through the grades, they confront more complex language needs. They need to develop conversational skills, and need to improve speech intelligibility so that a wider, less familiar circle of people in school and in the community can comprehend them. The need for comprehension and the ability to understand and follow instructions grows as your child grows and negotiates his way in the larger world. There is a lot to share and a lot to learn. Let's get started.

CHAPTER 2

Speech and Language Skills in School-Aged Children with Down Syndrome

When he is at home, six-year-old Kyle understands what his parents say, and follows directions very well. But, when he is at school where there is background noise, he has difficulty following instructions and sometimes runs and hides under the desk. The teacher says he has a behavior problem.

Devon, age 8, is a good reader, but when he is asked the names of his brother and sister, he struggles to say their names. He can point to their photos in a photo album. When his mom wrote the names under the photos, Devon was able to read their names, but he can't consistently say their names. When he wants to call his brother at home, he says "bo" for bro. For his sister, he says "Ti" for Tina.

Sometimes Lila, age 9, can say a whole sentence really well, but then she never says that sentence again. When her mother tries to get Lila to repeat words, Lila has great difficulty. She often ends up running out of the room in tears. Her mother says, "I feel that she can do better, but she doesn't try."

Ten-year-old Allen has excellent social skills. Whenever guests come to his home, he introduces everyone to each other, remembering all of the names correctly and saying the names clearly. But, when he tries to tell his parents about something that happened at school, he isn't able to relay what happened, who was involved, and why he is upset. This is frustrating for Allen and his parents.

Brian's speech has always been difficult to understand. In fourth grade, he began to withdraw from social situations. Brian was trying very hard but a combination of weak facial muscles, difficulty with sequencing sounds, and stuttering made his speech very difficult to understand. Brian was evaluated for an augmentative and alternative communication (AAC) device. Once he learned to use the system, he was able to communicate better at home and at school. The system has a speech synthesizer that "talks" electronically for Brian, once he formulates the message. He started interacting more with other children and joined a sports fan club at school.

Jennifer, age thirteen, has age-appropriate language comprehension and reading skills. She has an extensive vocabulary and speaks in long, grammatically correct sentences. Although others rarely have any trouble understanding her speech, she sometimes speaks too loudly or too quickly and her speech can sound slightly robotic—the rise and fall and cadence of her speech seem a little "off." People sometimes focus on how Jennifer talks, and are not listening to what she is trying to communicate.

Michelle is a fourteen-year-old who loves to talk and has a lot to say. She talks with friends on the phone, and with her sister at college. She also keeps in touch using email. She loves shopping and crafts, and is in jewelry making and baking clubs in her local community. Sometimes her conversations are rambling and go on and on, changing topics frequently. Although Michelle is very social and communicative, she doesn't always pick up on cues that her listeners are getting tired of a conversation or are having trouble following her.

Since you are reading a book about Down syndrome, you probably deduced that all of the children described above have Down syndrome. You undoubtedly also noticed that they each have at least some difficulties with speech and/or language, although their communication abilities vary a great deal. This underscores the fact that there is no one "Down syndrome profile" when it comes to communication skills.

There is a wide range of communication abilities in school-aged children with Down syndrome. Some children and adolescents with Down syndrome have excellent language comprehension skills, are able to process, integrate, and formulate language messages, and have speech that is easy to understand. Other children may have difficulty understanding more complex messages and instructions in school, but do better in the home and community, where less formal language is used and there are more contextual (environmental) clues. Some children have great difficulty with comprehension of auditory information, but respond well to written or picture instructions. Others have speech that is very difficult to understand. Most have a combination of speech and language challenges.

Research has confirmed what my clinical experience has shown: Children with Down syndrome often have more difficulty with speech and language than would be expected at their cognitive level. Within the channels of communication, people with Down syndrome almost always understand more than they can express. That is, their receptive language and comprehension is more advanced than their expressive

language. The output modalities—speech and writing—are more difficult for children with Down syndrome than the input modalities— comprehension and reading.

Why do children with Down syndrome have difficulty with speech and language? What do we know and what can we do to help children communicate? Over the past 25 years, we have learned a great deal about the speech, language, and communication skills of children with Down syndrome. This chapter will review some of the most important information that researchers have found about the types and causes of communication skill difficulties in children with Down syndrome. Note that this research was mostly gathered by studying children who have trisomy-21 (which is the case for about 95 percent of people with Down syndrome).

There is very little information on the speech and language characteristics of children with mosaic or translocation Down syndrome. In my clinical experience, however, children with these rarer types of Down syndrome have a wide range of communication abilities. They often share some of the same challenges with communication skills that children with trisomy-21 do, but may have milder symptoms. Some children with mosaic Down syndrome whom I have evaluated have only mild hesitations and fluency difficulties or mild speech intelligibility problems. Others have language profiles that are more similar to children with learning disabilities. Generally, they have the same communication strengths as other children with Down syndrome.

Your child won't have all of the problems described in this chapter, but she will have some of them. Identifying which areas are difficult for your child and which affect her speech and language development is very important. Identifying your child's particular challenges is the first step in doing something about them. Speech-language pathology treatment is not a general plan where the same treatment is used for every child with Down syndrome. Treatment is always individualized and it is based on your child's strengths and challenges. Depending on your child's needs, specific techniques and information can be used to help her make maximum progress in communication development.

Relative Strengths and Weaknesses in Communication Skills

As discussed above, there is no one Down syndrome profile when it comes to communication skills. There is wide variation in speech and language development. For example, children with Down syndrome have been reported to say their first words as early as 9 months to as late as 7 years of age, and to begin combining 2 words anywhere from age 18 months to 11 years.

Research has shown, however, that the strengths and weaknesses that children with Down syndrome have almost always involve some combination of certain areas of communication. How many of these difficulties a given child has, and to what extent, varies widely.

Children with Down syndrome usually do not develop at the same level or achieve at the same level in all language areas. This results in what speech-language pathologists refer to as an **asynchrony** of language skills—some skills are more advanced than others. Most notably, children with Down syndrome are usually better at comprehending language (receptive language skills) than at putting thoughts and ideas into words (expressive language skills). As explained below, however, there may also be other patterns of strengths and weaknesses.

RELATIVE STRENGTHS

You are probably used to hearing how your child compares with typically developing children developmentally or on tests of academic skills. For instance, SLPs and other specialists often use "norms" to determine how your child compares with the average skills level for her chronological age. So, they might report that your child is below average or is one year behind in vocabulary according to test scores. But, there is another way to describe your child's development by comparing your child to herself across various developmental areas. So, for example, you might hear that your child has a relative strength in reading compared to math. This doesn't necessarily mean that she reads on grade level or above, but that her reading stills are stronger than her math skills.

In language, pointing out relative strengths and weaknesses is sometimes known as *intralinguistic referencing*, and may involve comparing your child's language functioning in one area such as vocabulary to another area such as morphosyntax (grammar). So, the SLP might report that vocabulary is a relative strength from your eight-year-old if she scores at a seven-year-old level for vocabulary and a five-year-old level for morphosyntax (grammar). That is, compared to your child's grammar difficulties, vocabulary is a strength.

The three most common relative strengths in communication for children with Down syndrome are:

- Vocabulary;
- Pragmatics; and
- Visual learning of communication skills.

VOCABULARY

Vocabulary (semantics)—understanding the meaning of words and using them appropriately—is often an area of relative strength for children with Down syndrome. Studies have shown that children and adults with Down syndrome can continue to develop their vocabularies all their lives. The more experiences your child has, the more new words she will learn. There is no limit or ceiling to vocabulary acquisition, and the acquisition of new vocabulary words and concepts should be a focus through childhood and into adult life. There is a wide range of vocabulary level in individuals with Down syndrome. Many adolescents and adults have rich and varied vocabularies; others have more limited vocabularies.

Research has shown that for people with Down syndrome, vocabulary development is more advanced than grammatical development. The difference between vocabulary and grammatical development gets larger as children get older. That is, vocabulary gets broader and more advanced, while grammar often remains difficult.

See Chapters 4 and 5 for more information about semantics.

PRAGMATICS

Pragmatics, or the social use of language, is another area of language that is often a relative strength for children with Down syndrome. Pragmatics encompasses such skills as using social greetings appropriately and understanding the unwritten rules of conversation (for example, everybody usually doesn't speak at once, but waits their turn). With practice and experience, children with Down syndrome usually do well in these areas. Children with Down syndrome also generally learn how to formulate appropriate messages for their listeners. For example, they learn to speak to their teacher using different vocabulary and syntax structure than they would use with their two-year-old cousin.

In addition, most children with Down syndrome are skilled at the nonverbal aspects of pragmatics—for instance, using gestures and facial expressions to help people understand their messages. Other areas of pragmatics such as asking questions, requesting clarification, and staying on topic are more difficult for children with Down syndrome. With help from therapists and parents, however, they can usually make good progress in these areas. Working on social communication skills with your child is essential, as they contribute greatly to inclusion within the community. For a more detailed discussion of pragmatics, see Chapters 8 and 9.

VISUAL LEARNING

Visual learning of communication skills is also a strong suit for many children with Down syndrome. In general, children with Down syndrome are more successful at learning from watching and experiencing, using visual cues, photographs, and instructions than they are at learning through listening. In fact, research has shown that people with Down syndrome have specific difficulty with following directions and naming pictures when the stimulus is the spoken word (verbal stimulus). They have less difficulty reading the word or the instructions. For example, if the teacher says "Point to the door and the window," a child with Down syndrome will have more trouble following the instructions than if she reads an instruction to point to the door and the window.

This difficulty with auditory learning and strength in visual learning is why using signs, picture communication systems, modeling, and visual organizers are all successful strategies for helping children with Down syndrome learn. It is also why early reading experiences can help children with Down syndrome make progress in language skills (as discussed in Chapter 5).

RELATIVE WEAKNESSES

The difficulties that children with Down syndrome have with speech and language depend on the anatomical, physiological, and psychological conditions that they are dealing with in addition to Down syndrome. For example, children who have chronic middle ear fluid with resulting hearing loss tend to have language difficulties related to fluctuating hearing. Children who have tactile defensiveness (hypersensitivity to touch) around the mouth will have more difficulty with learning where to place the lips, teeth, and tongue to articulate sounds. Children who have a dual diagnosis of Down syndrome and autism spectrum disorder will probably have problems with social interaction in language (pragmatics) that other children with Down syndrome do not have. Thus, there are many possible combinations of relative strengths and weaknesses.

The difficulties that school-aged children with Down syndrome have with communication skills tend to include:

- Delays and difficulties in expressive language;
- Language skills below cognitive level;
- Expressive language below receptive language skills;
- Difficulties in morphosyntax (grammar);
- Difficulties with auditory memory;
- Difficulties with oral sensory and oral motor skills;
- Shorter phrases in speech;
- Difficulty with topicalization;
- Short conversations;
- Difficulty with clarification and repairs;
- Difficulty with requests;
- Reduced speech intelligibility;
- Childhood apraxia of speech;
- Metalinguistics.

DELAYS AND DIFFICULTIES IN EXPRESSIVE LANGUAGE

Using any modality, children with Down syndrome tend to be delayed in beginning to express themselves. By the time a child reaches age six, her language is still usually delayed to some extent, whether or not she has been using sign language or some other assistive technology to help her express herself. The delay is more noticeable in speech than in other modalities.

Some of the increasingly greater difficulties that are documented as children with Down syndrome get older are related to the fact that tests for older children rely more on language. For instance, tests for children above the third grade level assume that the child will be able to use language and reading skills to understand and answer questions on a test. The tests are supposedly testing aptitude or subject matter, but the test results will be greatly affected by the child's language abilities.

Unfortunately, people tend to judge your abilities by your expressive language. Parents often report that their older children with Down syndrome are the navigators on trips and know how to get to a favorite store or restaurant; that they often know how to work complicated electronic games and equipment; or have other useful, real world skills. If children have difficulty speaking, however, folks outside of the family and immediate circle may not believe that they have these abilities. The result is that people often underestimate the capabilities of someone with Down syndrome, and they are denied opportunities to show what they can do.

LANGUAGE BELOW COGNITIVE LEVEL

In children with Down syndrome, language level is often more impaired than would be expected based on the child's cognitive level. For example, a twelve-year-old who has the cognitive skills of a nine-year-old might have the expressive language skills of a five-year-old. In 2000, Sue Buckley, a British psychologist who extensively researches learning and development in children with Down syndrome, compared receptive and expressive language scores of children with Down syndrome with their scores on nonverbal cognitive tests. She found that vocabulary comprehension was about 1 year 6 months behind nonverbal reasoning ability, while grammar comprehension was about 2 years behind. When Buckley looked at expressive language skills, specifically sentence length and complexity in speech, she found that the teenagers were more than 3 years behind as compared to their nonverbal reasoning ability.

Another group of researchers (Abbeduto et al., 2003) compared the performance of children with Down syndrome on three nonverbal subtests on the Stanford-Binet Intelligence test (bead memory, pattern analyzing, and copying) to their receptive language, as tested on the Test for Auditory Comprehension of Language (TACL-R). They found that the children had more difficulty with receptive language skills than their nonverbal mental age would suggest. They also found that the children scored lower on the two grammar-oriented subtests of the TACL-R than on the semantics subtest. They therefore concluded that there was an asynchrony between understanding of grammar and nonverbal cognitive ability in children with Down syndrome.

RECEPTIVE-EXPRESSIVE LANGUAGE GAP

Children with Down syndrome usually can understand language more easily than they can express themselves. This results in an asynchrony of receptive and expressive language skills, also known as a "receptive-expressive gap." For example, an eight-year-old who has the receptive language skills of a typical seven-year-old may have only the expressive skills of a typical four-year-old.

This gap may be a problem if people who do not know your child well assume that she knows less than she does because she has trouble verbally responding to questions. At home, too, you might assume that your child doesn't understand what you say if she pauses before responding. Generally, as your child gets older, the questions she is asked become more abstract and more complex. But your child also has more life experience with age. So, the gap may appear to narrow at home, where experience helps her respond in familiar situations, but get wider in school, where language becomes more abstract and complex.

DIFFICULTIES IN MORPHOSYNTAX

Syntax is commonly referred to as grammar and refers to the order of words in a sentence and what function they serve. Morphology includes word parts (morphemes) such as prefixes and suffixes that signal structural relationships (for example, possession or past tense). Syntax and morphology are closely interrelated and they are usually studied together, so this area of language is currently known as morphosyntax.

Research has found that children with Down syndrome have more difficulties with expressive and receptive morphosyntax than do other children of the same mental age.

That is, even though an intelligence test might show that your ten-year-old is generally performing at the level of a typical seven-year-old, her morphosyntax (grammatical) skills would likely be lower than those of a typical seven-year-old. Grammar and word order are abstract, and more difficult to learn. In addition, many grammatical markers (such as the *–ed* that signals past tense or the *'s* used for possession) occur at the end of the word, are pronounced more softly, and are harder to hear. Expressive morphosyntax is the most difficult area, but researchers have found that even receptive morphosyntax presents difficulties for children with Down syndrome.

For more information on morphosyntax, including home activities, see Chapter 5. You may also wish to read some of the studies from researchers who have confirmed that grammar is a far more difficult area for children with Down syndrome than vocabulary is. For example, see these studies listed in the References: Abbeduto et al., 2003; Berglund, Eriksson & Johansson, 2001; Chapman & Hesketh, 2000; Fowler, 1995, Grela, 2002; Kumin, Councill & Goodman, 1998; Laws & Bishop, 2004; Miller, 1995; Miolo, Chapman, & Sindberg, 2005.

POOR AUDITORY MEMORY

People with Down syndrome generally have more difficulty remembering what they hear than what they see. This includes trouble remembering environmental sounds, as well as words and other verbal information. One study found that individuals with Down syndrome recalled less information than typically developing children with the same mental age when trying to remember stories and numbers read aloud (Bird and Chapman, 1994). Other researchers have suggested that children with Down syndrome have a specific verbal auditory memory deficit (Jarrolf & Baddeley, 2002; Miolo, Chapman & Sindberg, 2005; Vicari, S., Marotta, L., Carlesimo, G., 2004).

Children with Down syndrome usually have verbal memory spans that are well below those of typically developing children. For instance, children with Down syndrome tend to score poorly on the digit span tests that are often part of IQ tests (where they are asked to repeat longer and longer strings of numbers spoken by the examiner).

As discussed in later chapters, visual cues can be useful in helping children with Down syndrome remember the sounds of speech, as well as what was said.

DIFFICULTY WITH ORAL SENSORY AND ORAL MOTOR SKILLS

Oral sensory skills involve the ability to receive and process sensation in and around the mouth, including touch, perception, and feedback that help the child perceive where her tongue is in her mouth. Difficulties with these skills are discussed later in this chapter, in the section on sensory processing disorders.

Oral motor skills are the facial and oral movements used

for feeding and speaking. Difficulties in this area are related to low tone and muscle weakness in and around the mouth. Oral motor skills often improve as children with Down syndrome get older. Current best practice is to treat oral motor skill difficulties early through games and exercises and to apply the improved muscle skills to speech activities as early as possible. See Chapter 6 for activities that can help with oral motor skills.

SHORTER PHRASES IN SPEECH

One consequence of your child's expressive language delay and speech difficulties is that she will probably have shorter mean length of utterance (MLU) than other children. This means that, on average, her phrases and sentences will contain fewer words. Although this may be a problem in school for academic learning, it does not have to be a problem in daily living. Most of the time, it is possible to get our meaning across with short sentences. In addition, environmental stimulation and language intervention do make a difference. Research has shown that parents who are trained to help their children learn language can help improve their children's language skills, especially in the areas of mean length of utterance and structural complexity. Refer to Chapters 5 and 9 for information on increasing your child's MLU.

DIFFICULTY WITH TOPICALIZATION

Topicalization includes knowing how to choose topics, introduce topics, stay on topic, and end and change topics during the course of a conversation. Children with Down syndrome have particular difficulty staying on topic in a conversation or when telling a story or recounting an event that happened (for instance, at school). Difficulties with topicalization generally become more apparent in older children with Down syndrome. You will find some home activities aimed at helping your child with topicalization and other conversational skills in Chapter 9.

SHORT CONVERSATIONS

In the elementary and middle school years, most children with Down syndrome are unable to sustain a conversation very long. This is related to expressive language difficulties and difficulties with the structure of language, morphology, and grammar and with difficulties with topicalization. For most children with Down syndrome, difficulties in sustaining a conversation result from a combination of problems in knowing what to say and how to express what they want to say.

DIFFICULTY WITH CLARIFICATION AND REPAIRS

Clarification is the ability to ask for more information when you don't understand, and repairs is the ability to provide more information when you are aware that the person you are talking with does not understand what you are saying. For example, if your child's brother says, "Let's get that new video," your child may need to ask for clarification, "Now, or some other time?" or "Which new video?" Or, your child may need to make repairs if she is speaking with someone and says, "Jack said so." The listener may say "Who's Jack?" Your child will need to clarify whether this is a child in her class, her uncle, or some other Jack she knows. This skill is related to being able to understand and ask wh-questions, as well as the awareness that you need to ask for or provide additional information.

Asking others for clarification or giving listeners more information to fix a misunderstanding are difficult skills for most children with Down syndrome. See Chapter 9 for more information about clarification and repairs.

DIFFICULTY WITH REQUESTS

Children with Down syndrome often have difficulty knowing how to ask for information, which is related to difficulties with clarifications and repairs, above. They may also have difficulty knowing how, and when it is appropriate, to ask for other things. These difficulties are related to problems with morphosyntax. To ask a question or to make a request, you need to be able to formulate sentences—to put words in a sentence to make a question and to use "wh" words such as what or when—skills that are difficult for many children with Down syndrome. See Chapter 8 for information on how to help your child learn and practice requests.

REDUCED SPEECH INTELLIGIBILITY

When a child has reduced speech intelligibility, her speech is difficult to understand, especially by people who are not familiar with her speech. Intelligibility difficulties can be related to many problems, including difficulties with:

- oral motor skills,
- phonology (understanding when to use the different sounds of speech),
- articulation (being able to physically produce the different sounds of speech), and
- Childhood Apraxia of Speech (being able to put the sounds of speech in the right order).

Since intelligibility is a major problem for many people with Down syndrome, it is discussed in detail in Chapter 6.

CHILDHOOD APRAXIA OF SPEECH

Children with Childhood Apraxia of Speech (CAS) have difficulty sequencing speech sounds to combine the sounds into words, phrases, and sentences. It is a problem with motor programming. CAS is a condition that is found in typically occurring children, but also can occur with Down syndrome. It is an often overlooked contributor to speech intelligibility in children with Down syndrome and is discussed in Chapter 6.

METALINGUISTICS

Metalinguistics means talking about or analyzing language. These are skills such as analyzing a poem, or understanding and using metaphors, similes, and alliteration. Metalinguistic skills become more important in the middle school and high school academic curricula. These are abstract skills and are often difficult for children and adults with Down syndrome.

Reasons for Difficulties with Communication

Many of the sensory, perceptual, physical, and cognitive problems that can occur in people with Down syndrome affect communication skills. In later chapters,

Major Communication Difficulties in Children with Down Syndrome

Given the laundry list of potential communication difficulties that school-aged children with Down syndrome may have, you might be wondering which of these cause the biggest problems. In general (and there are always exceptions), the difficulties that have the biggest impact on a child with Down syndrome are:

1. the receptive-expressive communication gap;
2. difficulties with complex conversation skills related to morphosyntax (grammar);
3. speech intelligibility problems;
4. auditory memory weaknesses; and
5. topicalization.

Over the years, many researchers have confirmed that these are the major communication problems for individuals with Down syndrome. For more information, you may wish to read some of the studies listed in the references: Abbeduto & Murphy, 2004; Chapman & Hesketh, 2000; Chapman et al., 1998; Horstmeier, 1988; Kumin, 2002a, 2002b, 2002c, 2001b, 1994a; MacDonald, 1989; Miller & Leddy, 1999; Rosin & Swift, 1999.

all of these areas of difficulty will be discussed in detail. In this chapter, we will offer an overview of the most common reasons that communication can be a struggle for school-aged children with Down syndrome. For information about how these issues affect children younger than six, you may want to consult *Early Communication Skills for Children with Down Syndrome* (Kumin, 2003*)*.

Sensory and Perceptual Skills

In order to develop speech and language skills, children need certain fundamental sensory and perceptual skills. Sensory skills include the abilities to see, hear, touch, taste, or smell objects and people in the environment. They also include two lesser-known senses: 1) proprioception, which enables us to tell where our body parts are in space through feedback from our muscles, and 2) the vestibular sense, which enables us to balance.

Perceptual skills refer to the ability to give meaning to this sensory input. Thus, your child's ability to hear your

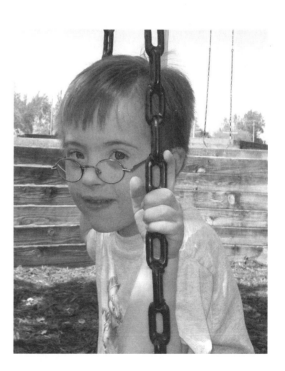

voice is a sensory skill; recognizing that it is Mom's or Dad's voice and interpreting the sounds you make as words with meaning are perceptual skills.

Clearly, children need to be able to hear what is being said in their environment in order to learn speech and language, but they also need perceptual skills to be able to make sense out of what they hear. They must also be able to see and focus on objects in order to learn the labels of objects. And they must be able to receive and interpret touch sensations in and around the mouth in order to learn how to make speech sounds. The sections below explore how sensory and perceptual characteristics of children with Down syndrome affect speech and language abilities.

AUDITORY (HEARING) SKILLS

The typical way to learn language is through hearing the language spoken in your environment. That's why people brought up in English-speaking homes speak English and people brought up in Spanish-speaking households speak Spanish. Infants are not preprogrammed to speak a specific language. They learn the sounds, meaning, and structure of the language they hear spoken around them; that becomes their native language.

Since the majority of children with Down syndrome have some degree of hearing loss, at least some of the time, relying on the auditory channel alone isn't sufficient for learning communication skills. Hearing loss, whether constant or intermittent, has an impact on speech and language development. Consequently, your child may need visual cues such as gestures, pictures, and reading to help stimulate language. In addition, children with Down syndrome often have difficulty distinguishing between what is being said and the background noise, especially in the classroom. We need to make the language pop out of the environment, so that children can hear it and learn.

Because good hearing is so essential to speech and language development, your child should be seen regularly by an otolaryngologist (ear, nose, and throat specialist), a medical specialist who can treat hearing disorders, and an audiologist, a professional who can evaluate hearing and provide therapy or assistive listening devices such as hearing aids. The Healthcare Guidelines for Individuals with Down syndrome of the Down Syndrome Medical Interest Group (DSMIG) recommend that children with Down syndrome have a routine annual hearing evaluation with more frequent evaluations when problems arise (see the Resource Guide).

HEARING PROBLEMS IN SCHOOL-AGED CHILDREN WITH DOWN SYNDROME

Children with Down syndrome may have one or a combination of the two broad types of hearing loss:

1. Conductive hearing loss, or
2. Sensorineural hearing loss.

Conductive Hearing Loss. A conductive hearing loss occurs when something prevents sound from being received by the outer and middle ear and transmitted to the inner ear effectively and consistently. The sound is most often blocked by fluid behind the middle ear, which may accumulate due to ear infections, allergies, or improperly functioning Eustachian tubes. Fluid may also accumulate because the ear canals in children with Down syndrome are often smaller and less angled, making it harder for any fluid to drain. Even excess cerumen (wax) in the ears can cause conductive hearing loss.

Fluid in the ear is a widespread problem among children with Down syndrome. Estimates are that 60 to 70 percent of children with Down syndrome have intermittent conductive hearing loss because of ear fluid accumulation.

A conductive hearing loss is generally not constant because it changes based on the status of the fluid or other similar issues. The most common hearing loss in children with Down syndrome is a fluctuating hearing loss, meaning that some days hearing is better than others. This can be very confusing to children, since the same speech sound may sound different on different days. (See Table 2-1 for examples of how one eight-year-old with Down syndrome misheard speech sounds during a bout of middle ear fluid.)

Fluctuating hearing loss also affects the development of speech sounds and the development of word endings and grammar. If your child doesn't hear all of the sounds clearly, she may have difficulty learning the sounds. If she can't hear all of the sounds in a word, she may have difficulty learning to include all of the sounds in the word. In English, final sounds in words (such as verb endings and possessives) are generally spoken more softly. It is very common for children with Down syndrome to omit the final sounds in words, and that is related to hearing loss. In school, if your child does not hear the teacher's instructions and does not respond to them, the teacher will usually think that she has a behavior problem, or doesn't want to follow the instructions. So, hearing loss may be one of the factors underlying problem behavior.

Table 2-1: Example of How Middle Ear Fluid Distorts Hearing

What Was Said	What Child Heard
Give her a *treat*	Give her *three*
I need something to *read*	I need something to *eat*
Let's go *get* Kathy	Let's *forget* Kathy
Keep *the ants* out	Keep *your hands* out
She has *measles*	She has *needles*
Pizza with *sausage*	Pizza with *dog spit*
Goody goody	Kitty kitty
Daisy	Baby
She was *born*	She was *boring*

Adapted from *Early Communication Skills for Children with Down Syndrome* (Kumin, 2003).

As children with Down syndrome enter school and progress through the early elementary grades, many have fewer ear infections. Many children, however, continue to have problems with middle ear fluid, due to anatomical differences such as smaller, narrower ear canals. Dysfunction of the Eustachian tube (the tube that connects the middle ear to the back of the nose) is common, so that fluid that collects behind the eardrum may not properly drain away. According to Dr. Sally Shott, an otolaryngologist who works extensively with people with Down syndrome, children in the six- to fourteen-year age range covered by this book often have unrecognized middle ear fluid and hearing loss. Currently, no information is available on how long middle ear fluid continues to be a problem. Dr. Shott is conducting research in this area (Shott, 2000; Shott & Heithaus, 2001).

Fluid in the middle ear (known as "glue ear" in the United Kingdom and Europe) is sticky and often blocks the Eustachian tube. This prevents the Eustachian tube from keeping the middle ear aerated. When fluid fills the middle ear, sound cannot pass through as well, and speech sounds muffled. Dr. Patrick Sheehan of the National Deaf Children's Society in the United Kingdom reports that many children with Down syndrome grow out of glue ear (middle ear fluid problems) as their Eustachian tubes grow, often by about age eight, but in some children, the difficulties last longer. Anecdotally, some children continue to have Eustachian tube problems through their teen years, and to require the treatments discussed below in order to preserve and maximize their hearing.

To minimize the effects on hearing, ear infections should be treated promptly. Antibiotics can sometimes help to clear up ear congestion. Some physicians prescribe antiobiotics on a prophylactic (preventative) basis. Often, small tubes need to be surgically implanted in the eardrum to allow fluid to drain away. In the U.S., these tubes may be referred to as PE tubes (for pressure equalization), tympanostomy tubes, or myringotomy tubes; in other English-speaking countries they may be referred to as grommets or ventilation tubes. The PE tubes allow air pressure in the middle ear to equal air pressure outside the ear. The surgery to implant these tubes is called a myringotomy. Ordinarily it is performed under general anesthesia by a pediatric otolaryngologist (ear, nose, and throat doctor) and is a short procedure, usually taking ten or fifteen minutes. Ear tubes are usually intended to be a temporary "fix" for fluid in the ears and come out on their own after several months to a year.

Inserting ear tubes can often make a remarkable difference in a child's hearing abilities. Some children with Down syndrome only need one or two sets of ear tubes, but many have multiple sets of ear tubes over a number of years. One mother told me that her son is still getting ear tubes put in (as the previous ones dislodge and fall out) at age 21.

Even when there are no active ear infections, parents need to ensure that their child receives regular ear examinations by a primary care physician or otolaryngologist and annual hearing tests to monitor hearing function, and to treat any problems that occur.

Sensorineural Loss. Some children with Down syndrome have sensorineural hearing loss or deafness. This is a more permanent type of hearing loss caused by damage to the inner ear, the auditory nerve, or both. It may affect the ability to hear at certain frequencies (pitches), and may therefore affect the ability to hear certain sounds. Although researchers have found a higher number of inner ear anomalies in children with Down syndrome, these findings have not been correlated with sensorineural hearing loss.

Children with this type of hearing loss often need hearing aids to amplify sounds. Hearing aids are generally small electronic boxes that are worn on the body in a pocket or strapped to the chest area (body aids) or miniaturized electronic aids worn in back of the ear or inside the ear canal. It is important to try to gradually get your child to wear them at all times, or as directed by the audiologist.

Mixed Hearing Loss: Many children with Down syndrome have a combination of conductive hearing loss and sensorineural hearing loss. The combination is known as mixed deafness or mixed hearing loss.

UNDERSTANDING HEARING TEST RESULTS

School-aged children with Down syndrome should have their hearing tested every year. Although your child's school or pediatrician may do a hearing "screening," this is not a good substitute for a thorough hearing test administered by an audiologist—a professional who is trained in using many different tests and strategies to measure hearing as accurately as possible and can evaluate your child in a soundproof room free of distractions. When hearing screenings are conducted at school or in a pediatrician's office, there is often a great deal of noise in the environment that makes the results inaccurate. Noises from the hall, chairs moving, people walking by, or babies crying in the doctor's office will all make it difficult to get accurate test results. Testing should be conducted in sound retardant acoustical settings (such as sound booths in an audiologist's office) to obtain accurate results.

Hearing test results tell you the *sound threshold*—the softest sound that your child consistently responded to on the test. They also tell you whether your child has more difficulty hearing sounds at particular frequencies (pitches) than at others.

Children with sound thresholds of 15 decibels (dB) or less have normal hearing. This means that they can hear sounds that are 15 decibels or softer. Children who have sound thresholds from 15-30 dB have a mild hearing loss. They will be able to hear vowel sounds clearly, but may have difficulty hearing some consonant sounds. For instance, they may have trouble hearing the final /s/ sound on the ends of plural nouns. They may also have difficulty understanding speech when there is background noise, such as in an open space classroom or the cafeteria.

Children who have sound thresholds from 30 dB to 50 dB have a moderate hearing loss. They have difficulty hearing sounds at normal conversational level, and need amplification to help them learn sounds and learn language. Children who have sound thresholds from 50 to 70 dB have a severe hearing loss and will usually need to wear hearing aids to be able to hear speech and learn to speak.

Children who have sound thresholds greater than 70 dB have difficulty learning to speak, and need ongoing treatment. Children with Down syndrome who have severe or profound hearing loss would have a dual diagnosis of Down syndrome and deafness. (When there is severe or profound hearing loss, the term *deafness* is often used.)

Most children with Down syndrome who have a hearing loss have a mild to moderate conductive hearing loss. Children with this degree of hearing loss usually still learn to use speech as their primary communication method. When children with Down syndrome have a severe or profound hearing loss, there needs to be consultation with the otologist (ear specialist) or otolaryngologist (ENT), audiologist, speech-language pathologist, and special educator to determine what method of communication will be most effective for the child.

Hearing in a Noisy Classroom Environment

In a typical elementary school classroom, the teacher stands about six to ten feet from children in the front row, and farther from children in the other rows. The background noise in a typical classroom is about 60 decibels. Measurements of teacher's voices have found them to be about 62-64 decibels. Because the teacher's voice is only a few decibels louder than the background noise, it is often very difficult for children with a mild to moderate hearing loss to make out what the teacher is saying.

Assistive listening devices and sound field systems can help amplify the teacher's voice so that your child can hear better. Generally, sound field systems are used for groups and to improve classroom listening in general. They help children with mild hearing loss. Radio aids or personal FM systems are used when an individual child, or a child with a moderate to severe hearing loss, needs assistance. Sound field systems transmit sounds from a microphone inches from the teacher's mouth to the listener's ear, so they amplify what the teacher is saying without amplifying the background noise. The goal is to produce a clear consistent voice that can be easily heard above any classroom noise.

Sound field or personal FM amplification are generally the systems used for children with mild hearing loss. Binaural FM (in both ears), behind-the-ear FM, or personal FM systems are used for children with moderate to profound hearing loss. Sometimes these are known as radio aids.

An audiologist can work with you to determine your child's needs and prescribe appropriate systems. Planning for hearing support should be part of the IEP process. If the need for sound field system support is written into your child's IEP, her school will be mandated to provide the system. Sound field systems can be helpful for many children in the class including those who have learning disabilities or difficulty with concentration. The sound field systems make the teacher's voice louder, without increasing the background noise, so the important messages stand out from the background noise.

VISUAL SKILLS

Children learn language by connecting a label with an object. To learn a word, it helps a great deal if your child can look at you in order to learn how to say the word. The ability to visually track, or follow a moving object, is also important in learning about concepts and learning to use words as labels. Vision continues to be important to learning as children grow.

Children with Down syndrome rely on and do well with contextual cues. That is, they pick up clues from what is going on around them (especially through vision) that help them with language comprehension. For instance, if your family visits an aquarium and you gesture to the sea life as you use a new vocabulary word, your child can easily figure out which creature you are talking about. This is why language skills at home and in the community are often much more advanced for children with Down syndrome than their language test scores show. Testing involves decontextualized language. There are no clues in the environment or in the test booklet that help you to figure out what is going on or what you are being asked to do. In a test, a question might be "What would you expect to see at the aquarium?" but there would not be any pictures or environmental cues. On tests, words usually stand alone.

If your child cannot see clearly or has difficulty focusing on objects, she will naturally have more trouble learning to attach particular words to particular objects.

Many children with Down syndrome have visual difficulties. At least 50 percent have strabismus, or muscle imbalance problems that cause one or both eyes to turn outward or inward. Nearsightedness (blurred distant vision), farsightedness (blurred near vision), and astigmatism (blurred vision at all distances due to irregularly shaped eyeballs) are also common problems. Since a child's eyes usually continue growing until late adolescence, it is not uncommon for vision problems to first appear or to evolve in school-aged children. Farsightedness may become less of a problem over time as the eye grows, but nearsightedness generally worsens.

These vision problems are all easily correctable and should not be allowed to interfere with your child's communication development. If you suspect a vision problem, you may want to ask your pediatrician for a referral to a pediatric ophthalmologist—a medical doctor specializing in evaluating and treating vision problems of children.

Despite some possible visual difficulties, visual perception is strong in children with Down syndrome. They have relatively strong visual memory and usually learn well through the visual channel.

TACTILE (TOUCH) SKILLS

Children with Down syndrome may have several difficulties related to touch that can affect speech development and speaking. These include difficulty with sensory awareness, hyposensitivity to touch, hypersensitivity to touch, or a combination of these problems.

Children with Down syndrome may have difficulty with sensory awareness. For example, if a child with Down syndrome chews a cracker or cookies, she will often not be aware if there is any food remaining between her lips, cheeks, and teeth. She will generally not use her tongue to clear the area automatically, but she can be taught to do this. She does not clear the area with her tongue because her body is not sending sensory feedback messages that tell her there is still food in her mouth. Usually, when you show the child her mouth in the mirror, she is surprised. In her mind, she has finished all of the food. She may also have difficulty with tactile feedback when speaking; that is, knowing where her tongue is and where it should be placed to produce a specific sound.

If your child has trouble processing sensations in her mouth, this can eventually lead to speech difficulties. If she is getting insufficient feedback, she may have more difficulty feeling where her tongue is touching when she tries to make speech sounds.

Some children with Down syndrome are oversensitive to touch (*tactilely defensive*) and may find any kind of touch around their face or mouth intolerable. If your child is tactilely defensive, she might not enjoy exploring objects with her mouth, resulting in limited practice exercising the lips and tongue.

Other children with Down syndrome are hyposensitive (less sensitive to touch than usual). Some of these children are sensory seeking. That is, they are constantly putting things in their mouth, licking, chewing, or sucking on non-food objects such as their shirt, fidgeting, and moving. They are focused on the input, and often have less awareness of the sensations and movements involved in speech. In speech-language therapy, and at home, activities such as using a mirror can help children become more aware of the articulators and feedback from their lips, tongue, and other articulators as they make various sounds.

If your child is either over- or under-sensitive to touch, consult an occupational therapist who is trained in treatment for sensory processing disorders (SPD), as discussed below. The occupational therapist can use activities and exercises to help your child learn to respond more normally to touch.

SENSORY PROCESSING DISORDER/ SENSORY INTEGRATION

To learn language effectively, children need to be able to simultaneously process and organize input from more than one sense. For example, to learn to pronounce a new word in science class, your child must be able to hear each sound in the word as the teacher says it and then figure out how to position her lips, tongue, etc. to make those sounds. And to learn which words correspond with which gradations of color, she must be able not only to see and recognize the colors, but also to know the difference between light and dark.

This ability to organize input from various senses and apply them to everyday life is known as sensory processing or sensory integration. It is the neurological process through which people integrate and interpret sensory messages from all seven senses: sight, sound, touch, taste, smell, proprioceptive, and vestibular. Approximately 20 percent of people have some kind of sensory processing disorder, but my clinical impression is that a much higher percentage of children with Down syndrome have sensory processing disorders.

Some children have difficulty with hypersensitivity to sounds. They put their hands over their ears even when the sounds in the environment are not too loud. They are very uncomfortable at baseball games and other sporting events where there are loud noises. This is known as an auditory integration problem. There are several different programs of auditory integration therapy (AIT) specifically targeted to address this problem. These therapies involve having the child listen through headphones to music that has had certain frequencies filtered out in order to "retrain" her hearing. AIT therapy is controversial, expensive, and sometimes administered by minimally trained practitioners. If your child has auditory integration difficulties and you seek out therapy, be sure that the program is administered by a certified and licensed audiologist.

Your child's sensory processing/integration ability often affects the way others view her and her behavior. For example, when a teacher calls on her, she expects your child to answer the question or follow instructions. That is, the teacher expects your child to hear what she says and then translate what she hears into the appropriate movements. If your child does not respond with the expected words or movements, the teacher may assume that she is willfully not following instructions. As a result, the teacher may assume your child is being noncompliant. Many children with Down syndrome are accused of having behavioral issues that are actually the result of sensory processing or communication difficulties.

Children with Down syndrome may have trouble processing input from more than one sense at once—for example, if they are asked to look and listen at the same time. They may also have trouble focusing on what is being said if they are overloaded by too many sensations at once—the sound of students walking through the hallway, the smell of poster paints, the reflection of sunlight on a nearby window. Sometimes when

children with Down syndrome appear to be hyperactive or impulsive, it is actually a sign of sensory integration difficulties. Sensory processing disorder and sensory integration problems of this nature not only make it difficult to learn communication skills, but many other skills as well.

An occupational therapist may be able to help your child overcome sensory integration problems. Some of the techniques that are used for SPD are development and implementation of a sensory diet at school as part of the IEP; pressure, icing, heat, and/or brushing; and Social Stories to teach appropriate reactions that may be affected by the SPD. A sensory diet is a plan to provide sensory activities on a schedule that will give each child the sensory stimulation that she needs so that she will not seek out sensory input in inappropriate ways such as by head banging.

An occupational therapist may already be a part of your child's education team. If not, the American Occupational Therapy Association can help you locate a therapist trained in working with children with SPD. See the Resource Guide at the end of this book for contact information. Also check the References and Suggested Reading list at the end of the book for publications that have suggestions about how to work on those difficulties at home.

Sensory processing difficulties are more common in children with Down syndrome than in children with typical development. They are even more common in children who have a dual diagnosis of Down syndrome and autism. Clinically, we have observed that many young children with Down syndrome seem to have some difficulties with sensory processing, such as tolerating loud noises, having their teeth brushed, getting haircuts, or handling mixed textures in their food.

Physical Characteristics

Children with Down syndrome frequently have differences in the muscles or structure of the facial area that can result in speech difficulties. These differences include:

- Low muscle tone (hypotonia)—muscles that are more relaxed and "floppy" than usual, and therefore more difficult to control. Muscles in your child's lips, tongue, and jaw might be affected. Although hypotonia can improve with age, it can continue to affect your child to some degree her whole life. For instance, she may never be able to make the complex movements with her tongue needed to make a clear /r/ sound.

- Difficulty moving the lips, tongue, and jaw independent of each other. (Speech-language pathologists call this "dissociation.")
- A mouth that is relatively small in relationship to tongue size.
- A tendency to breathe through the mouth due to enlarged adenoids or tonsils or to recurrent allergies or colds. This is something that improves in many children with Down syndrome with age and proper medical treatment. Regular visits with an otolaryngologist (ENT) can provide evaluation and treatment for the underlying medical causes for these difficulties.
- A high, narrow palate that might limit tongue movements for speech. The palate can often be widened through the use of a palatal expander—a device that is attached to the upper teeth and exerts pressure to widen the upper jaw. Consult a dentist or orthodontist who has experience with palatal expanders and with children with Down syndrome.

See Table 2-2 for a more detailed listing of physical differences that can lead to speech and language delays.

The problems above can all affect your child's *speech intelligibility* (how easily her speech is understood) in different ways. Your child may have trouble with:

- **articulation,** or the ability to move and control the lips, tongue, jaws, and palate to form sounds correctly and clearly;
- **fluency,** or the ability to speak smoothly and rhythmically;
- **sequencing,** or the ability to pronounce sounds in the proper order within words (for example, your child may say "efelant" for "elephant");
- **resonance,** or the tone and quality of speech sounds your child produces (for instance, whether sounds are too nasal or "twangy" or not nasal enough and sound as if your child has a stuffed nose).

Although the problems above can make speaking more difficult and frustrating for your child, they need not prevent her from communicating effectively. Chapter 6 suggests ways you can work with your child on specific factors affecting her speech intelligibility.

Cognitive Characteristics

Most children with Down syndrome have more difficulty learning because of the presence of intellectual disabilities (mental retardation). These intellectual disabilities can have an especially big impact on communication skills, because so much of language learning depends on cognitive or thinking abilities such as reasoning, understanding concepts, and remembering.

These problems will have a significant impact on your child's communication skills, but she can continue to make considerable improvement all her life. As a parent, you can help by providing language experiences as the basis for learning language

Table 2-2: Physical Differences That Affect Speech & Language

Physical Characteristic	Effect on Speech/Language
Low tone in mouth, tongue, pharynx muscles (hypotonia)	Articulation and intelligibility problems; imprecise speech; voice and resonance problems
Underdevelopment of midfacial bones, also known as midfacial hypoplasia	Articulation and intelligibility problems
Lax ligaments in TMJ (loose connections in the jaw bone area)	Articulation problems; imprecise speech
Drooling	Difficulty with sensory awareness and feedback for articulation
Open mouth	Articulation problems, especially for /p/, /b/, /m/, /f/, /v/
Mild blockage of nasal airways	Hyponasality (voice quality sounds "stuffy")
Velopharyngeal incompetence (difficulty using the soft palate and throat wall muscles to seal off the nasal cavity to keep air/sounds out of the nose)	Hypernasality (voice quality sounds too nasal); intelligibility problems
Mouth breathing	Hyponasality; articulation and intelligibility problems
Open bite (upper and lower teeth do not meet)	Articulation problems, especially for /s/, /z/, /sh/, /t/, /d/
Tongue protrusion	Articulation problems, especially for /t/, /d/, /s/, /z/, /sh/, /l/, /n/; intelligibility problems
Angle's Class III malocclusion with prognathism (lower jaw juts out in front of upper jaw)	Articulation and intelligibility problems
Tongue large in relation to mouth	Articulation problems, especially, for /t/, /d/, /s/, /sh/, /z/, /l/, /n/; intelligibility problems
Limited distance and range of motion for tongue movements	Imprecise articulation
Abnormalities of the neuromuscular junctions of the tongue	Articulation problems
Narrow upper jaw	Hypernasality; intelligibility problems
Palate height too low	Intelligibility problems
Palate height too high; v-shaped palate	Hypernasality; intelligibility problems
Irregular dentition (teeth)	Articulation problems

(continued next page)

Physical Characteristic continued...	*Effect on Speech/Language continued...*
Difficulties with coordination, accuracy, and timing of mouth movements	Articulation and intelligibility problems
Difficulty with graded jaw movements (making small, precise movements throughout the range of jaw mobility)	Articulation and intelligibility problems
Sequential processing difficulties	Problems with phonemic processing, auditory memory, morphosyntax (grammar)
Apraxia or motor planning difficulties	Delays in speech; groping and struggling to form sounds; intelligibility problems
Dysarthria or oral motor difficulties	Intelligibility problems
Sensitivities to touch, sound, or movement	Oral motor difficulties, and difficulty in learning to produce speech sounds
Otitis media with effusion (fluid) and fluctuating hearing loss	Delayed language development; difficulties with auditory discrimination (telling sounds apart), auditory localization (telling where sound is coming from), auditory association
Impacted cerumen (ear wax)	Delayed language development; difficulties with auditory association and localization
Sensorineural hearing loss	Difficulties with speech perception; phonemic processing; hearing differences between sounds
Conductive hearing loss	Difficulties with hearing conversational level speech; difficulty following instructions in school unless amplification is used
Auditory-motor and auditory-vocal processing difficulties	Difficulties with phonemic processing; auditory memory; grammar; reduced sentence length

concepts, by giving your child many opportunities to use old words in new situations, and by giving her plenty of practice in using new language skills. Later chapters explain how, specifically, to do these things.

Some of the specific cognitive abilities that are usually affected by Down syndrome are discussed below.

GENERALIZATION

Generalization is the ability to apply information learned in one situation to a new situation. For example, an older child who has learned to form the plural of the words "dog," "ball," and "train" by adding an "s" to the ends of the words might not be able to figure out that she can form the plural of a new word such as "flag" in the same way. She may learn a skill in one situation, and not automatically generalize it to similar situations. For instance, the child may have trouble following rules or laws. Although she may have a general understanding of the rule, she may need explanations as to how it applies in many specific situations. (She may understand that she should not take things that don't belong to her when she is in her brother's room, but when she is in a store, she may not understand that the toys in the store belong to the store and therefore she can't take them.) With training and practice, however, she can learn to apply a skill to different situations.

MEMORY

Memory is the ability to store and recall information, actions, and events. Memory can be divided into long-term memory and short-term memory. Long-term memory may involve skills learned over time, such as playing a musical instrument or swimming, or recall of information and events. Short-term memory is the memory that

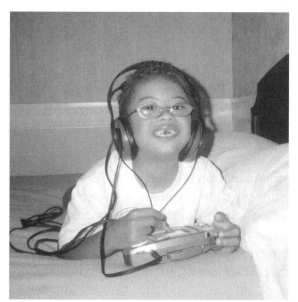

you use every day as you process information required to deal with situations as they are happening. Short-term memory is important for speaking and for processing language. Many, but not all, children with Down syndrome are better at remembering what they see (visual memory) than at remembering what they hear (auditory memory).

Auditory Memory. Auditory memory is another term for verbal short-term memory—retaining and remembering information that you have just heard. We use a process called the *phonological loop* to process and remember the sounds for speaking. The phonological loop is involved in short-term storage of verbal information. Children with Down syndrome have difficulty with the phonological loop. Remembering sequences of sounds and processing information about sound differences is an area of difficulty for them.

Ideally, auditory memory allows us to remember words long enough after they have been spoken so we can process and respond to them. Children with Down syndrome may have trouble with this, however. For instance, if the teacher asks your child to get out her social studies book, turn to page 55, and do the odd-numbered questions, she may only remember the first thing, getting out her book.

Since children with Down syndrome respond well to visual cues, your child may be able to follow instructions more easily if they are written on the board. Or she may need a picture list of the steps involved in conducting an experiment in science class. Auditory stimuli last for a very short time, whereas children can go back and reread or look again at visual stimuli. Children with Down syndrome may need more time to process information, and visual material (books, instructions on the computer screen) lends itself more easily to repetition. When auditory instructions are given, they can be taped so that your child can play them again (using a Big Mac switch or audiotape), or they can be programmed into a computer using synthesized voice, so that your child can hear the instructions as many times as she needs to.

In your child's IEP and in lesson plans, it should be very clear whether the goal of the activity is to work on auditory memory or if the goal is to learn specific subject matter (such as science or social studies). If the goal is to learn the curriculum, your child should not be penalized for her difficulties with auditory memory of the material. Instead, visual strategies should be used to help her learn.

Visual Memory. Working memory for visual-spatial activities appears to be stronger for children with Down syndrome than working memory for verbal activities. For example, if your child sees you demonstrate how to turn on the new DVD player, she is more likely to remember how to do it than if you tell her verbally, "Push the power button on top and then push the eject button on the right." Put another way: children with Down syndrome learn more easily by watching demonstrations than by listening to verbal instructions. They have stronger visual than auditory skills. This is why reading can be effective in helping children with Down syndrome progress in language. For more information, see Chapter 5.

ABSTRACT THINKING

Abstract thinking refers to the ability to understand relationships, concepts, principles, and other ideas that are intangible. Difficulty with abstract thinking may make it harder for your child to understand language concepts. Some subjects at school use unfamiliar vocabulary that is abstract. For example, in social studies, words such as government, democracy, and legislation are difficult because these concepts refer to things you can't see or touch. When a concept does not have a concrete referent, it is more difficult to grasp.

In reading, children with Down syndrome may be able to remember the characters, events, and setting, but may run into comprehension problems if the author expects readers to infer what is going on without directly stating it. Figurative language such as metaphors and similes can also present difficulties to children who are concrete thinkers. For example, if a character is described as being "as light as a feather" your child may struggle to understand what the author means, since she knows that people generally weigh quite a bit more than feathers. Proverbs such as a "bird in the hand is worth two in the bush" or "don't count your chickens until they are hatched" are also difficult.

PROCESSING SKILLS

Our brains are constantly processing information received from our senses. We take in, interpret, and respond to sights, sounds, and other types of stimulation in our environment.

Visual Processing, or the ability to take in, make sense of, and respond to things we see, is generally a relative strength for children with Down syndrome. Just as it is easier for children with Down syndrome to *remember* visual information than auditory information, it is also easier for them to *process* visual information than auditory information. Again, this is because visual information is not as fleeting as auditory information, so children with Down syndrome can take the time to make sense of it before it's gone.

This relative strength in visual processing is one reason that computer-based learning is so successful with children with Down syndrome. It provides visual cues that can be repeated as many times as desired. For similar reasons, perhaps, reading often is a relative strength for children with Down syndrome. It also means that pictures or written words or sign language will help children learn concepts more easily than spoken words.

Auditory processing, or how quickly and efficiently your child takes in, interprets, and responds to spoken words, can be a problem. Children with Down syndrome generally need more time to process and understand what is said to them, and may therefore be slower to answer questions or respond to instructions even when they aren't experiencing auditory memory problems.

Auditory discrimination, or the ability to hear differences between sounds, can also be difficult for children with Down syndrome. This influences whether the child can understand which word is being said—for example, "road" and "rose" or "land" and "sand" may be confused. Not surprisingly, middle ear fluid exacerbates this problem. Sensorineural hearing loss also makes sound discrimination more difficult. There are hearing tests that can be used to assess your child's sound discrimination abilities.

Word retrieval, or the ability to select the appropriate word to use in a given situation, is an issue for many children with Down syndrome. This problem may affect the complexity, accuracy, or length of the phrases and sentences your child uses. Sometimes when children are having difficulty with word retrieval, they may use words that are closely related to the word they are thinking of, such as saying "sock" instead of "shoe." Or they may say "you know" or "whatever." It is often frustrating for children or adults when they cannot retrieve the word they are thinking of.

Conclusion

Although the long list of communication problems that children with Down syndrome might have can seem daunting, much can be done to help overcome or alleviate the problems. As a parent, you can involve your child in activities and experiences that will help her overcome difficulties in many areas. And speech-language pathologists can use and explain special techniques, materials, and exercises that can help her optimize her communication skills. They can provide assistance through therapy for the challenges, as well as learning tools such as visual organizers that can enable your child to use her strengths to help her learn.

Learning communication skills is a process that continues over many years. Individuals with Down syndrome do not plateau at a certain point in language; they continue to learn and progress into adolescence and adulthood. As children and adolescents have new experiences, they learn more language, especially in the areas of vocabulary and pragmatics.

The older your child gets, the more you will probably notice that her language successes and challenges vary from one environment to another. At home and in the community, there are many cues in the environment that can help your child make sense of what is going on and speak and respond appropriately. In many situations, it is acceptable to use abbreviations, scripted phrases ("High five!"), and other predictable communication phrases ("See ya later") that children get to practice over and over. Your child may do very well with social language, greeting people, introducing them to one another, and giving and receiving help. In school, the academic language needed for tests and worksheets and for following instructions may be more difficult for her. One reason is that at school, there may be fewer contextual cues.

Try to stay aware of situations in which your child's speech and language meet her needs, and situations where she may need some additional supports for communication. This book can serve as a guide to assist you in finding the help that your child needs to be a successful communicator.

CHAPTER 3

An Overview of Speech-Language Evaluation and Eligibility

The first step on the road to increasing the effectiveness of your child's communication skills is a comprehensive speech and language evaluation. The purpose of a speech and language evaluation is to get an accurate picture of your child's present communication abilities in daily living activities, including home, school, and the community. The evaluation should clearly describe your child and should explore the best channels and approaches for him so that treatment can be planned to address any difficulties that he is experiencing. The evaluation should document what your child is doing to communicate, the areas in which he is successful, and any areas in which he is having difficulty. Speech and language evaluations may be completed for information on your child's present communication skills or documentation for a triennial evaluation, but the major reason for an evaluation, as I see it, is to plan an appropriate treatment program.

Usually, an evaluation will assess both your child's language and speech skills. The language evaluation looks at your child's:

- understanding (receptive language),
- language output (expressive language),
- language of social interaction (pragmatics), and
- use of sign language, gestures, communication boards, or electronic assistive communication devices.

The speech evaluation looks at your child's:

- respiration (breathing for speech),
- voice,
- articulation (speech sounds),
- oral motor skills,

- phonology (patterns of speech errors),
- fluency (smoothness of speech),
- rate of speech,
- resonance, and
- other characteristics related to speech intelligibility.

More information on what happens during language and speech evaluation will be discussed in Chapter 4.

Sometimes, an evaluation will focus on just language or just speech—depending on your child's needs or on time, procedural, or other constraints of the tester or the testing center. For example, let's look at the following scenarios:

Kimberly, age 10, is beginning to use sentences and have longer conversations and is experiencing some difficulty in being understood. She is already receiving language treatment in school but needs to be evaluated for speech intelligibility.

William, age 6, is not yet speaking and needs an assistive technology evaluation. The IEP team suggests that he go to a specialized center for an augmentative and alternative communication (AAC) evaluation.

Leo's speech is inconsistent. Sometimes he can say a word and sometimes he has great difficulty saying the same word. His mom read an article I wrote on childhood apraxia of speech (CAS). She would like an evaluation to determine whether Leo has CAS.

Sarita, a twelve-year-old girl with Down syndrome,, is having difficulty with language arts this year. When she needs to write reports, she uses a word processor but she has a lot of trouble organizing the material.

Brian, age 14, is in middle school. He is a very social and friendly young man. He wants to have friends in school and wants most of all to hang out with the guys. But when they use slang and the "in" expressions, Brian can't always understand them. Sometimes, he does what they tell him to do, and he gets into trouble.

Kimberly and Leo need speech evaluations, at this time. The issues they are currently experiencing are speech related, and the evaluations need to focus on determining and describing their speech difficulties so that treatment plans can be developed. William needs support or an alternative system for speech so that he can communicate. Although he is not yet speaking, he has a lot to "say." He will eventually require a speech evaluation to determine why he is not yet speaking and a language evaluation to determine the content for a communication device, as well as to plan language treatment. But first, he needs an Assistive Technology evaluation. Sarita needs a language evaluation to focus on her language organization skills. The evaluation can help to determine what kinds of visual organizers can be used in language treatment and in the classroom to help Sarita complete her assignments. Brian needs a receptive and expressive language evaluation. He seems to be having difficulty with abstract

language and may need help with social interactional and conversational skills.

Sometimes the type of evaluation a child receives depends on the setting. For example, the state technology centers focus on AAC evaluations (see Chapter 10 for more information). School-based speech and language evaluations focus primarily on language issues that relate to the classroom, but usually also include an articulation evaluation. Evaluations in a university or hospital center can be very comprehensive, if necessary, and look at a child's communication skills from all angles.

The general format of language and speech evaluations is similar, but the techniques and tests used are different. Therefore, this chapter will provide an overview of evaluation of communication, with the next chapter focusing specifically on language and speech evaluations. This chapter also explains the nuts and bolts of requesting and receiving speech and language evaluations through the public schools, since in North America, most children with Down syndrome receive their services through schools. The chapter concludes with some information for you to use during IEP meetings in advocating for the most appropriate speech-language services for your child.

Reasons for Testing

Some of the reasons that speech and language evaluations are completed are:

- *Child Find or First Call:* This is usually the first evaluation that determines a child's eligibility for speech and language services provided by the school system or early intervention program. States may refer to this evaluation by different names, but the purpose is to match your child's needs with the services available. Usually, Down syndrome is identified early so that a Child Find assessment occurs as part of early intervention. Sometimes, however, mosaic Down syndrome (MDS) is not identified until later in life, so Child Find may be involved with older children with MDS.

- *Screening:* The purpose of screening is to determine whether diagnostic testing is needed. Screening tests are short and have fewer test items than a comprehensive test. Sometimes kindergarten screenings just ask a child to give his name and age, and talk about his family. A positive screening just tells us that there is a need for further testing. Screening tests should not be used to diagnose or describe communication problems. In my work as a speech-language pathologist, parents often show me reports in which a diagnosis was made for their child based on a screening test, but this should not be done. Language and speech screening tests should be used only to determine whether further speech and language evaluation is necessary.

- *IEP development:* Language evaluation may be conducted for help in planning how your child's communication needs will be addressed on his individualized education program (IEP). The IEP meeting is usually held once a year, but may be held more frequently. The IEP should be developed to meet your child's individual communication needs as determined by an evaluation or by ongoing observation of your child's communication skills. The IEP should specify the tests that were used to determine the IEP goals and provide measurable goals for treatment. See Chapters 5-7 for more information on incorporating treatment into your child's IEP.

- *School placement/inclusion/transition to the workplace:* The purpose of a speech and language evaluation may be to evaluate your child's communication and determine whether he has the prerequisite skills to succeed in a certain setting. Speech and language testing for this purpose is best used to evaluate what supports your child will need in that setting—not whether he is "ready" for the setting. For instance, will he need speech and language services? Can his speech be understood by other children or by coworkers? Will the teachers or coworkers need information to help them communicate with your child? This testing should be used to analyze what supports an individual may need, not to exclude him from possible opportunities.

- *Triennial evaluation:* In the U.S., testing is often done every three years (triennial) in the schools to determine whether your child continues to be eligible for special education services, including speech-language therapy. But eligibility meetings or hearings may take place at any time if there are changes in your child's condition or performance or if you change school systems. Remember, the purpose of this testing is to determine whether your child *qualifies* for services through the schools, not whether your child *needs* services.

- *Baseline testing:* This testing is usually part of therapy. Its goal is to determine your child's skills before he begins receiving therapy for a specific skill. For example, if the SLP will teach your child to use the words *himself/herself,* what is your child's current ability to use these pronouns? If your child is having difficulty making the /s/ sound, is he having consistent difficulty or is he only sometimes experiencing difficulty (at the beginning, middle, or end of words or in all positions in words)? Baseline testing is a type of pre-testing.

- *Pre-testing and post-testing:* This is testing for a specific skill before and after therapy to determine your child's progress on that specific skill (such as using –ed to form past tense). Testing measures progress in a specific area or in development of a specific skill.

- *Specialized purpose:* Testing may be needed to see whether your child needs a specific type of therapy. For example, does he have auditory integration difficulties and should specialized therapy techniques be used? Specialized testing may also be done if the SLP needs to involve another professional such as an audiologist or occupational therapist in the evaluation. This may be the case if your child has difficulties with auditory processing and memory and organizational skills and could benefit from visual schedules or organizers. It also may relate to specialized equipment such as sound field auditory loop systems. The SLP and audiologist may work in collaboration with the classroom teacher and special educator to evaluate your child's needs and design an optimal system.

- *Consultant/second opinion:* Sometimes you want an outside opinion on your child's communication abilities. For example, consultant testing may be very helpful if your child is being considered for an augmentative and alternative communication (AAC) device. A center or a professional specializing in AAC testing will have a variety of equipment to try with your child, and the professional expertise and experience to prescribe and program an appropriate communication device for your child. For example, I am often asked to evaluate children with Down syndrome for childhood apraxia of speech. Many SLPs have not worked with children with Down syndrome who have CAS difficulties and overlook the diagnosis. Therapy techniques for the speech difficulties resulting from CAS are different from articulation therapy, so there is a need to determine whether CAS is affecting the child's speech in order to develop an appropriate plan for treatment.

Requesting an Evaluation

Most speech and language evaluations are completed as part of the IEP process required by the Individuals with Disabilities Education Act (IDEA). Under the law, every child with a disability is entitled to an evaluation in the areas of suspected difficulty, focusing on the educational needs of the child.

Because IDEA requires that schools assess children "in all areas of suspected disability," speech and language should always be tested in children with Down syndrome. A great deal of research and clinical experience supports the finding that communication difficulties are an area of suspected disability for children with Down syndrome. Parents should not be told, as I have often heard, that "in our district, we don't test speech until the child is talking." Or, "We don't test speech until children are three years old." The statute related to testing all areas of suspected disability refers specifically to the initial evaluation. Once communication is tested on the initial evaluation, it should be tested on at least an annual basis for IEP development, as well as every three years as part of the triennial evaluation process.

If your child is just entering elementary school and has not received an initial evaluation from your public school system, there are several ways to request one. First, if your child is just transitioning out of early intervention, you can ask your child's early intervention team who to contact. You can also call the special education office at your child's neighborhood school to ask how to start the process. If your child has already been tested to qualify for special education and has a current IEP, the procedure may differ depending on the age of your child, and your child's school setting and placement. Depending on the procedures used by your local school system, you may need to be referred for a speech and language evaluation by the special educator or the SLP, or you may contact the county or school system diagnostic center directly. IDEA 2004 has specific guidelines requiring that the evaluation be held within 60 days of receiving parental permission for the evaluation.

Subsequent testing is usually done on a regular schedule, once yearly before the IEP meeting to assess your child's progress and areas of need, and once every three years to determine his eligibility to continue receiving services. For children who are receiving special education services, a reevaluation must be conducted every three years (triennial evaluation). According to IDEA 2004, triennial evaluations are done to determine "whether the child needs special education and related services" and "whether any additions or modifications to the special education and related services are needed to enable the child to meet the measurable annual goals set out in the individualized education program of the child and to participate as appropriate, in the general education curriculum." (See the section "Evaluations and Eligibility" on page 59 for more on related services.)

Triennial evaluations may be done more frequently than every three years "if the local agency determines that the educational or related services needs, including improved academic achievement and functional performance, of the child warrant a reevaluation or if the child's parents or teacher requests a reevaluation." A reevaluation may not occur more than once a year unless the parent and the public agency (usually the local school system) agree otherwise.

The process and procedures will be different for an outside, nonschool-based evaluation, such as a university clinic or a Down syndrome clinic at a medical center.

SCHOOL-BASED VS. PRIVATE EVALUATIONS

Having the school evaluate your child's speech and language has both benefits and drawbacks. The major benefit is that the school SLP often knows your child, and has ongoing experience with your child's ability to communicate in daily activities at school. The school SLP also has access to your child's classroom teacher, special education teacher, and other specialists and can consult with them on questions related to the evaluation. Furthermore, school evaluations are provided at no charge to your family, through IDEA 2004 as part of a free and appropriate education (FAPE) with related services (SLP services are a related service).

A major drawback of school-based evaluations is that testing is designed to determine a child's eligibility for services and to determine areas of strength and difficulty directly related to IDEA guidelines. That is, the SLP will determine whether speech and language difficulties affect your child's ability to make progress in the general education curriculum. She will not be looking for all possible speech and language problems your child might have with an eye to optimizing his communication skills. For example, even though your child might have significant speech intelligibility problems, if he can communicate effectively in the classroom with an AAC device, the school may determine he does not need speech therapy.

School-based testing tends to focus more on language than speech, and the tests used are often prescribed by lists drawn up by the county or school district. There are hundreds of available tests in the marketplace, and a school system will purchase tests that can be used for many children within that school system. The school SLP may be limited in test choice because of these lists of qualifying tests and because of test availability within that school system. As a result, she may not be able to use the most appropriate tests for your child. Most school systems have criteria for eligibility, so the test scores determine whether your child is eligible for services.

Having said that, school-based speech-language pathologists bring a wide variety of skills and commitment to the evaluation process. Some have extensive experience working with children with Down syndrome, as well as with the teachers in your child's school. They observe in the classroom in addition to administering standardized testing. Others have little experience and assume that the communication difficulties they observe "go with Down syndrome" and can't be changed.

Another drawback to school-based evaluations is that families are not usually included in the testing sessions so they can't easily provide feedback (for example, if a test item is couch and you use the word sofa at home). However, IDEA 2004 specifically states that the IEP team must "review existing evaluation data on the child, including evaluations and information provided by the parents of the child." This means parents can submit videotapes or audiotapes to show how their child is communicating at home.

It is best, in my opinion, to consider the school's speech-language evaluation as one important piece of evaluation information for your child with Down syndrome, but not as the complete evaluation. There are two major reasons why I don't think a school-based evaluation is sufficient:

1. Most children with Down syndrome have significant difficulties with speech that need to be diagnosed and treated if they are going to achieve their communication potential as adults. However, most school-based evaluations focus on *language,* rather than speech. They may include articulation testing, but rarely include other speech areas that affect whether your child's speech is understandable (see Chapter 4 for information on areas of speech intelligibility evaluation).

2. School-based speech and language evaluations tend to underestimate the abilities of children with Down syndrome. Tests used in schools usually rely on verbal instructions. They don't offer visual prompts and cues. So, children with Down syndrome score lower than their capabilities if they have difficulties with auditory comprehension or auditory memory. The child may know the answer, but not understand what is being asked. In addition, school SLPs have limited time for evaluations and must sandwich them between therapy sessions and IEP meetings. As a result, they often cannot spend enough time with a child with Down syndrome to get a true picture of his abilities. The testing session should include time for your child to warm up to the new

situation and to get some practice in the kinds of items on which he will be tested. That takes time, and sufficient time is often not provided for school-based SLPs to conduct a comprehensive language and speech evaluation.

If you choose to supplement the school evaluation with a private evaluation, consider what you hope to learn from the private evaluation. What information will be helpful in determining the best treatment plan for your child? A private evaluation is more costly, and you want to be sure that it will provide the information that you and the school need to best help your child.

A private evaluation can take more time. It may be conducted over three or four sessions or be set up as *diagnostic therapy.* In diagnostic therapy, sessions can be designed not only to test your child's skills, but also to assess which treatment methods work well. For example, to get a better understanding of your child's articulation skills, the SLP may try various ways to get your child to improve his articulation of one or more sounds and observe which method works best with your child. The assessment tries to determine how your child learns and makes progress in speech and language; it is a prescriptive evaluation.

In Chapter 1, we discussed how to find a qualified speech-language pathologist with appropriate credentials. But, since there are no specialty credentials for those who have experience working with children with Down syndrome, how do you find the experienced professionals? In my opinion, your best resource is the local Down syndrome support group. Talk with the parents who have walked the road before you. Ask them about the professionals their family worked with, and ask for their recommendations.

If you are willing to travel for an evaluation, check the list of comprehensive Down syndrome centers across the United States and the world (you can find a list online at www.ds-health.com). Call and ask whether they have speech-language pathologists on their team who do evaluations. Or, check the university training programs in speech-language pathology (see the list of graduate training programs at www.asha.org). University training programs generally provide evaluations and treatment at reduced fees.

Another option is to check out the professionals who are writing and speaking about children with Down syndrome. Many have private practices or serve on university clinical faculties. I have many families calling me because of my work, and I have done speech evaluations at Loyola University in Maryland as part of our clinical training program. Because we conduct two-to-three hour, one-time evaluations, I don't do language evaluations as part of the one-time evaluation. I feel strongly that language evaluations need to be done over time, so that you can get to know the child. Language evaluations are best conducted as diagnostic therapy over three or four weeks, and supplemented by videotapes of your child communicating at home. It is very difficult to get an accurate assessment of language in an unfamiliar setting with unfamiliar people. Your child is unlikely to be communicating in his natural, usual way until he is more comfortable with the setting and with the people who are evaluating him. Speech intelligibility and speech production are less subject to change. In a one-time evaluation, you are more likely to get an accurate assessment of speech than of language. This is especially true if the family provides a videotape of their child speaking at home with familiar people, and if the parents observe the entire evaluation and provide feedback.

Insurance coverage for speech-language evaluations varies. Insurance is more likely to cover evaluation, rather than ongoing treatment. Still, many insurance plans do not even cover an evaluation. Certified speech-language pathologists are able to evaluate and treat independently, without referral. So, you can call a SLP directly for services. But, your insurance company may require referral from a physician, so it is worthwhile to investigate the preferred process for your health insurance coverage before scheduling an evaluation.

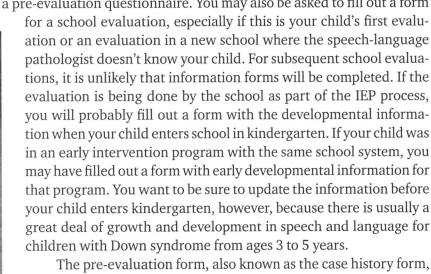

Elements of a Comprehensive Diagnostic Evaluation

A comprehensive speech and language diagnostic evaluation will usually include:

- Pre-evaluation questionnaire,
- Observation,
- Family interview,
- Playtime to develop rapport with the child,
- Formal testing,
- Informal testing,
- Feedback and sharing of results, and
- Recommendations and family counseling.

Before the Evaluation

When you call to schedule a private speech-language evaluation, you will probably be sent a pre-evaluation questionnaire. You may also be asked to fill out a form for a school evaluation, especially if this is your child's first evaluation or an evaluation in a new school where the speech-language pathologist doesn't know your child. For subsequent school evaluations, it is unlikely that information forms will be completed. If the evaluation is being done by the school as part of the IEP process, you will probably fill out a form with the developmental information when your child enters school in kindergarten. If your child was in an early intervention program with the same school system, you may have filled out a form with early developmental information for that program. You want to be sure to update the information before your child enters kindergarten, however, because there is usually a great deal of growth and development in speech and language for children with Down syndrome from ages 3 to 5 years.

The pre-evaluation form, also known as the case history form, will request information about your child's birth, medical history (especially ear infections and hearing), and developmental milestones (walking, toilet training). There will be questions regarding speech and language development and current speech and language skills. It is important that background medical, educational, developmental, and social information be available to the SLP as she diagnoses your child's speech and language difficulties. She may need to use amplification if your child has a hearing loss, or schedule breaks if your child has ADHD or other attention difficulties.

Some questions in the pre-evaluation questionnaire are designed to help the speech-language pathologists choose appropriate tests and materials for the evaluation. Your responses can also help the speech-language pathologist develop rapport when talking with your child. For example, does your child prefer watching *Aladdin* or *The Lion King?* Does he enjoy watching The Cartoon Network, The Food Network, or both? Will your adolescent be more likely to talk about movies or music, friends, or vacations? Is there a family event such as a wedding, Bar Mitzvah, first communion, or vacation that your child will want to talk about? The SLP needs to get an accurate picture of your child's conversation, and you know the topics that are most important to your child. Bring photographs to help your child remember and include the details. Or send photographs in if the evaluations are done in school, along with a note to the SLP to ask your child for the photographs.

Table 3.1 shows some areas that may be included and some typical questions that may be asked on a case history form.

Additional information related to specific speech or language considerations may be requested. See the next chapter on speech and language evaluations.

What to Expect during the Evaluation

Speech-language evaluations may be done in different ways. Some evaluations are scheduled for one time. For example, your child may have a two-hour evaluation in which all of the testing is done, after which you are given the results. Other evaluations are done over the course of several different sittings. You may be scheduled for a separate session to discuss the results, after all of the testing is completed. Still other evaluations are done as diagnostic therapy—for instance, a one-month evaluation period of half-hour or one-hour sessions during which the SLP gets to know your child and assess his communication ability. In addition, there is a recent diagnostic procedure known as Response to Intervention (RTI). It was developed for children suspected of having learning disabilities in order to match children with appropriate treatment methods. For more information on RTI, see the section on "Current Trends in Evaluation," on page 61.

For younger children or at a clinical, hospital-based, or university-based center, you will usually be present at the evaluation. If an evaluation is done in school, you may not be present, or might not even know exactly when the testing will be done. My opinion is that, if possible, you should always be present to observe the testing, so that you will be able to let the speech-language pathologist know whether your child is showing his typical skills. It is best for you to be an active participant in the process.

At the clinical center at Loyola University in Maryland, we use rooms with one-way mirrors. Families observe 100 percent of the evaluation. Since our clinic is part of the graduate student training program, the graduate students are in the room with the child, and the clinical faculty member is with the family on the other side of the mirror. The faculty member can explain what is happening in the evaluation and can also answer any questions that the family may have.

Table 3-1: Developmental History

EARLY MEDICAL AND DEVELOPMENTAL HISTORY

What maternal health problems(s) existed during the pregnancy with the child? _____
_____

Length of pregnancy _____   Birth weight_____

Describe delivery:_____
_____

General health of child at birth: _____
          Apgar score _____
Handedness: Left ☐   Right ☐   Ambidextrous ☐

At what age did the child master the following milestones:
- Crawl _____   • Use single word _____
- Walk _____   • Use two words together _____
- Sit _____   • Combine words into short phrases_____
- Toilet independently: • Talk in sentences _____
     bladder _____
     bowel _____

Has your child had sensory processing difficulties? If yes, please explain the difficulties._____
_____

Has s/he had therapy addressing sensory issues? _____

What strategies have been/are effective in addressing the issues? _____
_____

SPEECH AND LANGUAGE DEVELOPMENT

How was learning to talk encouraged at home? _____
_____

Has your child been referred to a speech-language pathologist or had speech and language services? _____

At what age did your child begin speech therapy services? _____

Describe the types of therapy goals/activities used from birth to 2 years? _____
_____

Describe the types of therapy goals/activities used from 3-5 years? _____
_____

What factors might have discouraged speech and language development? _____
_____

What speech/language problems did or do exist with other members of the family? _____
_____

Describe your child's communication skills, especially his/her:
- Strengths _____
_____
- Challenges _____
_____

Does your child speak in full sentences?_____

Does your child engage in conversations? _____ With peers?_____ With adults? _____

In speaking situations, do you feel that your child can make himself/herself understood to everyone? _____

If your child is not using words or is frequently hard to understand, has your child developed a gestural system to communicate?_____ If yes, please describe. _____

_____

Does your child use an augmentative/alternative communication system? _____

Please provide information about that system and whether it is meeting your child's communication needs. _____

_____

Do you feel that your child is able to understand age-appropriate conversation directed toward him/her? _____
If not, please explain. _____

AUDIOLOGICAL HISTORY

Have you ever questioned your child's ability to hear? _____

If so, what action have you taken? _____

If your child has had his/her hearing tested, please provide the following information for each testing date:
Where was s/he tested?_____
Date of testing: _____
What tests were used?_____
Results: _____

Does your child respond appropriately to verbal communication (e.g., directions, conversation, questions, etc.)?
If no, please explain. _____

Does your child have difficulty when there is background noise in the environment?_____

Is your child uncomfortable when there are loud noises; e.g., at a stadium or in the school cafeteria? _____

Does your child have Ear, Nose, and Throat (ENT) difficulties?_____

Is your child being followed by an otolaryngologist (ENT)? _____

SCHOOL INFORMATION

Does/did child attend day care?_____

Age entered school _____

What grades, if any, were repeated? _____ Skipped?_____

Child's attitude toward school _____

Child's relationship to present teacher _____
past teachers _____

Is the child experiencing any learning or social problems in school?_____

If yes, please explain. _____

_____

_____

Area(s) of greatest academic interest _____

Area(s) of least academic interest _____

Is your child included in the regular education classroom? _____

Is your child in an adapted program or receiving special services? _____

If yes, please explain. _____
_____

SOCIAL DEVELOPMENT

Describe your child's social skills *(e.g., is he/she independent, outgoing, cooperative, shy, neat, fearful, withdrawn, leader, etc.)*
_____
_____

What is his/her relationship to:
- Parents _____
- Brothers and Sisters _____
- Other Adults _____
- Other Children _____

Are there any behavior/discipline problems? _____ If yes, please explain. _____
_____

How and by whom are they managed? What strategies have been effective? _____

HEALTH

Please describe the following:
- medical or surgical treatment _____
- any past or present illnesses or accidents _____
- chronic health problems _____
- history of medications _____
- eating habits and diet _____
- sleep habits _____
- history of allergies _____

Are immunizations complete? _____ If not, please explain. _____
_____

Has your child been seen for any health or psychological service other than routine medical attention? _____

If yes, please explain. _____
_____

Is your child currently under medical treatment? _____ If yes, please explain. _____
_____

An important reason for family members to observe their child's evaluation is that language is very much affected by whether the child is shy or uncomfortable. In a new situation with new therapists who do not know your child, it is unlikely that your child will show his typical communication skills. With older elementary school or middle school children, it is more likely that they will talk with the SLP if she asks questions about a topic of interest to them. Parents are often frustrated during evaluations when they observe their child using shorter phrases than he uses at home. I have had parents tell me that their child "talks up a storm," although he was not doing that at the evaluation.

A second reason that it is important for you to observe your child's evaluation is that you can let the SLP know whether your child could have answered a test item correctly if it had been phrased differently. The tests used may have complex instructions that are difficult for your child to follow. This is often the case if the school is evaluating your child for eligibility for services, and is using more formal (standardized) testing. Standardized tests have standardized instructions for administration. This means that the speech-language pathologist may not have leeway to make changes in the way the instructions are given to your child and cannot adapt or change test items if she is going to use the test norms and the scoring system for the test.

I have observed many test situations where the child actually knew the answer but didn't understand the instructions, and got the item wrong. Your child may not understand that he is supposed to circle the one that does *not* belong, rather than the one that does. Or that he is to choose the antonym (opposite), not the word that means the same as the word presented. Or your child may know the object by another name. For example, the test item may be "present" and your child knows "gift," or the test item is "spectacles" and you say "glasses." Another reason you should observe your child's evaluation, if possible, is that regional differences in vocabulary and pronunciation also enter into test items. In some parts of the country, "soda" is "pop," or "Coke" is used as a generic term for soda. An ice cream soda may be called a "frappe" or a "cabinet" in different parts of the country. A rubber band may be called a gum band.

If you observe your child's evaluation, you will be able to let the SLP know if your child's performance during the evaluation matches what you are seeing at home. If this is not possible, prepare a video of your child to enable the SLP to see how your child communicates at home in a familiar environment. For example, videotape your child at home talking with his brother or sister or another family member. Again, you can submit a video of your child even if he is being evaluated at school. IDEA 2004 states that the evaluation team needs to consider material submitted by the parents when assessing the child and discussing eligibility for services. The parent is a member of the IEP team.

OBSERVATION

When you arrive for the evaluation, you will often be asked to play, read, or have a conversation with your child in a one-way viewing room. This is an opportunity for the SLP to see how you and your child communicate. There are two reasons for this section of the evaluation.

1. The SLP can get a more accurate picture of your child's skills when he is communicating with a familiar person—you.
2. The SLP will be able to observe how you and your child typically communicate. This observation can be used to make suggestions for continuing or changing certain communication interactions.

Parents should try to interact naturally, even though they know they are being observed and may feel self-conscious. The purpose of the observation is not to test or judge you. It is to determine whether the interactive communication strategies that you and your child are using are effective. If they are, it can help to reinforce what you are using. If not, the SLP can suggest changes or can teach or demonstrate effective strategies for you to use with your child to help maximize his communication. For example, the speech-language pathologist may be able to suggest certain:

- cues (such as giving your child the first sound in a word),
- scaffolds (such as giving an associated word to help your child recall the word he needs to say), and
- stimulation techniques (such as making sure your child is looking at you before you ask a question).

FAMILY INTERVIEW

During a private evaluation, the SLP will usually interview the family at the beginning of the evaluation. In the interview, she will ask about your concerns, and seek more information about your child's language and speech skills at home, at school, and in the community. She will also follow up on any information that is unclear or incomplete from the pre-evaluation questionnaire that you filled out. It is a good idea to check your child's baby book, or to bring it with you to the evaluation even when your child is older, because most of the information needed on speech and language development will probably be recorded right in your child's baby book.

When the evaluation is completed at a diagnostic center connected with the schools, parents may be part of the interview and evaluation. When the evaluation is completed in school, the questionnaire may be the only opportunity the family has to communicate with the SLP before the evaluations takes place. When evaluations occur during the school day, families are not likely to be included.

FORMAL TESTING

Formal testing is a major part of the evaluation. To understand your child's results, it helps to have a basic understanding of the different types of tests that are used:

- Standardized tests,
- Criterion-referenced tests, and
- Informal assessments.

STANDARDIZED TESTS

Standardized tests are often used. When a test is standardized, it means that the test has:

- *validity*—it measures what it is supposed to measure (for example, a picture vocabulary test has recognizable, clear pictures

so that it measures vocabulary not vision, or the test measures your child's ability to repeat words and not his ability to form sentences using words)
- *reliability*—scores are consistent (each time a given child takes the test he will get approximately the same score)
- *a standard set of instructions and standard administration procedures*—the instructions and administration must be given just as stated in the test materials
- *standard scoring*—the test results will be converted to scores that can be compared across children. For example, they provide language age scores (e.g., your child has the language skills of a typical child who is 5 years, 8 months old) or percentile scores (e.g., your child's receptive speech abilities are at the 15th percentile, meaning when compared to 100 children his age, 14 would score lower on the test and 85 would score higher), means (average scores), and standard deviations (measures the range of scores, or how the scores cluster around the mean)
- *norms*—norms are a profile of scores that report what is average, below average, and above average for comparable children who took this test (for example, "average" is often a standard score of between 85 to 115 or so)

As mentioned earlier, standardized tests usually present some difficulties for children with Down syndrome, because standard instructions mean that the examiner may not be able to repeat the instructions, or rephrase them, or allow extra time.

In addition, remember that most children with Down syndrome have more advanced language comprehension than speech production. More than three-fourths of children with Down syndrome have higher levels of comprehension and cognition than speech skills. This means that standardized measures of language production will probably underestimate a child's language comprehension ability and cognitive abilities. This is important to consider when using testing to determine what supports and adaptations for speech and language are needed for inclusion.

Norms and Their Drawbacks. Professionals often prefer using standardized tests because they provide norms for large numbers of children against which your child's scores can be compared. In the United States, most tests are normed by administering the test to large numbers of typically developing Caucasian middle class students grouped by age and gender. The test developers then determine what the average scores are for children of different ages and genders, based on test results. Some tests are normed on Black-American or Asian-American students. But, no current tests have been normed with children with Down syndrome. So, that means that your child's test score is being compared to test results of typically developing children, not children with Down syndrome.

Schools use test norms to determine eligibility for speech and language services. School systems develop their own criteria for eligibility. Generally, eligibility criteria for the schools state that your child's scores need to be 6 months, 1 year, or 2 standard deviations below the norms to be eligible for services.

You might think that using norms to determine eligibility would work to the advantage of children with Down syndrome. That is, since typically developing children learn speech and language skills at a faster rate than most children with Down syndrome do, children with Down syndrome are almost always delayed compared to test norms. So, they should almost always be sufficiently delayed relative to the norms to qualify for speech and language services, right? The answer is "yes" if your school system uses the chronological age of a child to determine whether he is below the norms. (For example, your school compares a child who is 7 years, 6 months old with the norms for a child who is 7 years, 6 months old.) But the answer is frequently "no" if your school system uses the mental age of a child to determine whether he is below the norms. (For example, if a child is chronologically 7 years, 6 months old, but his mental age has been tested at 5 years, the school would compare his scores with the norms for a 5-year-old.)

Even if your child qualifies for services on the basis of mental age because his skills are quite delayed, he may lose services the next time he is tested if his speech and language skills improve at a faster rate than his mental age (so there is now less of a discrepancy between his mental age and speech and language skills). See the next chapter for more information about how norms are sometimes used to deny speech services, in particular, to children who need them.

CRITERION REFERENCED TESTS

These tests evaluate how your child performs on a specific set of skills, such as auditory memory or morphology. They do not compare your child with other children—they just show whether your child has or has not achieved given skills. For example, a criterion referenced test might indicate that your child can understand and use plurals, understands but does not use possessives, and does not understand or use past tense.

Criterion referenced tests are helpful in planning therapy because they usually not only document which skills your child has mastered, but also which skills need to be mastered and the order that children typically develop the skills. Criterion referenced tests can often serve as guidelines for therapy, and as a means for assessing progress in therapy. We need more information about how children with Down syndrome develop specific language skills.

INFORMAL ASSESSMENT

Informal assessment is a very important part of a speech and language evaluation. During the informal portion, the SLP tries to observe and evaluate what your child actually does to communicate. In an older child, the informal assessment will evaluate your child's conversational ability and his communication interactions with others. The SLP might ask him questions about a favorite movie or a family trip or event. She will then observe whether your child can use greetings, introduce a topic, stay on the topic, use a variety of words, and use certain grammatical structures. During informal speech assessment, the SLP can listen and determine whether your child can say sounds in all contexts or only in certain situations—for example, when reading or when responding with automatic phrases such as "OK."

Also as part of the informal assessment, the SLP will evaluate your child's attention and on-task behavior, to best determine how therapy can be conducted. For example, can several activities be set up around the room, or does your child do better with no distractions other than the task at hand? Does your child respond better to visual instructions (written) or auditory instructions (oral)? Should the visual instructions be written text or picture icons? Can your child write? Use a keyboard to type? The informal assessment results will help in planning an effective treatment program.

Understanding Test Results

When you are given the results of testing, make sure you understand the reason that a test was done (such as to determine eligibility for services), the purpose of the testing (such as to assess comprehension), and what the results mean. Ask for a list of the tests used with the full titles and a brief description. Often SLPs who give these tests use acronyms such as TOLD or PPVT that are unfamiliar to parents. If the purpose of the testing is for help in writing your child's IEP, request a copy of the written report. During the sharing time or after you receive the report, be sure to ask questions about the testing, and about each test. Following are some suggestions of questions to ask about a specific test:

1. What does this test measure?
2. What is the format of the test?
3. What are the parts of the test?
4. Can you show me some sample items?
5. What does my child's score mean?
6. What problems do the test results highlight?
7. What therapy follows from the results?

There are many reasons that speech and language evaluations may be done at different ages and stages in your child's development. Most of these are integrally involved in service delivery decisions. That is, they will be used to determine whether your child qualifies for speech and language therapy at school, and if so, how much. Consequently, it is always very important that the evaluation accurately reflect your child's current abilities. If you do not feel that the speech and language test results are representative of your child's abilities, speak up. Videotape or audiotape your child, schedule another evaluation with the same examiner at a different time, or seek out another opinion.

Hold on to Those Records!

Your child's SLP will keep copies of all the speech and language tests she does, as well as notes on your child's progress. But SLP records don't often follow your child from one school level to another (e.g., elementary school to middle school), or when you move to another school district, or even when there is a change in SLP from one year to the next. Private clinics usually maintain records for seven years, but then archive or even destroy those records. Parents are the main case managers and information specialists for their child. Ask for copies of all evaluations as they are completed, and if you change SLPs, ask for copies of your child's clinical files and reports (e.g., evaluations, progress reports, session summaries). Keep copies of those records so that you can share them with other professionals.

DID YOU GET THE NEEDED RESULTS?

In discussing the testing results with the SLP, you should try to determine whether the results give you the data that you need. To determine this, you need to have a clear understanding of the purpose of the test (the information it can provide) and the reasons for testing (how will the results be used?).

To Design Treatment: The major reason for testing is to design and develop appropriate treatment approaches and materials. So, if auditory memory testing finds that your child has difficulty processing more than two spoken directions but he is able to follow complex directions when visual cues are provided, therapy should be designed to include visual cues. Or, if morphology testing finds that your child does not use plurals, and phonology testing finds that your child omits the /s/ and /z/ sounds at the ends of words, therapy must first be designed to teach your child to include the /s/ and /z/ sound at the end of words. Then therapy can help your child understand the concept of plurals and how to use plurals. See Chapters 5 and 6 for more information about designing treatment for language and speech difficulties.

To Document Progress: Sometimes the purpose of testing is to gather baseline data or pre- and post-test data. That type of testing focuses on whether your child needs work on a specific communication skill, what his abilities are before treatment, and how much progress he has made through treatment. For example, your child understands the concept of past tense and future tense, but is not using the correct word forms in speech. The baseline/pretest data shows that he uses the word "yesterday" to indicate the past without putting the verb into past tense—e. g., "I run yesterday." Post-test data indicate that he now can use the correct form of the verb: "I ran yesterday, I jumped down the step, I drank water," etc. This information may be part of a diagnostic evaluation or progress report. For samples of a diagnostic speech evaluation, diagnostic language evaluation, and language treatment progress report, see the Appendix.

To Determine Eligibility: This purpose for testing is most frequently used in school settings. As mentioned earlier, every school system or local education agency (LEA) has its own criteria for determining whether a child is (or continues to be) eligible for speech-language services. They are sometimes known as entrance-exit criteria. For example, on a specific test, your child must score 2 standard deviations below the norm for his chronological (or mental) age in order to qualify for services.

Professional speech-language pathologists do many evaluations. They are familiar with many standardized, criterion referenced, and informal measures that can be used to evaluate your child's speech and language abilities. Many of these tests will be unfamiliar to you. Feel free to ask questions so that you understand what the test results mean. Ask the SLP whether she has a written summary of the tests used in your child's evaluation, including sample items and a description of what the scores and results of the test means.

ANALYSIS OF INFORMATION

Following your child's testing, the SLP will take some time to analyze the formal and informal test results. Your input is valuable. If you feel that your child was not speaking or responding in his usual way, you need to let the SLP know. This is one of the reasons that I feel that observation of the evaluation by the family is important.

Based on test results and the SLPs clinical experience, she will summarize the evaluation findings in a written report.

FEEDBACK AND FAMILY COUNSELING

Once the SLP has evaluated the formal and informal testing results and the observational data, she will provide your family with the resulting information. Depending on the setting, the process of getting the results may be different. In school, parents may find out the results at the annual IEP meeting. The scores may be included in the IEP, but may not be written up as a separate document or report.

In a private setting, there may be a separate appointment to discuss evaluation results, or the SLP may be able to summarize the results immediately after the testing session and talk with the family. In a medical center or university center, whether the information is provided immediately or at a separate meeting may depend on whether you are at a local center or a distant one. My experience is that there is usually a separate session if the facility is near the family's home, and that results are provided immediately when families have traveled a greater distance for the testing. Either way, in private, medical center, or university clinics, the results are also usually provided in a written report that is sent to the family following the evaluation. That report will share test findings, the SLP's analysis of the information, and suggestions for treatment approaches. The report may also specify needed referrals to other professionals such as a sensory processing specialist, audiologist, or ENT physician.

If there is a face-to-face meeting, this is the time for you to ask the SLP questions about the testing. It is also a good time for the SLP to provide references and resources to help you and your family understand the diagnosis.

PUTTING YOUR CHILD'S EVALUATION IN PERSPECTIVE

Many view the goal of a speech and language evaluation as being able to diagnose and label the problem. The difficulty is that "labels" in the area of special education often put the child on a long road that does not lend itself easily to change. Labels may be limiting and lower expectations. "Labels have a way of drawing our attention away from understanding the individual as a complex and competent person. Rather, what we see is reinterpreted within the stereotypes associated with the particular disability category" (Kliewer and Biklen, 1996). When labels are used for children with Down syndrome, they usually highlight the individual's problems and weaknesses, not his strengths. A diagnostic evaluation should highlight both, and should concentrate on short-term and long-term goals and change.

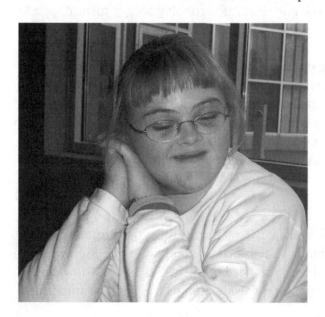

The diagnostic evaluation results should integrate the formal testing and informal evaluation findings, as well as your input about what you have observed to be easy or difficult for your child. The results should be a record of how your child is functioning in communication skills at that point in time. Phrases such as "Your child will never___" or "We have done everything we can" should not be part of the evaluation results. A speech and language diagnostic evaluation report should be long and detailed. It is not meant to be a screening; it is meant to describe your child's communication skills. The annual report in school settings will be brief and will be designed to assist in IEP planning. The comprehensive evaluation will be part of the triennial evaluation in schools, or part of a private practice, hospital-based, or university-based clinical evaluation.

A speech and language evaluation should help your family and your child (if old enough) to understand your child's communication difficulties and speech and language strengths. It is not sufficient for the SLP to give a diagnosis of "speech and language problems secondary to Down syndrome" or "Down syndrome speech." These diagnoses provide no useful information and do not point to appropriate treatment methods. The evaluation report (both verbal and written) needs to provide information about treatment options. It needs to be specific. That is why a period of diagnostic therapy can be helpful. It provides time and the opportunity for the SLP to work with your child, and observe which methods work well with your child and how your child learns best, rather than merely listing treatment options.

See the Appendix for an example of a comprehensive language evaluation completed at a university clinic. If you are paying for a private evaluation, you should expect this level of detail in the final report. Also see the Appendix for an excellent example of a school-based evaluation.

Perhaps the best description of my view of evaluation was given by Jason Kingsley in *Count Us In*: "Do the things that you *can* do" [That's what I see as the purpose of evaluation— to see what your child can do and what is difficult for your child] "and learn the things that you *can't* do. When you learn the things that you *can't* do, it then becomes the things you *can* do" (Kingsley and Levitz, 2007). That's what I see as the purpose of therapy—to help your child learn to do the things that are difficult for him. Evaluation and therapy are part of the same process leading to more effective functional speech and language skills.

Evaluations and Eligibility

As you probably already know, speech-language therapy is considered a *related service* under the Individuals with Disabilities Education Act of 2004 (IDEA). What you might not realize is that the definition of related service has changed. In prior legislation, related services were defined as services that are needed in order for the child to benefit from special education. Many children with Down syndrome were denied eligibility for speech-language pathology because they did not need the service "to benefit from special education." Now, special education is defined as supports needed for the general education curriculum, so that is a positive change. And related services are defined as services that are provided to enable the child to be involved in and make progress in the general education curriculum … and to participate in extracurricular and other nonacademic activities.

That means that before your child can receive speech-language therapy from the school, an evaluation must be completed to determine whether your child needs the therapy in order to make progress in the general education curriculum and/or to participate in other school activities. If so, he *should* be found to be eligible for speech-language services. It is possible, however, that you may have a struggle to prove that your child is eligible for speech-language services if your school system uses either discrepancy ratings or developmental models to determine who qualifies (see below).

In the past, many children with Down syndrome were denied speech and language treatment on the basis of discrepancy ratings. Using this system, the child's language test scores and intelligence test scores must be at different levels if he is to be found eligible for services. If the child's language scores are at the same level as his mental age test scores, he can be denied services. The justification is that his language function is commensurate with his intelligence level. The problem with this approach is that many intelligence tests are based on language and use language for the questions and answers. Thus, language test scores and standardized intelligence test scores are more than likely to be highly correlated.

IDEA 2004 discourages the use of discrepancy ratings for children with specific learning disability but does not address discrepancy ratings for children with other disabilities. It is possible your school system may still use discrepancy ratings. In my experience, school systems often focus on the discrepancy (or lack of discrepancy) between cognitive ability and language skills when determining eligibility for speech-language therapy.

If your child is denied speech-language services due to discrepancy ratings, you can request that a nonverbal intelligence test be used to assess your child's cognitive level. When that is done, there often is a discrepancy between the language and cognitive levels that will help your child qualify for services. Some nonverbal tests that can be used include the Leiter International Performance Scale, Revised (Leiter-R) and Test of Nonverbal Intelligence, Third Edition (TONI-3).

The Leiter Scale measures IQ and "logical ability" and provides norms for typically developing people aged 2 to 20 years. The TONI-3 assesses nonverbal intelligence, aptitude, abstract reasoning, and problem solving and provides norms for typically developing people aged 6 to 89 years 11 months. You can also ask your child's IEP team to focus on your child's scores on the nonverbal subtests of a typical IQ test such as the WISC-IV (Wechsler Intelligence Scale for Children, fourth edition) rather than looking at the full scale IQ. You can ask the evaluation team to work with the school psychologist or testing specialists to ensure that the nonverbal test sections or a nonverbal test's score are used as a comparison to language test results.

Another strategy is to remind your child's school that, under IDEA 2004, they are required to administer tests and evaluation materials "in the language and form most likely to yield accurate information on what the child knows and can do academically, developmentally, and functionally, unless it is not feasible to do so." This could include *sign language* and *augmentative communication* as ways to administer tests. Tests can be modified both in the mode in which the questions are presented, and the mode in which the child responds.

Another approach to using test scores to determine eligibility has been to use a developmental model. Using this model, your child's test results are compared to those of typically developing children at that chronological age. Usually, the school has specific entrance and exit criteria to qualify for speech and language services. For example, your child may need to score one year below chronological age, or 2 standard deviations below norms for the age (usually about 30 points) to qualify for services.

Services may not be continued if your child's scores, based on annual assessment, improve so that they are age appropriate. As explained in the section on Norms above, sometimes chronological age level is used and sometimes mental age level is used to determine eligibility through the formula.

A developmental model is often used to deny speech therapy for articulation problems. For example, if your child's chronological age is 7, the SLP may tell you that according to articulation test norms, children do not master the /r/ sound until 8 years of age, and that she would need to wait until your child is at least 9 to determine whether he is delayed. Or she may use mental age, and say that your 9-year-old has a mental age of 6, so she would not expect him to be able to say /s/ clearly, so she will need to wait and give him time to develop. Since children with Down syndrome frequently have oral motor difficulties and hearing loss, both of which affect articulation, I don't think that a developmental model as the criteria for eligibility is appropriate.

CURRENT TRENDS IN EVALUATION

There are current trends in speech and language assessment that may drastically change the way that evaluations are conducted. Due to the difficulties in testing discussed above, there is a growing recognition that many tests administered to children with Down syndrome do not provide accurate results that mirror the child's skills in daily living. The new methods of gathering information about a child's abilities described below can often provide a better picture of your child's speech and language skills.

PORTFOLIO ASSESSMENT

Portfolio assessment is increasingly being used in school settings. Rather than use one testing session to evaluate your child's speech and language skills, the school SLP maintains a folder of your child's progress over time, taking samples of his communication skills throughout the period. Scoring matrices (checklists that help organize the data) are designed that can document your child's progress over time. Audiotapes, videotapes, and written work may be used to assess progress. As a parent, you can also provide the SLP with videotapes (preferable) or audiotapes of your child at home, with siblings, friends, and grandparents engaged in communication. This can become part of the evaluation portfolio and can be available to the speech-language pathologists to help document your child's real-life communication abilities.

CURRICULUM/WORK OBJECTIVES MASTERY

Curriculum/work objectives mastery is another trend. Rather than trying to determine a language score for your child, the SLP analyzes the curriculum in school or the communication skills your child needs at work. Then, the SLP matches the communication demands at school or work with your child's abilities and determines what areas of communication will be addressed in therapy and what supports may be needed in school or the workplace. For example, the SLP might determine that your child has trouble following spoken and written instructions that include more than one step. Or he or she may find that your child has difficulty with abstract vocabulary in science (e.g., genus, species) and social studies (e.g., democracy, government). The SLP would then work on those skills with your child in therapy, rather than assigning your child a score based on his language abilities as the basis for a treatment program.

ARENA ASSESSMENT

This is a team approach to diagnostic evaluation. The team consists of a facilitator, the parent(s), and all specialists who work with the child. The team usually stands behind the child, but facing the facilitator. The facilitator is the person who usually interacts with the child. The facilitator chooses:

- a familiar activity, such as eating a snack;
- an age appropriate activity, such as playing with action figures or doing a puzzle;
- a graded activity (meaning an activity with a variety of tasks at different levels of difficulty), such as an obstacle course, to see how the child problem solves.

The psychologist, speech-language pathologist, occupational therapist, parents, classroom teacher, and any other professionals all observe the child as he participates in the activities. Each specialist has her own checklist and writes down her own observations related to her own area of specialty (communication skills, social-emotional skills, sensory motor skills, cognitive skills.) The team meets after the evaluation to share their findings with each other and the family.

RESPONSE TO INTERVENTION (RTI)

Response to Intervention is a system that helps the SLP choose an appropriate treatment method or compare several therapy techniques to determine which treatment would be most effective for a specific child. RTI is most often used for insight into helping children with AD/HD or learning disabilities with their educational difficulties, but it is applicable to children with Down syndrome.

Response to intervention is like diagnostic therapy. It is a system of instruction and intervention but the information is used diagnostically. It provides a window into your child's communication learning patterns. The SLP learns what works well for your child. RTI may enable her to see whether a specific therapy method works well, or to compare several methods and analyze which will be the best method to use in therapy, for your child, to reach a specific goal. RTI is a multitiered approach that involves close collaboration among a variety of specialists in the schools including speech-language pathologists.

REQUESTING AN ALTERNATE METHOD OF EVALUATION

Sometimes, when long, comprehensive language tests are used to evaluate children with Down syndrome, the results are not meaningful or applicable to planning treatment. For example, if test results show that your child's expressive language skills are far behind his receptive language skills, this doesn't provide specific, targeted information that can help to plan an appropriate treatment plan. In this kind of situation, ask the SLP if she can use criterion referenced tests, portfolio assessment, curriculum based assessment, and/or response to intervention instead to evaluate your child's needs.

What If the School Finds Your Child Ineligible?

Both of the situations described above place parents in a catch-22 situation. In situation 1, since cognitive testing is often based on language ability (both in understanding and following test instructions and in answering questions verbally), it is no surprise that a child's cognitive levels and language levels may appear similar. In situation 2, your child can only receive services when he scores below expected levels (certain cut-off scores). So, if your child improves, he can be denied services, and services will only begin again when his test scores fall a specific amount below age level. Some parents have told me that they permit the cognitive and language testing since the testing is mandatory to be eligible for services, but that they do not even look at the test scores because they feel that the scores do not represent their child's true level of intellectual or language function. One mom said, "I'm sure my son had very low scores, because they never again questioned his need for services."

What can you do if your child is disqualified from services on the basis of speech and language scores or cognitive scores because your school system is using one of the outmoded systems described above? I recommend reminding your IEP team that under the new IDEA regulations, your child's IEP must "meet the child's needs that result from the child's disability to enable the child to be involved in and make progress in the general education curriculum." Then give them specific examples of ways that your child's speech and language needs are preventing him from making progress in English, social studies, science, etc.

Contact the office of special education or the director of speech-language pathology within your school district. They are usually very aware of current regulations. They may have central office personnel who can consult with and serve as a resource for the school SLP and help her meet your child's needs. I know of several instances where such personnel met with the school SLP on a regular basis to help her learn how to adapt curriculum and how to modify the language on daily classroom worksheets.

If your IEP team is difficult to persuade and you can afford it, hire an educational advocate to help convince your IEP team that your child needs speech-language therapy to progress in the general education curriculum. Remember, under IDEA 2004, schools must include information provided by the parent in evaluations. The wording in IDEA 2004 is very specific in stating that initial evaluation and reevaluations must take into consideration, in addition to tests, "evaluations and information provided by the parents of the child, current classroom-based assessments and observations, and teacher and related service providers [SLP comes under this category] observation, and consideration of what the child needs to be successful in the general curriculum." This represents a major change and it means that eligibility decisions should be based on more than test results. Family input and teacher input should be taken into consideration when determining eligibility for speech-language pathology services

It may be helpful to get a private language evaluation to help persuade the school of your child's needs. You can also take video or audio tapes of your child's speech and language skills at home and in the community and request that the IEP team consider them. Outside information cannot be discounted or ignored. It must be part of the overall evaluation results that help determine your child's eligibility for services.

Even if your child is not "eligible" for services under your school's eligibility criteria, that doesn't mean that he doesn't need speech-language therapy. Need and eligibility are two different issues. Consider other settings such as an Easter Seals treatment center or other community clinic, a hospital-based or university-based treatment center, or a speech-language pathologist in private practice to help your child with speech and language skills. See Chapter 1 for more information on finding a qualified speech-language pathologist.

Your Child Is Eligible—Now What?

If your child is found to be eligible for speech-language therapy at school, the next step is to spell out what your child will work on, where, and when in his Individualized Education Program (IEP). Most likely, you are already well aware of what an IEP is, but if you don't, here is a brief summary:

The IEP is a written contract that is required under the Individuals with Disabilities Education Act for all students receiving special education services. It details, among other things:

- Your child's present level of performance in all areas where he needs assistance (i.e., results of formal and informal evaluations);
- Goals that state what your child is expected to learn during the course of the school year;
- The services (including special education or speech-language therapy) that will be provided to your child to help him achieve his goals;
- Where your child will receive the services and how often he will receive them.

IEPs are developed during one or more IEP meetings, which are attended by parents, teachers, therapists, and others who have knowledge or expertise that would be helpful in planning your child's educational program. You and your child's IEP team are supposed to work out his speech and language treatment plan during the IEP meeting. The IEP meeting is designed to be a process meeting when plans are discussed by the classroom teacher, specialists, and the family. Unfortunately, however, it is often the first time that parents have an opportunity to give their input. The professionals are interested in completing the process and having team members, including the family, sign the IEP at that meeting.

Meetings can be contentious and difficult. School personnel and parents often disagree about what is appropriate therapy. The schools are following the guidelines of IDEA and often want to provide the minimum of therapy to allow your child to access the curriculum. So, for example, even if your child can't speak in full sentences, if he can understand what the teacher says, the school may try to make the case that he does not need speech therapy. They are really saying that your child is not eligible for speech-language services according to the eligibility criteria the school system uses. In contrast, parents want school therapy to help their child reach his communication potential—to help him to communicate effectively in school and outside of school at home and in the community. So, generally parents are discussing *need* and schools are discussing *eligibility*.

The basic difference between what school systems and parents want out of speech-language therapy is most obvious when educators and parents talk about assistive technology. Many schools will evaluate a child for augmentative communication, and will purchase the equipment that the child needs. But, then they will only allow the child to use the system in speech sessions or in the classroom. They will not allow the child to take the communication device home after school, or on weekends or during the summer. And often, when the child moves from elementary school to middle school, the equipment does not go with him. It is considered the property of the school, not the child. In other words, the school is considering what the child requires to progress in the general education curriculum, whereas the family is considering what communication skills the child needs to function successfully as an adult. (See Chapter 10 for more information about AAC.)

What do I consider to be appropriate therapy? Speech and language therapy should provide for your child's present communication needs and prepare him for communication independence in adulthood, to the greatest extent possible. Therapy should be provided in the setting (or combination of settings) that will enable your child to achieve the speech and language goals on his IEP. (See next section.) Remember, however, that school therapy is not designed to meet all of your child's needs for communication help, just the needs that help him progress in the classroom. You may need to seek additional services outside the school setting to help your child reach his communication potential.

SERVICE DELIVERY MODELS

A combination of different ways of providing therapy ("service delivery models") may be needed to meet your child's individual needs. For example, group therapy sessions with four children who all need to focus on social language and conversation may be appropriate for him, but group therapy with four children who are working on different areas would not be appropriate. In the U.S., the most common service delivery models are:

- Pull-out
- Push-in
- Collaborative consultation, and
- Consultative services.

PULL-OUT THERAPY

Speech-language pathology services are often provided in a separate speech room, in individual or small group settings within the class day. This delivery model is known as "pull-out therapy," since your child is pulled out of the classroom. The benefit is that the speech room is usually quiet and your child can focus on speech. The drawback is that it is difficult to schedule sessions so that your child does not miss important class work. If your child is receiving group therapy, it is also difficult to schedule sessions so that children in the group have language difficulties that are similar.

PUSH-IN THERAPY

This is the term used when therapy sessions are held in the classroom. It is also known as classroom-based intervention. One benefit is that the SLP can use material in

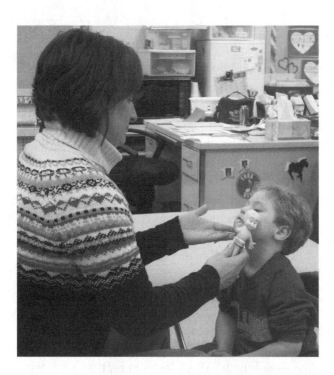

therapy that focuses on what your child needs to succeed in the classroom. The SLP has the opportunity to observe and work with your child in the classroom using the textbooks and materials used in class. The SLP can include other children in the sessions when doing conversational or social language activities. In both special education and general education classrooms, the SLP may lead a session on communication for the entire class.

The major drawback is that there are many distractions in the classroom. The classroom is often noisy and your child may be more interested in what is going on in class than on what the SLP is working on. Classroom-based therapy does not lend itself to certain types of therapy, such as oral motor planning problems for speech. But, classroom-based therapy need not be the only service delivery model used. Some children's IEPs may specify that they receive some of their therapy in the speech room and some in the classroom.

COLLABORATIVE CONSULTATION

When the term collaborative consultation is used in relation to speech-language pathology, it refers to the collaboration between the speech-language pathologist and the classroom teacher. Collaborative consultation works well when used in combination with push-in therapy. Since the SLP is right there in the classroom, the teacher can tell him or her what vocabulary and concepts the child needs to learn. She can also tell the SLP about any difficulties she's having understanding the child when he talks in class. The SLP can make suggestions to the teacher, and can work on strategies to increase speech intelligibility or to enable the child to answer questions, depending on what is needed. The SLP can observe the child trying to follow instructions and answering questions in class, and then the SLP can work on those things in therapy.

A benefit is that speech and language is not relegated to a brief time slot in a separate room. Instead, it can be integrated within the classroom and the curriculum, and become more a part of your child's daily life. In practice, it can be difficult for teachers and SLPs to find the time to collaborate effectively, and this model can't work unless they have the time to meet together to design the materials and to discuss and apply the methods.

CONSULTATIVE SERVICES

Sometimes the SLP does not work with a student directly, but is available to help school staff on a consultative basis. For example, if a teacher notices that your child is having trouble following spoken instructions in class, she might consult with the SLP about strategies that will help the child follow directions. Consultative service may be used when the child is not eligible for direct service because his communication problem is mild, or when the SLP is monitoring progress but does not feel that direct service is needed. Consultation should involve frequent observations of your child in the classroom and ongoing consultation with you and the teacher.

A drawback to the consultative services is that sometimes consultation becomes a once-a-term hallway conference between the SLP and teacher at the level of "How's Beth doing in class?" If your child is given consultative services, remember: you can communicate with the teacher and SLP about areas that concern you. You can try to get them to address your concerns, in order to get some benefit out of this model for your child. It is a good idea to ask for a home-school communication plan to ensure that you are in the loop, and that real consultation is occurring on a regular basis. For more information on home-school communication, see Chapters 5 and 6.

WHICH MODEL IS BEST FOR YOUR CHILD?

Both pull-out and in-class therapy are widely used in the schools. Most school systems use one or the other. My professional opinion is that each type of treatment has benefits, and that the type of treatment should meet the needs of your individual child, not be used system-wide. For example, classroom-based therapy may be preferable

for your child if he has goals related to learning language for academic subjects or following instructions, since the SLP will have access to the textbooks and worksheets that your child is using and will be able to observe how your child interacts with the teachers. In-class therapy is also useful for students who need to practice conversational skills, such as staying on topic, as there are always other children available for practice. But, I think that pull-out therapy is preferable for oral-motor exercises or intelligibility work, as these require individual focus and attention, away from the distractions of the classroom.

Remember that your child's IEP must be individually designed for his needs. If your child needs a combination of classroom-based and individual therapy, that should be provided (in the best of worlds!) in the schools, or through a combination of school-based and outside therapy. The bottom line is that the service delivery model that is used needs to meet the needs of your child to maximize his communication skills.

Disagreements with the School

What do you do if you don't agree with the IEP plan for speech-language services? First, consider the test results being used to develop the IEP. Are they an accurate representation of what you are seeing your child do at home? If not, you can videotape your child at home and submit the videotape to be included in the evaluation.

Remember, though, if you come to the IEP meeting and say that your child is performing better than the test results show, the IEP team could decide that he no longer qualifies for services. If you agree with the test results but feel that your child needs more therapy each week, the only criterion that you can address is how the language difficulties are affecting your child's performance in class. For example, if your child cannot complete assignments in class because he doesn't understand the verbal instructions the teacher is giving, he may need modifications such as written instructions or pictured instructions. If the classroom teacher and the SLP agree with your assessment, they may agree that the services should be increased. Usually, however, teachers and school SLPs will not be receptive to changing the service delivery models (direct, pull-out, push-in, collaborative consultation) and will state that this is what your child needs. (Although by law, services are supposed to be individualized, in practice, most schools use only a few service delivery models and are often unwilling to change them because they don't have enough SLPs and there is limited time during the school day to serve all children who need speech-language therapy.)

If you are unable to convince your child's IEP team to provide more therapy, I think the best path is to fight for a home practice program and a home-school communication program to be included. That way, you can follow through at home and increase your child's progress. If your child has a home program, he will get hours of practice in natural situations (if you follow through), rather than an extra fifteen minutes of therapy time during the week. Another possibility is to bring in results of outside testing by speech-language pathologists who specialize in working with children with Down syndrome, audiologists, or augmentative/alternative communication specialists (AAC) to document that your child needs additional services. This can be a long battle, and often by the time the decision is made to increase services by fifteen minutes a week, the school year is almost over.

Conclusion

Professional speech-language pathologists have knowledge and experience regarding the communication process. Other school personnel such as classroom teachers, special educators, reading specialists, school psychologists, and behavioral

specialists have knowledge and expertise in areas such as curriculum, behavior, and group dynamics that affect communication or that are affected by communication abilities. A speech-language evaluation should draw on the observations and expertise of school personnel as well as the family. Parents have a deep understanding of their child's skills and capabilities and likes and dislikes. They are aware of their child's speech and language strengths and challenges, and are an important information resource for both language and speech evaluations. The speech evaluation has its own circle of specialists, which may include dentists (pedodontists, orthodontists, prothodontists), pediatricians, otolaryngologists, occupational therapists, and oral motor specialists. Together, professionals and parents can collaborate to evaluate the communication abilities of a child, and to plan the best approaches to help the child progress in speech, language, and communication.

This chapter has provided an overview of the speech and language evaluation process. The next chapter will focus on the specific components of speech and language evaluations. If your child is about to be evaluated in school or if you are seeking outside evaluations, you will want to read the next chapter now. If your child's evaluation has already been completed or if you are heading into an IEP meeting without an evaluation, you will want to skip ahead to Chapters 5 and 6, which discuss treatment for language and speech, as well as using the results of the evaluations to write effective IEP goals for speech and language treatment.

CHAPTER 4

Evaluating Speech and Language Skills

The previous chapter covered the nuts and bolts of communication evaluations for children with Down syndrome, including the reasons for getting an evaluation, the school's role in providing one, and how parents can ensure that an evaluation best reflects their child's abilities. In this chapter, we take a detailed look at what specific speech and language skills are generally evaluated in a comprehensive evaluation and how they are evaluated.

Bear in mind that not all evaluations will cover all the areas discussed below. At times your child might have just a language evaluation or just a speech evaluation, but not both. For example, if your child is having a specific difficulty such as stuttering, the evaluation may focus only on that area. If your child is having behavior problems at school, a functional behavior assessment (FBA) may also include a language evaluation to determine what communication skills are affecting behavior and what communication messages underlie the problem behaviors. If conversation is a problem, the communication evaluation will focus on conversational skills.

This chapter will address all of these areas. In each area, there are many different tests that can be used to measure a child's skills. In this chapter, I will highlight some of the most widely used tests. Your SLP may, however, choose different tests to assess your child's speech and language skills.

THE LANGUAGE EVALUATION

What happens during the language evaluation will vary depending on how much language your child is using. If your child is speaking, a language sample during play or conversation will be taken. Often it will be videotaped or audiotaped so that the speech-language pathologist can analyze the sample later. If your child is not yet speaking, the evaluation may look at pre-language skills, use of sign language, and nonverbal communication. Individual tests may be used to assess each area (e.g., vocabulary) or a comprehensive test battery that assesses many different language skills may be used. The major sections that will be evaluated in a language evaluation are:

- Nonverbal communication
- Phonology
- Morphology
- Syntax
- Semantics
- Pragmatics

These terms are explained below.

Areas Assessed

NONVERBAL COMMUNICATION

Your child's nonverbal communication skills will be assessed, whether or not she uses speech to communicate. If your child is not using verbal or formal gestural communication (such as sign language), the SLP will need to evaluate:

- turn taking,
- visual skills such as reciprocal gaze (I look at you and you look at me) and joint referencing (we both look at something together),
- social gestures such as waving hi or bye or giving high-fives, and
- other pre-language skills.

The SLP will especially be interested in determining:

- whether your child appears to have communication intent (that is, she knows what she wants to communicate),
- whether your child tries to interact with people,
- how your child asks for help, and
- how she makes requests nonverbally.

The SLP will probably evaluate these skills by observation, through play, or through a parent checklist.

If your child is using a nonverbal communication system such as sign language or an augmentative/alternative communication device, the SLP will evaluate her lan-

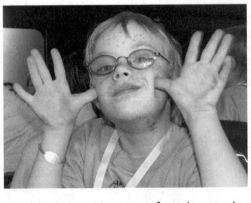

guage understanding and language usage of that system through play, observation, and carrying on a two-way conversation.

If your child is using speech, then the SLP will evaluate her gestures, facial expressions, and proxemics (use of space and distance) in the nonverbal communication section of the evaluation. Formal language tests are not usually used to evaluate nonverbal communication skills. The evaluation is usually informal, involving observation during conversation and/or narrative discourse (story telling). The SLP will watch to see whether your child uses gestures and facial expressions appropriately. She may ask yes and no questions to observe your child's head nod, or ask about a favorite cousin or a favorite video to observe whether your child's facial expressions match her happy words.

Usually children with Down syndrome correctly use nonverbal communication such as shaking the head yes and no, or shrugging the shoulders for "I don't know," or using a gesture for "come here." They rarely have difficulty with nonverbal communication. If difficulty is observed, further evaluation is needed to determine whether your child has another condition such as autism or nonverbal language disorder which may be affecting nonverbal communication abilities.

PHONOLOGY

Phonology is concerned with the patterns of sounds in the language, and how these sounds are organized in that language to form words. For example, in English, the /g/ sound can be followed by the /r/ or the /l/ sound for words such as *grow* or *glow.* The /s/ sound can be followed by the /l/ as in *slow,* but not by the /r/. Words in English don't begin with sr—for instance, srow is not a possible word in English.

Phonology also looks at the pattern of sound errors that a child uses, such as whether she always omits certain sounds from the ends of words. For example, perhaps your child can pronounce the /t/ sound, but she habitually leaves it off the ends of words. (She can say *to,* but she says *boo* for *boot.*) In fact, the most common difficulty that children with Down syndrome have in phonology is leaving out the last sounds in words (final consonant deletion).

Phonology also encompasses several important skills essential for reading and writing:

- The ability to discriminate between sounds (sound discrimination). For example, are two sounds the same or different?
- The ability to identify sounds. For example, what is the beginning sound in the word *leaf?*
- The ability to identify sound patterns (phonological awareness). For example, what rhymes with *cat?*

These skills are collectively known as phonological awareness skills. Children with Down syndrome due to trisomy 21 often have difficulty with phonological awareness skills. Some children with mosaic Down syndrome, however, have strong phonological awareness skills.

These skills are sometimes assessed to determine children's readiness to read. In the past, children with Down syndrome were sometimes not considered for reading programs because they scored low on tests of phonological awareness skills. Now, we know that children with Down syndrome can learn to read and that phonological awareness tests should not be used to deny them the opportunity to learn to read.

Teachers work with children on phonological awareness skills such as identifying rhyming words or words that start with the same sound in language arts. SLPs work on phonology in therapy by teaching your child to perceive and improve problems with her own speech sound patterns.

Your child's phonological awareness skills are usually evaluated during the language portion of the evaluation, whereas her ability to produce sounds correctly in speech are evaluated during the speech portion (see below).

To evaluate your child's phonological awareness skills, the SLP usually uses formal language tests, but phonological awareness skills are also tested on pre-reading and reading tests and on school readiness tests. An example of a test that may be used is the Phonological Awareness Profile (LinguiSystems, 1995). Test items would sample your child's expressive and receptive abilities in: rhyming, dividing words into syllables (segmentation), sound discrimination, and other similar skills. The examiner might read a word from a list of words, and ask your child to identify the middle sound or the ending sound in the word, to give a word that rhymes with the test item, or clap for each syllable in a word.

MORPHOLOGY

Morphemes are the smallest meaningful language components of words that have meaning, including root words, prefixes, and suffixes. For example, in the word *hands,* there are two morphemes. The root morpheme is "hand" and the suffix morpheme is "s," which tells us that the word is plural.

The morphemes in the English language are:

1. plurals (/s/ as in books, /z/ as in dogs, and /es/ as in houses);
2. possessives (John's book);
3. prepositions (in, under);
4. present progressive verb tense markers (e.g., the "ing" in cooking);
5. auxiliary and copula words (is, was);
6. past tense markers (e.g., the "ed" in mailed or folded);
7. pronouns (he, she, they, it);
8. articles (a, the);
9. conjunctions (and, but, because); and
10. meaningful root words (e.g., chair, arm chair).

Most of the comprehensive language batteries include subtests for morphology. The comprehensive language batteries such as the TOLD (*Test of Language Development-Primary*) and the CELF (*Clinical Evaluation of Language Fundamentals)* have subtests that assess morphology. There are also individual tests that focus only on morphology. An example of a formal test is the *Test of Language Development* (TOLD). There are subtests for Grammatic Understanding (receptive) and Grammatic Completion (expressive). For the receptive items, the tester would read a sentence and ask the child to point to the appropriate picture (e.g., "There are many balls"). For the expressive items, the tester would give the child a fill-in sentence and ask her to complete the sentence (e.g., "The book belongs to me. It is _____.")

A test item may probe whether your child uses the right morphemes to form plurals by asking the following using pictures: "I see a tree. Now I see two of them. How many are there?" (Answer: "two trees.") "I see a deer. Now I see two of them. How many are there?" (Answer: "two deer.") Or, the SLP may check your child's usage of verb endings with a series such as: "Ally is drinking the water. Now she finished. She _____ all the water."

SYNTAX

Syntax refers to the structure of language, including grammar and word order. Syntax also includes:

- subject-verb agreement ("I go," "she goes"),
- sentence length,

A Note on Standardized Language Tests

In children with Down syndrome, a preschool test or a test of early language development may still be used with an older child to assess which skills she has mastered and which she still needs to work on. Remember that norms for all of the tests are norms developed through testing children with typical development, not children with Down syndrome. There are no norms available for children with Down syndrome. In other words, the results of such tests will tell you only how your child's language skills compare to those of typically developing children, not to other children with Down syndrome.

- sentence complexity (e.g., using embedded phrases such as "This is the store that is having a sale"),
- being able to use a variety of sentence types—interrogatives ("Did Logan hit the ball?"; negatives ("Logan did not hit the ball"; active ("Logan hit the ball"; passive "The ball was hit by Logan",
- being able to use copula verbs (to be words, such as am, are, is).

Syntax practice usually involves making sentences, as well as making sentences longer and more complex. Some classes of words, such as pronouns and articles, are more difficult for children with language disorders to understand and use.

Syntax is abstract and is a difficult area for many children with Down syndrome. The child needs to understand when and why to use certain structures, such as in making a sentence into a question. For example, "You are going to the store" becomes "Are you going to the store?"

Morphology and syntax are interrelated. That is, you cannot use grammatically correct speech unless you also use correct morphology. For example, when you say the words "Megan's baby sister is crying" in proper grammatical order, you are also correctly using the morphemes to form the possessive of *Megan* and the present progressive tense of *to cry*. So when we talk about verb tenses, pronouns, word order, or how to make a sentence into a question, we are talking about both morphology and syntax. The area of language is now commonly referred to as morphosyntax.

During a language evaluation, the child is often given a situation and then required to ask a question. For instance: "John wants to go outside. What can he ask his mother?" Most comprehensive language test batteries assess syntax as part of their overall score. For example, *The Comprehensive Assessment of Spoken Language (CASL),* which is comprised of 15 stand-alone tests that can be separately administered and scored, tests understanding, expression, and retrieval of syntax information.

SEMANTICS   To evaluate semantics, the SLP looks at your child's use of vocabulary and meaning. As discussed in Chapter 2, this is a relatively strong area for children with Down syndrome. Research has shown that children with Down syndrome continue to develop vocabulary throughout childhood and into adulthood.

Usually, on tests of semantics, your child is asked to point to a picture (to test receptive language) or name it (to test expressive language). Typical vocabulary categories are animals, occupations, transportation, family relationships, foods, furniture and household items, and personal grooming items. For older children, vocabulary tests may also include questions about:

- synonyms or words with similar meanings ("Can you tell me another word for *light*?"),
- antonyms or opposites ("What is the opposite of *slow*?"),
- subordinates or one member of a larger class of things ("Name a fruit"),
- superordinates or broad categories ("What kind of food is an orange?")
- associated words or which words go together ("What goes with sock?")

As test items become more advanced, they may include *convergent* and *divergent* language skills. Convergent skills require your child to combine two or more attributes and come up with one word. For example, "I am thinking of a fruit that is red and crunches when you bite into it. What is it?" Divergent language skills often require your child to start with a broad category and name words that fit in that category.

For instance, she might be asked to name as many fruits as she can in one minute. Both of these types of questions assess your child's memory and word retrieval, but usually only the tests of divergent language skills are timed.

Vocabulary tests for older children and adolescents may include:

- word definitions ("What is a birthday?"),
- associations ("Tell me which words go together" or "Tell me which word does not belong"),
- semantic absurdities ("What is wrong with this sentence—The electrician painted the house?"), and
- flexible word use/multiple meanings ("What are all the meanings for the word *fall*?").

Most of the vocabulary tests that are used for evaluation are tests of single word vocabulary. That is, they just require your child to respond with one word or to respond to one word—for instance, by pointing to the picture that is named. When test results are reported to parents, they are often told that their child's vocabulary is at a 7 year 6 month level, but are not told that this score was based on a test of single word vocabulary. So, the score may make it seem as if the child's abilities are higher than they actually are, because these types of tests don't tap into difficulties with understanding and using vocabulary words in combination, in phrases, and in sentences.

Some tests such as the *Peabody Picture Vocabulary Test (PPVT)* and the *One Word Receptive Vocabulary Test (OWRVT)* assess only receptive vocabulary (language comprehension) at the single word level. The child is asked to point to the picture that matches the word being said by the examiner. Other receptive language tests such as *Test for Auditory Comprehension of Language (TACL)* are more complex and involve the child choosing a picture that represents a complex sentence such as, "Before he cleaned the kitchen, he loaded the dishwasher" or "The boy showed the DVD to his sister who was in the car."

Some tests such as the *Expressive One Word Vocabulary Test (EOWVT)* and the *Comprehensive Assessment of Spoken Language (CASL)* test assess expressive vocabulary (your child's ability to recall and say the correct word or words). The EOWVT is a test of single word vocabulary, whereas the CASL tests basic and advanced skills such as antonyms, sentence construction and sentence completion, paragraph comprehension, and pragmatic judgment. Other tests such as the *Wiig Assessment of Basic Concepts (WABC)* and the *Comprehensive Receptive and Expressive Vocabulary Test (CREVT)* assess both receptive and expressive vocabulary, including pointing to pictures (receptive) and defining words (expressive).

PRAGMATICS

Pragmatics refers to the social use of language and includes conversational skills, narrative discourse (retelling a story), topicalization (choosing, introducing, maintaining, changing, and ending topics), requests, greetings, and social interactive language. Social interactive language is generally a relative strength for children with Down syndrome, although some more advanced areas can pose difficulties. Retelling a story is often difficult, especially when the child is upset about something that happened. Usu-

ally, the child has difficulty providing details and an organized sequence in the story. Conversational skills are also usually an area of difficulty, because many children have trouble staying on topic and knowing what to include in a conversation.

To evaluate your child's skills in pragmatics, the SLP may use a standardized test such as the *Test of Pragmatic Language (TOPL)*. This test measures the child's ability to use language in social situations by presenting pictures and descriptions of various complex communication situations. For example, your child might be shown a picture depicting a social interaction. The examiner then tells her a story about the picture—for example, "Brian was trying to build a birdhouse to give as a gift for Mother's Day. He had a hammer but he didn't have the right nails. He went next door to ask his neighbor Fred for some nails. What did he say?"

The SLP may also evaluate some skills more informally, by recording and then analyzing a language sample. To get a language sample, she might ask you to send in photos of a family vacation or holiday celebration to get the conversation going. Or she may simply ask your child about her family or a family event. The SLP may then analyze the language sample to assess how your child introduces a topic, sustains a topic, changes topics, and starts and ends the conversation.

OTHER AREAS EVALUATED

Your child's language evaluation may also include an assessment of her comprehension ability. During this part of the evaluation, the SLP will focus on your child's receptive language and "understanding" skills such as auditory memory, auditory processing, following directions, making associations, understanding of wh questions (who, what, when, where, why), etc. Some test items might include following directions, recalling sentences, recalling a list of related words, recalling a list of unrelated words, and understanding written or spoken stories.

An example of a receptive language test is the *Test for Auditory Comprehension of Language (TACL)*. Some tests such as the *Boehm Test of Basic Concepts (Boehm)* and the *Wiig Assessment of Basic Concepts (WABC)* assess concept development such as *below* and *above, first* and *last,* and *closed* and *open.* The WABC tests both receptive and expressive skills, and is available in preschool and kindergarten-early elementary grades editions). First, the SLP asks the child to point to a pictured concept (receptive). Then she says, "You showed me ____," and gives the child a fill-in sentence with a different, many times opposite concept—"But this cat _____." The Boehm is a test of receptive language only which may be administered individually or to groups of children in the class. The child sees several picture choices, and is asked to put an X on the correct choice. These concepts are usually related to the terms used in school for instruction. They are tests of the child's ability to follow instructions.

The language assessment may also include evaluations of your child's reading and literacy comprehension and oral reading ability.

Some tests assess a variety of language skills. They are known as comprehensive language batteries. Some may also include subtests for articulation. The *CELF (Clinical Evaluation of Language Fundamentals)* is an example of a comprehensive, standardized battery for older children, and the *CELF-Preschool* is an example of a comprehensive test battery for earlier language skills (3 years to 6 years 11 months) that evaluates receptive and expressive language skills.

The *TOLD (Test of Language Development)* is a group of comprehensive language batteries for a wide age range of children. *The Test of Language Development-Primary (TOLD-P)* has nine subtests which measure areas of semantics and grammar, listening, organizing, speaking and overall language ability.

PARENT CHECKLISTS

In the informal evaluation, the SLP will try to make the assessment as real world as possible. Ideally, she would be able to observe your child's communication in daily life, but instead testing is done in a speech room or in the classroom. You, the family, observe your child's communication skills in everyday community situations. Current research is demonstrating that parents are accurate and reliable reporters of their child's communication performance. This means that parent checklists, as well as tests that use parent reports, can be effective in assessing your child's language skills. Research has shown that:

- There is a high correlation between parents' and professionals' judgments of a child's current developmental level.
- There is strong reliability between judgment of parents and professionals in determining whether a child needs referral for evaluation.
- There is a high correlation between parental reports of vocabulary and syntax level and the results of formal testing and language sampling results of professionals.

You are an important part of the information network that will enable the speech-language pathologist to get an accurate sample of your child's speech and language.

Collaboration between parents and professionals is essential to an accurate evaluation. If your child is being evaluated privately(through a clinic or a private practice), the SLP will likely involve you in the evaluation in several ways. For example, he or she may meet with you (by phone or in person) before the evaluation to discuss your concerns. He or she will probably send you questionnaires or checklists to fill out and send in as part of your child's case history. Depending on the physical set-up of the facility, the SLP may allow you (or even require you) to observe the evaluation through a one-way mirror. In school settings, however, the parents are often not included in the evaluation sessions at all, even though the test results are being used to determine whether your child qualifies for services through the schools.

If you think that your child will not show her abilities well in a formal testing situation and the SLP has not sought out your input, ask to fill out a parent checklist. The majority of the tests that have forms for parent input are language tests designed for young children under age 4. But they can often be used to describe speech and language in children with Down syndrome who are 8 or 9 years old and are delayed in communication skills. Some language tests that include parents' evaluation of their child's language as an integral part of the test are listed below. You can also provide input regarding what you see at home and in the community in written or oral form, by providing lists or notes to the SLP that become part of the evaluation.

Language Tests That Include Parent Input

The checklists and observational tools below ask parents to provide written responses to questions such as "When did your child begin to combine two words?" Or, "Circle the words in the following list that your child uses." The idea is that family members who are very familiar with a child's speech at home have a fuller picture of that child's communication abilities than an unfamiliar examiner who may not be able to get the best responses from the child.

- MacDonald & Horstmeier: *Environmental Language Inventory;*
- Wetherby & Prizant: *Communication & Symbolic Behavior Scale;*
- Sanford & Zelman: *Learning Accomplishment Profile;*
- Fenson et al.: *MacArthur Communicative Development Inventories;*
- Rescorla: *Language Development Survey;*
- Prather et al.: *Sequenced Inventory of Communication Development (SICD).*

THE SPEECH EVALUATION

A mother from Minnesota told me that her IEP team informed her that her ten-year-old son's speech was the way it was "because of Down syndrome." It would not get any better. And she just needed "to get used to it." When this mother asked for a diagnostic evaluation, the SLP and members of the IEP team said that an evaluation was not needed: "You already know the diagnosis—Down syndrome. We don't need a diagnosis." The mother sought out an outside evaluation at a university training program clinic in Minnesota. The diagnostic evaluation clearly delineated her son's communication strengths and needs. When she took this information back to the school and indicated that she was willing to go to due process if necessary to get the speech services her son needed, therapy was reinstituted. Now, almost two years later, her son continues to make progress in his speech skills, thanks to targeted therapy and diligent practice at home.

The fact is, there *is* no such thing as "Down syndrome speech." The good news is that there is no speech difficulty that is specific to Down syndrome. All of the speech difficulties that we see in children with Down syndrome are difficulties that other children experience too. There are speech therapy techniques that can target any of the difficulties. Each child has her own combination of speech difficulties that can be worked on in therapy, and each child can improve.

The bad news is that some speech-language pathologists and other professionals still believe that "Down syndrome speech" is a real diagnosis. They may not think it is necessary to look for the underlying reasons for your child's speech difficulties without your urging. Since effective treatment of your child's speech problems will depend on accurate evaluation of those problems, you need to understand what a good speech evaluation involves. That way you can advocate for an appropriate evaluation from the school, or, if necessary, seek a private evaluation for your child.

Requesting a Speech Evaluation

As explained in Chapter 3, children with Down syndrome often have both their speech and language skills evaluated in the course of one evaluation. There may also be reasons to have your child's speech evaluated separately from her language. For example, if your child has begun to stutter and is having more difficulty speaking, it would be wise to schedule a speech evaluation, even if it is not time for the triennial evaluation or for an annual IEP review. Or if your child's speech has become more hyponasal (your child sounds stuffed all of the time), it is time to check-in with the otolaryngologist (ENT) as well as the speech-language pathologist. Speech changes and language changes may occur independently, or at different times. If you are interested in a specialized service, such as therapy for apraxia using cueing systems, a speech evaluation may be needed in addition to any language testing that was done.

Whether your child is having both speech and language assessed or just speech, the procedures for requesting an evaluation are the same as described in Chapter 3 on page 43.

What to Expect During the Speech Evaluation

A comprehensive evaluation of your child's speech will include all the components listed in Table 4-1. Often, however, school-based speech assessments are not comprehensive. For instance, the SLP might assess your child only in articulation or fluency. Often, screening tests are used, rather than comprehensive speech testing.

If that is the case for your child and you believe that useful information could be obtained by assessing your child in some of the other areas discussed in this section, you have three choices. First, you could ask the school SLP to do additional testing of your child, perhaps showing her the information in this book about why such testing is often helpful for children with Down syndrome. If the SLP refuses to test or states that it is unnecessary, you could ask the school to pay for a private outside evaluation of your child's speech skills at their expense. Third, you could pay for an outside evaluation at your own expense.

Table 4-1: Diagnostic Assessment of Speech Sound Production Problems

  a. Case history including developmental speech history

  b. Parent checklist or report of speech at home

  c. Observation of parent and child

  d. Assessment of oral facial structures and function

  e. Comparison of feeding/eating, oral movements in play, and speaking

  f. Articulation and Phonology testing

  g. Stimulability testing

  h. Diadochokinesis (rapid speech movements; buttercup)

  i. Childhood apraxia of speech (CAS) testing

  j. Speech sample or conversational analysis (if possible)

CASE HISTORY

When you set up a private speech evaluation, you will usually be asked to complete a case history form. (As explained on page 47, you might also be given a case history form for a school-based evaluation, under certain circumstances.) The form focuses on your child's developmental history, and especially on speech and language history. Areas covered include information about the family, pregnancy and birth history, your child's medical and health history including hearing, developmental history, speech and language development, social development, educational history, and parental concerns regarding speech, language, and hearing.

Specific information that is collected for the speech evaluation includes: early medical difficulties and hospitalizations, nursing/feeding/eating history, developmental milestones, history of ear infections, fluid in the ear, use of antibiotic therapy or pressure equalization (P.E.) tubes, speech and language milestones, allergies, asthma, respiratory difficulties, and otolaryngological (ENT) difficulties. For an example of a case history form for speech evaluation, see the end of this chapter.

The background information from the case history form will enable the speech-language pathologist to choose appropriate assessment tools and plan the evaluation. How your child is evaluated will depend on whether she is nonverbal, vocal (using sounds), or speaking. If she is speaking, is she using single words, multiword utterances, sentences, or conversations? The formal and informal tests selected will be chosen to evaluate the level of speech your child is currently using to communicate.

PARENT INTERVIEW/ OBSERVATION

In a private speech evaluation, the first two parts are usually a family interview, and an observation of the family communicating and interacting with the child. The family interview will follow up and expand on the information you have provided in the case history. In the family interview, the SLP will gather more information on your child's nursing, feeding, and eating history because the information provides background on the functioning of your child's oral facial muscles in nonspeech activities. If your child is older, the SLP may ask about any current eating difficulties. For example, does your child have difficulty swallowing? When she has a full mouth of food, does she fail to clear the area out before she keeps eating? Is she propelling saliva or food out of her mouth while eating? The SLP will also be interested in your child's early sound-making history. Did she coo and babble? Did she play with sounds very little or a great deal? (You may want to look through your child's baby book or early intervention logs to refresh your memory about these details, especially if your child is older.) Questions will vary depending on your child's age and her current speech abilities.

During the interview, the SLP will also ask about the use of assistive listening devices such as hearing aids or a classroom auditory loop system. Under speech and language history, the professional is particularly interested in how your child has communicated as she developed, and on the status of her receptive language abilities. Did she use a transitional language system before she was able to use speech? What system was used: sign language (which system), picture communication board, Picture Exchange Communication System (PECS), high tech communication device, or other? Did/does your child use pantomime or gestures to communicate? What system is she using currently to communicate?

If your child is being evaluated by the school, you may or may not be interviewed or allowed to observe the evaluation. The older your child is, the less likely that you will be included in the evaluation. Remember, though: by law, you have a right to submit information about your child (such as audiotapes or videotapes) to provide information about your child's communication abilities outside of school.

PARENT CHECKLIST OR REPORT OF SPEECH AT HOME

On the case history form or during the interview, you may be asked questions about your child's speech at home. Is your child using speech? Does she say some sounds more easily than others? Which sounds does she have difficulty with? Does she have more difficulty when words are longer? There is no standard checklist or questionnaire that is used for speech. In the Appendix, you will find a speech questionnaire that I developed that you may find helpful.

OBSERVATION

Either before or after the interview, the SLP will observe you and your child speaking, usually through a one-way mirror. If your child is younger, you will be asked to play with her or read a book with her. If she is older, you will be asked to sit and talk with her. If your child is nonverbal, the SLP will be interested in seeing how she communicates and whether she makes sounds (this may be grunts or guttural sounds, rather than speech sounds) or attempts to say words as she uses the device. And if your child uses a communication board or a communication device, the SLP will observe to see how successfully she uses the device. Observing you and your child together enables the SLP to hear your child's speech in a comfortable, familiar interaction, and to observe how you interact with your child and respond to her speech.

The SLP often videotapes the parent-child observation so she can review it later. She may also use the tape when meeting with you, to demonstrate aspects of the communication interaction and to suggest methods that you can use at home. The SLP is looking for:

- speech sound characteristics (for example, whether your child has difficulty with sounds made in a specific place, such as the back of the mouth or sounds that require tongue elevation);
- nonphonemic characteristics such as voice, oral-nasal balance, and fluency; and
- consistency of sound errors.

All of these factors can influence your child's speech intelligibility—that is, the ability to be understood when speaking.

The SLP will compare what she observes to the results of the formal speech tests, discussed below.

Areas Assessed in the Speech Evaluation

After the SLP has gathered information on your child's abilities from your written responses and interactions with your child, as described above, the SLP will use standardized formal tests and informal observations and techniques to evaluate your child's speech sound production skills. She will also examine your child's mouth, lips, tongue, etc. to determine what physical reasons there may be for your child's difficulties with speech. See Table 4-1 for a summary of the parts of the diagnostic evaluation for speech problems in children with Down syndrome. See the Appendix for an example of a diagnostic evaluation for speech.

ASSESSMENT OF OROFACIAL STRUCTURE AND FUNCTION

Sometimes called the *oral peripheral examination* or the *oral motor evaluation,* this section of the evaluation looks at the anatomical structure and functional movement of the lips, tongue, soft palate, and other parts in and around your child's mouth. Your child will be asked to imitate some movements, and make specific "faces" (smiling, frowning, and raising the tongue tip to the top of the mouth), so the SLP can evaluate the movement patterns of her muscles. Your child will also be asked to spontaneously make movements with the articulators (lips, tongue, jaws, and palate); for example, throwing a kiss or blowing bubbles through a bubble wand to examine how well she pulls back and rounds her lips.

The SLP also examines the structural alignment and symmetry of the oral facial area. For instance, the SLP looks at your child's teeth and checks to see how well your child's upper and lower jaw are aligned. He or she will observe the anatomy and physiology of your child's lips, jaw, tongue, and hard and soft palate at rest and in movement.

Although many SLPs have observed oral motor skill impairments in children with Down syndrome, there is no definitive research on the incidence of problems with oral motor skills in individuals with Down syndrome. However, in a survey study of 1620 parents of children with Down syndrome, I found that 61 percent of the parents had been given a diagnosis of oral motor skill difficulty (Kumin, 2005, 2004a). Furthermore, a similar percentage of children had symptoms characteristic of oral motor skill difficulty, based on parents' reports of their children's symptoms when I analyzed the questionnaires. Parents also reported that their children had difficulty with low muscle tone in the face affecting feeding and speaking in infancy, but that the low muscle tone improved with age.

There is no standard oral motor examination form that is used universally. For the oral motor evaluation and for the feeding/eating evaluations, the SLP may use a published assessment protocol such as: *The Oral-motor/Feeding Rating Scale* (Jelm), *Oral-motor Activities for Young Children* (Mackie), *The Pre-Speech Assessment Scale* (Morris), and *The Dworkin-Culatta Oral Mechanism Examination and Treatment System* (Dworkin and Culatta). (See References section.)

Table 4-2 is a form I developed to use in oral motor evaluations which provides an outline of what is usually observed and assessed.

Assessment of Sensory Processing

To use speech, your child not only needs the motor skills discussed above, but also sensory processing skills. Sensory processing (sensory integration) refers to the way that people receive, manage, and interpret sensory stimuli. Through sensory processing, your child takes in messages from her senses of hearing, vision, touch, taste, and smell, and vestibular and proprioceptive systems and then makes sense of these messages.

Difficulty with sensory processing will affect how your child learns from the environment. In order to speak, she needs to hear speech sounds clearly (hearing) and get sensory feedback from the muscles in and around her mouth as she is learning to make the sounds (tactile and proprioceptive). For example, she needs to be able to feel where in her mouth her tongue goes when she pronounces the /t/ sound vs. the /r/ sound.

Children with Down syndrome frequently have difficulty with processing and integrating messages from one or more of the sensory systems, including:

- vision,
- hearing,
- touch,
- the vestibular system (sense of head position in space, as well as increases and decreases of movement),
- proprioception (inner awareness in the muscles and the joints),
- smell, and
- taste.

An occupational therapist trained in sensory processing/sensory integration therapy can assess and treat sensory integrative disorders as well as provide suggestions for activities to enhance oral motor treatment. If you have had an occupational therapy evaluation or if your child has had sensory integration therapy, be sure to bring the report and to let the SLP know about the sensory processing difficulties in the case history or as part of the family interview. If you haven't had an OT evaluation but the SLP suspects your child might have sensory issues, she may refer you to an occupational therapist.

Table 4-2: Oral Motor Evaluation

I. Structures at Rest

    A. oral muscle tone/jaw posture

    B. lip closure and muscle tone

    C. tongue position and muscle tone

    D. oral patterns

        1. drooling

        2. tooth grinding (bruxism)

        3. breathing

II. Oral motor Tasks

    A. lips

        1. movement

        2. strength

        3. puckering

        4. retraction

        5. compression

        6. coordination

        7. ability to maintain lip closure

    B. tongue

        1. strength

        2. range of motion

        3. accuracy and precision

        4. protrusion

        5. elevation

            a. internal (tongue tip to alveolar ridge in back of upper teeth)

            b. external ("touch your nose")

        6. depression ("touch your chin")

        7. lateralization (side to side movement)

            a. internal (touch inside of cheek with tongue)

            b. external (move from one corner of mouth to other side and back)

        8. coordination

        9. functional problems

            a. tongue thrust (tongue comes forward when swallowing, eating, or speaking)

            b. hypotonia or low muscle tone (weak or floppy tongue)

    C. Jaw

        1. alignment

        2. movement

            a. range of motion

            b. graded movements (ability to move smoothly in small increments)

            c. strength

FEEDING/SWALLOWING EVALUATION

As part of the oral motor evaluation, a feeding/swallowing evaluation may be included for your child if she spills food from her mouth or has difficulties with tongue thrusting during eating. (A feeding/swallowing evaluation is more often conducted for infants and toddlers who are having difficulty with feeding.) Sometimes, the feeding/swallowing evaluation is done separately by either a SLP or OT, or a team which includes both specialists. Some medical centers and schools have separate swallowing teams.

Children with Down syndrome frequently have problems with feeding and eating. Some of these include:

- losing food from the mouth due to inadequate lip closure and tongue thrusting (sometimes food is propelled out of the mouth),
- failure to fully chew foods,
- failure to completely clear the mouth area of food (resulting in food remaining in the mouth, around the teeth, gums, and cheeks),
- tongue thrusting (the tendency for the tongue to push out of the mouth while chewing and swallowing food, and while speaking), which can cause problems with swallowing, feeding, and speech.

The SLP will collect information from you about your child's feeding difficulties. She will also ask your child to eat foods with a variety of tastes and textures (e.g., dried fruit, crackers, pretzels, applesauce, yogurt) and drink a variety of liquids from a cup and a straw (e.g., milkshake, juice, water). The speech-language pathologist then observes how your child manages the food and drinks, looking at the strength and coordination of muscle function. If your child has feeding or eating difficulties, it will be important to address them in therapy, since speaking uses the same structures and muscles used in eating. Table 4.3 outlines areas that are usually addressed in a feeding/eating evaluation.

ARTICULATION EVALUATION

Previous chapters in this book have alluded to the difficulties with speech intelligibility that children and teens with Down syndrome often have. One of the major factors affecting intelligibility is articulation. Parents of children with Down syndrome report that they think articulation is the most difficult speech skill for their children. In studies, about 80 percent of the parents noted difficulties with articulation (Kumin, 1994). Meanwhile, in the professional research literature, studies have found that 90 percent or more of children with Down syndrome have articulation problems.

Table 4-3: Feeding/Eating Evaluation

    A. chewing

        1. soft foods

        2. crunchy foods

        3. chewy foods

    B. swallowing

        1. mixed solid/liquid (cantaloupe)

        2. solids

    C. management of liquids

        1. thicker liquids

        2. clear thin liquids

    D. clearing and evacuation (using your tongue to clear food from your mouth)

Articulation refers to the way we make speech sounds. More technically, it refers to how a person places and moves the *articulators*—the lips, tongue, teeth, hard palate, and velum (soft palate)—to produce speech sounds. Articulation errors are generally consistent. This means they usually do not significantly affect speech intelligibility for familiar listeners, since these listeners are able to substitute the correct sound in their mind as they decode the message. For instance, your child might say: "I shaw a shkwahl dump onto huh woof." Assuming you know that your child pronounces the /r/ sound like a /w/ and the /j/ sound like a /d/, and that her /s/ sounds tends to sound more like "shh," you can correctly translate this sentence as: "I saw a squirrel jump onto her roof." These types of errors can, however, mystify listeners who do not know your child's speech well.

COMMON ARTICULATION PROBLEMS

To date, there has not been a great deal of research into articulation disorders in children and teens with Down syndrome. What we do know is that:

- More errors are made on consonants than vowels. In one study, adolescents with Down syndrome made significantly more errors articulating the consonants in words

Understanding How Speech Sounds Are Written

Each individual sound in a language is known as a phoneme. Phonemes are written using the phonetic alphabet with the phonemes written between slashes. For example, /d/, /b/, /g/, and /l/ are phonemes. Some phonetic symbols are the same as the alphabet letters, but others are not letters. For example, the symbol / ʃ / represents the "sh" sound as in *ship*, the symbol / ð / represents the "th" sound as in *then*, and / tʃ / represents the "ch" sound as in *chin*. If phonetic symbols are used in written reports of your child's articulation test results, ask the SLP to give you a sample word for the sound.

than did adolescents who had intellectual disabilities due to other causes (Rosin et al., 1988). In another study of four children with Down syndrome, over 90 percent of the sound errors were on consonant sounds (Stoel-Gammon, 1980).

- Children with Down syndrome make more articulation errors on sounds such as /s/ or /r/ that typically develop later (Van Borsel, 1996) than on the earlier developing sounds such as /p/ or /g/. Later developing sounds are usually more difficult to produce.

- Articulation errors are consistent—that is, the child will make the same sound errors over and over. Sometimes, however, speech errors are inconsistent. That is, sometimes a particular child can produce the sound correctly in one word, but not in another word. These problems may be related to the other sounds in the word. For example, a child can say the /s/ in *store,* but not the /s/ in *sore.* That is because when she gets ready to say the /t/ sound in store, it puts her tongue in the correct place for the /s/ sound. Other children can produce a sound correctly at one time, but not at another time. This may be related to childhood apraxia of speech, which is discussed below.

- More articulation errors are made as words get longer. For example, *key* is easier to say than *monkey; play* is easier to say than *playground.* Longer words involve more movements that need to be made rapidly and precisely, so they are more difficult to say.

- Children with Down syndrome make more articulation errors in conversations than in single words (Kumin, 2002, 2004; Kumin & Adams, 2000; Stoel-Gammon, 1980). When a child reads a list of words or identifies pictures, she can focus on how to say the words. In conversation, though, she is focusing on the meaning she is trying to convey rather than on making the sounds in the words, so articulation is more difficult.

REASONS FOR ARTICULATION PROBLEMS

Children with Down syndrome have anatomical and physiological differences that usually result in difficulties with articulation (Kumin, 2001; Leddy, 1999; Stoel-Gammon, 2001). These may include:
- high, narrow palatal arch;
- a large tongue and/or low muscle tone in the tongue;
- relative macroglossia (an average-sized tongue in relation to a smaller than average upper and lower jaw, which interferes with the ability to move the tongue freely);
- short soft palate (this makes it harder to use the soft palate to keep air out of the nose, resulting in increased nasality);
- an underbite with the lower jaw jutting forward;
- upper jaw (maxilla) that is small and narrow;
- lower jaw (mandible) that has loose ligaments;
- oropharynx (the area of the throat just behind the mouth) may have inflammation, resulting in reduced nasality;

- nasopharynx (the area of the throat just behind the nose) may have inflammation; when combined with a short soft palate, this may contribute to increased nasality;
- tonsils/adenoids may be enlarged and result in reduced nasality (causing speech that sounds like the person is "all stuffed up");
- larynx may have structural differences or low muscle tone, affecting voice.

The SLP should identify which of these differences your child has during the oral motor evaluation described above. Medical or dental treatment can often help with these difficulties. Consult an otolaryngologist (ENT) or an orthodontist to discuss treatment options.

HOW THE SLP TESTS YOUR CHILD'S ARTICULATION

The SLP will evaluate your child's ability to produce the sounds of English. She is especially interested in the kinds of speech errors your child makes. When your child has difficulty with a sound, does she:

- substitute a different sound (for example, saying *fum* for *thumb* or *toup* for *soup*);
- have a distorted production (for example, making the /s/ sound with air coming over the side of the tongue or making the /l/ near the back of the mouth rather than in the front);
- omit the sound (for example, say *gas* for *glass* or *cown* for *clown*);
- add some additional sounds (for example, say *scupper* for *supper* or *blow* for *bow*).

The SLP will probably evaluate your child's articulation by showing her a series of pictures as part of an articulation test. The *Goldman-Fristoe Test of Articulation (GFTA)* and the *Photo Articulation Test (PAT)* are two tests widely used. Articulation tests enable the SLP to hear how your child produces all of the speech sounds. Most articulation tests have colored pictures or photographs representing each speech sound in different positions in the word. Some tests sample the sound in the initial (beginning), medial (middle), and final (end) position. For example, the words *fork, elephant,* and *knife* sample the /f/ sound at the beginning, middle, and end of a word. Other tests sample the sound at the beginning and end of the word only. Your child is asked to name the pictures, and the speech-language pathologist listens carefully and audio- or videotapes the test.

Using a test rather than just listening to your child speak ensures that every sound will be heard in a systematic manner. The SLP will compare the test results to your child's sound productions during the observation (the time when she was observing you and your child speak), and during the conversational language sample (the time that she talks with your child about some of your child's interests).

The results may be reported to you in several different ways.

1. The SLP may indicate which specific sounds in which positions in words are in error. For example, your child is having difficulty with the /s/ sound in the initial and final positions, the /r/ sound in initial, medial, and final positions, the /l/ sound in the initial position.
2. The SLP may specify the sound groupings that are difficult for your child. For example, your child is having difficulty with plo-

sive and affricate sounds, or your child is having difficulty with voiced sounds. (See Table 4.4 for definitions.)

3. The SLP may identify the speech structures or movements that are affecting your child's articulation. For example, your child has difficulty with tongue and palatal movement.

If your child has any of these difficulties, you will probably be told she has an *articulation disorder*. Articulation disorders can be defined as incorrect production of speech sounds due to faulty placement, timing, direction, pressure, speed, or co-ordination of the movement of the lips, tongue, hard palate, velum (soft palate), or pharynx (throat area). Therapy for articulation is concerned with teaching your child to physically form the sounds correctly. (See Chapter 6.)

Norms. As you may recall from Chapter 3, a child's scores on tests of language may be compared to "norms" for typically developing children. The same is true of tests of articulation. In typically developing children, articulation norms are considered very important. School systems use these norms to determine whether a child's articulation is sufficiently delayed to justify providing her with speech-language therapy. For example, if a child is six years old and is having trouble with the /s/ sound, speech-language treatment will usually not be provided because the majority of children do not master the /s/ sound until eight years of age.

In children with Down syndrome, the use of developmental norms is complex and questionable. Do you compare the child to children with the same chronological age, the same mental age, comparable mean length of utterance, or use other measures? Using developmental norms to determine eligibility for services assumes that maturation will solve the problem. For typically developing children, this is often true. For children with Down syndrome who have low muscle tone, other oral motor difficulties, and hearing difficulties, maturation will probably not result in correct articulation of all sounds.

Once therapy begins, services should be provided on an ongoing basis and build upon the skills that your child mastered in an organized way. If your child is making progress in articulation therapy, it doesn't make sense to stop therapy because she has mastered age appropriate sounds. If she has oral motor difficulties and/or childhood apraxia of speech, she needs ongoing therapy to help her learn the sounds that she can't say yet, even if the norms tell us that those sounds are mastered, on average, by 7-year-olds and your child's chronological age is 6 or her mental age is 5. It makes more sense to continue treatment so that your child can continue her progress in making sounds.

I believe strongly in teaching the sounds, not in waiting until the norms show that your child is eligible for services. See Chapter 6 for home activities you can use to help your child improve her articulation. If your child is not receiving speech therapy through the school, see Chapter 1 for help in finding private speech services.

PHONOLOGY EVALUATION

Steven, age 8, can say the /b/ sound at the beginning of words, so he has no trouble saying ball. But when the /b/ sound comes at the ends of words, he leaves the sound off. So, for example, he says the word bob as bo, knob as no, and corn on the cob as coco. He also pronounces the word mom as bo.

Table 4-4: Sound Groupings

In the written report describing your child's articulation, the SLP will describe your child's difficulties based on the manner of production, place of production, and voicing:

Manner of Production:

- *Stop sounds* (also known as plosive sounds) are made by stopping the air completely and then releasing it with a small puff or explosion of air. The stop or plosive sounds are P, B, T, D, K, G.
- *Fricative sounds* are made by sending air through partially closed articulators (the word "fricative" comes from "friction"). Fricative sounds are S, Z, F, V, SH, ZH, TH (thin), TH (this).
- *Affricate sounds* are combinations of a stop and a fricative sound. CH as in chime and J as in judge are affricate sounds.
- *Nasal sounds* are sounds where the breath stream is sent through the nose. Nasal sounds are M, N, and NG as in ring.
- *Glides* are sounds in which the articulation changes as the sound is being made. Glides are always followed by vowels. W and Y are glides.
- The *lateral sound* is made by sending the air stream through the sides of the mouth. L is the lateral sound.
- The *rhotic sound* is complex and involves air being directed in more than one direction. R is the rhotic sound.

Place of Production:

- Upper and lower lip (*bilabial* sounds): P, B, W, M, WH
- Lower lip and upper teeth (*linguadental* sounds): F, V
- Tongue between teeth (*interdental* sounds): TH (THIS), TH (THIN)
- Tongue tip behind upper teeth: T, D, L, N
- Tongue blade and upper gum ridge (*lingua-alveolar* sounds): S, Z
- Tongue and palate (*linguapalatal* sounds): SH, ZH (MEASURE), CH, J
- Front palate: Y
- Central palate: R
- Velum (soft palate) (*velar* sounds): K, G, NG
- Glottis (voice box) (*glottal* sounds): H

Voicing:

- *Voiced* sounds involve vibration of the vocal bands. When a sound is voiced, you can feel the vibration if you place your fingers on the Adam's apple area.

  Voiced sounds are: B, D, G, Z, TH (THIS), ZH, J, M, N, NG (only consonants)

- *Voiceless or unvoiced* sounds do not cause the vocal bands to vibrate.

  Voiceless sounds are: ALL VOWEL SOUNDS, plus P, T, K, F, S, TH (THIN), SH, CH

Cognates:

Sounds that are produced at the same *place of production* and in the same *manner of production*, but differ in *voicing* (one is voiced, the other is voiceless) are known as *cognates*. P and B are cognates. F and V are cognates. When one cognate is incorrectly substituted for the other, it is known as *cognate confusion*.

Katie, age 10, can say the /d/ sound and the /g/ sound, but when the sounds are together in a word, she makes both sounds the same. For example, when reading the book Make Way for Ducklings, *she referred to them as gugings.*

As explained in the language evaluation section above, phonology is concerned with the patterns of sounds in the language. Children with Down syndrome can have difficulties both in *hearing* these sounds and in *producing* these sounds in their own speech. Difficulties hearing the differences between sounds is a *language* problem, whereas difficulties making the sounds correctly is a *speech* problem.

During the speech portion of your child's evaluation, the SLP will be looking for ways that your child habitually produces sounds incorrectly—otherwise known as phonological processes. These speech mistakes are not due to problems physically producing the sounds, but with simplifications and patterns of production that affect production of the sounds at the right times and in the correct places in words. For example, Steven, page 90, can physically pronounce /b/, but omits the /b/ sound at the end of the word and substitutes the /b/ for /m/ in mom because he has swollen tonsils and adenoids, and air can't be resonated through his nose. Teaching him how to make the /b/ sound won't correct his difficulties. Katie couldn't say "ducklings" correctly because the back sound /g/ was affecting her ability to say the /d/ sound. Her tongue was anticipating the /g/ sound and so she also made the /d/ as /g/.

COMMON PHONOLOGICAL PROCESSES IN CHILDREN WITH DOWN SYNDROME

Phonological processes are simplification patterns that all young children use as they are developing the sounds of the language. For example, if the child cannot yet produce sounds in the back of her throat, she will make a corresponding sound in the front of the mouth. An example would be saying *tootie* for *cookie.* Or, if she begins a word that has two syllables, she may just repeat the first syllable (*wawa* for *water*). If she is getting ready to make a sound in the second syllable, she may substitute that sound in the first syllable (*lelloe* for *yellow*). Children with phonological disorders may be difficult to understand or may even be unintelligible.

Many people with Down syndrome, even those with relatively good speech, continue to use at least a few phonological processes into adulthood. For example, although the person may be able to say the word *you,* when producing multisyllabic words such as *music, computer,* or *beautiful,* she may substitute an "oo" sound (MOO-sic, com-POO-ter, BOO-ti-ful).

Children with Down syndrome tend to use more phonological processes as the length and complexity of their speech increases. For instance, they use more phonological processes in connected language samples than in picture-naming or imitative naming.

The most frequently used phonological processes in children with Down syndrome are:

- consonant cluster reduction (for example, saying *gas* for *glass*);
- final consonant deletion (saying *boo* for *boot*);
- stopping: fricative sounds such as /s/, /z/, or /f/ are produced instead as stop plosive sounds such as /p/, /b/, or /t/ (*toup* for *soup* or *dat* for *that*);

- gliding: liquid sounds such as /l/ and /r/ are produced as glides such as /w/ or /y/; for example, *lolly* becomes *yahyee* and *real* becomes *weal*
- vocalization: liquids at the ends of words are produced as vowel sounds (*mall* becomes *maw* and *door* becomes *doow*);
- fronting, or making all the sounds in the front of the mouth ("tootie" for "cookie");
- backing, or making all sounds in the back of the mouth ("gagi" for "daddy");
- weak syllable deletion ("hamger" for "hamburger").

HOW THE SLP TESTS YOUR CHILD'S PHONOLOGY

For the SLP to be able to assess phonological process use, your child must be using some speech sounds and using the sounds in combinations as words. A phonological evaluation will look at the patterns of sound errors your child makes in speech. The SLP will then describe your child's rule systems and patterns when making sounds in

What Is the Difference between Articulation and Phonology?

When we focus on **articulation,** we are concerned with determining whether a child is moving his articulators to form sounds correctly. That is, we are concerned with whether a child has the ability to pronounce particular speech sounds, such as the /s/ sound, correctly. Articulation is a production task.

When we focus on **phonology,** we are concerned with understanding what sounds typically appear in a language (such as English or Spanish), and in what patterns they appear. For instance, English contains the /s/ sound, and it can appear in many positions in a word, in many different consonant combinations (e.g., /sc/, /sn/, /sl/, /sm/, etc., but not /sd/).

When your child has difficulty forming and producing a speech sound, that is an articulation problem. When your child can say the sound in one context but does not include it appropriately in another context, that is a phonology problem. Technically speaking, your SLP would call this a **phonological process**—meaning your child is changing the rules of phonology and making her own simpler sound patterns). For example, she can say the /d/ sound in *do* but says *guck* for *duck* and *gog* for *dog*. The distinction is important because speech therapy techniques and approaches are different for the two problems.

Another difference is that learning to read can help a child with her phonology problems, but not her articulation problems. Reading often helps children learn about sound differences. Being able to read the letters in words that correspond to the sounds often helps children with Down syndrome move ahead in phonology—especially as they become aware of correct and incorrect sound patterns. Articulation problems are more difficult to treat because they are related to anatomical and physiological factors (such as dental underbites, missing or crowded teeth, or problems coordinating muscles). Articulation problems are also complicated by oral motor and motor planning difficulties. It's important for parents and SLPs to understand and identify the differences between articulation and phonology problems for each child, so they can target their activities appropriately to help with both areas.

speech. For example, does she always leave off final sounds (saying *ba* for *bat*)*?* Does one sound in the word affect other sounds (your child says *yeyow* for *yellow* because of the effect of the "y" but she can say the /l/ in *lamp* and *light* correctly)?

The SLP may evaluate your child's phonology informally or formally. Informal testing involves taking a sample of your child's speech in conversation or reading or both. This will usually be audiotaped or videotaped so that the SLP can review the results when writing a report. The SLP is especially interested in whether your child's production of speech sounds is consistent. That is, does she make the same errors or do the errors vary? If errors are inconsistent, are they affected by the length of the word or phrase and by the complexity of what she is saying? The SLP will inventory all of the sounds your child makes, and determine whether she is making many different sounds or few sounds. This information will help in identifying the speech sound difficulties for the evaluation, and developing an appropriate treatment plan.

There are three kinds of formal assessments for phonological processes:

- tests specifically targeted to measure phonological process use (such as *Hodson Assessment of Phonological Patterns);*
- tests that measure both articulation and the use of phonological processes (such as *Bankson-Bernthal Test of Phonology* or BBTOP; *Clinical Assessment of Articulation and Phonology* or CAAP);
- formalized systems of using the information from an articulation test (such as the *Goldman-Fristoe Test of Articulation*) and analyzing the responses through their phonological process patterns (such as the *Khan-Lewis Phonological Analysis (KLPA)*).

On the CAAP, for example, your child would be shown pictures and told a story about the pictures. She then would be asked questions about the picture, and would respond with a single word answer, such as *cage, cheese, swing.* The SLP would then analyze your child's answers to determine whether your child was leaving out the final consonants in the words (*ca* for *cat*), reducing the consonant clusters (*wing* for *swing*), or substituting another sound (*fing* for *swing*). The patterns that your child is using would be documented. The results would be used to determine what phonological processes your child needs to work on in therapy.

STIMULABILITY TESTING

Stimulability means that ability to repeat a sound correctly when a model is given. If your child does not use a sound correctly in speech, can she imitate the sound correctly? That is what stimulability testing is designed to find out. Stimulability testing is done after articulation and/or phonological testing is completed and the SLP has a list of sounds your child does not say correctly in words. Some SLPs test all sounds to see which are stimulable, but most test only the sounds that your child did not say correctly on the articulation test. The SLP simply says, "I am going to say some sounds. Say just what I say" or "I want you to imitate the sound that I say." With younger children, I sometimes use a speech hat, and the child has to say what I say when she is wearing the hat.

Perhaps your child does not say /t/ in speech, but she can imitate /t/ correctly. Or she cannot say /s/ or /z/ correctly in speech, and can only imitate the /s/ sound. The results will be reported as follows: Your child is stimulable on the /t/ and /s/ sounds but is not stimulable on the /z/ sound.

The Goldman-Fristoe Test of Articulation has a section that tests for stimulability. Stimulability testing helps the SLP prioritize which speech sounds to work on with your child in therapy. When choosing sounds to work on during treatment, the SLP will often begin with sounds that are stimulable.

DIADOCHOKINESIS TESTING

This is a means of listening to how your child produces sounds in sequences. Making sounds in sequence is an important skill because we don't speak in individual sounds, but in strings of sounds.

The SLP wants to hear how your child can produce sounds made with the lips, tongue, and palate, so she will ask your child to say *pa* as many times and as fast as she can for 5 seconds, then to do the same for *ta* and *ka*. She will record these numbers. Then she will ask your child to combine these sounds and say *pataka*. This may be difficult for your child, because pataka doesn't mean anything. If so, the SLP may ask her instead to say a real word, such as *buttercup* or *pretty kitty* to sample her ability to make rapid movements for speech.

The rate at which your child can produce these sounds and words is known as the diadochokinetic rate or the diado rate. The SLP may compare your child's results with norms developed on the *Fletcher Time-By-Count Test of Diadochokinetic Syllable Rate*. One group of researchers (Brown-Sweeney & Smith, 1997) found that children with Down syndrome had more difficulty with rapid syllable repetition than they did with other aspects of speech.

CHILDHOOD APRAXIA OF SPEECH EVALUATION

Many children with Down syndrome have difficulty producing consistently clear speech. At one time, your child may call her brother by saying, "Mitchell, come here," clearly and understandably. At another time, she may reverse the sounds in Mitchell's name, leave out words, or syllables and say, "Chell, come." Another time, she may grope and struggle and not be able to say her brother's name at all. Why can she say the name clearly one time, but not at other times? Why does she have difficulty ordering a drink in a restaurant, but then when the waitress asks, "ice or no ice," she very clearly says, "I don't care." And, why does she have less difficulty with a word in a short phrase than when the same word is in a long string of words, even though it's the same word? For example, she can say *pop*, but has difficulty saying *pop* when it's part of "Let's go get *pop*corn at the store now."

These difficulties and inconsistencies are typical of a problem with motor planning for speech that is known as childhood apraxia of speech (CAS).

The diagnosis of CAS describes difficulty in voluntarily programming, combining, organizing, sequencing, and producing consonant/vowel combinations. CAS is a descriptive label that is used when a child's speech difficulty is due to problems with oral motor planning—that is, in planning the motor movements and sequences of sounds for speech. Other terms that have been used to describe this difficulty include childhood verbal dyspraxia, developmental apraxia of speech, developmental dyspraxia, developmental verbal apraxia, articulatory dyspraxia, pediatric verbal apraxia, childhood verbal apraxia, and oral motor planning difficulties.

Many researchers have examined the nature of difficulty with childhood apraxia of speech in typically developing children. The most common signs of childhood apraxia of speech reported in these studies are:

- inconsistent productions (one time, the child can say a sound or a word clearly, but at other times, she has great difficulty with the same sound or word);

- difficulty with oral motor skills such as tongue movements;
- struggle and groping (the child seems to be working hard to talk, but the correct sounds are not coming out. Sometimes, you may even see her move her lips or tongue, but she is not saying the correct sounds);
- difficulty imitating sounds;
- poor sound sequencing (the child may be able to imitate or produce individual sounds, but when she tries to combine them into words, she has difficulty, especially as the word gets longer or more complex. So, she can say *ham*, but when she says *hamburger*, it may come out as *hangurber*. *Banana* may be *nabana*. Sounds and syllables are frequently reversed. This reversal is known as *metathesis*);
- increasing difficulty the longer the words or phrases are (the child may say *key* easily, but have difficulty with *monkey* or *monkey bars*).

Importantly, CAS does *not* appear to be related to cognitive level. Children with and without cognitive disabilities experience this difficulty.

CAS IN CHILDREN WITH DOWN SYNDROME

There has been limited research on childhood apraxia of speech in children with Down syndrome, but the findings are very clear. When formally evaluated with childhood apraxia assessment batteries, some children with Down syndrome meet the criteria for diagnosis of childhood apraxia of speech (Kumin, 2004a, 2004b, 2003a, 2003b, 2002a, 2002b, 2001; Kumin and Adams, 2000). Research is not yet available on the prevalence of CAS in children with Down syndrome, but in my clinical opinion, it is currently under-diagnosed.

Children with Down syndrome who are subsequently diagnosed with CAS often have strikingly similar developmental histories. Frequently:

1. They are late talkers compared to other children with Down syndrome. (Many do not speak until after age five.)
2. They were quiet babies; used little cooing and babbling.
3. They may have difficulties feeding.
4. They have limited sound repertoires; mostly vowels.
5. In saying early words, they often omit the first sound (*up* for *cup*).
6. Words may be said correctly, and then *disappear*.
7. They try hard, but struggle to say words.

When these children's speech is analyzed, the following characteristics are observed:

1. Inconsistent production of speech sounds;
2. Limited number of speech sounds in the child's speech;
3. Struggle or groping when speaking;
4. Muscle movements for nonspeech tasks are unimpaired (for instance, they can lick peanut butter from behind their teeth but have difficulty when asked to place their tongue behind their upper teeth for the /s/ sound);

5. Intelligibility decreases as word or sentence length increases (*light, lightning, lightning bug* would be increasingly difficult);
6. Failure to improve with regular articulation or language therapy;
7. Difficulty combining and sequencing phonemes (e.g., saying *efelant* for *elephant*);
8. Difficulty producing both consonant and vowel sounds (children with Down syndrome who just have articulation problems usually only have difficulty with consonants);
9. Omitting sounds and syllables in speech (e.g., saying *hamber* for *hamburger*);
10. Sound and syllable additions (e.g., saying *hamburgurgger*)
11. Automatic speech is easier (that is, frequently used phrases such as "I don't care" or "I don't know" may come out clearly, but the child has great difficulty in spontaneous conversation or when asked for a specific answer to a question);
12. Omits initial sounds in words and/or syllables (e.g., saying *ino* for *window*);
13. Difficulty saying unfamiliar words;
14. Difficulty imitating words;
15. Difficulty with rhythm, stress, and timing in speech.

HOW THE SLP TESTS FOR CAS

The current tests used for evaluating childhood apraxia of speech are descriptive, rather than objective. That is, the tests describe the child's speech patterns in sentences and conversations and rely heavily on analyzing the child's speech and sound imitation skills. Often, a conversational speech sample is used. The nature of the testing delays the time of diagnosis. By the time that children with Down syndrome are able to have a longer conversation of 50 to 100 utterances (the requirement for many tests) so that the SLP can analyze a language sample, they are often in middle childhood or adolescence. At that point, valuable treatment time has been lost.

Recently, some speech-language pathologists have recommended that children with Down syndrome be evaluated for CAS using different methods. Specifically, they believe that a diagnosis can be made based on a particular profile of speech and language development, as well as their speech output (Kumin, 2004a, 2005; Velleman, 2003). In 2004, I conducted a survey of 1620 parents to determine whether childhood apraxia of speech symptoms could be identified in children with Down syndrome by their parents. Parents were asked to respond to examples of speech characteristics of CAS found in daily living, such as "My child has difficulty imitating a word I say" or "Sometimes my child can say a word clearly but then he cannot say it again."

The most common characteristics these children had, according to parent report, included:

- decreased intelligibility with increased length of utterance,
- inconsistency of speech errors,
- difficulty sequencing oral movements and sounds, and
- a pattern of receptive language superior to expressive language.

Although many children with Down syndrome have *some* of these characteristics they do not make *inconsistent* speech errors unless they have CAS. In addition children with Down syndrome who do not have CAS tend to have the same amount of difficulty with shorter and longer phrases.

The survey also examined the impact of childhood apraxia of speech on speech intelligibility. Results indicated that children with Down syndrome who have clinical symptoms of CAS have more difficulty with speech intelligibility. That is, there was a significant correlation between CAS and parental intelligibility ratings.

The unfortunate fact is CAS is being under-diagnosed in children with Down syndrome. Only 15.1 percent of parents responding to the survey had been given a diagnosis of childhood apraxia of speech. Many more children showed characteristics of CAS in their speech in daily life (Kumin, 2004a, 2005).

Why is it important to accurately diagnose CAS if your child has it? Therapy that targets apraxia is different from traditional articulation therapy. Therapy for phonology is also different from traditional articulation therapy. So, it is important to identify the patterns affecting speech for an individual child so that the therapy can be designed to address the specific areas of difficulty underlying that child's speech difficulties.

If you read the above descriptions, and said to yourself, "That sounds like my child," then you want to find a speech-language pathologist who can evaluate whether your child has CAS difficulties. You will probably not be able to find a SLP who has a great deal of experience with children with Down syndrome who are dealing with CAS, but you should be able to find a SLP who has experience evaluating and treating children with CAS.

How Do You Determine Which Speech Sound Difficulties Are Affecting Speech?

Unless you are a speech-language pathologist, you may have found the preceding discussions of difficulties with articulation, phonology, oral motor skills, and childhood apraxia of speech somewhat confusing. In many cases, these four problems can cause speech difficulties that sound similar to parents, and so the descriptions of these problems can sound similar too. In addition, many, if not most children with Down syndrome have two or more of these difficulties, and some have all four. How can you tell which of your child's speech difficulties are attributable to which problem?

Difficulties with articulation, phonology, oral motor skills, and childhood apraxia of speech can be compared and contrasted based on seven factors:

1. Developmental patterns (what the general patterns of speech development are: stops and starts, delays, difficulty with feeding, etc.);
2. Error patterns (e.g., does the child have difficulties with all sounds that involve lip rounding or are her errors only on later occurring or more complex sounds);
3. Motor patterns (whether or not errors are due to specific underlying anatomical or physical difficulties);
4. Consistency (does your child always make the same sound errors or are the errors inconsistent);
5. Speech and nonspeech oral movement patterns (for example, blowing bubbles, eating, making speech sounds);

6. Nonphonemic acoustic features (characteristics of speech other than the way sounds are pronounced that affect how it sounds—e.g., rate, fluency); and
7. Speech productions in different situations (whether the child has more trouble speaking clearly in some situations or at some times than others).

See Table 4-5 on the next page for information on identifying speech and sound difficulties.

INTELLIGIBILITY EVALUATION

Intelligibility of speech is the "understandability" of speech. That is, is it easy or difficult for the listener to understand what the speaker is saying? Intelligibility sounds like an objective scientific term, but it is not. It is a subjective judgment made by a listener and can be affected by many factors. The speaker and her speech *are* important factors, and the difficulties in articulation, phonology, oral motor skills, and CAS described above all definitely affect a child's intelligibility. But there are other factors, as well, including:

- the familiarity of the listener (how often does the listener hear your child speaking);
- the type of message being communicated (a simple request to go get pizza vs. a complex description of something that happened at school);
- factors in the environment (such as noise or distractions)

Intelligibility is not static; it can vary greatly from one situation to another.

Speech intelligibility is a term that is used as a global description of a person's speech. You may be told by the speech-language pathologist that your child's intelligibility is fair or good, or that your child's speech is unintelligible. Or, a numerical rating system might be used, with 1 being completely unintelligible and 7 being completely intelligible. Labels such as poor intelligibility or scores such as 2, however, do not provide any guidance to enable us to help a child improve her intelligibility. Global descriptions do not help point the way to appropriate treatment. Unintelligibility is too broad a category, and it is a description rather than a diagnosis. Although it is possible to measure intelligibility globally through an adjectival (good-poor) or numerical (1-7) rating scale, it is not possible to treat intelligibility globally. To treat intelligibility, we need to understand the specific factors that are making an individual child's speech difficult to understand.

HOW THE SLP TESTS INTELLIGIBILITY

If your child is receiving a speech evaluation through the school, there is a good chance that the SLP will not evaluate her intelligibility per se. This is because schools do not usually consider intelligibility an issue that affects a student's educational progress. If your child is having a private speech evaluation, the SLP will usually note that she is easy to understand or is having difficulty with intelligibility. The SLP may or may not give your child an overall score for intelligibility, and may not evaluate all of the factors that affect intelligibility for your child. But there is a good chance that he

Table 4-5: Categorizing Speech Sound Difficulties in Children with Down Syndrome

Factor	Articulation	Phonology	Oral Motor Skills	Childhood Apraxia of Speech
Developmental Patterns	Speech development may be typical or delayed	Speech delays consist of using phonological processes beyond typical age	Often delayed in speech sound development; parents describe as quiet babies	Delayed; sound play mostly vowels. Quiet babies who don't coo or babble much
Error Patterns	Errors are substitutions, omissions, or additions of additional consonants. There may be one or many sound errors	Errors are not on specific sounds, but across many sounds; e.g., leaving off final consonant sounds	Errors are on sounds that have similar movements; e.g., if the child has difficulty elevating the tongue tip, will have difficulty with /n/, /l/, /t/, and /d/	Length and complexity of the sound combinations lead to error; more difficulty with sounds as words get longer; e.g., /k/ sound more difficult in monkey than in key
Motor Patterns	Child may or may not have difficulty with strength and coordination of oral facial muscles	No difficulty with motor patterns	Muscle weakness and decreased strength and coordination of oral facial muscles	No difficulty with muscle movement for nonspeech tasks; difficulties only with speech
Consistency of Sound Errors	Consistent sound errors	Errors based on patterns; consistent on those errors	Consistent	Inconsistent
Difficulties only with Speech Sounds?	Difficulties with speech sounds, and sometimes with nonspeech oral facial activities (e.g., chewing)	Difficulties with speech activities only	Difficulties with speech and non-speech oral facial activities	Difficulties with speech activities only
Acoustic Features (voice, resonance, fluency)	May co-occur with difficulty with voice, resonance, fluency	No difficulty with acoustic features	Difficulty with acoustic features is common	No difficulty with acoustic features
Situational Factors	No difference based on situation	No difference based on situation	No difference based on situation	Difficulties vary with different situations

or she will evaluate at least some of the "nonphonemic acoustic features" mentioned in Table 4-5. These factors include:

- Voice
- Resonance
- Fluency
- Rate
- Prosody

Voice Evaluation: Before a voice evaluation is done, your child should ideally be seen by an otolaryngologist (ear, nose, and throat physician). If possible, see a pediatric otolaryngologist because he or she will have appropriate sized equipment, and more clinical experience with children.

This section of an evaluation analyzes your child's voice: is it loud or soft, breathy or hoarse, etc.? It enables the SLP to determine whether your child needs to work on voice in therapy.

In my clinical experience, children with Down syndrome often have voice problems. Sometimes these problems are related to food allergies (such as to milk), otolaryngological (ear, nose, and throat) problems, or respiratory (breathing) difficulties. In other children, problems may be age related—for example, voice changes that come with puberty. Sometimes voice problems are the result of incorrect use of the voice. For example, a child who screams a lot may have a hoarse voice. Some voice problems will be evident early, but others may be more noticeable at later ages, when your child is speaking more. Specific laboratory equipment, such as the Visipitch may be used, or the computerized speech lab (CSL) may be used to analyze your child's voice difficulties. The SLP may also use videostroboscopy equipment to visualize your child's vocal folds and observe the function of her larynx (voice box). This enables the SLP to determine whether voice problems are due to a physical problems such as nodules or due to vocal abuse, and what the appropriate treatment might be (e.g., resting the voice, therapy for vocal abuse). The SLP will listen, with her trained ear, to your child say "ee" and "ah" and have your child describe a picture or engage in conversation.

Resonance Evaluation: Resonance refers to whether the air stream for speech is directed through the mouth or the nose as your child is saying specific sounds. In English, only three sounds are supposed to be produced with air going through the nose: /m/, /n/, and /ng/ as in *ring*. All other sounds are made with the air stream coming through the mouth.

Resonance patterns vary. Some children with Down syndrome are *hyponasal* (less nasal sounding than usual). They sound stuffed up, as if they have a cold all of the time. This is often due to swollen tonsils and adenoids, resulting in difficulty sending the air stream through the nose.

Other children are *hypernasal* and their voices have a twangy, whining quality. This is often due to a high palatal vault (the hard palate is high and narrow in many children with Down syndrome), short palate, or weak muscles in the palate and pharyngeal (back of the throat) wall. This results in difficulty in blocking off the nose, so the air stream travels through the nose for many or all sounds, and the child's speech sounds too nasal.

Sometimes, you can hear both hyponasality and hypernasality in a child's speech. The child sounds hyponasal on /m/, /n/, and /ng/ and hypernasal on the other consonants. Some children with this problem breathe through their mouths; others have swollen tonsils and adenoids, so air can't go through the nose.

The SLP will listen to your child's speech to determine whether she can modify the air for speech in the mouth and nose as needed for speech. The evaluation may be done by listening or by using specialized equipment such as the manometer or spirometer devices that compare the amount of air coming through the nose and mouth.

It is always important to have a full medical ENT (ear, nose, and throat) evaluation to examine causes for some of these conditions before a voice treatment plan is developed. Surgery is a medical decision that you and your physician make together. Inflammation of the tonsils and/or adenoids is frequently the underlying problem when speech is hyponasal. Children who sound hyponasal are also often mouth breathers.

If your child's speech sounds hyponasal (stuffed) before surgery to remove the tonsils or adenoids, the resonance will often be normal after surgery. If your child's speech resonance is normal before surgery, the resonance will often be hypernasal after surgery when the inflamed, enlarged tissue is not there to assist in closing off the nasal cavity and directing air through the mouth. (When there is inflammation, the muscles are not able to move the full distance, so the child will have gotten into habits that will result in inadequate closure of the nasal cavity after surgery.) In this case, speech therapy will be needed after surgery to retrain and strengthen the muscles. This type of speech pathology service is often covered by health insurance providers, but you need documentation to demonstrate that a change has occurred post-surgery that required therapy.

If surgery is recommended for your child and she sounds normal or hypernasal, ask for a pre- and post-surgical speech evaluation from a speech-language pathologist to determine whether therapy will be needed. If an evaluation is not done before surgery, it is sometimes difficult to document the need for therapy after surgery.

Fluency Evaluation: *Stuttering* or dysfluency is more prevalent in people with Down syndrome. Difficulties with fluency may include repetitions ("PPPeter hit me") or blocks (can't get the sound/word out). It is estimated that 50 percent of people with Down syndrome stutter at least some of the time. Sometimes children with Down syndrome have difficulties with fluency as they are developing language. But, more frequently, the fluency difficulty does not become evident until the child is using longer, more complex phrases and sentences during later elementary and middle school.

We do not yet know for sure whether fluency difficulties arise from difficulties with oral motor skills and breath stream or whether it is related to language load (how much your child is saying at one time) and complexity (how difficult the material is to formulate and say). Sometimes when a child is tense or anxious, the muscles have excessive tension and fluent speech is more difficult. Some children will therefore stutter more in school than at home. This could be related to language complexity or anxiety. Some children have difficulty only in certain situations—for example, when they have to answer difficult questions orally in class. I know some children who stutter in new situations with unfamiliar people, such as during the transition year from elementary to middle school. Sometimes fluency difficulties improve as the child becomes accustomed to a new situation.

At the Loyola University Center for Speech and Language in Individuals with Down Syndrome, we have been able to document that the fluency patterns that we are seeing in children with Down syndrome (ages 7 to 15) present the same characteristics as stuttering seen in younger, typically developing children. For example, repetitions are more common on the first sound in the word.

To evaluate your child, the SLP will listen to connected speech and determine whether there are dysfluencies or "stuttering-like speech." She will observe your child's breathing patterns, and look for muscle tension in her mouth and face. She will listen for and describe blocks (instances when it looks as if the speech locks or freezes in place or as if your child is choking on her speech) and repetitions of sounds in a word {e.g., b-b-b-baseball). She will ask you about the kinds of dysfluencies you have noticed, in case your child's fluency varies from situation to situation. She may ask you or your older child or adolescent to fill out a questionnaire, such as the *Stuttering Severity Instrument*, which asks questions about stuttering characteristics, situations in which stuttering occurs, situations your child avoids because of stuttering, and other similar information.

Rate Evaluation: Children with Down syndrome may have a rapid rate, slow rate, or uneven and changing rate of speech. This is an area that has not yet been studied by researchers, so we do not have facts and figures about the incidence and types of rate problems in children with Down syndrome. In my experience, rate of speech sometimes is a problem for children with Down syndrome. Rate is usually not a problem early on when children are using short phrases. Sometimes, however, the rate increases as children are able to say longer sentences. It also sometimes varies with different situations. For example, if your child is excited or upset, she may speak more quickly. Problems speaking too quickly are more common than problems speaking too slowly. Usually children with rate problems are capable of speaking either more slowly or more quickly. The problem is that they are not aware of their rate of speech.

To evaluate your child's rate, the SLP will engage your child in conversation, listen to her speech, and determine whether speech rate is slow, fast, uncontrolled and varying, or appropriate. This is a subjective measure, so she may also ask you your impressions about your child's rate of speech and what you have observed in different situations. She may then try to have your child imitate rapid or slow speech, to determine whether your child is able to voluntarily adjust her speaking rate.

Prosody: Prosody is the rhythm and melody of speech. I have seen some children with Down syndrome who use a monotone pattern in speech. But many other children speak with lots of variation and emotion in the voice. Some children have difficulty in some situations but not others. For instance, a child may be much better at using inflection when she's reading aloud than when she's spontaneously speaking.

In English, prosody is not a big problem because it does not affect meaning. In some languages, such as Chinese, your inflection actually affects the meaning of the word. Still, English speakers may make assumptions about a speaker based on her prosody. For example, if you are speaking in a monotone, they may conclude that you are bored or not very excited about what you are saying. Or other children may mock another child's monotone speech if it sounds significantly different from the norm.

Some test batteries have subtests that ask a child to repeat a sentence exactly as the examiner does. The examiner is instructed to vary the inflection, sounding calm or excited, or saying a statement such as "you're going" like a question. In my clinical experience, this type of test is very difficult for most children with Down syndrome. They are trying hard to repeat the correct words but they don't vary the inflection and emotion in the voice to match the examiner's models. When you listen to the same child telling about her grandfather's birthday party, or the family trip to her cousin's wedding, her voice is animated and she uses upward inflection for questions and downward inflection for statements.

I think that most children with Down syndrome use prosody appropriately; it is just out of their awareness. Usually, the SLP will not test specifically for prosody, but may listen for it in a conversation with your child during the observation of you and your child, or when she is informally evaluating your child's language. She may then comment to you about your child's use of prosody when speaking.

PUTTING RESULTS OF INTELLIGIBILITY TESTING ALL TOGETHER

At the end of the evaluation or at a separate meeting, your speech-language pathologist will hopefully not give you just a global rating for your child's intelligibility, but will be able to break down your child's speech difficulties according to the underlying causes. After all, the purpose for the evaluation is to develop an appropriate treatment plan. And it will be impossible to set good therapy goals for improving your child's speech without understanding what is causing any problems with intelligibility. The SLP should summarize formal and informal test results, and talk about what the results mean. She should give examples of what she is hearing in your child's speech, and how that affects speech intelligibility. She can explain some of the therapy approaches that she thinks would be appropriate for your child.

After the evaluation is completed, a written report should summarize test results, diagnosis, suggestions for treatment planning, suggestions for home program, and referrals to other specialists such as an otolaryngologist or audiologist. There is a comprehensive outline for intelligibility testing in the Appendix to guide you in making sure your child is properly evaluated.

For a comprehensive picture of the reasons behind intelligibility problems in children with Down syndrome, you may want to watch the DVD *What Did You Say?* (Kumin, 2006). The DVD includes many examples of children with Down syndrome speaking, illustrating different types and degrees of intelligibility difficulties. (See the Resources.) For an example of a comprehensive speech evaluation report, see the Appendix.

Conclusion

Speech, language, and communication skills are an important part of life for everyone. But, needs change over time. At 6, your child may be working on learning vocabulary and adjusting to school language and school rules. At school, she may play with friends at recess, and at home she may play outdoors with friends or watch videos or do other indoor activities with them. By middle school, adolescents are talking, networking, shopping together, talking about the school dance or clothing,

and gossiping about who's doing what to whom, and who's saying what to whom. They are communicating through speech via cell phone, or writing via text messaging, instant messaging, or email.

So, how do you keep up with your child's changing communication needs? One of the best ways is through speech and language evaluations conducted at regular intervals. IDEA states that reevaluations should be conducted at least every three years. But those evaluations are for the purpose of determining whether your child is eligible for special education and related services. They do not necessarily include a comprehensive speech and language evaluation. (For examples of what comprehensive speech and language and speech intelligibility evaluations should look like see the Appendix.)

If you have a home-school communication program, you will be "chatting" with the school SLP on a regular basis, and should feel free to ask her when she sees changes and growth in communication, and when an updated speech and language evaluation may be indicated. Don't ask whether an evaluation is *needed*. Most school SLPs are under guidelines that say that if they tell you that your child needs a service, the school system is required to fund that service. Thus, they are not likely to use or respond to the word "need." So, ask whether an evaluation would be a good idea, not whether it's needed.

Observe your child and seek out speech and/or language evaluations whenever you have questions for the IEP and treatment planning (within or outside of the school) that are not easily answered. When your child's evaluation is current and relevant, the results should point the way to appropriate treatment. When there are questions, concerns, or indecision, it is time for another evaluation. Evaluation leads to treatment. Treatment leads to improvement. Practice at home and in the community leads to improved communication skills. And that can lead to more interesting opportunities, friendships, and an improved quality of life for your child with Down syndrome. The cycle begins with evaluation.

CHAPTER 5

Language Treatment

Language is part of daily living and is best practiced during real life. That is why it is so important for the speech-language pathologist, your family, and the teacher to work closely together to help your child learn and practice language. Treatment cannot be effective if your child just learns language in the therapy room and does not use it in daily life at home, at school, and in the community. I am frequently asked how often language therapy should take place. My response is that the time in the therapy room is the smallest portion of the overall time that language interactions take place. How often should your child be involved in language activities? All of the time; every moment that there is interaction between your child and other people; every waking minute. And I say that seriously.

Not every moment is going to be spent in therapy sessions. But breakfast can be a language experience, as can every other meal. Bathing and grooming can be language experiences. Riding the school bus or being a passenger in a van, or riding to school with mom and siblings in the family car are all language experiences. Each trip, your child sees different vehicles on the road, different weather conditions, listens to the same or different songs and sometimes sings along with the words, sees familiar landmarks along the way and labels them, and talks to you about what is going to happen that day. Most of your child's day involves language in some way. That is why teamwork between the SLP, family, teacher, and other important people in your child's life is essential.

My bottom line is that language therapy that does not involve the family as an integral, ongoing part of therapy is not good therapy. What parents want and need to know is what is being worked on in the therapy room and how they can teach, practice, and reinforce the language concepts at home. During that morning car ride to school, should Mom or Dad try to make the child aware of red and green lights, of flowers and trees in bloom, of leaves falling to the ground, which vehicles are moving slowly and which are moving quickly, or possessive markers ("Jane's ice skates are in the car." "Whose baseball mitt is that? It's Brian's mitt.")? For your child to use and retain the concepts taught in language therapy, he needs to be aware of the words, use the words, and practice the words.

All parents are capable of helping their child with language, but they need information from the SLP on what to focus on during that week. Otherwise, language work is not as effective, and trying to help can become overwhelming for the family. You don't want home practice to become language treatment at the kitchen table every day for 20 minutes. That's like another therapy session. You want to comment and teach and stimulate in daily living, as the words are appropriate to the situation.

Formal vs. Informal Language Therapy

Chapter 3 discussed how children with Down syndrome (or other disabilities) qualify for speech-language therapy through the public school. If your child qualifies for school-based therapy, this can be an important service for him—*IF* he receives therapy that is appropriate for his needs and *IF* you (or the school) do not assume that therapy done at school without any home reinforcement will be sufficient.

As I can't emphasize enough, formal speech-language services are essential for most children with Down syndrome, but so too are informal strategies that parents use to teach and reinforce language concepts when their child is at home or out in the community. This chapter will provide an overview of areas that may be worked on formally in therapy but also include many ideas of ways you can work on your child's language skills at home.

Coordinating Home and Therapy Activities

Communication is a natural part of daily living. Your child should do most of his practice of language skills in natural settings. It is certainly better for him to learn the names of vegetables in the produce section of the supermarket, at the farm, or in your home garden than at school looking at pictures of vegetables. Your child needs to work on concept development in school, home, and community settings simultaneously. So, if your family knows that your child is working on past tense of verbs in speech sessions at school, you can highlight past tense as you talk with your child. At home, you can talk about clearing the dishes from the table, and then comment that you *cleared* them and *loaded* the dishwasher.

Communication between home and the school SLP needs to be frequent (at least once weekly) and ongoing. It needs to be two-way so that the SLP can let you know what your child is working on in therapy, and you can let the SLP know how practice is going at home, what is being used at home, and whether there are family events, trips, or crises that may affect therapy. If possible, there should also be daily communication in school between the SLP and the classroom or special education

teacher and daily communication between the teacher and the family. Your child's teachers play an important role in helping him improve his language skills. Teachers can help to reinforce the concepts being taught and can collaborate with the SLP so that language treatment sessions include the vocabulary and concepts that your child needs in class to learn the curriculum.

As a parent, you should not wait for your child's SLP to contact you to get involved in designing and providing language activities. You need to take on the role as information source for the SLP. Your child will learn language best when what is being taught is important to him, relevant to daily life, and can be practiced frequently in daily living. So, if you are going on vacation or to a family event, let the SLP know what kinds of phrases it would be helpful for your child to learn (e.g., "good to meet you" and "see you later"). Your child will be interested in the names of the unusual things he might see—trees or animals or landmarks and monuments—or relatives he will be meeting. This will be useful information that can serve as material for language treatment sessions. You are the major resource for providing that information for the SLP.

You also are the only one who can report to the SLP whether your child is carrying over to real life what is being worked on in therapy sessions. This helps the SLP know whether your child needs more practice, is ready to move on, or needs a different approach because he is having difficulty learning the material. Talk to the SLP and find out how she would prefer to receive input from you—through email? through notes sent in a communication book? through phone calls? through regular meetings?

For more information on home-school communication planning, see *Classroom Language Skills in Children with Down Syndrome* (Kumin, 2001). There are additional home-school communication forms in Chapter 6 and the Appendix.

PARENTS AS SERVICE COORDINATORS

If your child is receiving therapy both in school and in a private setting, the SLPs need to coordinate treatment with each other. The most common way is for them to work on different skills that your child needs to learn. For example, one might work on grammar and the other might work on making requests or on auditory memory and following instructions. At our speech and language center at Loyola University in Maryland, the clinicians working with the child coordinate therapy goals and treatment methods with the school SLP, and usually visit the classroom to observe the child in class and in language therapy sessions in school.

If your child's private speech-language pathologist does not take on the role of service coordinator, you, the parents, are often the coordinator of services. You are the only one who has an overall picture of your child's strengths and challenges in every situation at home, in school, and in the community. No one else sees your child in the morning and at night, at school and at your place of worship, at Scouts and at soccer, and ordering and eating pizza. You have the whole picture! You can let both SLPs know what your child is having difficulty with and what comes easily in daily language. You can share progress reports and test results from one SLP with the other. You can let both SLPs know what you are working on at home, and what progress or difficulties

Home-School Language Report

Child's name: **Sarah T.**   Date: **May 20, 2008**

We are working on: *(check those that apply)*

☑ Vocabulary

☐ Morphosyntax

☐ Following instructions

☑ Wh- questions

☐ Other (specify)

Therapy targets this week *(progress and difficulties):*

(1) Answering who questions: Sarah successfully answers who questions when a written cue card is used. She can answer with the name of the person when photographs of children in the class are used. She understands the concept of who.

(2) Vocabulary—names of professions: Sarah can name painter, builder, carpenter, teacher, chef (she says chefer), bus driver when looking at picture cards, but she has difficulty when using those words to answer wh questions.

Please work on the following at home:

(1) Use photographs of your family and real life activities. Ask Sarah WHO questions; e.g., Who is mowing the lawn? Who is grilling the burgers? Write who on an index card to use as a cue. When you ask the question, say the word who louder than the other words.

(2) When walking around the neighborhood or driving, talk with Sarah about the jobs people do. Ask who questions about the people. If Sarah has difficulty, you answer the questions so that she can hear a model. Then ask it again; e.g., Who is painting that house? The painter. Who is painting that house?

Home practice activities *(progress and difficulties):*

[Here, parent describes what they did at home and the successes and difficulties.]

you are observing. And, you can let both SLPs know what is reasonable and possible to address at home, so that the home activities don't become overwhelming.

I have worked in combination with school SLPs, and I know this kind of arrangement can work very well. I spoke with a family who was working with three SLPs at the same time. The school SLP was working on following instructions and the vocabulary that goes with academic subjects, one private SLP was working on speech intelligibility (specifically difficulties relating to childhood apraxia of speech), and the second private SLP was working on fluency difficulties. For that child, having therapy sessions with three SLPs was working well. It was what he needed at that time.

What Your Child Will Work on in Language Therapy

Language treatment can focus on linguistic areas and/or on channels. Linguistic areas are:

- Phonology (sounds of the language),
- Semantics (vocabulary and meaning),
- Morphosyntax (grammar, word parts including prefixes, root words, suffixes, tense markers, etc.),
- Pragmatics (language in use).

Channels are:

- Receptive language, including comprehension and understanding, and
- Expressive language, including formulating thoughts and sentences and then expressing them through speech, sign, assistive technology, or writing.

This chapter will focus on language treatment for semantics and morphosyntax. It will also discuss how both receptive and expressive language can be improved through therapy and home activities. Bear in mind, however, that when we address expressive language, we are not only addressing formulation of words and combining those words into sentences. We are usually also talking about speech. Therapy for speech will be discussed in Chapter 6. Information on treatment of phonology can be found in Chapter 6. Information on pragmatics can be found in Chapter 8.

How will your child's SLP decide what approaches to take and what methods and materials to use? Most likely, he or she will probably work on both channels and linguistic areas with your child. However, all treatment plans, through school services and the IEP process or through clinic or private practice, should be individually designed to meet the child's needs. The program plan should be based on the results of your child's comprehensive speech and language evaluation, and should take into account his:

- Hearing status,
- Sensory processing skills,
- Semantic skills,
- Morphosyntax skills,
- Pragmatics skills,
- Receptive language abilities,
- Expressive language abilities,
- Intelligibility of speech,

- Interests,
- Needs for school support,
- Needs for home and community.

SAMPLE
TREATMENT
PLAN

Robin is an eight-year-old girl who has good receptive language skills. She enjoys reading, and is very interested in nature, especially insects. Robin's family often goes camping and she enjoys everything about those camping trips. Her expressive language skills are limited, and she speaks primarily in three- to four-word phrases. She has difficulty with morphosyntax, and often leaves off word endings for plurals, possessives, and other markers. In second grade, the science curriculum includes units on trees, plants, and insects.

When Robin's treatment plan is developed, her interests, needs for school, home and community supports would all be considered. Since her interest in insects matches an area of study in school, as well as home recreational activities, that would be a good area to include in the plan.

The SLP can discuss with the classroom teacher and the family how the curriculum and home activities can support Robin's interest in bugs. Perhaps, she can do a science report or project on bugs. Robin can say the /b/ sound very well, so perhaps an oral report on bugs can be part of her treatment program. The SLP can ask the teacher for the vocabulary that will be included in the science units on plants, trees, and insects, and use that vocabulary in treatment. She can work with the family, so that they can label different bugs, plants, and trees in their camping experiences. Perhaps, Robin can photograph different bugs, label the photos, and write brief descriptions using the computer, creating a photo journal of their camping experiences. A pacing board can be used to increase her MLU to 4-5 word phrases, and some sentence forms can be taught through carrier phrases—e.g., "I see _____" (a beetle, a firefly, a butterfly).

IEP goals for speech and language for Robin might be:

- Robin will expand her MLU to use 4-5 word phrases in the classroom when giving oral reports 80% of the time.
- Robin will be able to use plural and possessive markers appropriately 80% of the time.

Treatment should be reevaluated on a regular basis through the use of progress reports. In Chapter 4, we talked about baseline, pre-testing, post-testing, and portfolio analysis. All of these are ways of evaluating progress in communication. For an example of a language treatment progress report, see the Appendix.

Semantics

As explained in Chapter 2, children with Down syndrome generally have a relative strength in semantics—they understand the meaning of words and concepts and have a varied vocabulary. This does not mean, however, that children with Down syndrome do not have difficulties with semantics. In fact, most studies have found delays in vocabulary development. There is a wide variability in vocabulary and concept development, however. Although most children with Down syndrome have a vocabulary deficit when compared to typically developing children matched for mental age, about a third of children with Down syndrome have vocabularies that are appropriate for their mental age—so a ten-year-old with a mental age of seven might have the vocabulary of a typical seven-year-old (Miller, 1995).

Clearly, even children with Down syndrome with relatively good semantic skills could benefit from therapy and home practice to improve their vocabulary.

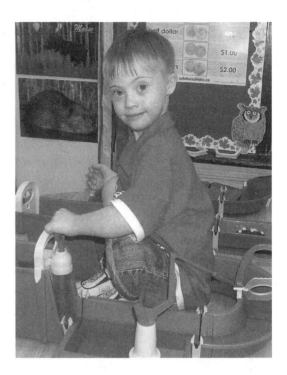

HOW THE SLP WORKS ON SEMANTICS

Often, the SLP will work on vocabulary with your child through categories. It is best when working with school-age children to choose categories that are part of the curriculum or vocabulary that will be useful for the child at home or in community activities. Typical vocabulary categories are animals, occupations, transportation, weather, family relationships, foods, furniture and household items, and personal grooming items. For older children, vocabulary categories might include insects, plants, and other science terms; terms that relate to history and social studies; and categories related to other academic subjects. Therapy activities will focus on helping your child:

- understand vocabulary words,
- learn to use vocabulary words, and
- practice vocabulary words.

The SLP will often use crafts or cooking activities to help your child understand the concepts and learn the words. For example, a session might focus on the words for different types of fruit, and the activity for the session might be making a fruit salad. Often, a single treatment session and a single activity may have multiple goals. So, one goal might be to help your child learn the names of a variety of fruits. Another goal might be for your child to learn how to answer yes and no questions. For example, "Do you like or do you want to put peaches in the fruit salad? Apple? Kiwi?"

The SLP may use board games, both commercially available games such as *Scattergories* or therapeutic games marketed to speech-language pathologists. The SLP may also modify games, such as by putting pictures of vocabulary words on a *Candyland* board, and having players say the word when they land on that square. During some therapy sessions, the SLP may use flashcards of the vocabulary words for practice. Digital photography has made it much easier to design appropriate individualized materials for children in therapy. The picture of the kitchen or bedroom can now be a photo of the child's actual bedroom at home. File folders work well for custom made game boards. They are easy to take with you and store.

How do you choose the words to work on in therapy sessions? Some vocabulary can be based on your child's home and community needs. What events are coming up for your family? Is there a big family reunion? Is your family going on a skiing trip? Is your child going to another state for Special Olympics? The SLP can work with your child on vocabulary related to any of these events.

Some vocabulary words can be based on the curriculum. This is a good area for the SLP and classroom teacher to work together. Some books have lists of vocabulary words that children are expected to master. If not, the teacher will often have materials from the county or state guidelines that include concepts to be mastered.

In school, semantics will include work on nouns, verbs, pronouns, adjectives, adverbs, and other parts of speech. In English or Language Arts, your child will be expected to learn these parts of speech and to identify examples of each. Your child will learn and practice pronouns such as I, you, he, and she, but will also be expected to know that a pronoun is a word that replaces a noun in a sentence.

Some sessions may focus on the development of concepts used in school for instruction (for example, *below* and *above* or *first* and *last)*. For older children, vocabulary work may teach synonyms, antonyms, subordinates (an apple is a fruit), superordinates (vegetable is the category for peas), and associated words (hat and gloves go together). One analytical vocabulary area that is difficult for many children with Down syndrome is describing how things are the same and how they are different. For example, an apple and a banana are both fruits and you can eat both of them, but they have different shapes, colors, and textures. Being able to switch from describing same and different characteristics with the same objects is an advanced language skill.

Beginning in about the third grade, language used in school textbooks and in the classroom becomes more abstract. New terms will be introduced in science, social studies, and other subjects. It is a good idea to have the speech-language pathologist work with the classroom teacher to pre-teach vocabulary words that your child will need for classroom learning. The SLP can review the textbooks and worksheets and consult with the teacher to catalog the vocabulary, so that it can be included in therapy sessions. That way, your child will be familiar with the terms when they are taught as part of classroom lessons.

In late elementary school and middle school, your child will encounter idioms (e.g., It's raining cats and dogs; I have butterflies in my stomach) and figurative language such as similes (this room looks like a pig sty) and metaphors (the king was a monster). There are practice materials available for teaching idioms which are usually found in books for teaching English to bilingual students or in books designed for children with language learning disabilities.

When the SLP is able to work on vocabulary proactively—to pre-teach words that the child will need to know in school, it gives the child an edge. The terms are more familiar to him when they are introduced in class. Some parents ask for information, right before summer vacation, on what will be covered in school during the following school year. They then choose summer vacation sites, day trips, and activities to help the child become familiar with the vocabulary and concepts he will encounter in the following school year.

Once your child has mastered the concepts or learned the vocabulary words, activities will focus on practicing the words. The therapist may have conversations with your child that focus on a specific category or topic so that he has the opportunity to practice the words. Once your child can use the word, the SLP may correct him when he uses the word incorrectly. Some activities may provide negative practice—saying the word correctly and incorrectly or identifying when it is used correctly or incorrectly. This is the time when home practice can be most useful.

Receptive and expressive vocabulary activities are also included in treatment for semantics. Receptive vocabulary deals with understanding vocabulary words and concepts. Expressive vocabulary deals with language output, and usually focuses on formulating and retrieving appropriate words, and on speaking the words. For example, your child might be asked to point to objects and pictures, and to name them. These kinds of activities work well with pairs of children, including siblings at home. For children who have severe speech intelligibility problems, expressive vocabulary work may involve formulating a message on a word processor or a voice output communication device (VOCA). (See Chapter 10.)

In later elementary and middle school, vocabulary activities can expand to include:

- word definitions ("What is a birthday?");
- associations ("Tell me which words go together" or "Tell me which word does not belong");
- semantic absurdities ("What is wrong with this sentence: The electrician painted the house");
- flexible word use/multiple meanings ("What are all the meanings for the word *spring*?" perhaps using a Slinky toy and pictures of flowering trees to demonstrate the multiple meanings);
- homonyms (words that sound the same but have different meanings, such as *led* and *lead*) and heteronyms (words that are spelled the same but have different meanings and pronunciations, such as the verb *lead* and the noun *lead*);
- *convergent* language skills (e.g., "I am thinking of a fruit that is red and crunches when you bite into it") and *divergent* language skills (e.g., "Name as many fruits as you can in one minute").

HOW PARENTS CAN WORK ON SEMANTICS

There are many enjoyable and interesting ways that parents can help boost their children's language abilities at home. Some of these activities help a child with just one area of language—such as semantics—while others are useful in helping the child improve his abilities in many areas of language. Bear in mind that just because I have grouped an activity under one area of learning doesn't mean that it can't be used to help your child with other areas of difficulty. As you are working your way through this book, I suggest you skim through all the activities to see which ones might be a good match for your child's interests, and be helpful in improving your child's communication abilities. If in doubt as to whether an activity would be appropriate for your child, ask your SLP.

Below are some activities that focus primarily on vocabulary building, but may also be helpful in teaching your child grammar, receptive language skills, articulation, and other skills.

HOME ACTIVITIES FOR VOCABULARY BUILDING

LEARNING ABOUT SHAPES

There are many terms used to describe shapes. The basic shape terms (circle, square) are usually taught in preschool or kindergarten. But, there are more advanced vocabulary words used to describe shapes of objects, such as spirals, tubes, squares, triangles, diamonds, rings, cylinders.

Foods come in different shapes and can be used to describe and learn a variety of words related to shapes. If a wide range of pasta or noodle products are available in your area, these can be used. If not, you can make a bread or cookie dough and cut the dough into various shapes.

If you use pasta, engage all of your child's senses. Feel the pasta, smell it, visually examine it. For younger children, try stringing the pasta on a piece of string or yarn and talk about which shapes are tubular and which are not. You can string macaroni or ziti or rings, but you can't string fusilli or orzos. For adolescents, buy pasta in different flavors and talk about tomato and spinach and how they flavor, as well as color, the pasta.

After you talk about the shapes, you can do several activities. You can pour some of each pasta into a bowl. Mix the various types well, and then sort the pasta by shape, and describe each shape. You can also use the pasta for craft activities. Glue the various shapes of pasta onto a piece of poster board, and when it is dry, brush or spray paint. Or, for older children or adolescents, glue the pasta shapes onto a shoebox, plastic box, or wooden craft box. Spray paint the design and the box. You have now made a decorative storage box that your child can keep or give as a gift.

There is always the old delicious standby. Cook and eat the pasta, and enjoy the shapes and the flavors!

SAND PICTURES OR BOTTLES

A summer crafts activity that can be used to stimulate many language concepts is a Sand Picture. This is a goal-oriented activity. The activity is to make a sand picture, but the goals are:

- To learn verbs involved with paper activities (measure, pour, close, mix, shake, dry, squeeze, take, put);
- To learn how to make requests ("May I have red sand," "Help me, please," "Hold the paper," etc.);
- To understand and use color names.

For a sand picture, first buy or scoop up some sand (a great beach or sandbox activity). Put some sand into 4 measuring cups. Put a few drops of red food coloring in the first cup, yellow in the second cup, green in the third cup, and blue in the fourth cup of sand. (If your child already knows these color names, mix blue and green to make turquoise or even yellow and green to make chartreuse.) Mix each sand-coloring combination separately until the sand is tinted the color that you want. This activity can also be done with just one color of sand for a younger child when you are teaching a specific color such as blue. Talk about mixing the colors with the sand. Take a large piece of poster board or thick paper. Put on glue, or squeeze on glue. Then put a small mound of sand on each glue area. Let dry for a while, and then shake off the excess sand. Have your child request glue, colored sand, and so forth as you go through the steps.

A variation on this activity is to make a sand bottle. These make terrific handmade gifts. Take a small empty soda bottle, then color the sand as in the sand picture activity. Put a funnel in the top. Slowly pour some sand into the bottle through the funnel.

Talk about the activity as you are doing it. Ask questions. "Do you want a lot of red, or a little red?" Ask your child, "What do we need?" Put in the colors slowly and sequentially until you have a design that you like. When the bottle is filled with a sand design that you like, place a cork or screw-on cap on top to seal the bottle.

This project can also be done with a small, squat bottle (such as a baby food jar). After you have poured the colored sand into the jar, you can insert a stick or pencil carefully into the layers and then draw up different colors of sand to make a design. Pebbles, shells, or other found objects can also be placed in the layers to provide additional interest. The small bottle can then be used as a paperweight.

LEARNING VERBS

It is often difficult to find interesting books about verbs and actions for older children. But, I'll bet you have boxes or CDs of photos that show people your child knows doing interesting things. Magazines can also be used to supplement your picture inventory.

With the help of these pictures, you can make your own verb book. Once you get started, it's easy to take pictures specifically for the book. How about

dad *grilling* hamburgers, mom *making* (or *brewing* or *mixing*) iced tea, grandpa *fishing*, grandma *shopping* for shoes with your child, brother playing baseball (*batting, catching, throwing*), sister playing soccer (*kicking, dribbling, passing*), mom *driving* the car. You can make the labels for the photos simple or complex, depending on your child's language level (e.g., *baseball, playing baseball, brother playing, My brother's playing baseball*). Mount the pictures in a photo album, or tape them on notebook paper and put them in a three-ring binder.

Photos can also be mounted on pages specific to a concept. For example, you can make a page for driving that shows photos and/or magazine pictures of people driving a car, driving a truck, driving a tractor or riding mower, driving a school bus, etc. This would help to teach the concept of driving and can serve as a reinforcement for experiences that your child has with drivers and driving.

To give your child experience with the actual verb, practice doing the movement, when possible—for instance, running, jumping, hopping—then reinforce with the photo book. Or you can use the photos to teach the concepts related to playing baseball and driving after you have done the real activity.

The verb book can be used for both receptive and expressive language activities. Once the pictures are in the album, you can ask your child to "show me playing baseball; show me driving." This is a similar activity to tests your child will encounter during evaluations such as the *Peabody Picture Vocabulary Test*, the *One Word Receptive Vocabulary Test,* and other receptive vocabulary tests, and is good practice.

EXCURSIONS AND TRIPS

Excursions and trips can provide many opportunities for learning new language concepts. For example, to teach your child the vocabulary of transportation, take a ride in a car, bus, train, or trolley, or visit the train station, bus depot, or airport. Comment on the size, number of people, the driver, the fare container, slot, or ticket. Take photos of the experience.

At the end of the day, for a younger child, buy a toy car, train, or bus so that he can recreate the experience in play. Recreate the experience with the toy

train or car and your play town with your child in play over the next few weeks. For older kids or adolescents, buy some postcards for an album or to send to friends. These may also be used as visual cues when talking about what you did on the trip. Make a poster or a collage with the photos and postcards, save them in a photo album, or make a book about the experience using the photos. You will help your child remember the experience and learn vocabulary that goes with transportation while talking about the day.

Trips involving food and cooking are often fun for families. For instance, you can arrange to go to the working area in the bakery and watch breads and cakes being made. Some supermarkets have in-house bakeries and will allow you to tour if prior arrangements are made. The local pizza parlor will usually allow you to watch the dough being tossed, the pizza being assembled, and baked. Is there a pretzel bakery or other commercial operation in your area? Our local area has an apple cider mill where you can watch the cider being made.

Sometimes, these companies have tours where you can watch all of the stages as the product is made. How about a trip to a dairy farm to watch cows being milked? Or a creamery to watch ice cream being made? Or a donut shop to watch the donuts being shaped, the fillings being put into the cream and jelly donuts, the powdered sugar and cinnamon sprinkled on top? These excursions are interesting for adults as well as children.

The culmination of any food tour is tasting the results. No ice cream tastes as good as the one you have just seen being made. Food trips are multisensory experiences. The sights, sounds, and smells stay with you, and the vocabulary concepts have added meaning. Be sure to take photos, and make a book about your trip with those photos so that you can relive the experience.

To teach concepts involving communication, consider a trip to the post office. Try to be there early in the day when your own mail carrier is there sorting the mail. After watching the process, buy a postcard or a stamp and have your child write a note or make a drawing or put a sticker on a card. Take photos as you and your child write, stamp, and mail the note. Send the card to someone you know well and ask them to take pictures as they open the card. Then, make a book about "Our Visit to the Post Office." Watching the operations in the back of the post office is interesting for older children and adolescents.

A radio or television studio is an interesting destination for older children or adolescents to talk about communications. For example, CNN in Atlanta has a tour that is fascinating for adults and older kids, and also lets visitors watch CNN news live from the newsroom through a large observation window. It may be possible to be part of the studio audience at a television show if you live near a studio.

Trips and tours provide new experiences for children and adolescents. Discuss what you are going to see before you go. Keep a list of some of the key words related to the excursion. Take photos and make a follow-up album or a personalized language learning experience book to help your child relive the experience.

HOLIDAYS

Preparing for a holiday can be an opportunity to learn and practice many language skills, in addition to being a lot of fun. Thanksgiving, because of the extensive food preparation, is a holiday for which there is always advance planning and preparation. You can use this planning process to teach your child organizational skills and language skills. Make lists with your child (words or pictures may be used depending on your child's skills at reading). Some suggestions are:

- Lists of guests
- Lists of recipes/finished dishes
- Lists of food and ingredients
- Lists of serving pieces
- Lists of dishes to be brought by others

The possibilities are endless and varied, depending on your own family traditions. You might include favorite dishes that are always brought by certain people—e.g., Aunt Sarah brings the sweet potatoes. Or you might list the category of food that different people are responsible for (vegetable, dessert, appetizer). This is a good way to practice asking and answering who questions, as well as learning about subordinates (specific examples) and superordinates (categories) You might ask your child to help make place cards for the table, and talk about the relationship of each person to the family. You might make a centerpiece or favors for each person to take home. If you will later want to review the holiday with your child, be sure to keep the lists, and take photos of the many preparations. The photos can form the basis for a personal book featuring holiday vocabulary.

FOOD ACTIVITIES

Preparing and eating food can be a very motivating way for children and teens to learn new vocabulary (and also sequencing skills; see below). Here is an example of an activity that is fun and can involve siblings and friends. It can be adapted for younger or older children.

You and your child are going to create an edible ocean with fish. It can be used for speech and language practice, and as a bonus can be eaten as dessert! Blue Jell-O is the ocean, and gummy fish and gummy sharks are the sea creatures. Take a round, square, or rectangular cake pan (glass pans are great, but disposable foil pans work fine, too). Make a batch of blueberry or blue raspberry Jello. When it is partially jelled, add gummy fish and gummy shark candies. (Since it is partially jelled, they will not sink to the bottom.) Chill completely. Carefully place some more gummy fish and gummy sharks on the surface of the Jell-O, partially submerging them.

This activity can be used as a language activity for colors; blue for the water, a single color for the sharks and fish, or multicolor sharks and fish. You can also talk about the ocean and sea creatures. In this case, you can read books about fish and sharks in the ocean, watch a video, and visit an aquarium. The food activity could be a follow-up to the trips and reading. You may also use the activity to focus on the articulation of the /sh/ sound. Each time you submerge a sea creature in the Jell-O, you say a word containing the /sh/ sound such as *ocean, shark,* or *fish.*

This activity can be easily adapted for different purposes and for a wide range of age groups. For older children and adolescents, you can use the cooking activity for auditory memory, auditory sequencing, following directions, measuring for math practice, vocabulary (verbs such as *measure, pour, stir*).

Use your imagination to come up with similar food-based activities to teach about other vocabulary—for instance, make a garden or swamp with "dirt" made from chocolate pudding or cookie crumbs and put gummy worms or frogs, or candy flowers in it. This activity can be enhanced by reading books about gardening and by actually growing a garden. Take photos as your child does the food activity, and as your child plants seeds and works in the garden. Use these photos to practice sequencing, staying on topic, and other language and speech skills in addition to vocabulary.

HOME ACTIVITIES FOR CATEGORIES

CLOTHES SHOPPING

Many language assessments test the ability to categorize. Many jobs and daily life skills involve the ability to categorize and organize. Here's a fun way to practice those skills. You can do this as a role playing activity with each participant taking turns being the salesperson and the customer, or if you really need to order from a catalog, you can do it as a real life activity.

Begin this activity by looking through your child's closet or drawers with him. Focus on how you would describe a piece of clothing. What is it (shirt, pants, socks, dress)? What color is it? What fabric? How does it feel? Is it for warm, cold, or hot weather? Who could wear it in your family? What size is it?

Take your child out shopping and continue the discussion. A shopping mall or department store that has a wide variety of items for various ages and members of the family is an especially good destination. Talk about different departments—men's and women's, shoes, and house wares departments. Generally, focus on how things are organized in the store. Then focus on how things are organized in each department. Talk about the size markers on the rack, look at how items are grouped, how colors and different items of clothing are separated.

Later, at home, look at some mail order catalogs. Your older child or adolescent may also be interested in looking at online catalogs available on various websites such as Lands' End, American Eagle, or Aeropostale. Find an item of clothing that is of particular interest to your child by clicking on the general category, such as shirts, pants, or footwear. Discuss the various types of information that are necessary to order the item, such as color, size, and order number. Use this as the basis for a discussion of what you need to include when describing something. For example, if you didn't specify the color, you probably would not get the color you wanted or the company might not even fill the order because the description was not complete. Look online or at a catalog and discuss the categories on the order form, such as size and color.

If you need to order an item, make the phone call or find the website and actually order the item. If you use online shopping, be sure to discuss that this is an actual purchase that you will receive and will be required to pay for. Only use this option if you feel that your child understands the financial ramifications of shopping online. When using mail order catalogs, look at the different items and how they are classified and described in the catalog. Relate these classifications to your closet and shopping experiences. These activities help practice skills of categorization.

After you have thoroughly discussed the vocabulary of clothing with your child, you can arrange a visit to another type of store that appeals to him. Many preteen girls, for example, would be especially motivated to learn about the vocabulary of accessories during a trip to a store such as Claire's or Libby Lu. There they can see and feel many different colors and styles of necklaces, earrings, hair clips, and the like. Likewise, many boys or girls would be motivated to learn the vocabulary of sports by visiting a sporting goods store and looking at (and trying out!) items such as basketballs, lacrosse sticks, inline skates, etc.

SORTING HOUSEHOLD ITEMS

During the course of our daily lives, we often sort items by category or other attribute. When we organize our house or workspace so that similar items are grouped together, it helps us find what we need more quickly and efficiently. Try to involve your child in routine sorting activities so he too can learn the value of putting things into categories.

Sorting laundry is a categorizing skill. Laundry can be sorted by item (all shirts), but also can be sorted in more specifically defined categories. For example, matching socks can involve sorting by size, color, and fabric or texture. Or we might sort all the dark items into one pile, which requires more judgment than putting all the black items in one pile. Putting away silverware involves sorting by shape and use. Emptying the dishwasher and putting things away also involve categorization skills.

There are many items to sort in the house. Try sorting toys by shape (separating the plastic farm animals from the little people that live in the dollhouse) or by type (separating the wooden blocks from the Legos). Then put them in the containers where they belong. Or, get a series of plastic bins, and sort the jumbled kitchen drawer, separating straws, coins, coupons, and twist ties. In a desk drawer, you might put together coins, pencils, stamps, paper clips, etc.

When you are sorting with your child, discuss the different categories and how you look for what the items have in common. Talk about multiple ways of sorting the same items. For example, you might have a red pencil, a green pen, a green towel, a red washcloth, a green glass, a red mug, a green baseball hat, and a red ski cap. You can sort these items by:

- color (red/green),
- function (things you write with, things you use when you are washing, things you drink from, things you wear on your head),
- texture (smooth things and fuzzy things).

What is the most sensible way to put these things into categories?

BEANBAG CATEGORIES

In this activity, your child gets to throw beanbags around while learning about categories. First, make or buy beanbags that are a comfortable size for your child to throw. Then, use shelf liner, the back of a wallpaper roll, or any long paper roll to make several game grids. Cut off a length of paper approximately three or four feet long? Draw lines with a marker to divide the paper into six to twelve blocks, sized so that your child can easily throw the beanbag into the block. If you live in a city with sidewalks or have a concrete driveway, you can use street chalk to draw the grid and the picture too.

This activity can be done in two different ways. One way is to discuss what objects go with a category. You might have a stack of pictures from a magazine. Label and discuss the pictures, and then divide them by categories. Some pictures are of food, others are of toys, others are of cars. The other way to set up the game is to choose categories that go with a concept. For example, mittens and a snowman are winter pictures, and a sandcastle, bathing suit, and goggles are summer pictures.

Then mount the pictures from each category on a separate paper grid, in the blocks you have drawn. You now have a couple of different game boards for your game. Place the game board on the floor. Have your child throw the beanbag. When the beanbag lands in a block, your child needs to name what is in the block. Or, you might ask him to make up a phrase, a sentence, or even a song with that word. To add another wrinkle, you might ask him to run over and pick up the beanbag, or hop or jump to the block with the picture. This game can be modified so that it is just right for your child.

At a more advanced level, players would need not only to name that insect, but to name five insects. Or the block could have written clues rather than a picture, such as "fruit, long and curved, yellow, has a peel," and the child would need to use word retrieval and convergent language skills to come up with *banana*.

Categorization, although a semantics area, also relates to topicalization, an area of pragmatics. When you understand and have practice with categories, you have a better understanding of what is on topic and what is off topic. This contributes to the ability to have longer, on-topic conversations. See Chapter 8 for more information on topicalization.

CATEGORIES IN NATURE

You can use things that you collect at the beach or in the park to teach your child about grouping and collections. You can go on a nature hunt with

the goal of collecting one thing, such as twigs for a campfire, or rocks or shells. Read a book about campfires and twigs or about rocks and shells. Collect many samples of whatever you have chosen to collect. Put them all in a pail or a bag. When you have collected many samples, sit down and look at what you have found. Discuss them with your child: How do they feel? What color (or colors) are they? How do they look? Where did you find them? If appropriate for your child, categorize the objects in different ways (e.g., by type of leaf, color, size, etc.). This can help your child learn how two objects can be both the same and different, a more complex language skill.

Another activity is to collect an assortment of things that you find interesting as you walk around, such as leaves and shells and rocks and wildflowers. When you have collected all that you want to, empty your pail or bag, and survey your finds. Decide how many different kinds of things you have and how to sort them. For example, you might sort your finds into pebbles (or little rocks), big rocks, and shells; or into white shells and rocks, brown shells and rocks, and purple shells. For older children or teens, check out a book from the library and see if you can identify some of the items you have collected. This is an activity that helps children learn about grouping and categories.

BOARD GAMES AND CARD GAMES

There are many commercially available games that offer a fun way for parents to teach their children about categories, as well as many other language, speech, and social skills. For example, Pictionary Junior is an excellent game for working on categories. To play the game, players take turns drawing people, places, or things indicated on a card. Each card is labeled with the category of the item, and other players are given that category as a clue to help them guess what is being drawn. The Appendix lists a variety of board games and card games that can be used to help all your children, with and without Down syndrome, improve their speech and language skills.

HOME ACTIVITIES FOR SAME/DIFFERENT

GROUPING SIMILAR OBJECTS

Knowing whether two items or a group of items are the same or different is a skill that children are expected to know by early elementary school. Being able to group cups with cups and spoons with spoons using objects, photographs, and/or line drawings is a skill often tested in school readiness tests and tests used in early elementary school.

There are many ways your child can learn and practice this skill at home. It is best to begin with objects that are familiar to your child, such as cars, teddy bears, cereal boxes. Show your child how to group them together as the same or different. If your child has difficulty understanding what same and different mean, teach him *same* by pointing to specific features. For instance, point out that two teddy bears both have eyes (Say "same"), both have two hands and two feet, both have fuzzy brown fur. Teach *different* by pointing out what makes the two bears different: This bear has white fur; this bear has brown fur (they are "different"; their color is "different.").

Once your child is able to group objects effectively, take photographs of the objects. Then have him sort the photographs into same and different. You can use two shoeboxes and make a "same" box and a "different" box so that your child can sort the photos. On the same box, have pictures of things that are the same or write the word "same." Once your child is able to sort and categorize the photographs as same and different, you may want to make a same and different book out of the photographs to use for practice. A magnetic photograph album or a sketchbook work very well.

Over time, help your child to progress from sorting photographs that are the same and different to sorting line drawings. Recognizing drawings of items is a stepping stone skill to being able to read and also a useful skill in following picture schedules.

If your child has a dual diagnosis of autism and Down syndrome or is more cognitively delayed, he may have trouble understanding that a picture stands for an object. To help him learn this concept, you may want to begin by having him manipulate small objects instead of photos of objects when learning about same and different. For example, have him sort plastic animal figures or cups and plates from a tea set. Later, attach those same objects to a color photo of the object. Still later, try separating the objects from the photos and see if your child can sort the photos. Eventually, progress to colored drawings and then line drawings.

WORKBOOKS

There are many workbooks for same and different available at educational bookstores, a toy or variety stores, or even supermarkets. These usually use line drawings. Start by tracing, copying, or cutting out those pictures and have your child sort them into "same" and "different" boxes, as described above. Once your child can sort the pictures, move on to workbook activities.

For younger school-aged children, the problem with workbooks is that the instructions involve more than identifying the same objects; you need to circle or underline the same pictures and that involves another step and good fine motor skills. So, start by having your child point to the pictures that are the same. Then, when this becomes easy for your child, move on to underlining and circling activities. Following instructions such as these is a necessary skill for test taking in elementary school.

DESCRIBING SIMILARITIES AND DIFFERENCES

Many activities related to identifying *same* and *different* are preschool and early school year skills. But there is a related skill that is much more advanced and can be worked on into adolescence—namely, the ability to tell how two items are the same and how they are different. For example, how are a cup and a spoon the same and how are they different? Usually, children will be able to tell how they are the same—e.g., you use both of them to eat. But, then how are they different? Being able to shift mindset to answer the second question is much more difficult for most children with Down syndrome, and for children with learning disabilities. To be able to say that you use a fork to eat and a cup to drink or you use a fork for solid foods and a cup for liquid foods is more advanced.

To work on this skill at home, you can create a visual aid to help your child identify the characteristics of an object. Make a list or chart that specifies characteristics or asks questions, such as color, size, shape, material, and function. Then line up two objects, such as Cheerios and Strawberry Mini Wheats. List the characteristics for each:

Object	Cheerios	Strawberry Mini Wheats
Color	tan	pink
Size/Shape	round	square
Made of	oats	wheat
Category	cereal	cereal
Function	eat	eat

Fill out the form together with your child. Then review the list with him to see how the two cereals are the same and different. Cheerios and Strawberry Mini Wheats are both cereals. Put an S next to the cereal line to indicate "same." Cheerios are tan and Strawberry Mini Wheats are pink. That's different. Put a D next to the color line, etc.

Catalogs are also wonderful for teaching and practicing same and different concepts. Page through a catalog with your child, commenting on how the items are the same and then discuss why they are different. For example, both are shirts, one is yellow and one is blue; or both are team shirts, one is for the Ravens and the other is for the Patriots.

HOME ACTIVITY FOR FOLLOWING DIRECTIONS

FOLLOWING RECIPES

Following recipes is a terrific home activity for a number of reasons. It is a practical skill that adapts well to speech and language practice. It involves following directions, sequencing steps, learning appropriate nouns (*cup*) and verbs (*pour*), as well as working with numbers and measurements for math skills. It provides opportunities to talk about vocabulary—for instance, what is the difference between *cut* and *dice, stir* and *whip?* Cooking or baking something for dinner also is helpful to the family and helps your child build self-esteem. Some guidelines:

- Use a cookbook with illustrations or photographs.
- Set out all of the equipment first.
- Gather all of the ingredients.
- Choose a recipe that can be enjoyed by family and friends.
- Begin with a recipe that has fewer than ten steps.

For example, let's say that you have decided to make tomato sauce for your child's favorite meal, spaghetti. First, get a colorful, easy-to-read cookbook from

the library. Write out the list of ingredients or read them from the book with your child. Gather, then measure, all of the ingredients. Tailor your child's participation to meet his skills. Can he read the list of ingredients? Can he assemble the ingredients as you read the list? Can he measure? Can he put the tomatoes in the pot? Stir the sauce? Talk about each step as you are working on it. Then, enjoy pasta with your very own tomato sauce for dinner.

You may want to take photographs of each step from picking the tomatoes or buying them at the store to eating the pasta with tomato sauce. Then you can use the photos as visual cues to review the steps in the activity. Also, use the photos as a visual cue to assist your child in retelling the events of his day. If your child is working on story telling skills, cue him to use words such as *next* or *then* or *after that* when retelling the sequence.

Morphosyntax

When Aidan, age 7, is telling his parents about the first grade field trip he went on today, he says, "Ride fire truck." His parents, who are very familiar with their son's speech, fill in the blanks to understand what Aidan meant: "I rode on a fire truck."

Nine-year-old Samantha is telling her mom about something that happened at school. "Billy push push, teacher mad. Her get red and yelling." Samantha's mom can figure out that Billy pushed someone, but did he push Samantha or someone else in the class? Was the teacher's yelling related to Billy pushing or did it happen at another time during the day? Samantha's difficulty with word endings, verb tenses, and pronouns affects her meaning. It is difficult to understand what she is saying.

Rory, age 13, just came back from a trip to his aunt and uncle's house. He said, "Wow, I ride in the new car. It is beautiful. And no top. The wind blow my hair." Rory has some difficulty with verb tenses, but his morphosyntactic errors don't affect his meaning. You can figure out what Rory is trying to tell you—that he rode in a new convertible and his hair blew in the wind.

Like Aidan, Samantha, and Rory, most school-aged children with Down syndrome have difficulties with morphosyntax. As a result, many speak using short, telegraphic phrases and it can be difficult to understand what they mean.

As discussed in Chapter 2, children with Down syndrome have more trouble with morphology (word segments) and syntax (grammar) than with semantics (vocabulary). Furthermore, the difference between vocabulary and grammatical development gets larger as children get older.

Morphosyntax, including word roots, prefixes, suffixes, word order, and sentence composition, is one of the most difficult areas for children with Down syndrome. They have greater difficulty in learning to use prepositions (e.g., *in, up, above*) and connectives (e.g., *and, but, or*) and other function words as compared to content words (nouns and verbs). This suggests that they develop adequate referential meaning (they know what the word is referring to and understand what the word represents) but have difficulty learning: 1) the grammatical category of words (whether a word is a noun, verb, or preposition) and 2) how you use the grammatical words correctly in a multiword phrase or sentence.

Researchers such as Ann Fowler believe that specific difficulties in learning syntax based on underlying sequencing difficulties cause major language learning problems in children with Down syndrome (1990, 1995). It is also possible that syntax presents more difficulty because it is more abstract. Or, then again, children with Down syndrome may have trouble hearing word endings such as suffixes and verb tense markers, as they tend to be said in a softer voice. Grammatical markers and word order become a concern when children are using longer more complex utterances, and more complex utterances are more difficult for children with Down syndrome, So, there may be multiple reasons why morphosyntax is difficult for individuals with Down syndrome. Researchers have not found definitive conclusions that can lead us to appropriate assessment and treatment strategies. There is a need for further research.

We don't know how great an impact oral motor ability and speech ability have on some of the morphosyntactic difficulties. For example, if the child does not produce plurals, we do not know whether this is due to difficulty in articulating the final /s/ sound, difficulty in understanding or using the plural marker, or some other reason. After all, in analyzing expressive speech, we judge whether the child is using plurals by whether he includes the final /s/. Perhaps a child is trying to use plurals, but because he leaves out or cannot say certain final consonants, we assume that he is not using the plural marker.

For whatever reason, the majority of children with Down syndrome do not use grammatical and morphosyntactic markers until at least age five. Most gradually learn to use possessives and tenses over the elementary school years, although some may still not be using these forms by the end of middle school.

Some researchers have shown that children with Down syndrome reach a period during late adolescence where there is a slowdown in morphosyntactic development and that they don't make much spontaneous progress beyond that period. Others have found no evidence of a critical period for syntax development or a syntactic ceiling (an upper limit to what they can learn). There has not been any research to investigate whether morphosyntax can continue to improve with treatment—that is, whether specific interventions can result in progress when children do not spontaneously improve their skills.

THE MOST DIFFICULT AREAS FOR CHILDREN WITH DOWN SYNDROME

In my experience, the areas of morphosyntax that are especially difficult for children with Down syndrome are:

- the use of regular (*walked, played*) and irregular (*sang, ran*) past tense;
- agreement of pronoun and verb (*he walks, they walk*);
- the use of personal pronouns (*her, hers, herself*);
- active versus passive construction (*Bob is hitting Boris; Boris was hit by Bob*);
- correct use of negatives (*he is not/isn't coming over*);
- correct use of positive and negative interrogatives (*When is he coming? Or Why isn't he coming?*);
- the use of articles (a, an, the).

HOW THE SLP WORKS ON MORPHOSYNTAX

Despite their difficulties with morphosyntax, children with Down syndrome learn grammatical structures in the same order as typically developing children do—just at a slower pace. This means that you and your child's speech-language pathologist can use the typical linguistic stages as a guideline in figuring out appropriate goals in morphosyntax for your child. See Table 5-1 on the next page. Criterion referenced tests (discussed in Chapter 3) can be used to develop a framework for language treatment. The test results will record the morphological and syntactic structures your child has mastered and provide a hierarchical list of the structures he still needs to learn.

After the SLP has evaluated your child and determined what his morphosyntax difficulties are, he or she will treat those specific areas. Treatment methods usually include:

- modeling,
- imitation, and
- pattern practice.

These methods are used together. For instance, the SLP and your child look at a picture together, and the SLP models saying, "The boy is jumping." Your child imitates "The boy is jumping." Once your child can imitate a given grammatical structure, you move on to having him label the pictures himself. Once he can label the pictures, the SLP provides multiple practice opportunities with that specific structure. In this case, the child might label a stack of 30 pictures all using the present participle verb structure—"he is walking … running … writing… coloring … painting … skiing … skating," etc.

The SLP may also use books or software to help your child with his morphosyntax problems. She would read a book to your child, pointing out the grammatical forms, and possibly pairing the practice with work on answering questions. See the box about *Bruno the Baker* for an example of how your SLP (or you) could use a book in this way.

HOW PARENTS CAN WORK ON MORPHOSYNTAX

In general, parents can work on morphosyntax with their children with Down syndrome the same way as they would work with their typically developing children. For example, when your child says something that is not grammatical, you can repeat it for your child correctly. For example, your child might say, "Go pool." Then, depending

Table 5-1: What Are the Linguistic Stages?

If you ever read accounts of research studies into children's language skills, you may come across references to the children being at, for example, "Brown Stage I" or "Brown Stage IV." What the researchers are referring to is the length of the children's typical utterance, as well as how far they have progressed in mastering the first fourteen morphemes learned in the English language and basic semantic skills. A description of the order in which young children typically learn to use morphemes was originally published by Roger Brown in his book *A First Language*—hence the references to "Brown stages."

These are the five stages and how they affect a child's morphosyntax:

Stage I: MLU of 1.75 words; reached by typically developing children at 22 months.

Children form sentences without using morphological word endings. For example, they say "Mommy shoe" to mean "Mommy's shoe" or "Baby cry" to mean "Baby is crying."

Stage II: MLU of 2.25 words; typically reached at 28 months.

Children use the following morphemes:
1. Present-progressive verb ending ("-ing"): For example, "Julie eating"
2. Preposition "in": "Billy in car"
3. Preposition "on": "bowl on table"
4. Regular plural ("-s"): "toys," "cars," "fingers"

Stage III: MLU of 2.75 words; typically reached at 32 months.

Children add the use of the following morphemes:
5. Past irregular verbs: "toy broke," "you fell down," "Susie came home"
6. Possessives: "Mommy's cars," "Joey's shoes"
7. Uncontractible copula (using "to be" words without contractions): "What is that?" "Where are they?"

Stage IV: MLU of 3.50 words; typically reached at 41 months.

Children add the use of the following morphemes:
8. Articles (the, an, a): "the ball," "a hat"
9. Past regular tense endings ("-ed"): "Kelly walked yesterday."
10. Third-person regular tense endings ("-s"): "Josh carries teddy," "Susie sees cookies"

Stage V: MLU of 4.00 words; typically reached at 45 months.

Children add the use of the following morphemes:
11. Third-person irregular tense endings: "Mom does"
12. Uncontractible auxiliary (full form of "to be" used as a "helping verb": "The dog is barking."
13. Contractible copula (contracted form of "to be" used as the only verb in sentence: "Brian's silly," "Where's mommy?"
14. Contractible auxiliary (contracted form of "to be" used as a "helping verb": "The dog's barking."

*Reprinted from Kumin, L. **Early Communication Skills for Children with Down Syndrome, 2nd edition** (Woodbine House, 2003).*

Bruno the Baker

To illustrate how a book can be used to teach and reinforce morphosyntax let's look at the book ***Bruno the Baker*** by Lars Klinting (1997). This book can be used to practice the -er ending to mean "one who"—for example, *baker* is one who bakes. It can also be used for verb tense markers, subject-verb agreement, word sequencing, vocabulary, and asking and answering questions.

Here's how to plan what to teach with the book:

1. Read the text to yourself.
2. Note the information that you would like to try to teach in particular parts of the book (you will want to highlight this information by increasing your volume, or by using emphasis or more emotion in your voice).
3. Decide what question you will ask immediately after reading the section.

Next you will read the book together with your child, asking your questions and waiting to see if he can answer them. If not, you will model the answer. If your child is a reader, you can point out the answer, or use highlighting tape to note the answer. *For example:*

You read: "Who is that knocking on Bruno's window? It's FELIX." Then you ask, "WHO is knocking on Bruno's window?" If your child says, "Felix," move on. If not, point to the name in the text and the illustration, and say, "It's FELIX.... Who's knocking on the window? FELIX" (provide the model). Then ask the question again, and look to your child to answer. If he cannot, provide a visual cue for the /f/ sound and see if that will help him say Felix.

Another example:

You read: "First Bruno melts the butter." Then you ask, "What does Bruno do first?" ("He MELTS the butter") (point to the picture, if necessary). Repeat, if necessary: "What does Bruno do first? He MELTS the butter."

You read: "After Bruno and Felix blend the mixture well, they pour the batter into the cake pan."

You ask: "Bruno and Felix mix the batter well. Then what do they do?" (They POUR the batter into the cake pan.) (In this case, you are highlighting more complex morphosyntax: "they pour"; "he melts.")

on how many words he can use in a sentence and his language learning goals, you can model a more correct version for him. For instance, if you are working with him on prepositions, you might repeat: "Go TO pool."

Another natural way to work on morphosyntax is to read aloud to your child, emphasizing the specific morphemes that your child is having trouble with. This is similar to the strategy described above for *Bruno the Baker,* except you are not asking your child to answer questions using proper morphosyntax, but are highlighting the structures he is working on. For example, *Bedhead* by Margie Palatini (2000) is a book about a boy, Oliver, who wakes up with bedhead hair on the day of his class photo. There are many examples of past tense including: "He yawned,

He yanked, Splashed some water, swished some mouthwash…they spritzed him and sprayed him. And they gooped, glopped and moussed him." If your child is working on past tense, when you read the book with him, emphasize the past tense markers by making them louder—e.g., "he yankED."

Cueing systems can be used to help. For example, you can use a pacing board with the words written under the dots, or you can write up cue cards so your child can read the words. If your child is leaving out the "-ed" ending, you can write a cue card where the "ed" is in a different color such as red to emphasize the word ending.

HOME ACTIVITIES FOR ASKING AND ANSWERING QUESTIONS

LOOKING AT FAMILY PHOTOGRAPHS

Being able to ask and answer *wh* questions (*who, what, when, where*) is an important skill. You can use the same photographs you use for vocabulary prac-

tice, above, for practice in asking and answering these questions. "*Who* is making iced tea? *What* is grandma making? *Who* is playing baseball? *What* sport is Fred playing?" You also can do the practice in reverse, with your child asking you questions about the pictures.

Adapt this activity to your child's speech abilities. For example, you can answer for your child, "Walking," and then have him imitate you. Or you can ask, "What is grandpa doing? What is Bob doing?" and your child can answer, "hitting," or "he is hitting," or "he is hitting the baseball" depending on his speech and language skills. With an older child who is more advanced, you can also get into discussions about subtle differences in verbs— e.g., *stare, look, glance,* or *walk, jog, sprint.*

Later on, when your child has mastered many verb concepts, the book can become a cherished memory book, or it can continue to be expanded to include more high-level verbs—"He is sending a fax"; "She is peering through a microscope."

NEWSPAPER ADS

A wonderful source for material for *wh* question practice is the advertising pull-out sections of your Sunday newspaper. It is also a resource in which the items changes from week to week, but the basic format usually remains the same, so it will look different, but familiar to your child.

Pull out the supermarket section and ask: "What do you want to buy?" If your child does not give an answer, provide some cues in the form of questions. "Do you want to buy juice? Do you want to buy cereal?" or "Which cereal should we buy?" Then, try a clothing store advertisement. "What should we buy?" If there is an ad for men's, women's, and children's shorts, ask "Who needs these shorts?" Or if your child is working on colors, ask, "What color are these shorts?"

Once you have used two or three different ads, ask questions such as, "Where can we buy shorts?" "Where can we buy M & M's?" "Where can we buy a hammer?"

Later, take the ads with you when you go shopping with your child. If possible, buy some of the items he expressed an interest in. In the store, you can work on *where* questions: "What did you want to buy? Right, graham crackers…. Where are the graham crackers in this store?"

THE SPORTS PAGE

Another part of the newspaper that lends itself well to *wh* question and answer work is the sports section. As above, the format is familiar. The names of the teams are familiar, but the information is different every day, so the sports page is excellent for *asking and answering* therapy and home activities. Looking at the sports page is also an activity that can be a lifelong interest and activity.

Some questions you might ask:

- Which teams played baseball last night?
- Did the _____ play?
- What was the score?
- _____ was injured, so who played first base?
- Why do you think they lost?
- Did the golf tournament finish up yet?
- Where are they playing?
- Who won the green jacket?

An interesting book that teaches people how to read the sports page and how to understand sports stats is *Reading the Sports Page* by Jeremy Feinberg (1992).

HOW AND WHY

"How?" and "why?" are among the most difficult questions for children with Down syndrome to answer. One reason may be that to answer many *why* questions, you need to have an understanding of cause and effect, a cognitive skill that is usually delayed in children with Down syndrome. For example, to answer "Why did you take off your coat?" you need to remember and verbalize what prompted you to take off your coat: "I was too hot," or, "I couldn't run fast with it on." Other *why* questions are phrased in the negative, and negative sentence constructions, in my clinical experience, are a particular area of difficulty for children with Down syndrome. For example, "Why can't we go?" or "Why don't you like this show?" both require an understanding of negatives.

To answer *how* questions, you may need to understand cause and effect ("How did that mud get on the rug?") or you may need to be able to sequence a series of actions ("How do you play this game?"). Again, both of these are difficult for children with Down syndrome.

As children with Down syndrome are learning to answer *why* questions, they may grasp that these questions are usually answered with a *because*, but still not know how to formulate an answer correctly. For instance, if you ask your child why you should turn the TV on for him, he might answer something like, "Because, just do it!" He probably knows why he wants to watch TV (he wants to see if a favorite show is on, for instance) but doesn't know how to respond to the question.

Answering *why not* questions is especially difficult. For example, a child may say, "I can't do the book report" and his mother may ask, "Why not?" The child may not really know the reasons. That may be why he is asking for help.

When your child is learning to answer *why* questions, it can be helpful to give him a choice of answers. For instance, if you have asked him, "Why are you laughing," and he doesn't answer, you could then ask: "Did I say something funny?" "Did you see something funny?" He can then answer yes or no. Then you could say, "So that's *why* you are laughing. *Because* Stef said something funny!" You can also frequently model the use of *because* in everyday speech. For example, tell your child: "I'm happy BECAUSE you brushed your teeth without being told." Or, "We need to go shopping BECAUSE we are out of milk." When your child cannot answer a question, give him choices, and then follow up with a correct model. Providing suggestions and then providing a model for a correct response are good strategies.

It may take even longer for your child to understand how to ask and answer *how* questions because *how* can be used in so many ways: "How's it going?" (in what manner); "How do you open this?" (in what way); "How did that happen?" (what was the sequence of events leading up to it). You and your child's SLP may need to choose specific usages of *how* that are important for your child to know how to ask and answer at that point in life, and directly teach the usages to him, one by one. For instance, when your child is starting school, it may be most important for him to understand how to answer variations on "How are you?" As he gets older, it will probably become important for him to be able to ask "How do you …?" when he doesn't know how to do something (and before he gets frustrated).

Other suggestions for working on how and why at home include:

● If your child is younger, role play with puppets, figurines, etc., during imaginative play. For example, have the mother puppet ask *why* and *how* questions.

● Make photo books showing *why/because* and *how* scenarios. For instance, photograph an important event such as a party, and put them in a photo album with *why* and *because* captions. "On June 8th, we had a party. Why? Because it was George's birthday. George had chocolate cake because that is his favorite…."

● Planning for trips is an activity that is good for practicing *wh* questions. Why are we going to Uncle Dave's house? How will we get there? Who else is coming? What will we eat? Why do you have to sleep on the sleep sofa? What holiday are we going to celebrate? Provide models as needed. Then take photos of the trip and use them for question and answer practice when you get home.

- Read published books that emphasize *wh* words. Joke books use *wh* questions quite a lot. Knock-knock jokes always include "Who's there?" and are good choices. A delightful joke book is *Giggle Bugs* by David Carter (1999), which comes with a push button for a laugh track. Some examples are: "Why does a Hummingbird hum? Because it doesn't know the words." "Why don't Banana Bugs ever get lonely? Because they hang around in bunches." Some of the language is sophisticated and can be used to work on double meanings: "Why do some bugs become Baker Bugs? Because they need the dough." You could even

Good Books for Asking & Answering Questions

Wh Questions

Conrad, P. *The Tub People.*

Cooper, H. *Pumpkin Soup.*

Davis, K. *Who Hops?*

Gomi, T. *Where's the Fish?*

Handford, M. *Where's Waldo?* (and other books in series)

Hutchins, P. *What Game Shall We Play?*

Hutchins, P. *Which Witch is Which?*

Kraus, R. *Whose Mouse are You?*

Kraus, R. *Where Are You Going Little Mouse?*

Martin, B. *Brown Bear, Brown Bear, What do You See?*

Miller, M. *Guess Who?*

Rink, C. *Where Does the Wind Blow?*

Stamaty, M. *Who Needs Donuts?*

Tafuri, N. *Whose Chick Are You?*

Waber, B. *An Anteater Named Arthur.*

Why Questions

Arnold, T., et al. *Why Did the Chicken Cross the Road?*

Bang, M. *The Grey Lady and the Strawberry Snatcher.*

Cendrars, B. *Shadow.*

De Paola, T. *Hey Diddle Diddle and Other Mother Goose Rhymes.*

Emberley, B. *Drummer Hoff.*

Fox, Mem. *Hattie and the Fox.*

Hutchins, P. *Don't Forget the Bacon.*

Knowlton, L. *Why Cowboys Sleep with Their Boots On.*

Lawrence, J. *Harriet and the Promised Land.*

Patterson, F. *Koko's Kitten.*

Taback, S. *This Is the House That Jack Built*

write an adaptation, "because they knead the dough," and discuss the different meanings of *need*, *knead*, and *dough*. This would be a very high level language skill.

- Create a personalized game board to practice *why* and *why not*. First, make a game board as described in the section on "Homemade Game Boards" in Chapter 6. Have a card deck with activities such as "Let's go swimming." The player who picks that card has to tell either why we should do that (e.g., "I like to splash") or why not (e.g., "It's winter and we only have an outdoor pool near our house.") Or, "Let's make a snowman. Why? It's fun. Why not? It's not snowing." If a player can answer, he can move his token forward one space. If not, he stays where he is and another player has the option to answer and move ahead.

- Read children's books that have an interesting plot. They lend themselves to questions. An example is *Funny Frank* by Dick King-Smith (2001). In the book, eight chicks are hatched and a character named Jemima names them all. Seven of the chicks played in the grass, but Frank walked right to the pond. Frank is a chicken who wants to be a duck. Why does he want to be a duck? He wants to swim. What does he do? Read the book and follow up with questions for each page or chapter. As you are reading, note the words that answer the questions you will ask and emphasize those words by saying them louder, and, if your child reads, pointing to those words in the book.

- For practicing *how*, try the book *How do Dinosaurs Eat Their Food?* by Jane Yolen (2005). It's a book about eating and manners, and includes many *how* questions which lend themselves to longer answers, and also *does* questions, which are good for practicing yes and no answers.

- See the box on the previous page for some other books that focus on *wh* questions, and on asking and answering questions.

HOME ACTIVITIES FOR PREPOSITIONS

SINGING PREPOSITIONS

Use the song *The Bear Went Over the Mountain* to help your child learn about and practice prepositions. The original song's words are: "The bear went over the mountain, the bear went over the mountain, the bear went over the mountain to see what he could see."

You can use the same tune but vary the words to help your child learn and then practice the prepositions *over* and *under*, *on* and *in*, *around* and *through*, *in front of* and *behind*. Begin with you and your child pretending to be bears. Use a small brown cape or other prop to make the activity more fun. Or, use your child's name instead of bear. This can be done with siblings or friends using each child's name as they are doing the movement activity.

You can create a small obstacle course inside the house with pillows, bolsters, toy slides, etc. or outside in the yard to use. You also can use the playground for this activity.

Demonstrate each activity and sing the appropriate words to the song. For example, "The bear went over the pillow," or "The bear went under the slide." If your child is able to sing only one or two words in sequence, focus on *under, over, through*, etc. by making these words louder when you sing.

If your child responds well to this activity, then you can use the song for many movements and directions—for instance, "Joshua walked up the steps" or "Meghan jumped over the puddle."

As an alternate activity, you might want to read and act out the book *We're Going on a Bear Hunt*. In the story, the children who are looking for a bear repeatedly encounter obstacles and then exclaim: "We can't go **over** it. We can't go **under** it… Oh, no! We've got to go **through** it."

SIMON SAYS

You can play a variation on Simon Says to help your child learn about prepositions and prepositional phrases. At first, you play "Simon" and say and model what you want your child to do. Make sure you include a variety of prepositions in your instructions. For example: Simon says…

- Put your hand *on* your head.
- Put your finger *under* your chin.
- Stand *next to* the chair.
- Sit *under* the table.
- Put your hands *on* your hips.
- Put your hands *up*.

Later, just say the instructions (without modeling them) and see if your child can do them without watching you. Of course, at this point you should sometimes "forget" to say "Simon says" so you can catch your child doing the action when he was supposed to wait for you to say "Simon Says."

HOME ACTIVITIES FOR VERB TENSE

As discussed above, verb endings are especially difficult for many children with Down syndrome to master. Your child will likely need to hear verbs used in daily life and have his attention drawn to the endings many, many times before he is able to use tenses correctly.

At some point when your child is learning to use tenses, you may notice that he has learned the rules too well. For example, he may have learned how to form the regular past tense with an -ed, but now is applying that rule to irregular verbs or exceptions to the rule. For instance, he may object to someone sitting in a seat by saying, "I had-ed that seat first!" Or, he may tell you, "I falled-ed off the swing." Or then again, your child may be looking for a favorite book at the bookstore or library. He knows he needs the author's name to find it, so he asks you, "Who writed this?" or "Who wroted this?" He is aware that he should use past tense and that -ed is involved with past tense, but he's not quite sure how to form it.

When a child does this kind of overgeneralizing of a rule, that is a good thing! It means he is well on his way to figuring out how that morphosyntactic rule works. You can give him models for the correct production for exceptions, and help them learn those exceptions. ("Barbara Parks WROTE it." "I'm sorry you FELL. Are you hurt?") But, most of the time the rule will apply, so he will more often be right than wrong.

Here are some ways to work with your child on verbs:

- Make a habit of chatting with your family at dinner about the best thing (or something interesting) that happened to them that day. Or you might ask who they played with (ate with, sat next to) that day. If your child uses the wrong verb form, just pleasantly repeat what he said, emphasizing the correct ending or form. "You ATE with Dylan? How nice!"

- Look at photos of past events or vacations and talk about them with your child, casually working on past tense and *wh* questions as you do so. "What did we do? We went on vacation" (irregular verb past tense). "Where did we stay? We stayed at the lake. Who was there?" etc.

- Choose a "verb of the week" and use it many times per day in present tense, past, and future tenses. For example, make a point of using the words *drink* and *drank* (and later, *drunk*) many times before, during, and after a meal. Or, if your child enjoys singing along with music, use the words *sing* and *sang* frequently when your child is singing or has finished singing.

- Keep a family journal or help your child keep a journal. At least a couple days a week, have him dictate or write some things he did that day. If he tells you in present tense, clarify— "Are you eating with Jack NOW? No, that was at lunch. We need to say 'I ATE with Jack.'"

- Describe a physical activity that passes quickly, using the present tense and the past tense—for instance, "I am jumping. I jumped. I am running. I ran." This can also be used for activities that involve choice—"I am picking an apple. I picked the apple." If your child still enjoys playing with dolls, action figures, toy cars, or stuffed animals and lets you play along, you can sometimes narrate what you are doing using these verb forms. For example, "I *am driving* my car to the store. Whoops! I *drove* too fast!"

- Use children's books to provide opportunities to hear many examples of verb tenses and pronoun-verb agreement. For example, *Ruby Lu, Empress of Everything* by Lenore Look (2006) is a story about a young girl whose cousin, Flying Duck, emigrates from China and comes to live with the Lu family. Flying Duck is deaf and uses Chinese sign language. The book is about challenges, not only adapting to a new country, but also about fear of swimming lessons, going to summer school, and other challenges of childhood. There are many examples of past tense verbs; e.g., "Ruby liked the parties....Ruby liked the noise and excitement....The telephone rang all the time....Everyone wanted to meet the newcomers."

● Have your child pick out a monthly calendar that he likes and hang it in his room. Help your child to write upcoming events on the calendar. Talk about them using the future tense. "Tomorrow you have swimming lessons. That means we will go to the Rec Center.... This is the day we will fly to Disney World."

HOME ACTIVITIES FOR PRONOUNS

It is common for young children to make mistakes with pronouns. Some children mix up the masculine and feminine pronouns and say things such as "He's a nice girl" or "Daddy got a bandaid on her finger." Others use the wrong form of a pronoun and say things such as "Him going to fix the car" or "Her make burgers for supper." And some overgeneralize rules and say things such as "Mines is pink" (after all, you would say "Hers is pink" and "Yours is pink," so why shouldn't it be "Mines"?).

Children with Down syndrome often persist in making these errors longer than usual. In my clinical experience, however, they usually learn to choose the right gender and form of pronouns with enough repetition over time. What is more difficult for them is to learn pronoun-verb agreement—that is, to use a singular verb with a singular pronoun and a plural verb with a plural pronoun— for example, I am swimming; we are swimming. He swims; they swim.

Subject-verb agreement is an abstract concept. The best way to help your child learn this is through practice. At school, he will probably work on this skill with worksheets. At home, you can try several games:

● Gather several family members or friends together, including at least one person of each gender. Choose a leader. The leader does a physical activity. She says, "I walk" (run, jump, hop, crawl, etc.). The other people have to do the same action and say, "I walk." Then they take turns pointing to another player and describe what he is doing. ("He is walking" or "He walks.") When you want to practice "they," choose two leaders. They jump. This is a good activity to involve siblings at home, or older children in school who come to assist in a lower grade class. It takes some advance planning. You can give them a list of activities they will demonstrate.

● Make a pronoun board game. Make a game board from a file folder or use the board from another game your child enjoys. Then, look through magazines or your family photos for pictures of men, women, boys, girls, and groups doing actions your child can describe (playing soccer, throwing a ball, eating, smiling, sitting, etc.). Glue the pictures to index cards and put them in a stack in the middle of the board. Players take a turn choosing a card. If they can correctly state what the person is doing ("He is swinging" or "he swings") they can roll the dice and move ahead. (To get your child to say "is swinging" vs. "swings," you can try asking, "What is he doing?" or "What does he do?")

- For an older child who is learning the parts of speech in school, try reading *I and You and Don't Forget Who: What Is a Pronoun?* by Brian Cleary and Brian Gable (2004). This book, and the others in the "Words Are Categorical Series," teaches the rudiments of grammar with silly rhymes and drawings that appeal to elementary school children.

HOME ACTIVITIES FOR PASSIVE VS. ACTIVE VOICE

Most of us don't use passive voice that much in everyday speech. For instance, we say "Kathy made the pie" instead of "The pie was made by Kathy." "Brendan hit the ball" instead of "The ball was hit by Brendan." "I signed the letter" instead of "The letter was signed by me." So, since children with Down syndrome have to hear many more repetitions of something before they learn to understand and say it themselves, passive voice can be very difficult for them.

I have observed that children with Down syndrome sometimes interpret meaning by word order when a sentence is in passive voice. For example, they interpret "the truck was hit by the car" to mean the "truck hit the car," since they are used to the subject coming first in the sentence.

The differences are easiest to demonstrate by using play activities. Use toy vehicles, stuffed animals, or action figures and interpret what you say. You may first need to demonstrate. Once your child understands active and passive, he can listen and then demonstrate what he hears. For example, show him the difference between:

- The truck hit the car. The truck was hit by the car
- The cat chased the dog. The dog was chased by the cat. The dog chased the cat. The cat was chased by the dog.
- The boy hit the ball. The ball was hit by the boy. The ball hit the boy.

What you are trying to convey is how the meaning is changed by the way you say the sentence.

If your child is frequently confused by passive voice in daily life, you may need to make a deliberate attempt to use it more in your speech. It may help for you to phrase things both in active and passive voice at times. For example: "This picture was made by you? *You* made it?!"

HOME ACTIVITIES FOR NEGATIVES

Negatives ("He is not coming" or "He's not coming") and negative interrogatives ("Why isn't he coming?") are difficult structures to use. If your child is working on these structures in school, or appears ready to work on them (i.e., he understands the concepts of negatives and negative interrogatives and has sufficient speech to say the longer phrases), you can try to provide examples of these structures. Do this in real situations in daily living as they occur. For example, ask your child, "Are you unhappy? (or not happy). Why aren't you happy? It's taking a long time to get to Grandma's house. There's a lot of traffic. Will you be happy when we get there?"

● Play direction-following games where you give some instructions in the positive and some in the negative. For example, see if your child can color a picture following your instructions: "Color his hat blue. Now color his scarf, but don't (or do NOT) use green." Or, "Don't use any red for the flowers." You could also use a felt board or Color Forms. Tell your child what to put on the board, using negatives: "Now put the big red square on the board. Don't put it by the blue circle."

● Browse through a library, bookstore, or online bookseller for children's books that include negatives. One example of a book that can be used for teaching and practicing negatives is *Giraffes Can't Dance* by Giles Andreae (2001). This is a spirited book with many different animal characters dancing. Your child can use the repetitive phrase, "Giraffes can't dance," to practice the negative contraction.

● If you have some time to kill while driving or waiting in a restaurant or doctor's office, ask silly questions and let your children answer in the negative or the positive, starting with one-word answers and working up to longer sentences. For instance, you could ask, "Do you want to eat fried worms? sleep in a dog house?" In the beginning, your child could simply answer yes or no. Later, he could answer with "Not me!" or "I don't!" or "I don't want to."

HOME ACTIVITIES FOR ARTICLES

Working on articles involves both receptive and expressive language skills. First, your child needs to understand the difference between the definite article (*the*, which we use to refer to a specific person or object that we have in mind) and indefinite articles (*a* or *an*, which we use when we are referring in general to a type of person or object, but not to a particular one).

You can help your child practice his receptive understanding of articles through play. For example, when he is playing with toys that have multiple parts, note the difference between *a* or *an* and *the*: "Give me A game piece. No, I want THE car." Or "Give me a car. No I want the red car." This practice lends itself to crafts activities as well. For instance, if you are beading a necklace, ask for a bead, then say, "No, I want the red bead." Scrapbooking is another craft where there are many choices, and it lends itself to practicing articles. Recipes are yet another activity that work well for practicing articles. For example, "Give me a measuring cup. No, I need the bigger one." Or, "Give me the red sprinkles for the cupcakes." Eventually, you can talk about how *a* can refer to any, but *the* is more specific to bring the difference between articles into your child's awareness.

Once your child understands articles, he needs practice using them. If he tends to leave out the article when he speaks, a pacing board can be helpful (see Chapter 8 for information on using pacing boards). If your child is reading, the pacing board can be used with sentence strip cards with the article in bold print—for example, Get **a** drink.

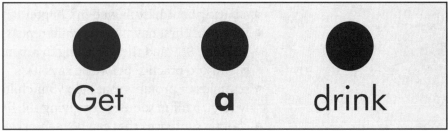

Pacing board with print cues

If your child's language level is more advanced, you can use barrier games to practice using articles. See Chapter 9 for information about barrier games.

Again, you can use books to help your child understand the differences between articles. One book that can be used to practice using articles is *Martin Bridge: Ready for Takeoff!* by Jessica Scott Kerrin (2005). In this early chapter book, Martin is building a rocket decorated with flames, for the science fair. His friend steals the idea. There are many examples of *a, an,* and *the* in this book. In reading the book and in talking about the story, your child will get practice with understanding and using articles.

Channel Based Therapy

In the sections above, emphasis is on improving specific skills within a linguistic area (semantics or morphosyntax). As you probably noticed, however, some activities are focused on improving your child's understanding (receptive language) while others are focused on improving his speaking (expressive language skills). Sometimes, rather than focusing on one of these linguistic areas in particular, your child's SLP will use channel based therapy. This simply means that the SLP will focus on either improving receptive language or expressive language in general. Or, perhaps, your child's long-term goals on his IEP might focus more generally on improving receptive or expressive language skills, while short term goals focus on a specific area of language.

RECEPTIVE LANGUAGE THERAPY

Receptive language therapy includes helping your child learn to follow directions with multiple parts, similar to the instructions given in school. To boost your child's receptive language, the SLP might work with your child on:

- comprehension exercises, such as following instructions on a worksheet;
- reading activities, such as figuring out the topic of a paragraph;
- experiential activities, such as learning about the meaning of prepositions while playing on a playground; and
- specific comprehension of vocabulary, morphology, and syntax.

Expressive language therapy focuses on topics in vocabulary, similarities and differences, morphology, syntax, and increasing the mean length of utterance, or MLU (the number of words your child typically uses in his sentences). This type of therapy would occur after your child had worked on these issues in receptive therapy, and would teach him to say words correctly to state his meaning.

To help your child increase the length of his sentences, the SLP may use:

- a pacing board, explained in Chapter 8;
- rehearsal (first having your child repeat a phrase or sentence after the SLP and then learning to repeat it to himself, perhaps silently, to practice before he says it)
- scaffolds or prompts that help your child say something correctly (e.g., a fill-in sentence or giving the first sound in the word);
- scripts (sentences that can be memorized for specific real-life situations such as answering the phone); practicing that script in role playing and then in real situations.

The goals for therapy may target speech and oral motor skills, or encoding a language message and then producing it. One channel, such as reading, may be used to assist your child with another channel such as expressive language or written language.

Some schools (and SLPs within those schools) use a channel-based approach called "whole language" for all students, not just those receiving speech therapy. Using this approach, reading, understanding, writing, and expressive language are taught as a whole. Often, thematic activities are used in conjunction with specific books. For example, your child might read a book about weather, and also have experiences with weather reporting, building a weather station, drawing pictures or taking photographs of different weather conditions, etc. SLPs and teachers who use the whole language approach do not teach in discrete linguistic units, such as focusing on plurals or verb tenses. Rather, they teach in larger themes using meaningful multisensory experiences to teach concepts.

Teaching Language Skills through Reading

Many children with Down syndrome learn more easily through the visual channel—that is, through seeing rather than through hearing. The written word stays in a book or on the computer screen as long as the child needs to look at it, whereas speech is rapid and fleeting. In many children with Down syndrome, otitis media with effusion (OME), fluid build-up, and fluctuating hearing loss are problems that interfere with reliable hearing and with learning solely through hearing. Because of these factors, children with Down syndrome may be able to learn to read words before they can say the words, and may be able to learn and understand concepts more easily through reading than through hearing.

When children with Down syndrome learn to read at an early age, reading can become a door to learning language. Sue Buckley, a British psychologist who has extensively researched the educational and developmental needs of children with Down syndrome, believes that many children with Down syndrome can be taught to read between two and three years of age. In case studies, she has confirmed that children with Down syndrome can read as early as two years of age.

Sue Buckley suggests introducing reading when the child can match pictures, select pictures to demonstrate comprehension, and has a comprehension vocabulary of 50-100 words. Although not every child will succeed in reading at an early age, Buckley believes that all children will derive speech and language development benefits from working on reading (Buckley & Johnson-Glenberg, 2007). She believes that one of the reasons that children with Down syndrome have language delays is that their language learning is held back by difficulties in accessing language solely through the auditory channel (hearing), and that reading provides another channel for learning language.

WHAT DOES THE RESEARCH SAY?

Research has shown a positive link between reading and communications skills in children with Down syndrome. Studies have demonstrated that progress in reading has led to progress in spoken language and in short-term memory skills. Studies have confirmed that students with Down syndrome who have higher reading levels also have higher language levels. The studies, however, do not take into consideration that both reading tests and language tests tap into language ability, so we would expect that there would be a high positive correlation. Other studies have demonstrated that children with Down syndrome often have a higher reading level than would be predicted from their cognitive level. And those studies generally use nonverbal testing to determine cognitive level.

Generally speaking, when we look at the relationship between understanding of language (receptive language) and spoken language (expressive language) in children with Down syndrome, there is evidence that receptive language is more advanced. However, in studies of reading skills in children with Down syndrome, the opposite has been found. That is, word reading skills are generally more advanced than reading comprehension skills. Studies have shown that reading comprehension skills tend to be at least one year behind word reading skills.

Buckley and her colleagues at Down Syndrome Education International in Portsmouth, England (formerly The Down Syndrome Educational Trust) have studied reading in children with Down syndrome for many years. What have they learned about the relationship of reading to other factors? First, they have found a relationship between vocabulary comprehension and word reading. That is, being able to read helps children with Down syndrome acquire and understand new vocabulary and sentences. Second, they have found no significant relationship between phonological skills and early reading. In other words, children with Down syndrome do not need phonological skills in order to begin to learn to read. This is an important finding, because phonological skills such as letter recognition, rhyming, and sound blending have been thought to be pre-reading readiness skills for typically developing children. For many years, children with Down syndrome were not considered as candidates for reading programs because they had low scores on phonological skills readiness tests.

Although teachers and clinicians may need to use different approaches when teaching children with Down syndrome to read (see below), they certainly do not need to delay reading instruction until the children have mastered phonological pre-reading skills. In addition, there are programs available that can be used to work on phonological readiness skills. They include *Earobics,* software that is currently used by audiologists and SLPs to increase auditory and phonological awareness skills, and *FastForward,* an intensive, computer-based program for increasing auditory processing skills that is administered by professionals trained in using the system.

Another very important finding from Sue Buckley and her colleagues is that there is a positive relation between inclusion and the reading skills of children with Down syndrome. In studies of children in mainstream schools and special schools in the United Kingdom, they found that children who were fully included in mainstream classrooms had more advanced reading and language skills. They were more advanced in language comprehension, vocabulary comprehension, grammar comprehension, sentence memory, and auditory and visual digit span.

Finally, it is important to know that there is a wide range of reading skills in children with Down syndrome. In multiple studies of children from ages 7 to 14 years, Buckley and colleagues have found reading levels from 5 years 5 months to 10 years. Other researchers have also found this wide variability in reading level, but have found, in general, that many children are able to read at a lower elementary school level. By young adulthood, some individuals with Down syndrome are able to reach a 14- to16-year-old reading level (Buckley & Johnson-Glenberg, 2007).

WHAT READING PROGRAMS ARE HELPFUL FOR CHILDREN WITH DOWN SNDROME?

Many school systems use a phonics approach to reading. They begin with phonological awareness activities such as sound recognition, sound letter correspondence, rhyming, sound blending, and word segmentation. They then progress to helping children learn to "sound out" words in reading. As we have discussed above, phonological awareness activities such as rhyming and word segmentation are difficult tasks for most children with Down syndrome. Some may be able to learn to read using the phonics approach, but others need to use a logographic, whole word visual approach. That is, at first they need to learn to recognize words by sight, and perhaps later move on to being able to sound out words phonetically.

All children, when they are learning to read, rely on a logographic (whole word) strategy in which they memorize the whole word pattern and then recognize and remember that pattern when they read the word. Children with Down syndrome may rely on the logographic pattern for a longer time. Sue Buckley has noted that children with Down syndrome are able to use alphabetic and/or phonic spelling strategies once they can read and spell words on about the level of a typical seven-year-old. That is, they learn to understand phonics as they experience print and make progress in reading.

Some of the programs that are currently being used to teach children with Down syndrome to read are:

- *See and Learn;*
- Pat Oelwein's book *Teaching Reading to Children with Down Syndrome: A Guide for Parents and Teachers* (Woodbine House, 1995);
- *Love and Learning;*

- *EReadingPro Reading Kit*
- *The Learning Program (Down Syndrome Foundation of Orange County)*

SEE AND LEARN

The *See and Learn* program is based on the research of Sue Buckley and colleagues at the Down Syndrome Educational Trust in Portsmouth, England. It is a system for using reading to support the development of vocabulary and grammar. It is designed for very young children, aged 2 to 3, but may be appropriate for older children with language delays who are not yet reading. To start, the child is taught a 30 to 40 word sight vocabulary, with the words carefully chosen at a level matched with the child's comprehension skills. Once the child can read these words, the words are combined into meaningful sentences. Next, personalized books are created using these sentences, so that the child can read a book. For more information, see the website at: www. downsed.org/see-and-learn.

TEACHING READING TO CHILDREN WITH DOWN SYNDROME

This classic book by Patricia Oelwein is a step-by-step guide to using a language experience approach to teach reading skills to children with Down syndrome. Using this program, parents and professionals develop the materials for a child using photos and objects in his own environment. Pictures of family members, trips, activities, and games are all used to teach language and reading. The system is visually based, and begins with teaching sight words by having the child match, select, and then name (read) the word. Phonics is taught later through word bingo and other games and through a word family (rhyming words) approach. The book's appendices include basic sight vocabulary words and materials and illustrations for games. For further information, visit the Woodbine House website at www.woodbinehouse.com or call 800-843-7323.

LOVE AND LEARNING

Love and Learning is a multisensory system for teaching reading developed by Joe and Sue Kotlinski to teach their daughter, Maria, to read. There are six learning kits available that gradually progress from teaching the alphabet and the corresponding sounds to conversational skills. Each kit teaches the child between 50 and 150 sight words. Each learning kit has three parts. An audiotape lets the child hear the sounds and words spoken in a clear, slow manner. The tape is played at bedtime or playtime. A videotape repeats the same words. For example, the letter b is shown and pronounced, then the word *bus* appears and is pronounced, then we see a picture of a bus, followed by a real live example of Maria getting on the school bus. Books accompany the audio and video tapes and provide for reinforcement and reading practice for the new words. For further information, call 313-581-8436 or visit www.loveandlearning.com.

EReadingPro READING PROGRAM

The EReadingPro (newer version of Out of the Box) Reading Program is based on the whole-word approach, and is aimed at helping children begin to understand that a word represents a "thing." The program focuses on teaching written words in a clear, precise, and repetitive manner. The program's core vocabulary consists of 130 individual words (food, environment, belongings, etc.). Abstract words are presented on flashcards, and are shown separate from pictures in order to avoid visual distraction when the child is learning the written word. Flash cards, printed in red, are presented quickly, and are shown many times. Only five to six flashcards are presented during each ten-minute session. Kits are available that come with sentences and artwork that parents can use to make books, based on words in the core vocabulary. An EBook format makes it possible to download books. For more information, visit the website at www.ereadingpro.com.

THE LEARNING PROGRAM

The Learning Program was developed by the Down Syndrome Foundation of Orange County (California) to supplement traditional education in reading and math through direct instruction and materials for home teaching. The literacy portion of the program uses the whole word approach and is based on the work of Patricia Oelwein and Sue Buckley. The program stresses the need to follow the child's lead, make learning fun, and ensure success. Families who use the literacy program begin by working on sight word acquisition with their child, then gradually introduce alphabet and phonics activities. Most of the materials needed are available free on the DSFOC's website, and include sight-word readers and worksheets. For further information, visit the website at www.dsfoc.org/learning_program/index.html.

GENERAL STRATEGIES FOR HELPING YOUR CHILD READ

In language learning and in learning to read, there are ways to design learning that can make it easier for children with Down syndrome to master new skills.

- Learning should be pleasurable. Do not put pressure on your child to learn to speak or read at home or in therapy; provide opportunities, but allow him to move at his own pace.

- It is easier to learn a new skill if it is broken down into smaller steps. This way, the child can be successful in mastering each small step.

- Don't get stuck on mastering "prerequisite" skills. Many authorities believe that *phonemic awareness*—knowing the relationship between each sound and its letter and being able to sound out words—must be mastered before a child can read. But, some children may not master this skill, and yet still be able to learn to read through a visual or whole language approach. (See the discussion of Sue Buckley's research into this very issue, above.)

- There are many pathways to learning a new skill such as reading. Try to match your child's learning styles to the approach chosen.

- Follow your child's interests. Choose books that are interesting for him, as well as on the appropriate reading level.

- Choose reading materials that focus on experiences that will be familiar to your child. Research has shown that children have better reading skills when the subject and people or characters are familiar. If you can't find books at your child's level on topics that interest him, make your own. On many photo developing websites such as Kodak Gallery and Snapfish, you can now upload photos to personalized books and add your own text, ending up with a customized, illustrated book. You can also glue snapshots to paper and handwrite your own captions beneath. Personal journals and diaries work well, if your child can write, word process, or dictate the descriptions to you.

● Provide many opportunities for practicing a new skill. When your child knows the letters h and c, choose books that have many examples of those letters in them. For example, the book, *The 500 Hats of Bartholomew Cubbins,* would be a good choice. Reading the book can also lead to a discussion of how the letter c can sound like /s/ as in *city* or /k/ as in *cow.* Follow your child's timetable. Children with Down syndrome may need more practice, and may take longer to master a specific skill. Don't get discouraged. Try to provide a variety of materials and practice, so that your child doesn't get discouraged, and continues to move forward.

● Show pleasure in your child's new accomplishments.

● Provide experiences that will help your child generalize the skills learned. You don't want him to only be able to know the word *red* when it is a colored square on an index card or a red block. Provide multisensory experiences to help him master the concept of "redness" as it relates to a variety of experiences.

● Use technology to practice reading skills and increase your child's motivation to learn. For example, turn on the closed captions when your child is watching movies on TV, look into "talking books" on the computer, and, if your child likes music, get him a karaoke machine that shows the lyrics on the TV screen, or help him learn to select his own songs on his MP3 or iPod.

HELPING YOUR CHILD WITH PHONOLOGICAL SKILLS

Even though Sue Buckley and her colleagues have found that children with Down syndrome don't need to have phonological awareness skills before they learn to read, learning these skills will help your child make progress in other skills such as word recognition and decoding. When teachers talk about reading skills, they include the five areas of phonological awareness, phonics, vocabulary, reading fluency, and comprehension. According to Buckley, children with Down syndrome have difficulty with rhyming tasks and segmenting tasks (dividing words into syllables). Phonological instruction can help.

TEACHING ABOUT RHYTHM AND SYLLABLES

Rhyming skills are based on the sounds of the language, and are important skills that help children learn about the sounds of words and word parts. When children can rhyme words, we know that they can hear similarities in sound patterns. Some ideas for working on rhymes include:

- Read books with rhymed texts, such as *Sheep, Sheep, Sheep, Help Me Fall Asleep; Is Your Mama a Llama; In the Tall, Tall Grass; Sheep in a Jeep;* and *Pigs Aplenty, Pigs Galore.* Using rhyming books helps children learn that language is playful and fun. See the box below for some books that are good for working on rhyme.

- When you're reading a book with a strong rhyme, pause at the ends of sentences and see if your child can guess the rhyming word that comes next.

- Read some poems from a book together. Shel Silverstein's books have many delightful rhyming and nonrhyming poems. See if your child can tell you which ones rhyme and which ones don't.

- Play a rhyming variation of "I Spy" when you are waiting with your child in a doctor's office or restaurant. For instance, say, "I see something that rhymes with moon.... Need a hint? You use it to eat with" (spoon).

- Make up riddles for your child that use rhyme. For example: "I am thinking of something that is good for sleeping on. It rhymes with head."

- Sing or play a recording of the "Name Game." Help your child learn to sing his own name to the song: "Dan, Dan, Bo-van; Banana, fanana, Fo-fan; Me, my, mo-man, Dan...." If he cannot sing the song, introduce the practice by clapping to the words. You are familiarizing your child with the activity and also practicing rhythm and prosody.

- Make a "Go Fish" game with cards showing pictures of words that rhyme (dish/fish, boat/coat). Use pictures from magazines or take your own photos and glue them to index cards. Or just write the words if your child can read. Have players ask each other: "Do you have anything that rhymes with _____?" The person who collects the most rhyming pairs is the winner.

TEACHING ABOUT SYLLABLES

It is also important for children to become aware of the number of syllables in a word. One way to help your child develop this awareness is to purchase a drum or bells or make your own musical toy that can be pounded on. Say a two-syllable word, such as *pancake* or *birthday,* and pound out the syllables on the musical instrument. If your child can read, you can write the word down for him and underline the different syllables or draw a slash between them to help him see where one syllable ends.

When your child can pound out two-syllable words, increase the number of syllables and the number of words—for example, *pancake house, pancakes with syrup, railroad train, birthday cake, birthday party.* Using an instrument to pound out the syllables also helps children in producing longer words in speech.

Some books have verses that lend themselves to rhythm, clapping, and banging a drum. *Chicka Chicka Boom Boom* by Bill Martin (2000) and *Tanka Tanka Skunk* by Steve Webb (2003) are good examples of books that lend themselves to work on syllables and rhythm. *Tanka Tanka Skunk* explicitly points out how many "beats" (syllables) are in animal names such as *kangaroo* and *caterpillar.*

Books to Help with Rhythm, Rhyme, & Syllabification

Some children's books that focus on rhyming and other phonological awareness activities are:

Rhythm and Rhyme

Cox, P.R. & Cartwright, S. *Fat Cat on a Mat Board Book.*

Cox, P.R. & Cartwright, S. *Big Pig on a Dig.*

Cox, P.R. & Cartwright, S. *Ted In a Red Bed Board Book*

Degen, Bruce. *Jamberry.*

De Paolo, Tommie. *Andy, That's My Name.*

Eichenberg, Fritz. *Ape in a Cape: An Alphabet of Odd Animals.*

Emberley, Barbara. *Drummer Hoff.*

Fleming, Denise. *In the Tall, Tall Grass.*

Gregorich, B. *The Gum on the Drum.*

Gregorich, B. & Witty, B. *The Raccoon on the Moon.*

Hennessey, B. *Jake Baked a Cake.*

Ochs, C.P. *Moose on the Loose.*

Pomerantz, C. *The Piggy in the Puddle.*

Seuss, Dr. *The Cat in the Hat.*

Shaw, N. *Sheep on a Jeep.*

Shaw, N. Sheep out to Eat.

Sound Identification and Phonological Awareness

Edwards, P. *Four Famished Foxes and Fosdyke.*

Fox, Mem. *Night Noises.*

Hawkins, C. & Hawkins, J. *Jen the Hen.*

Hawkins, C. & Hawkins, J. *Mig the Pig.*

Hawkins, C. & Hawkins, J. *Pat the Cat.*

Hawkins, C. & Hawkins, J. *Tog the Dog.*

Most, B. *There's an Ant in Anthony.*

Otto, C. *Dinosaur Chase.*

Seuss, Dr. *There's a Wocket in My Pocket.*

Writing

Writing is another expressive language output system. Very little research has been done on the language component of writing in individuals with Down syndrome, although Sue Buckley has found that children with Down syndrome who were taught to read in the preschool years were the best writers.

In addressing the difficulties children with Down syndrome have in expressing themselves in writing, we need to separate out the motor component of writing and the language component. Children with Down syndrome often have difficulties with the fine motor skill of writing, whether or not they have difficulty formulating what they want to say in writing. Working memory difficulties can also contribute to difficulties with writing. When writing a story, the child needs to remember what he just wrote and plan what he wants to say next.

Using computer software to help write sentences, paragraphs, and stories has been demonstrated to be helpful for individuals with Down syndrome. Dr. Laura Myers has worked with children and adolescents with Down syndrome on writing sentences, personal journals, and stories. She has found that the ideas, as well as the vocabulary individuals were able to use when word processing their thoughts, were more advanced than the words that they used while speaking (for example, "I like to be

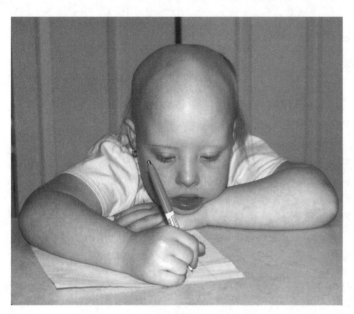

quiet. Then I can hear God talk to me."). Meyers, who developed the first simple talking word processor to use in her research on the written language skills of children with Down Syndrome, believes: "...the keys to effective computer use by children with language disabilities are to implement the computer both as an access tool and as a personal meaning tool; that is, to use the technology to provide access to speech and text, link it to their personal meaning systems, and thereby allow them to participate in the natural processes of language learning" (Meyers, 1994).

Computer assisted instruction can help children learn to write through word processing or speaking. Programs are interactive, hold the child's interest, and provide instant feedback. Computer programs that can be used for writing (many times in combinations) include word prediction software, spell checker, thesaurus, speech-to-text, and text-to-speech. Software is available that can help children learn to write sentences and stories. Some software programs that can be helpful in teaching children written language include *Simple Sentence Structure* (Laureate Software); *Co-Writer* (Don Johnston, Inc.); *Write Outloud!* (Don Johnston); *Dr. Peet's TalkWriter* (Hartley Courseware); *Kidworks II* (Davidson); *Storybook Maker* (Hartley); and *WiggleWorks* (Scholastic).

At home, you can help your child improve his expressive language writing skills by encouraging him to keep a journal or diary. The constancy and regularity of the activity is important.

A journal can be kept in a diary, or a notebook. If your child enjoys thinking about his daily experiences, but does not enjoy the physical process of writing, help him start a journal on the computer. He could also dictate his words to you. Your child might want to combine his writing with photographs in a photo album or make his own photo book using an online photo developing site.

It may help to encourage your child to focus on one experience each day. Which one? The best one? The experience that was the most fun? An experience that involved school or recreation in the community? Only give your child as much assistance as he wants, since the idea is for him to express his own thoughts in writing.

Conclusion

Language is complex. As long as this chapter is, it did not begin to cover all the areas of language that children with Down syndrome may need help with, at home, at school, and in the community. This chapter focused on language therapy, what would occur in treatment, and activities you can do at home to support and reinforce what is happening in therapy sessions. The focus was on semantics and morphosyntax and on both receptive and expressive language. Chapter 7 focuses on language and speech issues in school. Chapter 8 focuses on language and speech issues at home and provides more activities for practicing communication skills at home. Chapters 9 and 10 address pragmatics skills and conversation skills.

In the school years, from ages 6 to 14, therapy and home practice can focus on a very wide variety of language areas. For an outline of comprehensive language treatment areas and for a treatment planning guide, see the Comprehensive Language and Speech Treatment plan in the Appendix.

CHAPTER 6

Speech Treatment

Since we have now established that there is no such thing as "Down syndrome speech," it should be clear that speech treatment for your child needs to be individualized to her needs. As with language treatment, the most important first step in planning speech treatment is to obtain a comprehensive evaluation of your child. Treatment would then target the specific factors that are affecting your child's speech intelligibility. For example, if your child had difficulty with the /r/ sound, articulation

therapy would focus on the /r/ sound. If your child deleted final consonants sounds, therapy would address that problem. If low muscle tone was a factor, therapy would focus on strengthening the muscle tone in your child's face, lips, and cheeks. If your child did not look at the speaker's face, therapy would focus on eye contact.

There is no specific speech treatment plan recommended for all children with Down syndrome. Rather, your child's treatment plan should include objectives to address each factor that affects her intelligibility, and benchmarks to measure the improvement for each factor.

Speech Therapy at School

As explained in Chapter 3, whether your child will receive speech treatment at school, and if so, how much, depends on eligibility criteria, not on need. Your school system has specific criteria that it uses to decide whether a child can receive speech services. Usually, the child's scores on specific speech tests (chosen by the school system) need to meet the eligibility criteria. The criterion score may be 6 months or 2 years below chronological age level or mental age level. Sometimes, eligibility is based on average scores so a standard such as 2 standard deviations below the average score according to test norms might be used. Remember that none of the test norms were developed based on children with Down syndrome.

For articulation, scoring is often based on developmental norms. So, if your child only has difficulty with sounds that are not usually mastered until age 8, and your child is 6, she would not receive services. Sometimes the norms are compared to mental age scores. For example, your 10-year-old child might have a mental age score of 6. If the sound she has trouble with is not mastered by typically developing children until age 8, she would be denied services.

If your school system uses these kinds of eligibility criteria, you should be aware that they were developed before the most recent regulations to IDEA were passed. According to IDEA 2004, special education and related services are provided to help with problems that "impact progress in the regular educational curriculum." Therefore, school systems should not be using rigid cutoff scores to determine which children qualify for speech therapy. The deciding factor should be whether your child's speech difficulties are preventing her from progressing in the regular curriculum.

In practice, it can be difficult to prove to schools that speech intelligibility difficulties affect classroom progress. See the box below, however, for examples of types of arguments that might convince your IEP team that your child needs speech service. For an individual child, speech difficulties may be affecting progress in reading, accuracy of test scores, and behavior in the classroom. When parents provide information about speech difficulties, they are often told that "this is Down syndrome speech. And there isn't much we can do about it." That is not true, but it is typically the message that is sent to families in the schools. Schools are usually more accepting of proof that language difficulties affect progress in the regular educational classroom.

In practice, if your child is receiving language therapy at school, but has not been approved for speech therapy, the SLP may work on at least some speech difficulties with your child. For instance, Megan may be seeing the school SLP to work on her difficulties with language (perhaps using the /s/ for possessives). If the SLP notices that Megan is having a hard time saying /s/ correctly, he or she would likely work with Megan on articulation even if she is not technically supposed to work on speech with Megan.

If your child does receive speech therapy through the school, you may still have problems getting the services provided in the way you think is appropriate (see the box on service delivery models on page 65 in Chapter 3). The service delivery models usually depend on the practices of your school system. Although all IEP decisions are supposed to be individualized, parents often hear that "children with Down syndrome are seen in groups." Or, even that "We don't have children with Down syndrome and normal children in the same group" even when the articulation difficulty (e.g., /s/ production) is the same. Neither one of these statements are legal, but the situations frequently occur. Another problem is that there is a shortage of school SLPs across the country. Consequently, you may have a difficult time getting truly individualized therapy from your school if there are not enough therapists to meet the demand.

To add insult to injury, many parents have trouble getting their private health insurance to cover speech therapy because insurance companies don't want to pay for developmental services. Policies may pay to *rehabilitate* speech but not to be proactive, and teach it to begin with. My opinion is that all children with Down syndrome need and benefit from help with articulation and speech sound production. It is difficult to understand why insurance companies and schools do not question the need for physical therapy to help a child who has low muscle tone learn to walk, but they routinely question and deny services to the same child when the low muscle tone is in the muscles of the face and mouth and is affecting the ability to speak. The child needs help to learn to articulate, just as she needs help to learn to walk.

Examples of Ways Speech Difficulties Affect Progress in the Curriculum

- Perhaps your child is still learning to read and one of the major ways the teacher assesses reading progress is to have her students read aloud. If the teacher can't understand your child's speech, she can't help your child progress in reading.

- Perhaps your child's writing skills are lagging. Consequently, she has the accommodation of answering questions on tests or worksheets orally while an aide or teacher writes them down. Again, if the aide can't understand her speech, how is she going to accurately transcribe your child's speech so the teacher can determine what she is learning?

- Perhaps your child's behavior is impeding her ability to progress in the general education curriculum. She gets angry, frustrated, or confused at times and the teacher can't understand her when she tries to explain what the problem is. When this happens, she has a meltdown and ends up learning nothing for an hour.

GETTING INVOLVED IN YOUR CHILD'S THERAPY PROGRAM

Given that your child may not be receiving speech services in the ideal setting or as often as you would like, how can you maximize the benefits she gets from her therapy? In my mind, the most important part of therapy for speech sound production difficulties is that the family is provided with home-school communication and a home practice program. Speech difficulties often involve daily practice, and this won't happen in school therapy. But if the school SLP and the family works together, articulation difficulties can be worked on, practiced, and improved.

In a private therapy setting, you usually have a couple of minutes at the end of the session to talk with the SLP. In schools, speech-language pathologists have large caseloads and are often not provided with any time during the day to communicate with families. So, it is helpful to develop a home-school communication and a home practice sheet, to make it easy for communication to occur.

Communication needs to be two-way. The SLP needs to keep you up-to-date regarding what your child is working on in therapy, how she is progressing, and what you can do to help. It is just as important for the SLP to get feedback from you so that she knows whether your child is generalizing the skills she has learned in therapy to her home and community. She needs to know whether your child has practiced the sounds or exercises and how she has progressed. The SLP needs to know where your child has had success, and where she has encountered difficulties.

Below is an example of a home-school communication sheet for articulation. (See the Appendix for a blank form.) The same form can be used for work on Phonology and Oral motor skills. The example shows effective communication between the SLP and parents. There is specific information on what is being worked on in therapy and specific home activities for follow-up. There is space for the parents' comments about how their child is doing at home, in practice, and in daily life, so there can be two-way communication between the SLP and home.

The form on the next page was developed for home-school communication. The purpose of "therapy targets this week" is for the SLP to provide information for your family about what is being worked on in therapy sessions. The purpose of "progress and difficulties" is for the SLP to let your family know what successes your child has had in therapy sessions or the classroom, what sounds you can correct at home, and what are being worked on in therapy, but are not yet ready to be worked on at home. You can also provide feedback to the SLP on how your child is doing at home in daily life in these specific areas. In addition, you can let the SLP know about family events, visits and trips, celebrations, and illnesses that are currently important in your child's life. This information can serve as the basis for materials chosen in treatment. For example, if Uncle Joe is coming to visit, and your child is working on the /j/ sound, *Joe* can be on his word list. If he then learns to say Joe correctly, think of all of the positive reinforcement he will get during this visit.

The bottom section of the form is for a home practice program. Let's say your child is working on the /s/ sound in therapy, and that she cannot say the sound correctly. In therapy sessions, she is working on keeping her tongue behind her teeth. The SLP may suggest for home practice that you time how long your child can keep her tongue behind her teeth at rest with her lips closed and then with her lips rounded and slightly protruded. Or, if your child is working on the /s/ sound, and needs help in learning to listen to /s/ sounds but is not yet ready to say the /s/ sound, the SLP may suggest that you read books about sunflowers, snakes, or the Sahara desert to provide practice in hearing the /s/ sound. In the "progress and difficulties section," you would provide feedback on how the listening practice had gone. Or the SLP might send a practice sheet home when your child can say the /s/ and ask you to practice the words. Then, you would send back a filled-in sheet documenting your child's practice.

Unfortunately, all too often communication between the school SLP and parents is nonexistent or ineffective. On page 158 is a real-life example of poor home-school communication. The goals are vague. The SLP mentions general areas such as fluency, but not what she is specifically working on in treatment. There are no home activities that can be worked on. The report was not even proofread—it says increase sounds in error. If your child brings home reports of this nature, see if you can persuade the SLP to use the Home-School form in the Appendix instead.

Home-School Speech Report
(Example of Effective Communication)

Child's name: Brian P.   Date: 5/30/08

We are working on: *(check those that apply)*

- ☑ Articulation
- ☑ Phonology
- ☐ Oral motor skills
- ☑ Other (specify): fluency

Therapy Targets This Week:

Brian is working on the /sh/ and /ch/ sounds. He had been leaving the sounds off at the end of words, so this week's goal has been to include the final /sh/ and /ch/ in words.

Progress and Difficulties:

Brian is able to correctly make both sounds when he focuses on it. Sometimes we use the mirror so he can see how the sounds are made.

Home Practice Activities:

Ask Brian to be in charge of telling you what to wash and watch. All day, whenever he sees something that needs washing, he can announce that to you—for example, Wash the dishes, wash the dog, wash my shirt, wash my shorts, etc. Same thing with the word watch—watch out, watch the baby, watch TV, watch the leaves blow, etc.

Progress and Difficulties at Home:

Speech and Language Therapy Note
(Example of Ineffective Communication)

Child's name: Alex   Date: 5/14/08

Current Concerns of Family:
Misarticulated sounds; dysfluencies

Goals:
Increase fluent speech
Increase sounds in error

Progress:
1. good practicing "slow easy speech" and pausing at punctuation
2. good attempt at correct pronunciation

Homework:
Practice fluency booklet

Suggestions Discussed with the Family:
Give wait time
Model sounds

What Your Child Will Work on in Speech Therapy

In speech therapy, the SLP will target the areas that affect how understandable your child's speech is. The areas that affect the way that your child makes sounds are:

- oral motor skills,
- articulation,
- phonology, and
- Childhood Apraxia of Speech (CAS).

Other speech symptoms that the listener might hear (speech symptoms that affect speech intelligibility) are difficulties with:

- voice,
- resonance,
- prosody,
- rate,
- fluency, and
- loudness.

In school therapy, articulation, phonology, and fluency are the areas that are most likely to be targeted. SLPs in private practice might address any or all of these areas. In addition, factors such as eye contact, complexity of what your child is saying, and the length of what she is saying may contribute to how well she is understood.

Therapy to Strengthen Oral Motor Skills

Articulation treatment that includes strengthening oral motor skills is an effective treatment approach for children with Down syndrome. Some researchers suggest starting treatment to address low muscle tone and sensitivity issues in the mouth and face area within the first year of life. By the time they are six, many children with Down

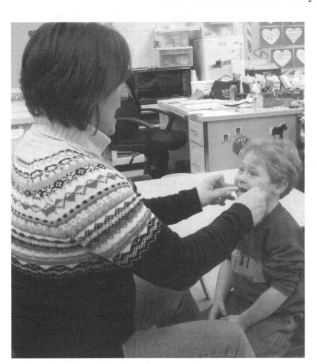

syndrome have strengthened their muscles but often still have difficulty coordinating the individual movements into words, phrases, and sentences. Continued low muscle tone can lead to speech sounds that are basically correct but sound slushy or imprecise. By later elementary school, many children with Down syndrome have improved their oral motor skills.

There has been very little research that documents the success of specific treatment methods for oral motor difficulties. School guidelines often state that they will treat speech and language difficulties using "evidence-based practice." Since there *is* no body of research on proven techniques, some schools no longer treat oral motor difficulties. However, in my clinical experience, working on oral motor skills does strengthen oral facial muscles and does improve speech. If your child is not eligible for oral motor therapy through the school system, you may need to seek services through private practice, university, hospital-based, or community-based clinics.

Oral motor treatment may involve working on:

- nonspeech movements of the mouth and face (such as smiling);
- movements with vocalization (saying /a/, /ba/, /la/);
- movements with speech (mouth movements involving real words such as *bee* or *me*);
- speech exercises (for example, saying your name five times);
- jaw stabilization work including bite blocks and exercises, to enable the child to make fine smooth movements (graded movements) and to move the jaw independently (dissociation);
- whistles, horns, straws, and blowing exercises;
- feeding therapy, if needed, to help the child chew, swallow, and clear her mouth of food; and
- myofunctional therapy (also known as orofacial mycology), as needed. This type of therapy is an oral facial muscle retraining program that requires a lot of home practice. It can help the child swallow food correctly and learn not to protrude the tongue when eating or speaking. It is usually provided in combination with orthodontic care and braces. Orthodontics helps change form and myofunctional treatment helps change muscle movement and function.

There is anecdotal evidence (but no definitive research yet) that mastering nonspeech movements also helps a child with speech movements. It makes sense that if a child learns how to round her lips, she will be able to round her lips to make the /w/ sound. Sara Rosenfeld-Johnson, CCC-SLP (1999), has developed sets of horns and straws arranged in a hierarchy of difficulty to strengthen the muscles in and around the mouth. Using her program, oral motor treatment involves using straws, horns, whistles, and musical instruments to help the child develop and practice oral motor skills.

When nonspeech sound practice is used with children with Down syndrome, it is best to work on movements that are clearly needed for making speech sounds, such as rounding the lips for /w/ and /u/. As soon as your child can approximate speech sounds, nonspeech tasks should be phased out as a therapy goal because the goal is speech. The movements should then be practiced through sounds and words. Nonspeech tasks may still be used as a warm-up activity at the beginning of a treatment session to heighten awareness of the tongue, lips, etc.

Professional materials that may be used in treating oral motor skills include: *Oral Motor Exercises for Speech Clarity* (Sarah Rosenfeld-Johnson, Innovative Therapists International); *Oral Motor Activities for Young Children* (Elizabeth Mackie, Lingui-Systems); *Can Do Card Decks* and *Oral Motor Game Cards* (Super Duper); *Oralympics* (Super Duper); and Sarah Rosenfeld-Johnson's *Talk Tools*.

Therapy for Articulation

FROM TESTING TO TREATMENT

Chapter 4 explored the major types of articulation problems that children with Down syndrome may have, together with the underlying causes for these problems. In my experience, most children with Down syndrome in the six- to fourteen-year age range have at least some articulation difficulties, and these difficulties can be targeted in therapy. This is borne out by researchers, who have found that over 90 percent of people with Down syndrome have articulation errors.

The results of your child's articulation testing may be reported to you in several different ways:

1. The SLP may indicate which specific sounds in which positions in words are in error. For example: your child is having difficulty with the /s/ sound in the initial and final positions, the /r/ sound in initial, medial, and final positions, and the /l/ sound in the initial position.
2. The SLP may specify the sound groupings that are difficult for your child. For example: your child is having difficulty with plosive and affricate sounds. Or, your child is having difficulty with voiced sounds. (See page 91 in Chapter 4 for explanations of sound groupings.)
3. The SLP may identify the speech structures or movements that are affecting your child's articulation. For example: your child has difficulty with tongue and palatal movement.

A comprehensive diagnostic evaluation is always needed so that the SLP can choose appropriate treatment options based on your child's specific speech symptoms. For children who are not yet speaking by age six, speech difficulties such as childhood apraxia of speech (CAS) and severe oral motor difficulties should be considered, as well as cognitive and language reasons that the child is not yet speaking. If the difficulties are found to be based on CAS or oral motor problems, speech therapy should begin immediately. If the difficulty is based on cognitive and/or language problems, therapy will need to focus on those difficulties rather than specifically on speech output. In either case, a child who is not yet speaking by age six should be evaluated for an augmentative/alternative communication system (AAC) or should be using sign language. The child needs to have an effective communication system at every age. For more information on AAC, see Chapter 10.

HOW THE SLP WORKS ON ARTICULATION

There are many different therapy approaches to articulation difficulties. For children with Down syndrome, the SLP will ideally evaluate what factors and combinations of factors are contributing to the articulation difficulty. That is, rather than simply trying to get your child to produce better /s/ sounds, the SLP needs to work on the problems underlying her difficulties with /s/ sounds. Does your child have low tone or weak muscles? Then therapy must work on strengthening the oral facial muscles. Does she have difficulty moving the tongue muscles separately from the lips and jaw? Then therapy must work on dissociating (separating) tongue movements from other articulation movements. Does she have motor planning difficulties that are affecting speech? Then a treatment program for Childhood Apraxia of Speech must be used to help her learn to produce sequences of speech sounds.

The goals for treatment and the benchmarks to measure progress must be individually designed to target the specific problems affecting articulation for each individual child. Here are some examples:

- For a child who has difficulties with making the /s/ sound, an appropriate goal might be: Brian will produce the /s/ sound correctly in the initial, medial, and final positions in single words 90% of the time by June 1.

- For a child who has difficulties with raising the tongue tip and therefore cannot correctly produce the /t/, /d/, /n/, or /l/ sounds, an appropriate goal might be: Alexis will be able to elevate the tongue tip and touch the alveolar ridge 90% of the time during practice sessions by the end of the marking period.
- For a child who has motor planning difficulties and is leaving out unstressed syllables (e.g., saying *hanger* for *hamburger*) an appropriate goal might be: Quinn will be able to correctly pronounce three-syllable words with 80% accuracy when reading words.

See the Resources list for articulation, oral motor strengthening, and motor planning materials that are used in the treatment program at the Loyola University Center for Speech and Language in Children with Down Syndrome.

Since articulation focuses on the structures and muscles used to produce the speech sounds, articulation therapy focuses on helping your child learn to control, move, and use the articulators to produce the phonemes. There are several different approaches that are used:

1. the traditional therapy approach (sound by sound);
2. therapy that targets the place, manner, and voicing of the error sounds (distinctive feature approach);
3. therapy that strengthens oral motor skills without directly working on speech sounds (oral motor approach).

Oral motor work has been discussed in the section above. There are also many treatment approaches to working with children who have Childhood Apraxia of Speech. If your child has CAS, some of these approaches may be used in combination with the approaches used for articulation problems in general. That will be discussed later in the chapter.

THE TRADITIONAL APPROACH

If your child's SLP uses the traditional therapy approach, he or she will target one or more specific phonemes; for example, /s/. The SLP will choose which phonemes to work on with your child based on the results of the oral motor examination, articulation testing, and stimulability testing. For example, perhaps your child had trouble using the /l/, /r/, /s/, /z/ sounds during the speech evaluation but the SLP could get her to make the /l/, /s/, /z/ sounds in isolation (not as parts of words). Because your child was physically capable of making the three sounds, the SLP will probably choose those sounds instead of /r/ to work on. In addition /r/ is a later sound developmentally and has very difficult placement. The SLP will also consider your child's name and other factors that will affect the relative frequency of occurrence of sounds. For example, if your child's name is Sarah Solan, she will be saying the /s/ sound frequently.

Within any language, certain sounds are used more frequently than others. In English, the /n/ and /t/ sounds have a high frequency of occurrence, while the /v/ and /ch/ sounds have a low frequency of occurrence. (Think of the sounds people choose first on *Wheel of Fortune*.) So, even though the /s/ sound is more difficult to make than /l/, the SLP will probably choose to work on /s/ first. Some SLPs base their decision more on developmental norms and would choose /l/ first, but I don't agree with that choice, especially since the child could make the /s/ sound in isolation. Be aware that it *is* a choice and a judgment call.

Therapy will first provide your child with auditory stimulation and sound discrimination training for the chosen sounds. This will be done by having your child listen to the sound in isolation and in words in the initial, medial, and final position. Often the SLP will do this by reading children's books, and asking your child to raise her hand or hold up a sign when she hears the sound. In other words, sound discrimination involves learning to hear the difference between the therapy sound and other sounds that are similar. Then, your child will be taught to produce the sound. This may involve looking at photos or diagrams and practice looking in the mirror. Over time, your child will practice the sound in isolation, syllables, and in a variety of positions in words, phrases, sentences, and conversation.

The traditional method is too slow moving for children who have multiple articulation problems, as many children with Down syndrome do. Usually, the SLP does not move on to the next level until your child is able to produce the sound correctly 80 or 90 percent of the time. For children with CAS who have inconsistent sound production, they may never be able to say the sound 10 times and get 8 or 9 out of 10 tries correct. So, the traditional therapy approach is not an appropriate approach for children who have CAS.

DISTINCTIVE FEATURE THERAPY APPROACH

Another method focuses on patterns in your child's articulation problems that are related to anatomical and physiological differences. The SLP analyzes which speech sounds your child has trouble with, according to:

- place (where in the mouth the lips, tongue, or other structures come together to produce the sound);
- manner (the way in which the air stream is modified as the sound is being produced);
- voicing (whether or not the vocal cords vibrate in producing the sound).

See Table 4-4 in on page 91.

Therapy then focuses not on a sound but on a common pattern of errors. For example, your child might have trouble with all sounds that involve placing her tongue on the alveolar ridge (the gum ridge behind the central upper teeth). The SLP would teach her to lift her tongue and place it behind the teeth on the alveolar ridge. The theory is that learning the correct placement and movement would generalize to all sounds that are made in that place. So, if your child worked on tongue elevation for the /t/ sound, her tongue elevation should also improve on the /d/ and /n/ sounds, without needing to work on those sounds directly. Therapy might also focus on manner of articulation. So, the SLP might teach her how to valve (hold in) and then puff a bit of air for stop sounds. Again, the expectation is that when your child learns to hold and explode the air for one sound such as /t/, it will carry over to all other stop sounds.

This is a better approach for children with Down syndrome because it focuses on the placement of the articulators and the movements needed to make multiple sounds. Sound errors in children with Down syndrome are affected by anatomical differences and oral motor skills and a distinctive feature approach targets areas of difficulty that affect your child's difficulties across more than one sound. Typically, the distinctive features approach enables them to make quicker progress in their articulation than the traditional therapy approach does. This is because the distinctive features approach addresses movements that contribute to making multiple sounds. So, when your child learns to make the movements correctly, she can generalize them more easily to other speech sounds.

Teaching through Sight vs. Hearing

Traditional articulation therapy begins with helping the child to hear and discriminate the target sound, as described above. Research has shown, however, that children with Down syndrome often have a short-term memory deficit for verbal information. That is, they have trouble remembering what they have just heard. So, for children with Down syndrome, this phase of a traditional articulation approach may not be effective. Indeed, they may get stuck in this phase and not move forward to the next phase of treatment.

Since many children with Down syndrome learn better through seeing than hearing, it makes sense to include reading and visual stimulation, and not to rely solely on auditory stimulation, during articulation assessment and treatment. For example, the SLP can use books and worksheets to help your child work on identifying a specific sound such as /p/. The SLP would need to pair seeing the letter with hearing the sound. This strategy can make it easier for children with Down syndrome to identify and learn the sounds.

WHAT ABOUT MEDICAL TREATMENTS FOR ARTICULATION PROBLEMS?

No surgical approaches, to date, have been shown to improve articulation for children with Down syndrome. In particular, partial glossectomy, a surgical intervention in which the tongue is reduced in size, has not been shown to improve articulation in children with Down syndrome. In one study, pre- and post-operative articulation tests and a six-month follow-up test showed no difference between children who had tongue reduction surgery and a control group who did not have the surgery. Although tongue reduction surgery affects tongue size (anatomy), it does not change articulation performance (function).

In some cases, orthodontics can be helpful with articulation difficulties. For example, if your child has a tongue thrusting pattern, she will usually be treated by an orthodontist and speech-language pathologist working together. The orthodontist can use braces to improve the tooth alignment (occlusion), but this will only change the shape of the interior of the mouth (the anatomy or form). At the same time, the speech-language pathologist can use exercises to correct any imbalance between the strength of the muscles of the lips, tongue, and jaw, thus changing the function (the physiology or function) as well.

Braces or strengthening exercises alone are usually not enough. If only braces are used, the tongue will again begin to exert outward pressure against the teeth as soon as the braces are removed. If only exercises are used, the mouth size and shape may still lead to tongue thrusting. Both the anatomical and physiological factors need to be changed. Braces are not usually prescribed until the child is at least seven or eight years old. Palatal expanders can be designed for the child with a high narrow palate to help widen the palatal vault. (See the information on palate expanders in the section on Resonance, below.)

An innovative approach that combines technology with treatment is the use of electropalatography—a biofeedback system that provides visual feedback regarding where the sounds are being made. In a case study of a nearly eleven-year-old girl who used velar fronting (producing sounds in the front of her mouth rather than the back), therapy targeted teaching her how to make back sounds. Before treatment, the child always tried to produce the /k/ sound by placing her tongue behind her teeth as if to make the /t/ sound. At the end of a fourteen-week treatment program using electropalatography, she was placing her tongue correctly for the /k/ sound 87 percent of the time (Gibbon, McNeill, Wood & Watson, 2003). This method is currently being used more in England than the United States, but it is a visual and tactile learning method that has potential for treatment.

HOW PARENTS CAN WORK ON ARTICULATION

How do you know what to work on at home? How do you know when to correct your child's pronunciation? The best way to know what to do is to work in partnership with the SLP through a home practice program. This means you and the SLP need to communicate frequently with a home-school report such as the one included earlier in the chapter. That way, you know, from week to week, what activities you can do at home to help your child progress.

If you are not getting feedback from the SLP, here are some general suggestions:

- Use a mirror and games to heighten your child's visual and tactile awareness of the articulators and articulation movements. For example, play *Simon Says* using a mirror and moving the lips and tongue into funny faces.
- Read books with and to your child to help her learn to tune into individual sounds. For instance, use books that have repeating phrases that include the sound your child is working on in therapy sessions. If your child is working on /m/, use a book such as *Five Little Monkeys Jumping on the Bed.* Every time that the phrase comes up, your child is getting practice making the sound.
- Practice speech movements, using a lip or tongue Olympics game (see Double Dare game below).
- Practice sound production through songs and games.
- When your child correctly says a sound that she is working on in therapy, comment on it: "You made a terrific /s/ sound that time."

Using a Speech Calendar. One way to ensure that you work on these areas at home is to use a speech calendar. For each month, copy, draw, or create on the computer a monthly calendar. You can use a purchased calendar that matches your child's interests, such as a railroading calendar, or a calendar with dogs, or you can use a date book planner for older children. For each day, list an activity that would be timely and appropriate for your child to practice.

If you are working with a speech-language pathologist, coming up with activities to list on the calendar is a wonderful collaborative project for parents and professionals. For an older child, activities might involve practicing a speech sound by ordering

"French fries" in a restaurant today or finding three things on the menu that begin with the letter "f," or asking a question to find out what kinds of soda the restaurant serves. For a young adult, the speech activity might be to start a conversation or to make a phone call on a particular day. (You can include language activities on your calendar, in addition to speech activities.)

The activities you note on the calendar can build on each other. One autumn day, you can go leaf picking and the next day, trace the leaves and describe them. You will be practicing the /l/ sound as you describe the leaves and do the craft activity. You can take photos as you find the leaves, and use the photos as another day's activity to call Grandma and tell her about the trip or to write a personalized book about the trip. For an adolescent or young adult, one day's activity might be choosing a recipe that has the target sound—for example, tacos. The next day, the activity might be making a written or pictorial list of the ingredients. Then, buy the ingredients and try the recipe. Finally, eat and enjoy the food that you made. Once your child can say a sound correctly, she can interview family and friends. For example, if your child can now say the /f/ sound, she can ask friends and family, "What's your favorite food? What's your favorite color? What's your favorite ice cream flavor?"

For younger children, use a star or sticker to show that the daily activity was successfully completed. For older children, use a check. You can use the monthly calendar to document which activities were practiced and mastered. Choose activities that are short and practical, relate to what your child is working on in therapy, and can be practiced as part of daily life.

HOME ACTIVITIES FOR FOCUSING ON THE ARTICULATORS

When we work in therapy on articulation, we often focus on lip movements. These home activities help your child become more aware of lip sensation and movement. Be sure to use only the activities that are safe for your child. For example, do not blow bubbles with bubble gum if your child will swallow the gum.

- Gently stroke your child's lips with an ice cube, then show her how to smack her lips together.
- Suck hard on a Popsicle. Feel the ice on your lips. Look in the mirror and see the color on your lips.
- Put lip balm on your lips. Smack the lips together and feel how they almost stick together.
- Hold the lips tightly together and move them as a unit from side to side. This may also be done after rubbing with ice or using lip balm.
- Put lipstick on your lips. Then blot with a tissue held between the lips.
- Put lipstick on your lips. Make kissing marks on a piece of paper.
- Tighten your lips around food such as carrots or pretzels. Suck to a count of five, then release. Or see how long you can hold the carrot or pretzel stick in your mouth.
- Blow on whistles that have different-sized mouthpieces.
- Play a harmonica, a recorder, or a kazoo.

- Blow across the top of an empty or half full bottle of soda and make a musical note. Collect a number of empty bottles and fill them with different amounts of water so your child can experiment with making sounds of different pitches.
- If you have a real musical instrument around your house, such as a trumpet, flute, or saxophone, teach your child how to make a sound on it.
- Make popping sounds with your lips.
- Blow bubbles through a bubble wand.
- Play a game of air soccer, and blow a balloon or ping pong ball across a table and over the edge to make a goal.
- Make kissing movements and sounds. Pretend to blow them through the air.
- Blow bubbles using bubble gum.
- Smack your lips at each other, making kissing sounds. Start five feet apart. Move closer and closer until you are kissing each other. Then move farther and farther away until you can no longer hear the lip-smacking sound.
- Make gulping sounds. Pretend that you are gulping down a whole can of soda.
- Hold your lips open. Pull them together quickly. They will make a sound. Then open them quickly. They will make a pop. It will almost sound like "oom-pah."
- Look in the mirror; hold a family competition to come up with the scariest or the funniest faces.
- In *Simon Says* games, use direction such as: "Simon Says throw a kiss, or smack your lips, or stick out your tongue, or blow up your cheeks, or click your tongue on the roof of your mouth, or put your tongue in your cheeks (look in the mirror at the imprint it makes), or move your tongue from side to side on the outer corners of the mouth, or move your tongue from side to side inside the cheeks."

Double Dare. Play a team game such as "Double Dare" involving activities and physical challenges. Make the activities lip and tongue movements. Here are some examples to get you started:

- Put peanut butter on the top lip only. The contestant must lick it off in a specified time.
- Put a marshmallow on a long string. Your child has to get the marshmallow into her mouth using only her tongue, teeth, and lips. (Only use this activity if there is no danger that your child will swallow the string.)
- Take a bit of flavoring or syrup, put it in the middle of the alveolar ridge (upper gum ridge behind center teeth) touch your tongue and release on that spot 10 times in a row.
- Play tongue basketball. Place a Cheerio or Life Saver on the alveolar ridge. When you hold it in place with the tongue, that's a basket. Try to make 10 baskets in a row.

- Time how long you can hold a Cheerio on the alveolar ridge.
- Hold a clean Popsicle stick or craft stick firmly between your lips. Balance a Cheerio or raisin on the end and see if you can walk across the room without dropping it. This takes muscle control and coordination.

HOME ACTIVITIES FOR HEIGHTENING AWARENESS OF DIFFERENT SOUNDS

CHOOSE A SOUND OF THE WEEK

One way to develop sound awareness is to focus on a specific sound each week, providing practice for hearing the sound as it occurs in daily life.

For example, you can focus on the /p/ sound. Rent a pirates or penguins DVD and listen for the /p/ sound. Watch a sports event on TV featuring a team such as the Pittsburgh Pirates that has the /p/ sound in its name. Older children can look at maps and find cities that start with /p/. Plan your shopping trip to include lunch at a pizza place. Stop at the pet shop to look at the parrots. Play "I Spy" and point out all of the things you see around you that start or end with the /p/ sound. Have a snack of popcorn or pudding or peanut butter on crackers. Be sure to say the sounds because you want your child to get used to hearing the sound.

USE BOOKS TO TEACH SOUND AWARENESS

Identifying sounds is part of the area of phonological awareness which is considered a pre-reading skill. There are many workbooks and activity books that have worksheets for sounds. Just be sure that you say the sounds so that your child has many opportunities to hear the sound. You can choose books in the library that have many instances of the target sound. The first few times that you read the story, your child will be listening to see what happens. Once your child is familiar with the story, then begin to focus on the sound. To heighten awareness, when you read the stories, make the /p/ sound louder. Later, clap or hold up a card that has the letter on it every time you read a /p/ sound. When your child is able to hear and identify the sound, have her clap or hold up a card each time that she hears a /p/ sound. It is easiest to hear the initial sound in the word, so the /p/ in Harry Potter will be easier to identify than the /p/ sounds in Captain Underpants.

Reading books that have many examples of a specific sound helps your child learn to identify the sound and discriminate the sound from other sounds. Later, when your child can make the sound, reading books aloud can provide opportunities for her to practice the sound production. For children who are beyond the picture book or early reader stage, it is a little more difficult to choose books that include words that include a given sound, since chapter books usually include a wider selection of words. Here are some suggestions for finding books for older children and teens to help with sound awareness:

1. Look for "novelizations" of TV series or movies that your child enjoys that include characters whose names have the target sound. For example, books based on the *Pokemon* series include a great variety of creature names (Pikachu, Bulbasaur, Meowth, etc.), one of which is bound to include your child's target sound. And the *High School Musical* movies star several characters whose names include the /r/ sound: Troy and Gabriela, Ryan and Sharpay. Novelizations are often available on several reading levels.

2. Browse your library or bookstore for book series that include characters whose names include the target sound. These might be books that your child is capable of reading herself, or that she enjoys hearing read aloud (for instance, the Harry Potter books may be too difficult for your child to read herself, but she may enjoy listening to them—and picking out the /r/ sounds in the names Harry, Hermione, Ron, and Dumbledore). (See Table 6-1 for a list of some popular series that may be appropriate for children with Down syndrome aged 6 to 14.)

3. Read poems with the target sound aloud. Shel Silverstein and Jack Prelutsky both have many collections of poems that children enjoy, and your librarian can point out other good books.

4. Check out a nonfiction book from the library on a topic that interests your child and that features many instances of your child's target sound. For instance, if your child likes cats and is working on the /s/ and /sh/ sounds, you can read about Siamese, Abyssinian, short-haired, and Persian cats. Or if your child likes baseball, you can read about different teams and the various players. If he is working on the /r/ sound, you can read books about Cal Ripken and if he is working on the /f/ sound, you can read books about the Baseball Hall of Fame in Cooperstown, New York.

You can find more resources for choosing children's books at the end of the book.

USE SONGS TO TEACH SOUND AWARENESS

Sound awareness can also be a focus when you are listening to songs. Since we are talking about children up to the age of 14 years, listening to music is a very popular pastime. Here is how you might use a song for sound awareness practice:

Let's say that your child is listening to songs from *High School Musical*. There are several popular songs with repeating phrases. Your child happens to be listening to "We're All in This Together" (which repeats "we're all in this together" many times). Your child is working on the voiced th sound (as in *the*). She says "togeda" instead of together. First, you can sing the repeating verse, "We're all in this together," while looking in a mirror with your child. Clue her

Table 6-1: Book Series

Here are some popular children's series, with the names of recurrent characters in those books. The reading levels are approximate—bear in mind that some books in a given series may be written on a slightly lower or higher reading level than others.

First or Second Grade Reading Level

- *Amelia Bedelia* (Peggy Parish): Amelia Bedelia, Mr. and Mrs. Rogers
- *Andrew Lost* (J.C. Greenburg and Debbie Palen): Andrew, Judy, Uncle Al, Thudd
- *Arthur* (Marc Brown): Arthur, Buster, D.W., Mr. Ratburn, Pal, etc.
- Flat Stanley (Jeff Brown): Stanley and Arthur Lambchop
- *Henry and Mudge* (Cynthia Rylant): Henry, Mudge, Patrick, father, mother
- *Jenny Archer* (Ellen Conford): Jenny, Beth, Mrs. Pike
- *Junie B. Jones* (Barbara Park): Junie, Gracie, Lucille, Oliver, Mrs., Teacher
- *Little Bear* (Else Holmelund Minarik): Little Bear, Owl, Cat, Duck, Hen
- *Magic Treehouse* (Mary Pope Osbourne): Jack, Annie, Morgan
- *Nate the Great* (Marjorie Weinman Sharmat): Nate, Annie, Oliver, Rosamond
- *Pixie Tricks* (Tracey West): Violet, Sprite, Sport
- *Stink* (Megan McDonald): Stink, Judy, Mouse, Webster, Sophie

Third Grade Reading Level

- *Aliens* (Jonathan Etra, Steve Bjorkman, Stephanie Spinner): Richard, Henry, Aric
- *Boxcar Children* (Gertrude Chandler Warner): Henry, Jessie, Violet, Bennie
- *Cam Jansen* mysteries (David Adler): Cam Jansen, Eric Shelton, Mr. and Mrs. Jansen
- *Fudge* (Judy Blume): Peter, Fudge, Tootsie, Sheila, Jimmy
- *Judy Moody* (Megan McDonald): Judy, Stink, Rocky, Frank Pearl, Mouse
- *Little House in the Big Woods* (Laura Ingalls Wilder): Laura, Mary, Pa, Ma, Jack
- *Spiderwick Chronicles* (Holly Black): Jared, Simon, Mallory, Thimbletack, Mulgrath
- *Time Warp Trio* (Jon Schieszka): Joe, Fred, Sam

Fourth Grade or Above

- *Alice* (Phyllis Reynolds Naylor): Alice, Lester, Donald, Patrick, Pamela, Elizabeth
- *Amazing Days of Abby Hayes* (Anne Mazur): Abby, Jessica, Casey, Ms. Kantor
- *Anastasia* (Lois Lowry): Anastasia, Sam, Mr. and Mrs. Krupnik, Robert, Henry, Sleuth
- *Harry Potter* (J. K. Rowling): Harry, Ronald, Hermione, Dumbledore, Snape, Hagrid, Voldemort, Neville, etc.
- *Henry Huggins* (Beverly Cleary): Henry, Ribsy, Beezus, Scooter, Ramona
- *Narnia* (C.S. Lewis): Peter, Susan, Edmund, Lucy, Aslan
- *Ramona* (Beverly Cleary): Ramona, Beezus, Mr. and Mrs. Quimby, Howie
- *Sammy Keyes* mysteries (Wendelin Van Draanen): Sammy, Casey, Heather, Marissa
- *Series of Unfortunate Events* (Lemony Snicket): Klaus, Violet, Sunny, Count Olaf, Mr. Poe

into your tongue movement when you are making the /th/ sound. Your tongue is out of the mouth and between the teeth, and then you quickly retract it. Next, you make up a sign, such as putting your thumbs up in the air, when you hear the /th/ sound. First let her listen and watch for the sound as well as hear it while you both sing the song. Then take the focus off the visual and ask her to listen for the sound. You might lie on a beanbag chair or turn your back or begin dancing, any position so that your child cannot focus on watching your face, only on hearing the song. You can also shift from singing the song to listening to the song on the radio or CD.

You can also use songs for sound production and practice. When a song has a predictable repeating phrase, you can practice that phrase with your child. For instance, if your child is working on the /g/ sound, you might encourage her to sing "Get Your Head in the Game" from *High School Musical*. Once your child is able to sing that phrase, whenever it comes up in the song, she can sing it loudly. This is a painless, enjoyable way to practice sounds.

HOME ACTIVITIES FOR PRACTICING SOUND PRODUCTION

READING

Once your child is able to produce sounds (even if incorrectly), you can use books to stimulate her to practice sounds. As described above, when reading aloud you can highlight the words that begin or end with a targeted sound by drawing out the sound or saying it louder. Then ask your child to imitate the word from your model. Or, if your child is able to read the book herself, take turns reading aloud. For example, you read one paragraph or sentence aloud, emphasizing the target sound, then your child reads the next paragraph. If she can read the main character's names and other high frequency words, but not all of the words in the book, pause and point to the words she can read as you get to them and let her read them aloud. If your child is just beginning to get the hang of reading, you can read books with predictable phrases, pausing to let your child say the repeating phrase (e.g., "Brown bear, brown bear, what do you see?").

For children who are not yet using much speech, choose books with many pictures of things they enjoy looking at. Point out pictures of objects with your child's target sound(s) and encourage her to repeat the name after you. Many children enjoy hunting for things hidden in the pages of the *I Spy* series of books.

Try not to correct your child's production of the sound until she is able to make the sound correctly. You don't want to put pressure on your child until she is ready to make a sound. For example, if your child has difficulty with the /r/ sound, try reading any of the series books that include characters with "r" names. Or choose a book where the characters use a catch phrase that your child can chime in on. For example, the villains in Pokemon books always say, "Team Rocket's blasting off at the speed of light; surrender now or prepare to fight!"

The speech-language pathologist will work with you to determine when it is appropriate to correct your child's production. Once your child can make the sound correctly, then reading aloud can provide practice in producing the

sound. You can also ask your child questions about the book to provide practice in making the sound while speaking rather than reading, and while answering questions. Reading is usually easier because the letter gives you the visual cue, whereas with answering questions, your child has to formulate the answer (language) in addition to saying the sound (speech).

To determine whether a book is appropriate to use for stimulation on a specific sound, simply preview the book yourself. What you are looking for is what sounds words begin and end with in the book. Are there one or two sounds that are used more than others? For example, a children's book about Aladdin has many /l/ sounds. *The Three Little Pigs* has many final /f/ sounds (the wolf appears many times in the story) and can engage your child in practicing the /f/ with the repetitive phrase "I'll huff and I'll puff and I'll blow your house in." *Sherman the Sheep* by Kevin Kiser (1994) not only has many examples of the /sh/ sound, but also has a song that repeats throughout the book:

> "We're sheep! We're sheep!
> We're brave and we're bold.
> We go where we want,
> And not where we're told.
> Cause we're sheep! We're sheep!"

Nonfiction books that engage your child's interest while practicing sounds are very useful. For example, if your child is working on the /sh/ sound, and enjoys sports, how about choosing a book about the Chicago Bulls such as *Team Spirit: The Chicago Bulls* by Mark Stewart (2008)? The book can be used to listen for the /sh/ sound, practice the sound, and can lead to a discussion of sound-letter correspondence since the /sh/ sound in Chicago is written as Ch. The book can also be used to learn to ask and answer *wh* questions. Who is the mascot of the Chicago Bulls? Who is the coach? Who's your favorite player?

Remember that you are looking and listening for sounds, not alphabet letters, so the /th/ as in *the* is a /th/ sound, not a /t/ sound as in *toe*. Some books have many examples of one sound. Other books can be used to target multiple sounds. For example, in the book, *Hop on Pop*, the following sounds are included:

- *initial p:* past, Pat, pop, pup
- *final p:* hop, pop, cup, jump, pup, up, top
- *b:* back, ball, bat, bad, be, bed, bee, big, bit, bump, but
- *m:* me, mother, mouse, Mr., Mrs., must, my, am, bump, him, jump, tomorrow

- *f:* fall, fast, fish, fight, father
- *k:* call, came, can, cat, cup
- *s:* say, see, sent, sing, sister, song, sat, sad, snack
- *final l:* all, tall, small, ball, will, hill

When you go to the library or bookstore with your child, talk with the librarian and ask for suggestions of books that focus in on your target sound. Or, look through the books yourself; just use a different "set of glasses." You are looking for many examples of a specific sound. When you look at books in that way, you can find many wonderful books on topics and at a level appropriate for your child.

You may also want to try making your own books to target particular sounds. For instance, if your child is working on the /p/ sound, you could make popcorn with your child, listen to it pop, and pour it into the bowl. Take photos. Then make your own book about Popping Popcorn. Make a J book and fill it with photos or pictures from magazines or digital photos of things that begin with J such as *jar, jam, jelly,* and *jelly beans.* Then read *Bread and Jam for Frances* or one of the *Junie B. Jones* books to reinforce the /j/ sound.

Another idea is to buy or collect old calendars. Many calendars have twelve pictures on a similar topic, such as dogs. You can make a book with the pictures and put in your own titles—big dog, little dog, dog with a hat, dog and cat—then laminate and bind. You can use the pictures to tell a story. You can use a digital camera for an "All about Me" book that includes pictures of your child's family and friends, typical activities, and a special event such as a birthday party or a trip. Then use the photos as cues to talk about what is pictured. Try to focus on the specific sounds your child is working on.

FEED THE DOG

Depending on your child's interests, this activity may be called Feed the Rabbit His Carrots, or Feed the Dog Some Bones. First draw or make out of construction paper the face of a rabbit or a dog. Mount the face on the bottom of a paper lunch bag, making a paper bag puppet. Cut an opening for the dog's mouth. Another alternative is to mount the animal face onto one side of a shoebox that has been covered with construction paper. Cut slits in the top of the shoebox. Make twenty to thirty construction paper carrots or dog bones that will easily fit through the dog's or rabbit's mouth. On each carrot or bone, write a word that includes your child's practice sound, or mount a picture that includes the sound. For example, if your child's sound is /s/, write the words or have pictures of *sun, house, sofa, sandwich,* etc.

Then your child picks a carrot or bone, saying the word (perhaps five to ten times) for practice. Then she can feed the carrot to the rabbit or the bone to the dog, by placing it through the slits in the bag or the box. When she has finished feeding them all, you may want to give her a prize.

HOMEMADE GAME BOARDS

Portable game boards enable your child to continue speech and language practice while you are away from clinic or school. They are inexpensive, easy to carry, and highly adaptable for various speech and language activities. They can also be used with a wide variety of ages, from childhood through adolescence. For example, you might design a board as a way of practicing vocabulary words related to transportation or to practice the production of the /r/ sound.

To make a portable game board, purchase some file folders. Choose folders in several colors if you plan to make games for different purposes. (For example, you may want to make one board to practice the /r/ sound, one board for the /l/ sound, and boards for vocabulary words related to household articles and transportation.) Open up the folder. You now have a fairly large, flat surface. Draw a road, a ladder, a grid, or other pathway with spaces. Draw a starting point and a finishing point. The finishing point may have a glowing sticker or a rainbow or a jackpot of gold.

To make a speech sounds game, in each space, place pictures or words for your child to practice saying. A game board for /r/ might include *reindeer, roof, roller blades, rat, raccoon, rope, rain, radio,* and *rabbit.* A game board for transportation might include *train, car, plane, bicycle, motorbike,* and *truck.* You can use magazine photos, stickers, or drawings in the spaces. You can also take your own photos and cut out the outline of the featured item or use your printer to shrink down a digital photo so it is small enough to place in a space.

Vary the rules for the game depending on your child's age and sophistication level. You may want to use a single die or a pair of dice to decide the number of spaces each player will advance. Or, you can construct a spinner using a circle with numbers, and a cardboard arrow held in place with a paper fastener. Wherever the spinner lands will determine the number of spaces to advance. You may also want to make instruction cards (cards that instruct you to go backwards or forwards two spaces), or a pile of cards with various instructions that you choose from when you land on "Draw a Card." Each player uses a marker such as a colored button, coins, small toy car, or animal.

Game boards can be laminated or covered with plastic contact paper to make them more sturdy. You can write the title of the game or the topic area right inside the manila folder tab. When you are at home, the folder game boards can be easily stored in a file box or file cabinet. You may wish to refer to *Teaching by Design: Using Your Computer to Create Materials for Students with Learning Differences* by Kimberly S. Voss (Woodbine House, 2005) for tips on making polished-looking spinners, game pieces, etc.

SPEECH STEPS

When your child needs to practice saying a group of words or practice following a series of commands, this home activity can make the practice more fun. Either activity may be used for boys or girls, depending on their interest in movies or sports.

To play the game, you will need some carpet samples in different colors. (Many stores are willing to give you discontinued samples.) Place them on the floor in the pattern of a road or path. At the end of the road, place a prize or a treat (go out for lunch, rent a DVD). Place each practice card or item on a carpet sample. When a player steps on the carpet, she need to do the activity described or label the word on the card. For example, if your child is working on /r/, there might be pictures or photos of rabbit, rainbow, ring, and rain on the carpet samples and she has to pronounce each word to go on to the next one. You can make this more fun by playing marching music or other music. You might want to make the path markers out of yellow construction paper and play the song, *Follow the Yellow Brick Road,* from *The Wizard of Oz.*

A sports variation on the same type of activity is to trace your child's footprint, then cut out construction paper footprints. Place the footprints on the floor. Put an activity or a practice card on each footprint. The footprints should lead to some sports activity. For example, a Nerf basketball hoop, where your child gets to take some free throws, or a T-ball stand, or a goal and a ball to kick. Or your child might win a baseball card, and when she has collected a specified number of cards, she can go to a ball game.

KARAOKE SINGING

Many children and teens with Down syndrome enjoy hearing themselves sing, so why not use singing to sneak in some sound production practice? You can purchase a karaoke machine that hooks up to your television, together with specially made karaoke music CDs. When you insert the CD into the machine, the words of the song appear on the TV screen. If your family owns a video game system (Playstation, Xbox, etc.), there are also karaoke games that work on the same general principle. (Be careful if you invest in one of these video games, though, because some of them rate your singing at the end, which can be discouraging for a child who thinks she is a good singer, but isn't.)

If your child is reading, she can read the words on the TV screen and then try to sing or say them into the microphone in time to the music. If your child can't read, you or a sibling will have to teach her the words first. In either case, it can be very helpful for a child to hear her own pronunciation through the microphone.

TELLING JOKES

Look for children's joke books that include jokes, riddles, or knock-knock jokes that use your child's target sounds. Your child will need to practice saying the riddle so that people will understand the question she is asking them, as well as the punch line. For instance, to work on the /sh/ sound: "What did the ocean say to the shore? … Nothing, it just waved." Or, for /z/: "What goes zzub, zzub, zzub? … A bee flying backwards."

CHOOSING APPROPRIATE ACTIVITIES FOR YOUR CHILD

When is it appropriate to work on the activities described in this chapter? Or to read books that focus on specific sounds? Or to correct your child when she makes a sound incorrectly?

Children with Down syndrome learn sounds at different ages. Some eight-year-olds carry on long conversations, while other eight-year-olds are using three- to five-word sentences or using a few spoken words augmented by signs or another communication system. So, look at any of the activities in this chapter as possibilities. Try a few that you think your child might enjoy. If your child has difficulty, ask the SLP what activity might be a bit easier for your child. Try the activity again every few months to determine whether your child is ready at that time. If an activity is too easy or boring for your child, then make it more complicated and a bit harder. If it is too hard, simplify it, and come back to the more difficult items once your child has mastered the simpler ones. For example, you may show a photo of *grass,* which has the /r/ sound in a blend of two consonants /g/ and /r/. If your child struggles with this word, back up to *rock,* where the /r/ is a single sound. Once your child is saying /r/ well, then come back to *grass.*

Sometimes two activities may seem the same but one will be easier for your child than the other. For example, your child might try blowing two horns. One is easy for her because it has a wide mouthpiece and does not require too much breath pressure. Another horn is difficult because it has a very small mouthpiece so your child has to compress her lips hard around the mouthpiece and use a lot of breath pressure. Both activities are horn blowing.

When do your start correcting your child if she is saying a sound incorrectly? For example, she is seven, and she says she is "seben" and also says "seben" during math class. First, you want to separate practice from daily speaking. When she says the number for daily speaking, her focus is on meaning—on getting her message across. In daily living, you want to focus on her message. If you correct her at that time, it usually decreases speaking attempts. When she is practicing, she is learning to make the sounds. During practice times, you can heighten auditory awareness by making the /v/ sound in *seven* louder and more pronounced. Also heighten her visual awareness by using a mirror and having her watch your mouth while you say the /v/ sound. Teach her how to make the /v/ sound. Then practice it, perhaps by making a photo book of about the number seven. There are seven of each item, and your child needs to count the items.

Only when your child is able to say the sound in words in practice the majority of the time should you try correcting her in daily speaking. And, even then, it should be with respect—when you are alone or within the family in situations that will not embarrass her. Remember the distinctions that we made in the beginning of the book among speech, language, and communication. If you correct speech in situations that are difficult for your child, you run the risk of her deciding not to communicate, deciding that speech is just too hard, and giving up. Focus on one or two sounds. Focus on sounds that she is successful with in speech sessions or in practice sessions. And be sure to correct her only in comfortable situations, when she feels free to try again.

Phonological Processes

As Chapter 5 discusses, phonological processes are sound simplifications that all young children use as they develop speech (for example, leaving the ending consonants off of words or substituting the /f/ sound for the /th/ sound in *thumb*). Children with Down syndrome use these processes longer than other children, however.

Researchers have found that children with Down syndrome use more phonological processes as the length and complexity of their speech increases. That is, they use more phonological processes in generating their own sentences in conversation than when they are naming pictures spontaneously or imitating names spoken by others.

To determine which phonological processes your child is using, the SLP will do a phonological process analysis. Phonological process analysis is a method for analyzing sound errors in speech through an exploration of the substitution patterns the child makes. A phonological process analysis might look at, for example, whether your child makes all sounds in the front of the mouth, or whether she leaves off all of the final sounds in words.

When the SLP analyzes the phonological processes that your child uses, he or she can figure out the rules or patterns that your child is using to simplify speech. Phonological processes are not based on the articulation and oral motor abilities of the child. For example, a child may say /fum/ for thumb. If the error was based on articulation or oral motor ability, we would assume that the child has difficulty saying the /th/ sound. But, this child may also say /thun/ for sun, proving that she can make the /th/ sound. She just does not make it in the right word at the right time. This tells us that she has a different logical rule system in her mind. She has developed it although no one has taught the rule to her. Phonological process analyses are used when your child is able to produce sounds correctly in some contexts but not in others or when your child uses simplifications in her speech that follow definite patterns.

If your child is receiving speech-language treatment for phonological processes, the SLP will focus on correcting your child's patterns, rather than the individual sounds. For example, treatment for final consonant deletion will focus on making your child aware that final consonants affect meaning and that she is leaving off those final consonants.

Here are some sample IEP goals for children working on phonological processes:
- For a child who omits final sounds in words, an appropriate IEP goal might be: Sarah will include the final sound in single-syllable words with 90% accuracy by the end of the school year.
- For a child who is having difficulty making back sounds (k and g), an appropriate IEP goal might be: George will be able to produce the /k/ and /g/ sounds in words 80% of the time when reading a list of words.

The Cycles Approach and the Minimal Pairs approach are the most common approaches to treatment for phonological process use.

THE CYCLES APPROACH

The Cycles Approach was developed by Barbara Hodson and Elaine Paden (1990) to help children who had many sound errors and whose speech was unintelligible. The Cycles Approach has been shown to improve speech in children with Down syndrome.

The Cycles Approach targets specific phonological patterns and works on each pattern in a very specific manner. Hodson suggests that only one phonological pattern should be targeted during a session so that the child can focus in on that pattern. Within any pattern (e.g., final consonant deletion), the child may have several or many sounds that are produced using that phonological pattern. For example, she may say "boo" for *boot* (omitting /t/ sound), "do" for *dog* (omitting /g/ sound), and "pho" for *phone* (omitting /n/ sound). This is in contrast to articulation difficulties. If a child has articulation problems with the final /k/ sound, she may say "boo" for *book* and "too" for *took* (leaving off the final problematic /k/ sound), but she should be able to say phone correctly, because it ends with a different sound.

The SLP may focus on a specific pattern (such as final consonant deletion) for two to four weeks, targeting a different phoneme (sound) each week. Through the different sounds, the child gains practice in hearing and producing the correct pattern. A treatment cycle can last from five or six weeks to fifteen or sixteen weeks, depending on the number of phonological "deficiency" patterns the child uses, and the number of phonemes the child can work on within that pattern. Phonemes are chosen for treatment based on whether the child is stimulable on those sounds—that is, the child can imitate the sound correctly when a model is provided.

Treatment sessions are usually 40-60 minutes per week. Each session follows a seven-step instructional sequence:

1. Review
2. Auditory bombardment
3. Target word cards
4. Production practice
5. Stimulability probing
6. Auditory bombardment
7. Home program

Review. At the beginning of each once-weekly session, there is a review of the practice word cards. These are cards that the child made in step number 3 during the previous session.

Auditory Bombardment. In this part of the session, the child listens to the SLP reading words containing the target sound and the target phonological process. For example, if final consonant deletion is the phonological process being targeted and /p/ is the sound being targeted, the word list might include the words: *soup, top, cup, lip, cap, mop, hip, stop, chop, hop, pop, cop.* The child listens to the words being read for about two minutes, and there are approximately twelve words on the list each week.

During the auditory bombardment/listening activity, the child uses amplification—usually an auditory trainer. This makes it possible for the child to hear and attend to all of the sounds in the word, even the final sounds or unstressed syllable sounds, which are often said more softly. The use of mild amplification is particularly helpful for children with Down syndrome who often have fluid in the middle ear and a fluctuating hearing loss. The speech-language pathologist will read the words correctly while the child listens. Once the child is capable of producing the target sound correctly, the SLP may also produce the sound incorrectly and then contrast that with the correct production.

Target Word Cards. During this part of the session, the child helps to make word cards that will be used for practicing the target sound and phonological process. Hodson believes that it is very important for the child to participate in developing these materials, and that this activity helps motivate the child to use the cards and practice the words. The child may draw a picture, color a picture, or paste pictures on three to five large index cards. The child (if she is able) or the SLP writes the name of the picture on each card.

Production Practice. A variety of games are used to enable the child to practice the target sound. Multisensory stimulation, including auditory, visual, and tactile cues, is used to help the child correctly produce the sound. For instance, she may look in the mirror to see her teeth on her lower lip when she says /f/, touch her lower lip at the spot where you make /f/, and listen to the sound of /f/. The child is then expected to be able to correctly produce the sound. For children with Down syndrome who have low muscle tone in the mouth and face or who have Childhood Apraxia of Speech, the Cycles Approach may need to be modified to include additional cues and additional oral motor practice during the session.

Play, games, or experiential activities (depending on the child's age and abilities) may be used and a new activity is usually introduced every five to seven minutes to maintain the child's interest. There is also practice in conversation during each session.

Stimulability Probing. This part of the session is designed to determine which sound will be targeted in the next session. The target sound is chosen based on which sounds the child can imitate from a model. So, if the child has been working on the /p/ sound and the phonological process of final consonant deletion, the speech language pathologist may check whether the child can imitate final /t/ as in *pot,* final /d/ as in *bad,* final /k/ as in *back,* and final /g/ as in *dog.* The target sound for the next session would be chosen based on which of those four sounds the child was most successful in imitating.

Auditory Bombardment. The listening activity using the word list that was used as the second activity in the session is now repeated. Again, mild amplification is used. The SLP reads the words, and the child listens for about two minutes.

Home Program. The home program is discussed with the child and the parent in the last part of each session. Each week, the home program has a listening component and a production practice component based on the target sound and words used during the therapy session. Parents are asked to read the word list to the child at least once daily. The child is asked to practice the words on the five target word cards daily.

Most therapy programs progress to a new sound when the child has reached a specific criterion level. For example, the child and therapist will move on to a new sound when the child is able to produce the /p/ in the final position 90 percent of the time. The Cycles Approach is different. During each session, a new target sound is targeted and the target sound from the past week is reviewed. If, during review, the SLP observes that the child has not mastered the target sound from the previous week, the target sound is recycled and is used as a target during the next session. Thus, each sound is worked on for about one hour during a session and is then reviewed at the next session. At least two sounds are worked on for each phonological process, so each process is worked on for at least two hours during a specific cycle. If the sound and phonological process are not mastered, they are worked on during the next cycle. This approach mirrors the way that children develop language and speech. They may say a word or sound once, and then come back to it later on. When children are acquiring language, they rarely practice one sound or one word constantly until they master that word or sound.

For typically developing children who have unintelligible speech, three to six cycles of phonological treatment sessions or thirty to forty hours of treatment sessions and additional home practice are needed for the child's speech to become intelligible. We have no information on the progress of children with Down syndrome using the program, although the program has been used for children with Down syndrome. In my clinical experience, however, children with Down syndrome need to work on each sound for multiple sessions.

MINIMAL PAIR CONTRAST APPROACH

Minimal pairs are pairs of words that differ by only one sound (phoneme)—for example, *dig-big, bat-cat, dot-dock, bat-back* (notice, one sound may be two alphabet letters, but it still is only one sound). Using minimal pairs in therapy is based on the theory that if you contrast word pairs that differ by only one sound, the child will learn that individual sounds affect meaning, and that using two different sounds will affect the meaning of the word. Minimal pair contrasts may be used with sounds at the beginning or end of the word. The child may listen to lists of words, read lists of words, or identify pictures. The focus of the treatment is not on sound production, but on awareness of the differences. So, this method would work best for a child who says a particular sound correctly in some, but not all positions in a word—for instance, she says the /t/ in *top* but does not say the /t/ in the final position in *lot*.

Here are the steps involved in minimal pair contrasts treatment:

1. Choose a sound contrast to be worked on in treatment based on the child's phonological process errors.
2. Choose picture cards or word lists that contain the minimal contrasts targeted; e.g., *sip-sit, soup-suit, sap-sat.*
3. Teach and provide practice in listening to minimal contrasts and indicating which is which without expecting the child to say the words. For example, have the child listen to the word the SLP says, and then point to the picture, "Soup," "Suit."
4. Pretest the child's production of the target sounds. For instance, can the child correctly say the /p/ and /t/ sounds? If not, the SLP must teach the child how to produce the /p/ and /t/ sounds. The minimal contrasts method does not specify what approach to use to teach the sounds. That is left up to the SLP.
5. The SLP says the minimal pair contrast words. The child then tries to imitate her. (It is assumed in this method that the child can do that. If she cannot imitate the words, the SLP goes back to step 4 and teaches the sound productions.)
6. Provide practice for the child in producing the words with the minimal contrasts. Different types of activities can be used. For example, the card pointing activity in step 2 can be used, but this time, the child says the words and the speech-language pathologist points to the cards. Or, if the words were *jump-dump*, the child may say the word and then be allowed to do the activity—e.g., jump on a trampoline and dump blocks out of a dump truck. Or the SLP may use a Go Fish type game with the child, as described in the section called "Let's Match Up" below.
7. Help the child progress to using the target word in a carrier phrase such as "I saw the soup." (A carrier phrase is one that acts as a fill-in framework for the target word, such as "I want" or "I saw.")

8. Provide practice in using both minimal pair contrast words in a phrase such as "I saw the soup and the suit."

When a child uses the phonological process of final consonant deletion, the SLP may work with her using something called the open syllable program. In this program, the SLP uses a booklet with many small black and white drawings that represent words with minimal contrasts. These are used in a series of games and activities to help the child practice making the final sounds in words, and learn that these final sounds affect meaning.

Minimal pair contrast therapy is really designed for children who can produce a sound correctly but are not using the sound in the correct place or in the correct word. This is not usually the situation with children with Down syndrome, whose sound production is complicated by low muscle tone or motor planning problems. But the method is still useful for children with Down syndrome when we are teaching sound production. By using minimal contrast pairs, it often makes it easier for the child to hear the difference between two sounds. It also makes it easier to teach and then re-inforce the production of a sound by contrasting it with another sound.

HOME ACTIVITIES FOR PHONOLOGICAL PROCESSES

ACTIVITIES FOR FINAL CONSONANT DELETION

- Make two identical sets of cards showing pictures or words with final sounds that are hard for your child to distinguish. Give one set to your child and the other to another player. Set up a barrier between the two players, such as a file folder standing on end. Then your child arranges her cards in a row from left to right and reads them off to the other player. The other player puts his/her cards in the order that the child reads/says them, then you check to see if you have them in the same order. Then the players switch roles.

- For added interest, play the game above with players in different rooms. Have your child go into another room with a cell phone or walkie-talkie and call up the other player and tell him or her the order of the cards.

- Play a variation of the game called "Pin the Tail on the Donkey" called "Pin the Tail on the Dog" (or maybe rat, since that has a final sound and a long tail). Discuss that the final sound on a word is like the tail on the dog or rat; it needs to be right at the end. Say the word with the final sound attached and you get to pin or tape the tail on the dog. (You can draw a picture of a dog and let your child color in segments each time she says a sound correctly, or use a picture of a dog from a magazine and let your child tape the tail on.) Tape small pieces of tail segments with words that have final sounds all around the dog. If your child says the word and pronounces the final sound correctly, she can put that segment on the tail.

- Play "Let's Match Up" as described in the box on the next page.

Let's Match Up

This awareness activity adapted from the Go Fish card game is an example of a home activity to help children learn to include final sounds when speaking. If your SLP uses the minimal pairs contrast approach, she may use a similar game with your child in therapy.

- Make two copies of pictures of objects that only differ in the final sound, such as *boat*, *bowl*, *bone*, and *bow*. There are lists of such words in speech therapy books on "minimal contrasts" or you can make up your own.
- Mount the pictures on unlined index cards or cardstock, creating a deck of playing cards. For example, there would be two boat cards with pictures of boats, two bow cards, two bowl cards, and two bone cards.
- Give each player a number of cards (you can use three, five, or seven cards).
- Taking turns, players request specific cards so that they can make pairs. The player with the most pairs wins. For example, your child might ask, "Do you have any boat cards?" Now, if she does not pronounce the final sound correctly or omits the final sound, the other player may hand her the wrong card, not the one that she wants. This creates awareness that the final sound affects the meaning of the word. Both listening and production practice can be included in the game.

ACTIVITIES FOR FRONTING AND BACKING:

- Talk about the fact that some sounds such as /p/ and /l/ are made right in the front of the mouth and other sounds such as /k/ and /g/ are made at the back of the mouth. Use a mirror to see the front sounds and touch your throat area to feel the back sounds.

- Get an action figure, a Disney figure, or a toy animal and talk about its front and back. Have a list of words (or pictures for nonreaders). Say the word, and then have your child show you the front or back of the figure depending on where the sound is in the word. For instance, if you are working on the /g/ sound and you say the word *go*, your child should show you the front; for the word *big*, she should show you the back.

FOR WEAK SYLLABLE DELETION:

- Children who use weak syllable deletion leave out a middle syllable in a multisyllabic word. To bring this omission into your child's awareness, use a drum, tambourine, or a pacing board to pound out, count out, or touch the number of syllables in a word. (A pacing board is a strip of paper, cardboard, or other material with large dots in a row that can be used for marking syllables. See Chapter 8 for a description.) For example, say or pound out: *ham-bur-ger*, *base-ball-bat*, *ice cream cone*. Once your child is able to do the activity, you might want to develop a separate list of words that she is having difficulty saying. When you model the word,

emphasize the syllable that is usually omitted or say it louder for words on which your child is leaving out syllables. Another possibility is to "sing" the word in a three-part rhythm: "ham-bur-ger."

● Play catch and throw the ball to your partner as you say each syllable of the word. Or throw a dart or bean bag for every syllable.

● Say a multisyllabic word or phrase while you are using the item you are naming. For example, have your child say "trampoline" when she is jumping on the trampoline, "DVD" while she is walking over to get one, or "refrigerator" while she is opening the door.

FOR CONSONANT CLUSTER REDUCTION:

● Consonant cluster reduction occurs when your child omits one consonant in the cluster, such as by saying "gas" for "glass." To practice these sounds, model how to add an "a" sound after the first consonant sound and emphasize the two sounds in practice. For example, for "glass," say, "ga-lass." Sometimes children enjoy doing a dance while practicing these clusters.

● Make a list of words with consonant clusters that give your child trouble. Look for words that are words both with and without the omitted conso-nant (e.g., black and back, clap and cap, slip and sip). Make two cards for each word, illustrating them if your child cannot read the words. To play the game, arrange one set of cards in a 3 x 3 or 4 x 4 square. Your child draws a card from the other set. If she says the word correctly (drawn out with an extra syllable, as above), she can put it on the matching card.

Phonological Processing and Awareness

Two other areas of phonology should be mentioned: phonological processing and phonological awareness.

Phonological process**ing** (not to be confused with phonological process**es**) refers to the child's or adult's ability to perceive sounds that she hears. This may include:
- remembering or holding onto the sound,
- distinguishing between sounds,
- processing a sequence of sounds, and
- the speed with which children can process sounds.

Speech-language pathologist Anne Fowler has researched this area and found that many children with Down syndrome have great difficulty with phonological processing.

Phonological awareness (also known as metaphonology) is the ability to identify and manipulate the sounds of the language. It usually includes skills such as:

- segmenting words into their constituent sounds (*map* into m-a-p),
- combining sounds into words (s-n-o-w into *snow*),
- alliteration or identifying words that begin with the same sound, and
- rhyming words (*hat, cat, rat, sat, mat*).

Phonological awareness is related to reading development. Many of the reading and language arts skills that are tested and taught in the early elementary school years are phonological awareness skills.

Many early learning workbooks, activity books, and software programs address this area. Most of this material is not worked on until kindergarten and first grade, because segmenting words or combining sounds into words are more advanced phonological skills. Phonological awareness is generally taught as part of the language arts curriculum. See Chapter 5 for more information about phonological awareness and reading skills.

Therapy for Childhood Apraxia of Speech

As explained in Chapter 5, Childhood Apraxia of Speech (CAS) is a disorder that results in difficulty planning, coordinating, producing, and sequencing speech sounds. CAS interferes with the child's ability to say sounds and to combine them into syllables, words, phrases, and conversations. The speech difficulty is inconsistent, with the child making the sounds correctly sometimes, reversing sounds other times, and struggling and groping still other times. Although most children learn the sounds for speech by listening to and watching adults and other children around them and then practicing these sounds through verbal play, this is not true for children with CAS. These children must be taught the skills needed to program and sequence the movements for speech and must practice them deliberately and often.

Children develop motor skills, including speech production skills, through experience and practice. Although speech is a motor output system, it is based on well-functioning input systems such as vision, hearing, and touch. If your child is not able to integrate all of the incoming sensory information, it will be difficult to organize and sequence the movements necessary for precise, articulate speech.

Children need to process all incoming sensory input in order to develop the motor plans needed for speaking. The theory is that listening to the sounds in your environment helps develop sound perception and that during early speech motor practice (such as cooing and babbling), templates in the brain are developed for producing the speech sounds. These templates serve as a quickly accessible recipe for the necessary movements to produce sounds and sound sequences. For most people, these make the motor planning process almost automatic. Motor learning for speech depends on the development of strong templates (or motor plans) and those plans develop through experience.

Children with Down syndrome have many sensory (vision, hearing, touch) and motor deficits (low muscle tone, weak muscles) that can affect the ability to gain such experience. When children have developed strong motor plans, they can produce rapid, precise, sequenced speech, almost automatically. Children who do not have adequate practice to develop these templates have a difficult time planning speech output. They may need to consciously plan the many aspects of speech that are automatic for typically developing speakers. We can provide practice, in therapy and at home, to help children learn the movement patterns for sounds and combinations of sounds so that they can become more automatic.

The typical kinds of articulation therapy described above are not sufficient for children with CAS. Typical articulation therapy methods can help them with some problems, but not others. For instance, oral-motor therapy can help to strengthen the child's muscles, but not improve her motor planning abilities.

Treatment approaches used by SLPs for CAS include:

- Oral motor therapy (practicing the movements for speech sounds, as described on page 159)
- Phonemic and articulation therapy (teaching your child how to make the sounds and combine sounds into syllables), as described above in the sections on therapy for articulation and phonological processes
- Visual cueing (providing a hand cue that your child can see). Some approaches are:
    - Visual-tactile (Strode and Chamberlain): where the child learns to make certain movements that cue her as to where the speech sound is made. It may also involve picture or photo cues.
    - Physical cues (prompts), where the therapist touches the area on the face where the sound is made.
    - Cued speech: a system originally developed by R. Orin Cornett to help deaf people speech read (lip read). The system involves helping people "see" the sounds of English by using specific hand shapes to represent each consonant sound in a word and placing them in specific places around the mouth to indicate the vowel sounds. A few speech-language pathologists have begun advocating using this method specifically for children with Down syndrome, although to date there has not been any research into its effectiveness with children with Down syndrome.
- Multimodal or Total Communication approaches are often used, meaning that you always use the spoken word in addition to signs or cues.
- Prosodic approaches (melodic intonation therapy) use singing and rhythm to help the child learn sound combinations. The SLP and child tap out the number of syllables or sing the syllables with a strong rhythm (almost like an opera). This appears to engage additional areas of the brain.
- Shaping approaches (such as the Kaufman Praxis Treatment Kit) break words down to the level of complexity that your child can

say, moving the word immediately into functional expressive vocabulary use, and then building the word up through shaping procedures. For example, your child can say *na,* but cannot say *banana.* You would show your child *banana* many times, having her say *na,* and then building up to *nana,* and finally to *banana.* If her name is Jordan, she might start out by using /da/ when giving her name, then building to /oda/, then odan, then ordan, then Jordan.

All of these approaches were developed for children with CAS who do not also have Down syndrome. Since each child with Down syndrome has her own combination of speech difficulties, some methods will work better for some children than other methods. In our clinic, we often use a combination of oral motor, cueing, and shaping approaches. Most SLPs who have experience working with children with CAS are familiar with these approaches, so if one doesn't work with your child he or she could try another.

Regular practice is critical to the success of CAS therapy, and the SLP should provide a home practice program for you and your child to work on together. Also see the pages below for some suggested home activities.

HOME ACTIVITIES FOR CAS

- *Practice consonant-vowel combinations.* For example, you might encourage your child to singing along to songs with "lalala." Or teach your child to say "ta-da!" with a sweeping hand gesture when she has accomplished something. It's practice and it's fun.

- *Imitate sounds your child makes.* The rationale is that it is difficult for your child to imitate sounds you make, and the sounds she makes may be inconsistent. So, by repeating the sounds she makes and then having her say the sound again, you are trying to help increase the consistency of the correct sounds, and also trying to help her set up the motor templates through practice.

- *Accept word approximations.* Work with the SLP to know where your child is in sound making. For example, if she says "go" for "grow," she may still be having difficulty with consonant blends such as "gr."

- *Use singing and melody with speech.* You use a melody your child knows or make up your own. Try modeling singing a word or phrase for your child and see if she can imitate you. A rap song format can be good for practice.

- *Teach scripts for daily living.* Scripts are words, phrases, or sentences that your child can repeat verbatim in many situations in everyday life. For example, expressions such as "OK," "See you later," and "What's happening" can be used for many purposes. She doesn't have to stop and figure out word choices and word order.

- *Use familiar verbal routines with gestures.* For instance, with a younger child, do *Eensy Weensy Spider* and other hand rhyme songs; with an older child, try hand-clap routines such as *Miss Mary Mack.* Your child doesn't have to say any of the words at first. Let her participate with the gestures.

● *Read books with repeating lines and predictable phrases for practice so your child can participate. (Five Little Monkeys Jumping on the Bed, Chicken Soup with Rice,* and *Henny Penny* are examples.)*

● *Work with an SLP to use cueing systems that will help your child make specific sounds, as described above.* For cueing systems to be effective, they must be used consistently in all settings—for example, pointing to the throat for the /k/ sound, which is made in the back of the mouth. Every time that Kathleen would say her name, her mom would cue her that /k/ is a back sound by pointing to the throat

Therapy for Perceptual Speech Symptoms

In addition to the problems producing the sounds of speech that are described above, children with Down syndrome may have a variety of problems that affect the quality of the sounds they produce. These factors are sometimes jointly referred to as *perceptual speech symptoms* because they are heard and noticed (perceived) by the listener. These factors include:

● voice,
● loudness,
● resonance,
● fluency,
● prosody, and
● rate.

Many children with Down syndrome need treatment from pediatricians, otolaryngologists (ENT specialists), audiologists, and occupational therapists, in addition to speech-language pathologists, for some of these factors that may affect speech intelligibility.

VOICE

The areas of voice that can be worked on in therapy include volume, pitch, and voice quality. Before voice therapy is begun, a medical consultation should always be done to determine whether there are medical conditions underlying the difficulty or whether there are medical difficulties arising from the problem (e.g., vocal nodules from vocal abuse).

From the results of the evaluation, the SLP can determine whether your child needs to learn the appropriate skill or whether she can do it correctly, but needs help in generalizing the skill. For example, many children speak too softly merely because they are shy or are not aware of the need to speak up. They just need help in becoming aware of volume, and practice in using their louder voice more of the time during the day.

Other children speak too softly due to breathing difficulties. Their breathing is shallow and weak and does not provide sufficient power for a louder voice. These children need to work on respiration in speech therapy. The SLP may use exercises to strengthen the muscles of the diaphragm and abdominal area. She may have them

practice deep breathing, or may use exercises such as vocalizing while exerting pressure on a table top.

Some children shout and misuse their voice (vocal abuse). To help children become aware of loudness and get it under their control, the SLP may use practice and role playing. It can also be helpful to read children's books that focus on loudness such as: *The Quiet Noisy Book*, *The Very Quiet Cricket*, or *Noisy Nora*.

Vocal pitch refers to the highness or lowness of the voice. The SLP can measure habitual pitch (what your child is using everyday) and optimal pitch (what would be best for your child's age, gender, and use of the voice). She can then work with your child towards using optimal pitch in daily living. The SLP uses musical scales, awareness activities, and practice.

Voice quality refers to whether the voice is hoarse, harsh, or breathy. This is based on what you and the therapist hear. Often voice quality difficulties are related to medical issues such as a laryngeal web or a vocal nodule from vocal misuse. Voice problems may also be related to allergies such as milk allergies. When working on voice, you always want a team approach involving the SLP and the pediatrician or otolaryngologist. Treatment may be team treatment or it may involve medical interventions followed by speech therapy.

Published materials such as *Voice Adventures* (Super Duper), *Using Your Best Voice* (Communication Skill Builders), and *Remediation of Vocal Hoarseness* (Teaching Resources) may be used in therapy sessions.

Treatment of Voice Problems

The evaluation needs to determine whether your child is *able* to use her voice correctly and whether she *does* use her voice correctly.

If she is not able to use voice correctly:

What is the underlying cause? (e.g., shallow breathing)

- Structural-anatomical
- Muscular-physiological (weak chest and diaphragm muscles)

In this case, the goal of therapy is to work on the underlying cause. A child's team may include an otolaryngologist, pediatrician, and other medical specialists.

If she is able to use her voice correctly, but does not:

Is it due to:

- Poor habits
- Vocal abuse

In this case, the goal of therapy is to reinforce correct use and eliminate bad habits and abuse.

HOME ACTIVITIES FOR VOICE

- If your child can use a loud voice, but doesn't use it in the right situations, have her practice whispering, speaking softly, speaking at a conversational level, speaking loudly, and screaming. You can make cue cards with cartoon characters whispering in someone's ear, shouting through a megaphone, etc. Then you are the director and hold up the cue card so your child practices that level of loudness.

- Play a variation of Simon Says where the leader gets the other players to imitate what she is saying at the volume she is using. For instance, Simon says "talk like this" and then whispers "I have a secret" or yells "Help, help, help!" Once your child can understand the different levels of loudness, Simon can say "whisper" or "shout."

- Make a game board from a file folder and either number the spaces 1 to 4 or color them four different colors. Then write a number (or color) on the backs of a stack of index cards. On the other side, write up some fun scenarios where you might need to use different volumes when speaking. For example, you might have to yell if you have fallen into the quicksand and you might need to whisper if you are in the movie theater and need to use the bathroom. Roll the dice and move ahead that number to see which color (or number) of card you need to take. Then act out the scenario on the card, using the right volume. If you are correct, stay on that space; if you are wrong, return to the space that you started from.

- If your child is older and is still having a lot of trouble choosing the right volume to use, make a chart listing times it is appropriate to whisper vs. yell. For example, whispering would be appropriate during a religious service or in a movie theatre; screaming would be appropriate at a baseball game when your team scores a run. Also consider making a Power Card to help her remember how loudly to speak in certain settings (see page 264, Chapter 9).

RESONANCE

As Chapter 4 explains, some children with Down syndrome are hyponasal (less nasal sounding than usual). They sound stuffed up, as if they have a cold all of the time. Other children are hypernasal and their voices have a twangy, whining quality. Sometimes, you can hear both hyponasality and hypernasality in a child's speech. The child sounds hyponasal on /m/, /n/, and /ng/ and hypernasal on the other consonants. Again, it is always important to have a full medical ENT (ear, nose, and throat) evaluation to look for swollen tonsils and adenoids or other causes for these conditions before a treatment plan is developed.

HYPERNASALITY

Sometimes hypernasality is due to weak muscles. If so, your child's SLP will work on strengthening the muscles of the soft palate and the posterior pharyngeal wall (the back wall of the throat) through an exercise program. If, on the other hand, the hypernasality is due to a high vaulted hard palate, the SLP will work in partnership with a dental specialist. An orthodontist can design palatal expanders for your child to widen the palate and make it broader and lower. Usually, expanders are not used until a child's permanent molars come in.

Finally, if the hypernasality is due to a short palate, your child's ENT may recommend surgery such as *pharyngoplasty*—an operation in which tissue from the palate and back of the throat is repositioned so as to prevent air from escaping through the nose. A prosthodontist—a dentist who specializes in making implants and in cosmetic dentistry—may make an appliance (known as an obturator or speech appliance) to help your child make velopharyngeal closure (that is, to help the muscles close to divert the air stream from the nasal cavity to the oral cavity for sounds other than /m/, /n/, and /ng/).

When hypernasality is due to structural problems rather than weak muscles, families often consult a maxillofacial team (also known as a cleft palate team) at a major hospital center. These teams include ENTs, prosthodontists, and maxillofacial surgeons who can consult and determine which intervention would work best for your child.

HYPONASALITY

If hyponasality is the problem, it is usually related to inflammation and excess tissue, usually of the tonsils and adenoids. This often occurs in conjunction with allergies and mouth breathing. This is an issue that needs medical intervention.

When surgery or medications reverse the inflammation or other difficulties, your child's muscles may need retraining. Because of the excess tissue, the muscles have been moving less to make closure and the air has not been able to resonate through the nose. When the excess tissue and inflammation are gone, the muscles may not be achieving closure and your child may suddenly sound hypernasal. It is important to document your child's pre-surgical speech, so that if therapy is needed after surgery, you can prove that there has been a change in resonance and that speech therapy is needed. The SLP can do a brief evaluation to document your child's speech before surgery. It will usually consist of audiotape or videotape of your child saying prolonged vowel sounds (/a/ and /ee/) and reading words or sentences that have nasal and oral sounds in them (e.g., "name," "book," and "Beth's number is not in my cell phone").

RATE

How fast does your child speak? Some children with Down syndrome speak rapidly, but others speak slowly. The first consideration is whether your child can use an appropriate rate of speech. The next step is to determine whether she is aware of what is appropriate for different situations, and whether she can modify her rate to fit the situation. Therapy will focus either on teaching your child to use an appropriate rate, or on bringing rate into her awareness and then helping her learn how to modify her rate as needed.

HOME ACTIVITIES FOR RATE
- Make sure your child understands the concepts of fast and faster, and slow and slower. You might read the story of *The Tortoise and the Hare*, and talk about slow and fast. Or you might demonstrate (or let your child demonstrate) fast and slow with your VCR or DVD player. When you fast

forward, everything moves faster; when you let the movie go at its normal speed, it is slower. If you have a tape recorder that will allow you to adjust the speed of playback, you can demonstrate clearly what fast and slow speech sounds like.

- If you have the opportunity to attend an auction or watch one on TV, let your child experience what very fast speech sounds like and then talk about whether it would be a good idea to talk that fast in daily life.

- Have fun saying a rhyme or singing a song very fast and then very slow.

- Set up a race course and race a toy car and a very slow animal. The person operating the race car must talk very fast while the person with the animal must talk very slowly.

- Come up with some kind of discreet visual signal to let your child know when she needs to slow her speech down.

PROSODY

Prosody is the general term for the rhythm, pitch, and inflection (rise and fall) of speech. In English, we use prosody to differentiate between statements and questions, with our voice going up at the end of a question and down for a statement. Prosody carries the emotional quality and musicality in your speech.

When someone has difficulty with prosody, we say that they are speaking in a monotone. Although some children with Down syndrome have difficulty with the prosody of speech, there has not been any research that describes the prosodic patterns. In speech therapy, the SLP

may work with your child to bring prosody into her awareness. He or she may have your child speak as if she is singing an opera, or have her say phrases with different prosodic patterns—for example, with an upward inflection for a question. Then, they will practice appropriate prosodic patterns.

HOME ACTIVITIES FOR PROSODY
- Help your child learn more about the musicality of language by singing words as a game, as if you were in an opera. For instance, sing, "Good morning. How are you?" with a lilting, upward inflection. Or sing, "I had a terrible day!" with a dramatic, downward inflection.

- If your child can read, have her read a few sentences aloud to you without "expression" or with "expression." You guess which one she is doing. Then you read aloud with or without expression (in a real monotone). When you are reading books with your child, enthusiastically point out whenever she is reading aloud with expression.

- To bring prosody into your child's awareness, play a game with your child in which you have to say everything like robots (in a monotone) for three minutes or so. Set an alarm, and when it goes off, you have to speak like people again. When the alarm goes off again, switch back to being robots.

- Get a voice recorder such as the Voice Scrambler by Wild Planet Toys, which has settings to change your voice to sound like a baby, chipmunk, robot, etc. Play your child's voice or your voice back normally and then robotically. See if she can hear the difference.

FLUENCY

Fluency refers to the smoothness and flow of speech. When someone has dysfluencies or stuttering, they may have *blocks*—the jaw, lips, and tongue seem to lock in place and the child struggles but can't get the sound out. They may also have *repetitions*—the child is trying to say the first sound in a word but repeats the sound over and over and can't move on. Stuttering in children with Down syndrome may be related to "neurogenic stuttering," which means that it is related to neurological transmission in the brain and the chemicals involved in that transmission.

During evaluation, the SLP will try to determine your child's patterns: Does she block or repeat on specific sounds? in specific situations? Does she tighten specific muscles when she is breathing for speech? Once the SLP has described your child's patterns, she will work on the specific areas that your child needs help with. The method that we generally use in the clinic is to teach children to move their tongue, lips, and jaw in a relaxed and gentle manner and to close them in a smooth and relaxed way. This is known as *gentle onset*. Once the child can use the gentle onset method with single words, the focus shifts to practicing that skill in daily conversation.

Although current therapy methods can help children with Down syndrome learn to better control their fluency, the underlying difficulties often remain. We still have more to learn to successfully treat fluency difficulties in children with Down syndrome.

HELPING YOUR CHILD WITH FLUENCY AT HOME

What should you do when your child is stuttering and you know what she wants to say but she is not getting the words out? It is best to just wait. Keep eye contact and wait for your child to speak. If your child blocks on certain sounds, try not to inadvertently encourage her to avoid that sound, for instance, by suggesting alternative words with the same meaning she could use.

The goal is to promote successful experiences, so that your child will realize that although there are times when she is not fluent, this does not define her speech and her being. She is a person who sometimes stutters, not a stutterer. Here are some ways to build up her feelings of success:

- Usually, children have less difficulty and are more fluent when singing and when reading than when they are speaking. You might tape record your child while singing and then play back the fluent speech.
- Look for other situations that will promote and help your child practice fluency. For example, if your child enjoys reading aloud and is more fluent when reading, perhaps she can read a story to younger children during the school day or at a day care center after school each week.

How Long Do Children with Down Syndrome Need Speech Treatment?

During the elementary school years, most children with Down syndrome can benefit from speech therapy for articulation, oral motor difficulty, Childhood Apraxia of Speech, fluency, and voice or resonance problems. In adolescence, therapy sessions may involve repetitive practice related to these same issues. Once they reach their teens or young adulthood, some young people with Down syndrome may be more willing to be responsible for practice sessions. That is, they may be motivated to improve their intelligibility for their own sake or to promote friendships and relationships, not just to please their families or to earn a sticker.

Studies have shown that people with Down syndrome can continue to improve their speech into young adulthood and beyond. So, if your older child or teenager is motivated to work on her speech, ensuring that she continues to receive speech-language therapy can be very valuable.

Sometimes, however, as children with Down syndrome enter their teens, they are no longer receptive to treatment—perhaps because it makes them feel different in a bad way when they are pulled out of the classroom to do therapy. In adolescence, people with Down syndrome, just like other people, don't want to be reminded of what is difficult for them. They may also be "burned out" on therapies and need a break. Also, parents may ask to have therapy suspended—for instance, if they think their child loses too much instructional time or because the school-based therapy hasn't been especially effective and home activities are never sent home. Sometimes a teen who has lost interest in therapy will become more interested in improving her speech after she leaves school and has a job or is involved in community activities.

Table 6-2: Speech Therapy Across the Lifespan

Below is a general roadmap of the skills children with Down syndrome need to work on in therapy at different stages in life. Not all individuals with Down syndrome will need therapy for all of these areas, but most could benefit from therapy in many of these areas. Regular speech evaluations can help to assure you that your child is receiving appropriate therapy for her individual needs. The ideal situations would be to have a speech-language pathology consultant who can advise you at all stages and suggest appropriate home communication experiences.

I. Early Childhood (ages 4-7)
  a. Chewing and eating
  b. Drinking
  c. Hearing
  d. Sensory processing
  e. Oral motor skills
  f. Combining sounds into words
  g. Increasing repertoire of sounds (articulation)
  h. Phonological processes
  i. Childhood Apraxia of Speech

II. Later Childhood (ages 8-12)
  a. Combining sounds into longer words
  b. Increasing repertoire of sounds (articulation)
  c. Phonological processes
  d. Childhood Apraxia of Speech
  e. Oral motor skills
  f. Fluency
  g. Rate
  h. Resonance
  i. Myofunctional (tongue thrust) therapy

III. Adolescence to Adulthood (ages 13-21)
  a. Using sounds in longer conversational speech
  b. Childhood Apraxia of Speech
  c. Oral motor skills
  d. Fluency
  e. Rate
  f. Resonance
  g. Myofunctional (tongue thrust) therapy

As your child nears transition age (by age sixteen or sometimes before) her IEP team will need to include goals and services to prepare her for life after high school. For example, she might need goals for intelligibility or to develop survival speech skills for social and work situations. As your child enters the transition phase, your child's SLP will ideally consult with people in the community (such as job trainers) to find out what your child needs to learn. Then the SLP would focus on the speech skills, vocabulary, etc. that your child needs to learn to succeed outside of school.

At any age, if your child cannot use speech to meet her communication needs, augmentative communication should be considered. Augmentative communication devices—with or without speech synthesizers—can enable a child whose speech is unintelligible to find her "voice" and to communicate with the people in her world. The need for support and assistive technology to enhance classroom learning and participation should also be considered. If your child's speech cannot be understood, she may require the assistance of a classroom aide. She may need modifications in the curriculum to enable her to respond in a mode other than speech, and to complete projects such as oral book reports through another channel. For more information on augmentative and alternative communication, see Chapter 10.

Conclusion

Speech treatment must be individually planned for each child or teen with Down syndrome. The treatment plan should be based on the results of the comprehensive evaluation, and should address each of the areas in which your child is experiencing difficulty. See the treatment planning form in the Appendix. Remember that different therapy approaches are used for articulation difficulties than for phonological process problems, although your child may need to work on both areas. Also remember that you, as a parent, should be an equal member of the team designing a treatment program for your child. Your participation in your child's home therapy program is essential if your child is going to make good progress in speech and language skills. You are an important partner.

Always be sure that your child has a way to communicate while she is still learning to speak intelligibly. After she is using speech, note whether there are situations where she is not understood and be sure that she has a supplementary or alternative system to ensure that her message will be understood. For more information on augmentative and alternative communication, see Chapter 10.

We need to learn more about speech intelligibility, so that we help children and adults with Down syndrome communicate better. It is important to understand the complex factors that affect our judgment of intelligibility, and to evaluate and treat the factors that affect the intelligibility of the individual child or adult. As children and adults are included within school, the workplace, and the community, being able to be understood is increasingly important. When you can speak intelligibly, more opportunities come your way. Given more opportunities, you have more chances to show what you can do, and even more interesting jobs and activities may be available to you. This, in turn, improves the quality of your life.

CHAPTER 7

Communication Skills at School

Jocelyn likes to do everything well. She was very successful in kindergarten and really liked her kindergarten teacher. Now, it is the beginning of the year in first grade and Jocelyn has been coming home crying most days. She hates first grade. Her papers come home with many red Xs. On some worksheets, you are supposed to circle the answer, but on others, you are supposed to draw a line between two pictures, or put an X on the one that doesn't belong. She is often confused about what she is supposed to do, and when she does the wrong thing, the teacher seems angry.

Brandon loved first and second grade. In third grade, he began having stomach aches in the morning. He tells his mom that he can't go to school because he's too sick. Mom has noticed that, on vacation and snow days, he feels just fine. The teacher has said that Brandon is so good in class. He's quiet and never gives her trouble, but he doesn't complete the assignments.

Samantha is in fourth grade. She rides the school bus every morning, but is usually crying by the time she arrives at school. Some of the other fourth graders are bullying her and calling her "Four-Eyes" because she wears glasses. Samantha doesn't know what to say to them.

Allen is in fifth grade. He loves to be with other children in school, but he gets into trouble because he pushes other kids at recess. The teacher has observed the class on the playground, and she reports that Allen is tugging on the other kids' arms or patting their backs. He really isn't pushing them. She thinks he needs to know how to ask someone to play with him, or ask whether he can join their group playing a game.

Hannah is in the seventh grade. This year, she and her mom have been getting into battles about homework. She forgets to write down assignments, and her notebooks are a mess. Hannah wants help, but when her mom tries to help, she says her mom is doing it wrong. There is too much homework to be done in middle school, and each teacher wants the assignments completed in different ways.

As children enter elementary school and begin spending hours of their day in the classroom, the ability to communicate with teachers and classmates and to learn from the written and spoken word becomes of paramount importance. For many children with Down syndrome, however, the school setting is fraught with communication problems. All of the situations above reflect typical difficulties that children with Down syndrome experience with communication, language, and speech skills at school.

School is based on language. Walk through the halls and look into the classrooms. Teachers are giving instructions. Students are reading books and completing worksheets. They are working together on a team project and talking with each other. One student feels sick and tells the teacher. She sends him to the health room, and the first question he is asked is, "What hurts you?" and he is expected to answer. At school, students are expected to listen, understand, and speak. Classroom interactions, class assignments, and daily instruction rely heavily on verbal interaction skills. Even the instructions for lining up and for boarding the bus rely on language.

Skills Needed for Success in School

Educators have lists of the skills that are needed for school success. Language and communication skills affect each of these areas. Communication skills that have been identified as important to school success are:

1. **Appropriate behavior** (This is often related to communication skills. All behavior communicates something important)

2. **Following rules and routines** (When a child does not follow the rules, it is usually blamed on his unwillingness to follow the rules. Hearing loss and sensory processing disorder, as well as auditory memory problems, are underlying factors that need to be considered)

3. **Flexibility** (Is the child able to adapt when rules and situations change, such as during assemblies or fire drills or when he needs to transition from one activity to another—from reading to math or from lunch to physical education)
   - Able to deviate from routines when necessary, and
   - Able to make transitions.

4. **Receptive language skills**
   - Has good listening skills
   - Able to follow teacher instructions
   - Able to follow long, complex directions
   - Able to recognize when there is a communication breakdown and what needs repair

5. **Expressive language skills**
   - Able to answer questions
   - Able to ask for help
   - Able to ask questions
   - Able to share information verbally
   - Knows how to introduce and sustain topics
   - Able to request clarification when direction is unclear
   - Able to repair conversational breakdowns
   - Able to change registers to communicate with peers & school personnel (uses language appropriate for the situation)

6. **Interpersonal skills**
   - Participates in peer routines at lunch, recess, and in class
   - Able to interact verbally and socially with peers
   - Able to interact verbally with adults
   - Able to decode and understand the teacher's nonverbal cues
   - Understands turn-taking rules
   - Takes turns appropriately in conversation
   - Knows how to request a turn
   - Uses appropriate greetings for different situations
   - Focuses attention on speaker/eye contact
   - Understands the background that someone brings to communication (knows the level and amount of information the listener needs or the speaker needs to provide)

7. **Academic skills**
   - Understands the teacher's expectations for performance in an activity
   - Understands the teacher's expectations for the form and complexity of a response
   - Completes assignments well and in a timely manner
   - Uses appropriate learning strategies
   - Uses effective organizational skills
   - Knows test-taking strategies
   - Uses textbooks and reference books effectively

In addition, students need to understand and use the language of the curriculum in classroom, homework, and testing situations. Textbooks and testing procedures rely heavily on language abilities in speaking and writing, listening, and following instructions that are presented verbally. Schools tend to focus on the areas of language and mathematics. From the earliest years--when reading and math skills are emphasized--to the late high school years--when students take the SAT, ACT, and other post-secondary admissions tests--results are scored as language and quantitative skills. The conclusion is that schools consider language and mathematics as the most important skill areas.

Why Students with Down Syndrome Struggle with Communication Skills at School

As you can see by reading the long list of skills, students need abilities in both receptive language (comprehension) and expressive language to succeed. As in other areas of life, children with Down syndrome usually have fewer problems with comprehending language at school than with using language to express themselves. But even in the earliest years of school, many students with Down syndrome struggle with receptive language skills such as following spoken instructions due to difficulties with auditory memory.

As children progress through the grades, the language in school becomes increasingly more abstract and more complex. Teachers and textbooks provide fewer visual cues, and instructions for assignments rely on grammatical structures that are difficult for children with weaknesses in morphosyntax to understand. For example, even if a child with Down syndrome knew the answer, he might not be able to understand a question that is phrased like this: "Discuss the reasons that the colonists did not want to move westward."

Academic language relies on subtle language distinctions, such as *primary* and *secondary,* or *most important* and *least important* that can be difficult for children with Down syndrome to grasp. Watching others and doing what they are doing—which is often how children with Down syndrome cope in community activities such as Scouts or sports activities—is frowned on at school. In school, you usually are not allowed to look at what everyone else is doing. That's copying and cheating. School is more competitive than cooperative. Even when children work together in a group assignment, the end goal is to get a high grade.

For the educators and researchers who compile the lists of skills needed for school success, it goes without saying that they expect students to be able to communicate intelligibly with teachers and peers. Unfortunately, as discussed in Chapters 4 and 6, speech intelligibility is a problem for many children with Down syndrome in the elementary and middle school years. Your child may have good language skills. But if people can't understand his speech, those people will usually stop listening. Adults will nod their heads, and make general comments, pretending to understand what your child is saying even when they don't. Children are more blunt, and will probably say, "I can't understand you."

When adolescents are using slang and colloquialisms and more abstract language in long conversations, it is difficult for adolescents with Down syndrome to keep up with the conversation and take their turns. Class discussions in middle school are often abstract. What we have seen at our clinic is that some older children and adolescents begin to stutter at that time. We don't know if this has to do with coordinating the breathing, voice, and speech movements for longer utterances or if it is related to taxing the system when both language and speech are complex, or if it is related to stress, avoidance, and anxiety.

Handling Communication Difficulties at School

The communication skills identified above as essential for school success can be categorized in several ways. In *Classroom Language Skills for Children with Down Syndrome* (Woodbine House, 2001), I discuss many of the language skills in detail, in chapters focusing on:

- the language of the curriculum,
- the language of instruction,
- the language of the hidden curriculum,
- the language of educational testing,
- the language of classroom routines, and
- social interactive communication.

In this book, however, I do not have the luxury of devoting so much space to language issues at school, and I also need to focus on speech issues at school since this book covers both speech and language. Consequently, in this chapter I will focus on the broad types of speech and language skills listed above that are most often problematic for students with Down syndrome aged about 6 to 14. These include:

- Following rules and routines,
- Following instructions for assignments,
- Asking and answering questions,
- Requesting help and clarification,
- Understanding the language of the curriculum,
- Using language socially (pragmatics),
- Understanding abstract language on tests and in the curriculum.

UNDERSTANDING RULES AND ROUTINES

FOLLOWING
RULES,
ROUTINES, AND
INSTRUCTIONS

To follow classroom routines and rules, your child needs to be able to follow directions and understand the expectations for classroom discipline related to behavior and speaking in class. Classroom routines might include getting to class on time, sitting in your seat ready to work, beginning a task, staying on task, and completing a task, shifting tasks as indicated by the teacher, lining up and dismissal procedures, and lunch, assembly, and fire drill procedures. There might also be routines related to when to talk and when not to talk, and how to work in cooperative learning groups.

Understanding routines and rules is basically a receptive language and memory skill. Most children with Down syndrome are relatively good at this skill when the rules and routines remain constant. In fact, many children with Down syndrome thrive on routine. Transitions, however, are more difficult. Shifting tasks or finishing up one subject area and shifting to the next are often major problems.

In the classroom, there are often models for behavior and lists of rules. This can be helpful for children who can read and those who learn best from visual models, which is true for most children with Down syndrome. So, children with Down syndrome often learn classroom routines very well. Then, why do they get into trouble in class for not following routines? For one thing, once children with Down syndrome learn a routine, it can be difficult to get them to deviate from it. So, when the teacher changes the routine—for instance, by altering the order of the subjects or making room for a speaker in the schedule—children with Down syndrome may have difficulty adapting.

Visual Schedules. Visual schedules are very helpful for children with Down syndrome, especially when there is a change in schedule and the teacher can point out the difference. What we have found works well in therapy sessions is to have a written or picture list of activities, depending on the child's age. To make the picture schedule, we select photographs or line drawings to represent each activity, cut them to the same size, and laminate them or cover them with clear packing tape. We then attach one piece of Velcro to the back of each picture and the matching piece of Velcro to the schedule. At the beginning of the session, all the activity photos are attached to the schedule, with the first one to be completed on the far left. (Schedules can also be constructed vertically so that the child reads the schedule from top to bottom.) When the child finishes the activity, he removes the picture of that activity, and puts it in the completed folder. All activities need to be completed in that session.

For an older child or teen, it may be important for the teacher to post the schedule of activities for the day or period on the board, or to be given a written list of the tasks to accomplish that day or period. Children who can read can check off, or place a sticker next to, each activity as it is completed.

Social Stories. For children who have great difficulty dealing with changes in routine, it may be helpful for the teacher or aide to make a Social Story to read on days when there are changes to the routine. (See Chapter 8 for information on Social Stories.) In this situation, collaboration between the classroom teacher and the speech-language pathologist could have many benefits. The SLP could write a Social Story about situations in which your child needs to make transitions, emphasizing the need for flexibility and change. The SLP could read the story with your child and the other children in therapy and discuss how you behave appropriately in those situations.

Modeling Behavior. Understanding the language of classroom routines will be most difficult for children at the beginning of the school year. And routines will be more difficult for children with Down syndrome if the teacher gives verbal instructions to explain what to do, rather than modeling or showing what to do. Routines often involve long strings of verbal instructions that may be difficult for children with Down syndrome to follow. But, routines are repeated frequently, so there are visual models and many opportunities for practice.

You may want to ask the teacher to set up a buddy system to help your child learn routines. In the lower grades, children are often eager to volunteer for such a special assignment. Your child can then model what his buddy is doing—such as putting completed math papers in the blue folder attached to the bulletin board. Your child could also learn routines by modeling the classroom aide, if there is one.

FAILURE TO FOLLOW ROUTINES

The language of routines includes classroom behavior and the teacher's expectations for what is appropriate in the classroom. You have probably heard that behavioral difficulties are often forms of communication. When a child does not follow a routine that he has learned, he is trying to communicate something to us. For example, the teacher may indicate that it is time for students to close their math books and take out their reading books. If your child doesn't change over from one subject to another, he knows he will get into trouble. And yet he may not do what the teacher asks. There may be many reasons: he has not finished the math problems, he doesn't like the story the class is doing in reading, there was a lot of noise in the hall and he didn't hear the instructions, or he has a headache and feels itchy from a label in his shirt. We always need to ask what it is that the behavior is telling us.

If your child has good expressive language skills, the teacher can ask him directly why he is deviating from the routine. But many children with Down syndrome, especially in early elementary school, do not have the speech skills to explain their actions and may not even understand *why* questions. In this situation, both the teacher and your child can grow increasingly frustrated, and your child can end up trying to communicate with behavior that the teacher considers "bad" or inappropriate. If your child often gets in trouble for inappropriate behavior, you should request that the school conduct a Functional Behavior Assessment (FBA). (See box below.) You may want to ask the school to use the form for *Describing and Analyzing Behavior* (in the Appendix) to help develop a Behavioral Plan for your child.

UNDERSTANDING INSTRUCTIONS

When long strings of verbal instructions are given, it is difficult for children with Down syndrome to understand and follow the instructions. As explained in Chapter 2, auditory memory is a significant weakness for most children with Down syndrome. They may also process information much slower than the teacher is used to. As a result, they may not respond soon enough for her liking. Children with Down syndrome can also have difficulties with attention or hearing the teacher's voice against a noisy background. For example:

> *When Isabel was in kindergarten, the teacher called her mother one day to express concerns about Isabel's language comprehension. She wasn't sure that Isabel could understand her when she told the class to line up and follow her to the cafeteria. Isabel had gotten left behind in the classroom that day because she had failed to follow these instructions. In fact, Isabel was completely capable of understanding the teacher's instructions but had been engrossed in coloring and was not paying attention. Her mother told the teacher that Isabel often tuned out instructions unless someone said her name to get her attention first. Once the teacher started*

What is a Functional Behavior Assessment?

As the name suggests, the purpose of a functional behavior assessment (FBA) is to assess the function (purpose) of a behavior. Done properly, it can be a very useful tool to unravel the reasons for a problematic behavior and point the way to more appropriate communication for the child. It should never be proposed as some kind of punishment or last-ditch resort before the child is removed to a more restrictive placement. The FBA should lead to a positive behavior intervention plan (PBIP) to help reinforce good behavior and extinguish behavior that is noncompliant or troublesome.

The theory behind FBAs is that all behavior has a purpose, and that children who are less verbal often use their behavior to communicate. According to behavior analysts, the broad messages that children attempt to communicate are often:

- I want attention.
- I want to escape from a demand or situation. (I don't want to do this.)
- I want a particular thing.
- This feels good to me.

When an FBA is conducted properly, everyone who has witnessed the child's problematic behavior provides information related to:

- the antecedents (what happens before the behavior),
- the behavior, and
- the consequences (what happens after).

For example, perhaps there is a point every day when James flops down on the classroom floor and refuses to budge. What happens before this behavior? (What are the antecedents?) Does the teacher announce that it's time for math? Has James just come in from running around at recess? Are other children being chosen to collect papers, but not James? etc. It is also important to figure out what the setting events are. That is, what situations make the behavior more likely to occur for a given child? Examples of setting events in school are a change in schedule, a fight on the bus on the way to school, or a headache. Who is present when the behavior occurs? Who is absent when the misbehavior

occurs? (Does James only flop down when the classroom aide is out of the room?) Clearly describe the behavior that occurs, providing any details that are observable.

Next, look at the consequences of the behavior. What is occurring that reinforces the child for his behavior and makes him want to do it again? What happens once James is flopped down on the floor? Do many adults and children come over to James and cajole him to get up? Does he get to sit there while the other children have to do math? Does the teacher call his mother and get her to talk to him on the phone?

Someone who is trained in FBA (a psychologist, special education professional, etc.) also observes your child to try to get an idea of what triggers the behavior and what your child is gaining through it. Once the person conducting the FBA has an idea of what purpose the behavior is serving your child, he or she proposes alternative ways for your child to communicate his message. For example, perhaps the behavior analyst determines that James is trying to communicate that he needs a break from sitting at his desk writing. He or she could then work with the teacher and the SLP to figure out a more appropriate way for James to communicate this message—perhaps by using a cue or by showing a small card that says "I need a break." For 5 minutes, James can go to the water fountain or walk down to the office and visit with a designated adult. Breaks can be in response to James's indicated need or breaks can be prescheduled. The teacher could add some writing breaks for James into the schedule to keep him from tiring so rapidly—perhaps by having him get up to wipe off the board periodically or by sending him down to the office with a note for the vice principal.

using Isabel's name before giving instructions, there were no further problems with her getting left behind.

Some modifications/accommodations in the classroom that can help students with Down syndrome follow spoken instructions include:

- Keep spoken instructions short. Give one instruction at a time and wait until the child responds before moving on. For example, the teacher says, "Take out your math books." She waits for the child to get his book out and only then says, "Turn to page 25."
- Present spoken instructions slowly.
- Provide pictured or diagrammed instructions.
- Provide demonstrations. If instructions relate to completing written class work or a test, if possible, use a transparency or pass out a sheet with the sample items so that the child can follow along as you explain what to do. For example, if he is answering questions on a worksheet that involves matching, is he supposed to put the letter of the correct response, or draw lines from one column to the other?
- Provide written instructions for students who can read. If instructions are written on the board, make sure they stay up until the child with Down syndrome is done with his work and that he can see them clearly from his seat.
- Tape record directions for the child so he can replay them.
- Have the aide repeat or interpret directions for the child.
- Ask the child to restate the directions to demonstrate his understanding. (This should be done discreetly, so the child is not put on the spot in front of the whole class.)
- Ensure that the child has a way to ask for instructions to be repeated or re-explained. For example, a less verbal child might be given a small placard to hold up that says "Please repeat."
- Seat the child in such a way that it is easy for him to see and hear the teacher and for the teacher to see him.

If your child needs accommodations such as these, they can be written into his IEP. The teacher will then be required to ensure that these adaptations for your child are made (although if there is a classroom aide, he or she may be making some of the adaptations). Be sure that the implementation plan is included in the IEP. The most common reason that adaptations don't happen on a daily basis is that there in no one person designated as the person responsible for them.

In addition to having accommodations to help him follow instructions, your child should also be learning instruction-following skills. That means he should have goals focused on these skills in his IEP. Here are some examples of possible goals:

- Kate will be able to follow spoken instructions using the following concepts: underline, circle, on top of the page, on the bottom of the page, in the upper right hand corner, in the upper left hand corner, by the end of the marking period.
- Samuel will be able to follow instructions involving same and different concepts by December 1.
- Lila will be able to follow 3-stage directions by June 1.

HOME ACTIVITIES FOR FOLLOWING INSTRUCTIONS

- Make a game board from a manila folder (as described on page 189, Chapter 6) to help your child practice following instructions. For example, spaces on the game board might say, "Clap your hands," "Jump 3 times," "Stand up," etc.

- Look for commercially made games that involve following instructions and are right for your family members' ages and stages. For example, *Cranium Hullabaloo* includes an electronic game console that announces instructions such as "Touch your nose to a circle" and "Jump on a square shape." The old standby *Twister* is good for children who are learning their left from their right. ("Put your left hand on green.")

- Play Simon Says. Use increasingly complex instructions as your child gets better at following them. For instance, you can move on to two-step instructions once your child can follow one-step instructions: "Turn around two times, then sit down."

ASKING AND ANSWERING QUESTIONS

To ask or answer questions, either verbally or in writing, requires expressive language skills. Since expressive language is almost always a relative weakness for children with Down syndrome, they often have trouble showing what they know in class by asking and answering questions.

RESPONDING TO QUESTIONS IN CLASS

In elementary and middle school, students are usually asked to respond to

questions in two ways—either verbally or in writing. Both of these modalities can be difficult for children with Down syndrome, who often have fine motor problems in addition to delays in expressive language. Ideally, your child's teacher(s) will make accommodations for your child during class to help him respond to questions; e.g.,

1. Put your name and date in the heading of the page.
2. Include a title for your essay.
3. List at least 3 facts about Columbus the man.
4. Write at least 2 sentences about his discovery of America.
5. Write at least 2 sentences about what Columbus did after he discovered America.
6. Write a conclusion telling why Columbus is remembered.

1. Here are some suggestions to help with instances **when questions are posed verbally, and your child is supposed to respond verbally** (but can also respond with gestures, signs, etc.):

   - The teacher can give your child extra time to come up with his answer. For example, she can tell him before the lessons begins which question she will ask him in class. Or she could say, "In a minute I'm going to come back to you. I will ask you to tell me who wrote the Declaration of Independence."
   - The teacher can rephrase questions so the child only has to answer with a one-word (or signed) response, a short phrase, etc., depending on his expressive language abilities.
   - The teacher can simplify questions to make it clearer what she is asking for. For example, instead of asking, "Which was *not* a reason that settlers moved West?" She could ask "What was one reason the settlers moved West?"
   - The teacher can use visual cues and samples of correct answers. He or she can model how to answer the first questions for your child.

2. Here are some suggestions to help **when questions are posed in writing, and the child is supposed to respond in writing**. (For many more strategies, see *Classroom Language Skills for Children with Down Syndrome*.)

   - Provide multiple choice answers and let the child circle or underline the correct response.
   - Provide a written model showing how to answer the first question.
   - Have the child fill in the blanks rather than write a sentence.
   - Provide a checklist or other organizer to help the child understand what should be included in his answer. For example, a list can be designed to help him focus on what needs to be included in a book report.
   - If the child can read, but not write, provide cut out words that he can choose from and glue to the worksheet. Or explore using a word processor with voice recognition software to write.
   - Use assistive technology to reduce demands on fine motor skills and/or make it easier for the child to communicate in writing. One evaluation system that is used to determine what types of technology could support the child is the SETT (Student, Envi-

ronment, Tasks, Tools) Framework. See the Assistive Technology Report for Alex on page 317 for an idea of how assistive technology can help children with Down syndrome with writing and organizational demands in the classroom.

Again, it is not sufficient simply to provide accommodations to enable your child to better answer questions. If this is a major area of difficulty, his IEP should include goals that will help him learn to answer questions. Examples of goals:

- Martina will be able to answer questions in writing that ask for 2 reasons by March 15.
- Saki will be able to verbally answer questions that ask why an event happened by December 1.
- Lou will be able to answer questions related to what happened by June 1.

ASKING QUESTIONS IN CLASS

Asking questions in class is difficult for many children with Down syndrome. Sometimes, this is related to shyness and not wanting to stand out, especially in middle school. For other children, the reluctance to ask questions may be related to difficulty in formulating *wh* questions, or in knowing what to ask. There are different types of questions, and some teachers are open to one type or another, but not every type of questions. Some types of questions asked in class are: clarification of information, clarification of instructions, and questions on the subject. (See the section below on "Requesting Help or Clarification" for information on those types of questions.)

Your child may be more willing to ask questions in class if his teachers make it clear that they welcome questions. Most teachers welcome questions on the curriculum (the subject matter). For example, they will gladly answer a question such as: "Why did the colonists have all of those extra houses?"

Here is how one middle school science teacher encourages her students to ask questions: She makes preprinted slips of paper that say: "Science Question Card – Awarded for outstanding effort and/or excellent thinking. Because . . . questions are a good thing!" She hands out the slips to students who ask questions in class and periodically allows them to trade the slips in for small rewards like bags of pretzels, bookmarks, or erasers.

If teachers express that your child has trouble asking questions in class, it is important to pinpoint whether your child's problem is related to difficulties phrasing and articulating questions or to reluctance to speak up in class. If your child does not have the language skills to formulate a question, you and the SLP should work with him on *wh* questions, as discussed in Chapter 5. Also see the Home Activities for Asking and Answering Questions, below. If the problem is more related to your child's reluctance to talk in class, see the box below.

ANSWERING QUESTIONS ON TESTS

Unlike with classroom work, where the teacher can make modifications to help your child understand and respond to questions, making modifications to the language may not be allowed during testing situations. This is especially true if your child is

When Children Are Reluctant to Speak in Class

Sometimes a child with Down syndrome may have the ability to ask or answer questions in class, but is reluctant to do so. Some possible reasons include:

- He is shy and doesn't like to talk in front of groups.
- He is anxious and afraid that his answer will be wrong.
- He is conscious that his speech is hard to understand.
- He is afraid he will stutter.
- He has been teased in the past and is afraid children will make fun of him.
- He thinks the teacher may react negatively to his question. For example, perhaps when children ask to have questions repeated, the teacher says things such as, "Why weren't you listening the first time? I'm not going to repeat it." Or, "It's written on the board." Or, "Can't you hear me? Everyone else heard me."

As you can see, these are the same reasons that a typically developing child may hesitate to speak up in class. However, when a child with Down syndrome doesn't speak in class, teachers (and classmates) are probably more likely to conclude that he isn't learning the material. Teachers may stop expecting your child to participate in class if he never answers, and he may eventually begin to tune out.

In this situation, it is important for the teacher to set up situations where the child can contribute in a nonstressful way. For example:

- Ask the child to participate nonverbally. For example, rather than saying the name of a state capital, he can point to the capital on a map.
- Help the child play a leadership role in what he is good at. For instance, if he is a reader, let him check off names on a class list to help the teacher or give out programs at a school event.
- Reward all children for participating in a class discussion.
- Phrase questions asked of the child so that he only has to use one or two words to answer. If he is very shy about speaking in class, begin by asking just yes or no questions that he can answer either verbally or with a nod or head shake. For instance, instead of asking whether a snake is a reptile or amphibian, ask "Is a snake an amphibian? A reptile?"
- Let the child answer in a soft voice, rather than making him speak up loudly enough for the whole class to answer. The teacher can move close to him when he answers.

taking standardized tests or if your school system expects all children who are taking general education classes to take exactly the same tests.

Another reason that answering questions on tests can be difficult for children with Down syndrome is that the language of testing is highly *decontextualized*. That is, there are few, if any, cues in the context to help you figure out what the material is about. On tests, there are generally no illustrations and no manipulatives. You can't look around the room for clues, or follow what other classmates are doing. The words stand alone, and you need to interpret and respond to those words with no cues.

In elementary school, the language of testing may include questions on reading comprehension, topic sentences, appropriate titles for a story, analogies, and word problems. Specific terms such as *underline, circle,* or *mark within the lines* may be used in giving instructions for the test. In later school years, testing may include terms such as: *the reason that, evaluate the factors, the best answer, the one that does not belong, which was not a reason, which was the main reason, what is your hypothesis, analyze the relationship,* etc.

If your child is required to take unmodified tests, it is important that he be systematically taught the vocabulary he will encounter in test instructions. If your child is receiving speech-language therapy at school, you might request an IEP goal such as:

Henry will be able to respond to decontextualized instructions such as [*whatever is appropriate for his grade level*] with 80% accuracy in test taking situations.

When developing your child's IEP, it is also important to determine what modality (channel) will be used for questions and what modality will be used for responding. Will your child write an answer, circle, fill in a bubble, or answer verbally? IDEA states that testing should be conducted in the child's language that he uses every day. Can your child respond when the test stimulus items are spoken? When they are in written form? When your child responds, can he use speech, typing, writing, multiple choice pointing?

Testing Accommodations for Students Who Use AAC Systems

Each local educational agency or state department of education should have guidelines indicating the testing accommodations that are typical and approved. However, so far many agencies have overlooked accommodations for AAC users. Parents, teachers, and related service personnel need to discuss the purpose for testing for the student and the accommodations he may need to be successful.

The language of IDEA suggests that testing accommodations should include allowing your child to use his typical mode of communication to respond to tests. If your child is using an AAC system, this should be considered a part of his "typical mode of communication" when determining how test questions will be presented and responded to. Some examples of accommodations include:

- Presenting test items through a communication board or with picture symbols;
- Providing written directions rather than verbal;
- Interpreting verbal instructions with sign language;
- Reading test questions aloud to the student;
- Using text-to-speech software to compose answers; and
- Responding with an AAC voice output system.

The need for possible accommodations and modifications to tests are discussed in IDEA 2004 and No Child Left Behind legislation. The list of accommodations and alternate testing procedures is still developing, even though state departments of education have developed plans and lists of approved accommodations. Be prepared to ask questions regarding your child's participation in these assessments and what accommodations can be made if he uses an AAC system. If the members of your child's IEP team can't answer your questions, request that they refer your questions to school system administrators or even the state board of education.

HOME ACTIVITIES FOR ASKING AND ANSWERING QUESTIONS

- Ask your child's teacher what kinds of questions your child is expected to answer in class, or look at the written work he brings home. Does he need to answer *true/false* or *fact/opinion* questions? Is he asked to *summarize* things in his own words? Whatever the vocabulary, try to find ways to work it into your daily conversations with your child and other family members: "Well, you may think the Ravens are the best football team. But that's just your opinion! In *my* opinion...." Or: "It's a long story. Let me *summarize* what happened."

- Reinforce your child for asking and answering questions at home. Let him know that this is a valuable skill and that he can do it. For instance, sometimes when he asks you something, reply "Good question! Let's ask Dad." Or praise his answering abilities: "That's an interesting answer!"

- Make sure your child feels as if his questions are welcome. If at all possible, don't act exasperated by his questions, even if you don't have time to deal with them at the moment. Instead, say something like: "That's an important question. I'll answer it after dinner when I have more time."

- If he doesn't use complete sentences or spoken words to ask questions, model the complete question for him. For example, if he says "Mall?" or "Go Mall?" try to model the words he would use. So you would say "Are you telling me 'I want to go to the mall?'" rather than "Do you want to go to the mall?" Or if he gestures to the mashed potatoes on the table indicating he wants more, model "More?" for him, if he is able to say one word, "More potatoes?" if he is able to say two words, etc.

- Play 20 Questions. First let your child think of something, and you ask questions, trying to guess what he is thinking of. You can either use one question structure to help your child learn that structure (for example, "Is it an animal?" "Is it hot?" "Is it something in our house?"). Or you can vary the types of questions you ask to expand your child's knowledge of structures: "Can you eat it?" "Does it come in different colors?" "Have you seen one?" "Would you like to have one of these?" Then, switch roles and let your child ask questions about what you are thinking about. Traditionally, the questioner is supposed to ask "yes" or "no" questions, but you can allow all sorts of questions if that is easier or more useful for your child. ("Where does it live?" "What color is it?" "How big is it?")

- Have your child interview friends and family members just for fun. Have him tape record or videotape their answers if he enjoys using technology. Help your child think of the questions to ask beforehand. For instance:
    - What's your favorite sport?
    - What's your favorite team?

> ○ Who's your favorite player?
> ○ What's your favorite tv show?
> ○ What's your favorite movie?
>
> ● Do the activities related to *wh* questions included in Chapter 5.

REQUESTING HELP AND CLARIFICATION

In class, children need to be able to ask for clarification if they do not understand the instructions, and to ask for help if they do not know how to answer a question, do the exercise, open a pudding cup at lunch, etc. If your child cannot use speech to do this, or if his speech is not understandable, he needs another way of asking for clarification, making repairs, and asking for help. The SLP, family, special educator, and classroom teacher can collaborate to determine whether a small card or a visual cueing system might be most effective for your child. For example, he might be taught to make the sign for help or hold up a small card that says, "Please help." Raising his hand is usually not sufficient because children raise their hands for so many different things, and teachers often say, "Put your hands down."

If your child needs to learn to ask for help, this should be included as a goal in his IEP so teachers and other staff can help him work on the skill in the natural environment (the classroom). Here is an example of how this goal might be worded for children of different ages and abilities:

- For a less verbal child who can't use speech to ask for help, an IEP goal might be: Devon will ask for help at appropriate times using his help card 90% of the time by the end of the marking period.
- For a more verbal child who can use speech to ask for help, an IEP goal might be: Cheryl will say "I need help" when she does not understand the instructions 90% of the time by May 1.

In addition, if your child is likely to require repetition of instructions, simplified instructions, written instructions in addition to spoken instructions, or any other change to the way instructions are given in class, this should be spelled out as an accommodation in his IEP. That way, your child's need for additional clarification will be documented and teachers will be less likely to respond impatiently when he requests help or clarification.

In addition to understanding *how* to ask for help or clarification, children with Down syndrome also need to understand that it is okay to ask for help. This is a big issue for many children. In early elementary years, children are often too timid to ask for help. Some children are so shy that they barely speak above a whisper when called on in class, and do not initiate any kind of talk with a teacher or classroom aide, much less ask for help when they need it. In later grades, children may not ask for help because they don't want to be seen as different or less competent than their classmates. If other students are doing the assignment and seem to understand it, they may not want to raise their hands and admit they don't know what to do or that they need more time to work.

One eighth grader got a number of zeroes in a general education reading class because she didn't understand the instructions on written assignments, but would not ask for clarification. Instead, she would either do the assignment wrong or not finish it. She brought many unfinished papers home and her mother would look at them with her and ask why she didn't finish them. Then she would tell her mother—in an extremely articulate way—what she didn't understand about the directions. Her mother would explain what she needed to do, and then she would complete the assignment and turn it in late and get downgraded for lateness.

The only way that children will feel free to ask for help is when they know that they will not be penalized or ridiculed for asking for that help. We all need help, at times, but feel reluctant to ask for that help if we are afraid that we will be "punished" by lowered grades, negative comments, or other consequences that we would rather avoid. A buddy tutor can sometimes be helpful, but the relationship needs to be set up so that the tutor and the child being helped do not get disciplined for talking when they are trying to work together. Asking for help is a difficult issue.

In the next chapter, there is a fuller discussion of conversational breakdowns, requests for clarification, and repairs. These are skills that can be worked on in speech-language therapy sessions.

UNDERSTANDING THE LANGUAGE OF THE CURRICULUM

What is the language of the curriculum? It is the vocabulary and language level of the material included in the curriculum for each subject. For example, what specific language concepts does the child need to know to master the objectives for fourth grade social studies and science? There are differences from one subject to another. There are also differences between different grade levels. For example, a first grade textbook is much more likely to have pictures and other visual cues than an eighth grade textbook is. A science textbook is more likely to have diagrams and charts than a literature book is.

For children without disabilities, their success in school is largely determined by how well they master the language of the curriculum in each subject. That is, if they do not learn the grade-level vocabulary and concepts in a particular subject, they will fail the class. Children with Down syndrome are often not expected to learn all, or even most, of the language of the general education curriculum—depending on the goals in their IEPs. However, if they are included in general education classes, they need to understand enough of the curriculum to meet their individual goals in each subject and to participate meaningfully in class. If they are not in inclusive classes for some or all subjects, there will still be specific vocabulary and concepts they are expected to master.

Children with Down syndrome tend to have the most difficulty with the language of the curriculum when there are no visual or environmental cues to the meaning. For example, science and physical education are usually hands-on and provide many contextual cues during instruction. Social studies and language arts generally involve more lecture, fewer visual cues and models, and more use of language in which there are no environmental cues (decontextualized language). In science, when the teacher is talking about a seed, the child is likely to be looking at or holding a seed. In social studies, when the teacher is talking about the colonists, there are many fewer cues in the environment. This decontextualized language is much more difficult for children with Down syndrome.

Another way to put this is that children with Down syndrome have trouble with abstractions—with understanding terms such as *democracy, culture, economy, imperialism, mass, energy, theme,* and *motivation* that can't be visualized. Time concepts are particularly difficult for many students with Down syndrome to grasp, so it follows that "when" questions will be hard for them to answer. These questions are even more difficult when the topic relates to another time or era. So, a class unit on nineteenth century America may be difficult to understand.

In addition to having difficulties understanding abstract language in the curriculum, children with Down syndrome often have more trouble with polysyllabic words that may be hard for them to read, spell, say, or remember—regardless of whether the concepts are abstract or not. For example, they may struggle to learn and understand words such as *metamorphosis, photosynthesis, alliteration,* and *capitalism.*

COLLABORATIVE CONSULTATION

Your child's teachers should work with you to identify the language of the curriculum that your child may struggle with and develop strategies to help him learn it. Ideally, since language is so integrally involved with learning the curriculum, the speech-language pathologist and the special educator should be following up on this information and designing exercises, worksheets, and experiences that will help your child learn the concepts that he is expected to master in each subject.

How can the classroom teacher, SLP, and special educator collaborate to help your child progress in the curriculum? The classroom teacher is the specialist on curriculum—that is, what children in her class need to learn. The special educator has knowledge in adapting and modifying learning experiences and behavior based on a child's strengths and limitations. The SLP has knowledge about speech and language and has experience in observing, analyzing, and modifying speech and language for both the speaker and the listener (your child and the teacher).

In the collaborative model, the SLP might help the classroom teacher learn how best to give instructions to your child, how to adapt language on written worksheets, or how to design visual cueing instruction sheets that can help your child complete written work or follow classroom instructions. For example, many math worksheets use complex language. Often, when your child has difficulty with word problems, he can actually do the math that is required but he can't figure out what he is being asked to do. The SLP can work with the teacher and often with the classroom aide to help modify worksheets.

In addition, the teachers and SLP can collaborate to help your child master vocabulary that he is responsible for learning. For example, the teachers might let the SLP know ahead of time what vocabulary your child needs to learn so that the SLP can pre-teach those words to him in therapy. The teacher can also share word lists from textbooks with the SLP.

Another circumstance where it is critical for the SLP, special educator, and the classroom teacher to work together is when a puzzling problem behavior arises. If your child cannot explain what the problem is, the SLP and teachers might work together to determine what he might be communicating through behavior. They can then come up with a positive behavior intervention plan that will consider the relationship between communication and behavior for your child. In addition, they can identify communication skills to include on your child's IEP that he can use instead of the problem behavior.

The special educator can work with the teacher to modify curricular expectations through the IEP process. The classroom teacher will know what the curricular expectations are for children at your child's grade level, but the IEP will specify what the goals are for your child for that year. When the class is working on a unit about Latin America, your child's responsibilities may be to learn about the products of the country, while the class may be expected to memorize additional information about the government, population, and products.

For more on school-based language skills, see *Classroom Language Skills for Children with Down Syndrome* (Kumin, 2001).

THE PARENT'S ROLE IN TEACHING THE LANGUAGE OF THE CURRICULUM

Parents often need to take the lead in making sure their child's teachers and SLP understand that their child needs extra work on language of the curriculum, and

that someone needs to be continually making lists of words in each subject that he will be responsible for learning. Ideally, you might meet with teachers and the SLP at the beginning of the school year to discuss these issues and determine who is going to make these lists, how, and when. During the school year, every time the class starts a new unit in science or social studies, how will the parent, SLP, or other person responsible for making the list find out what words the child needs to learn? Otherwise, parents often don't find out that a new unit has started until their child brings home homework that he can't understand.

Unfortunately, I have spoken with many parents who have been told that the classroom teacher and the specialists do not have time to make lists of vocabulary words and concepts that their child needs to learn. Instead, it is often left to the parent to review the textbooks and make those lists, and then to send the material to the teacher or SLP. This can occur even if your child's IEP clearly states that it is the responsibility of a teacher, inclusion specialist, or another staff member to teach these concepts. Parents may have to choose between wasting weeks or months arguing with the staff that they must do this preparation for their child or just taking the situation into their own hands and doing the work themselves.

Sometimes, you may be able to get word lists for the next year before summer vacation. If you want to be as proactive as possible, ask for copies of the curriculum for the following school year, late each spring. Many textbooks will have lists of core vocabulary words for each chapter. Over summer vacation, you can then schedule trips, watch videos, and read books with your child that will introduce the vocabulary and concepts that he needs to learn for the coming year. For example, you might take a trip to a colonial village restoration or a swamp or marsh habitat. See the Home Activities for the Language of the Curriculum, below, for more ideas for teaching and reinforcing vocabulary and concepts at home.

MONITORING SPEECH NEEDS

As was discussed in Chapter 3, the purpose of related services such as speech-language therapy is to enable children to make progress in the general education curriculum. As was also discussed, children with Down syndrome are often denied speech services on the grounds that they do not need to be able to speak any better to progress in the curriculum. Clearly, however, it is important to regularly revisit this issue.

Not only do children need to understand the vocabulary for each subject, but to ask and answer questions in class, they need to be able to say the words, as well. (Or else they need an AAC system that enables them to ask and answer questions.) In addition, there may be classes where it is important for them to be able to read aloud intelligibly or to give oral presentations.

There is a need to regularly evaluate the level of speech skill that will be required in your child's classes and then to determine how he can communicate best in the classroom for his subjects. That means that there is also a need to regularly reevaluate whether your child's speech and language services are sufficient, and whether he now needs speech therapy, if he was found ineligible before. Refer back to Chapter 3 for information on requesting a reevaluation.

CLASSROOM STRATEGIES

Here is a sample of classroom strategies that can help students with Down syndrome learn the language of the curriculum. For more ideas, please see *Classroom Language Skills for Children with Down Syndrome*. Books on teaching children with AD/HD also frequently have useful suggestions for making lessons more hands on and visual.

- **Use role playing** when possible to help the student grasp abstract concepts. For example, if the student needs to learn the difference between socialism and capitalism, have class members act out running a business in a socialist country vs. a capitalist county.

- **Use a variety of visual supports.** For example, teachers should write down important words on the board or an overhead projector when they are lecturing, and refer to pictures, charts, or graphs. Or they can use Venn diagrams to clarify the similarities and differences between two concepts.
- **Use hands-on activities** vs. straight lecture whenever possible.
- **Introduce a small number of new concepts at a time.** Relate the concepts to what the child already knows.

- **Give students an overview of the information** before beginning the lesson. This is the "Here is what we are going to do" approach. This helps children focus on the purpose of the lesson. For example, "Today, we are going to learn how the Revolutionary War ended."
- **Give students study questions before they read the material.** Discuss what they need to look for in the textbook. If students are reading about deserts, it helps if they know what information they need to look for. Do they need to know how much rainfall deserts get? About the animals that live there? If they do not know the questions ahead of time, they need to remember all of the information as equally important and try to retrieve all of the information. This is very difficult for most children with Down syndrome.
- **Highlight important points to be learned.** For example, underline or use a color highlighter to draw attention to important information on worksheets or have the child do it.
- **Cue students in to what is really important in the lesson.** The teacher might say, "This is really important. Are you listening?"
- **Talk with the child individually at short intervals** to check whether he is understanding the material. This can be done with a peer partner or a classroom aide.
- **Provide feedback about written class work in a timely manner** to make sure the child is on the right track. For instance, give him feedback after he has completed the first three questions on a worksheet.

HOME ACTIVITIES FOR THE LANGUAGE OF THE CURRICULUM

- **Use music to help your child learn.** If you can create songs or jingles, it may help your child memorize and retrieve information for school. For example, if he needs to learn the order of the planets, you might make up a rap song that helps him remember them. Children who have musical intelligence often have a rhythmical way of speaking, and may unconsciously hum to themselves or tap on the desk as they work. This skill can be used to help children with Down syndrome tap out the number of syllables in a word, or tap to expand the number of words that they use in a sentence.

- **Make up silly mnemonics,** with or without picture illustrations to help your child learn and remember vocabulary words. For example, talk about how an acute angle is a cute little angle smaller than 90 degrees and draw a picture of an acute angle with a smiling face. Or tell your child that the *main* reason the U.S entered the Spanish-American War was because the *Maine* was blown up.

- **Visit science, history, art, and children's museums** and look for concrete objects that can help your child learn about and understand concepts he is learning about. While you are there, browse the museum shop. Museums often have games on specific topics and are good sources for subject-focused activity books, as well. The science center, natural history museums, and American history museums will all carry books geared to children that focus on specific topics.

- To help your child with **map skills needed for social studies:** When you are at the local mall, follow a printed map or directory. Look at the large map on the wall at the mall and then use the small printed brochure map or directory at home to play that you are walking around the shopping mall. Likewise, get a map or directory when you go to the zoo or the museum. Show your child how you figure out how to hold the map depending on where you are standing and the landmarks that are visible.

  When you are planning a trip to a city or to an amusement park, get a map and a directory, and talk about the places you will go. When you are there, use the map to determine the directions you need to walk in— north, southwest, etc. Be sure to point out the legend or key and use it to find things like the restroom. After the trip, include the map in a scrapbook or photo album with your photographs so that you can use it when talking with your child about the things you saw and did.

  When you are planning vacation trips, show your child where you are going on a map. Talk about how you need to drive west for 200 miles and then south for 50, etc. Point out topographical features such as rivers or mountains that you will cross or fly over. Point out the cities and the states or provinces that you will be in, both on the map and when you actually enter and leave them.

- To help your child make real-world connections to **social studies concepts about government:** Around election time, be sure to include your child in discussions about voting, your rights and responsibilities as a citizen, etc. Talk about why there are campaign ads on the TV and in your mailbox. Take your child to your polling place, let him see your ballot, let him witness you casting your vote (if that is allowed in your community). At local parades, wave to the mayor or your congressman as he/she drives by and tell your child what that person's job is. If you're in the state or provincial capital, point out where the governor lives. When your child is spending his own money, talk about the sales tax that makes the price higher and what it's for. These kinds of experiences can help your child understand abstract concepts such as *democracy* and *taxation without representation* he will encounter at school.

- To help teach and reinforce **science vocabulary and concepts,** look for ways to bring the language of the curriculum into your daily life so it's meaningful to your child. For instance, if he is studying weather, talk about whether there will be any *precipitation* today; if he is studying butterflies, point out milkweed in the field where monarchs like to make *cocoons;* if he is studying astronomy, look for *meteors* at night or show him the *constellations* you recognize; if he is learning about Newton's Laws of Motion, tickle him to wake him up in the morning and comment: "Newton was right. A body at rest tends to remain at rest unless acted upon by an outside force!"

- To help your child learn the **parts of speech** he will need to know in reading and English class, play *Mad Libs* (commercially available books where you create a silly story by asking people to give you a noun, adjective, etc. to fill in the blanks). Ask your child for a noun, and then tell him that means a person or thing. Or let him tell you he needs an adjective, and then you say, "OK, you need a word that describes somebody or something. . . . How about SLIMEY?"

  You can also use the game *Apples to Apples, Jr.* to reinforce the difference between nouns and adjectives. This game involves laying down an adjective card (such as *dangerous*) and then putting down the noun card that you think is best described by the adjective (such as *shark*).

USING LANGUAGE SOCIALLY AT SCHOOL

If you look back at the long list of communication skills important to a child's success in school, you will see that not all of them are related to communicating about academics. There are also many social interactive skills related to socializing with peers and adults.

Social interactive communication includes communication with peers and all school personnel (including other teachers, administrators, cafeteria workers, maintenance staff, bus drivers)—in the classroom, at lunch, recess, and on the school bus. At school, we need to make a distinction between speaking for academics in the classroom, and school activities that occur outside of class, which tend to be more social in nature.

Children with Down syndrome are often relatively better with the social use of language than with some other language skills. For instance, many are good with greetings (verbal and nonverbal) and use short phrases such as "awesome" or "no way" appropriately. During school activities such as clubs, children can often rely more on nonverbal communication and scripts. I have met many preteens and teenagers with Down syndrome who are managers of sports teams or participate in after school activities. Often their job is to set up equipment or organize materials for the team. Participation requires smiles and high fives, greeting, and comments, but does not usually require a lot of speaking.

Other areas of social interactive communication can be harder for students with Down syndrome. For example, skills such as knowing how to join a conversation and making appropriate contributions to conversations can be especially problematic. Chapter 8 discusses social language and chapter 9 discusses strategies to help your child with conversational skills. In this section I will focus on some social interaction skills that are specific to the school setting.

BEING INCLUDED IN CONVERSATIONS

All too often, children with Down syndrome are not fully included in their peers' conversations. Sometimes this occurs if a child has little or no intelligible speech, so classmates conclude that he doesn't have much to say. It could also occur if the child with Down syndrome doesn't seem to be interested in, or know much about, the topics his peers talk about. For instance, classmates might be reading and discussing Harry Potter books and movies, but the child with Down syndrome reads simpler books and has never seen a Harry Potter movie. Or the classmates might want to discuss current rock bands, while the child with Down syndrome still prefers Disney songs. An aide can also present a barrier to inclusion in conversations, if peers think they should talk to the child's aide rather than him, or avoid talking to the child since the aide is always sitting by his side. The problem of being excluded from conversations is often worse at school sponsored social events, such as middle school dances, than in the classroom.

Friendship Circles. Friendships are based on common interests and shared activities. One common strategy used to help students with disabilities make social connections is to set up friendship circles. A friendship circle is usually organized by an adult and may be written into the IEP. Peers are invited to join the circle, and then meet as a group, talk about how they can support the child with Down syndrome, and participate in his support network. This is helpful for some children to get the friendship ball rolling, but other families feel that this is akin to paid workers, rather than natural friendships.

Interest Lunch Days. Another strategy that can work in elementary schools is to ask school staff to set up interest lunch days, where tables are set up for children interested in dogs, cats, electronic games, camping, stamp collecting, etc. so that friendships can develop based on common interests. Even children who are not yet speaking can participate in interest lunch tables by bringing in a relevant item to share with others at his table. It is helpful for adults—such as parent volunteers—to monitor the tables to get conversations going on the right track. It's an extra bonus if the participating adult also shares that interest.

Making Sure Aides Don't Hinder Conversations. Aides can be very helpful. They are often involved in modifying worksheets, and in helping your child respond to worksheets when a channel other than speech is used in response. They can assist children who have difficulty with transitions. Sometimes, however, they can block your child from interacting with other people.

In one instance, I observed a twelve-year-old-girl who had very poor speech intelligibility and was very attached to her aide. The aide was obviously very dedicated to the child, and had traveled with the family from her home about 500 miles to be there for the child's evaluation at Loyola University in Maryland. The aide had developed practice materials for the child, when the SLP had refused to work on childhood apraxia symptoms. But throughout the evaluation, the girl sat in the aide's lap and talked to no one else. That aide was not helping the child communicate with the people around her. She was a barrier to communication with anyone but her. In another instance, I observed an aide at school who kept the child's communication cards zipped away in her fanny pack and did not allow the child to use the cards freely to communicate.

If your child receives services from a personal or classroom aide, it is very important to ensure that the aide is not a roadblock to conversation for your child. Here are some suggestions:

- Observe the aide and your child at different times of the day, both during classroom activities and during unstructured times such as recess. Either you or the SLP can make the observations.
- If the aide is communicating for your child, suggest nicely and discreetly that your child needs to get more practice speaking up for himself in class. Perhaps let the aide know how she can prompt your child to communicate on his own and then gradually phase out her prompting. Or, ask your child's SLP to make these same suggestions to the aide.
- If the aide is hovering around your child and discouraging other children from approaching your child, ask the teacher if it would be possible to encourage the aide to circulate around the room to help other children who need assistance, not just your child. Or, discuss how it might benefit your child for the aide to take a break during certain times of the day.

See the next chapter for information on helping your child improve his conversational skills in general.

INFORMAL LANGUAGE

Children and teenagers at school use informal language including slang, abbreviations, and the "in" terms. If "awesome" is the term currently being used, you don't want your child to say "cool" or "rad." If other kids IM each other after school and use abbreviations like MBFF (my best friend forever) in their speech, your child should learn about these abbreviations too.

It is also important for your child to learn what *not* to say. He may pick up culturally inappropriate or outdated language if he watches DVDs or reruns of old series or if he doesn't realize that most kids in his local community don't use the slang that characters on his favorite series use. He also needs to learn which slang will get him in trouble if he uses it at school—"bad words" that he may hear in the locker room or on the bus that shouldn't be used in the classroom.

At home and in speech sessions, members of your child's communication team need to help your child learn the appropriate words for social interaction. Some suggestions for helping at home include:

- Get input from siblings and peers who know what language is "in."
- Don't laugh or smile when your child uses a bad word because that is just likely to encourage him. Instead, give a short negative response, such as: "We don't say that word in our family." But don't give the word a lot of attention.
- At another time, talk to your child about words that can get you into trouble.
- If your child uses AAC, make sure that he has a way to use current slang, not just formal, grown-up language.

THE GOOD NEWS

Studies of children with Down syndrome who are included in regular education classrooms show that they reap many social interactive benefits. One of the benefits of inclusion in schools and in the community is that children with Down syndrome have appropriate peer and adult models, more learning opportunities, and more practice with social interactive communication. We see by watching young adults with Down syndrome today and comparing them with young adults of thirty years ago who were institutionalized or in very restrictive settings what a difference these opportunities have made! Researchers have confirmed that children with disabilities gain from socialization with their peers and make many advances in communication, social skills, and skills for daily living.

IS SPEECH AN EFFECTIVE COMMUNICATION SYSTEM FOR YOUR CHILD?

Some children with Down syndrome enter elementary school using an alternative to speech, such as sign language or the Picture Exchange Communication System (PECS). Ideally these children's IEPs include goals and strategies to enable them to transition to using more speech as they progress through the early elementary grades. Many succeed in making the transition, but others don't. Other children start elementary school using speech as their primary system but then begin to struggle—usually because of speech intelligibility issues.

How do you determine whether speech is meeting your child's communication needs at school? Here are some things to look for:

- signs of frustration,
- signs of withdrawal,
- behavior issues becoming more of a problem, especially if they could be related to ineffective communication,
- unhappiness, especially in the morning when your child is preparing for school.

If you or a teacher are concerned that your child's speech is ineffective, talk to your child's SLP and ask him or her to observe your child in class and provide suggestions for modifications. Observe yourself to see how your child communicates in class. Do you have any insights into any behavior problems that you might notice? Then if behavior issues continue, ask for a functional behavior assessment (see pag 204).

Your Child's Social/Emotional Intelligence

Despite the problems with social interaction skills children with Down syndrome can have at school, these skills are often a relative strength for them. In my experience, children with DS usually are better at interpersonal than intrapersonal skills. These are also referred to as interpersonal and intrapersonal intelligence by Howard Gardner in his works on multiple intelligence.

Interpersonal Intelligence refers to the ability to understand people and relationships. This intelligence often contributes to life success, and to being well-liked by people. People with interpersonal intelligence are often very understanding, can take different points of view, and can act as mediators or leaders seeking consensus. They learn well through the use of cooperative learning, group projects, and partnering. When they know another person well, adults with Down syndrome can tune into that person accurately and effectively. They may remember personal data including birthdays, and may sense when the other person is feeling low or is very happy. This area is usually a strength for older children and adults with Down syndrome. Children and adults with interpersonal intelligence enjoy socializing and group activities.

Intrapersonal Intelligence refers to the ability to understand oneself and to act on that understanding. This intelligence helps people choose jobs, situations, and relationships at which they can do well. People with strengths in this area often work best independently, at their own pace. Because of verbal limitations, older children, adolescents, and adults with Down syndrome may have difficulty explaining why they feel a certain way or what they would need to feel better. Although they may know that they are having difficulty with a peer at school or with an employer in a job setting, they may have difficulty expressing their feelings. The individual with Down syndrome will look sad and upset, but it is often difficult for family members, teachers, or counselors to figure out what is at the root of the unhappiness.

The interpersonal and intrapersonal intelligences are often grouped together. They are sometimes referred to as EQ, the emotional quotient, SQ, the social quotient, EI, emotional intelligence, or SI, social intelligence.

Whether or not your child has any communication problems at school, IDEA 2004 mandates that assistive technology needs should be evaluated at least annually when the IEP is written. So, the need for a word processor, synthesized speech, and electronic communication systems should be considered to assist and supplement speech in the classroom. Low tech options such as a language board or sign language or cued speech should also be discussed. See Chapter 10 for in-depth information about assistive technology that can be helpful for increasing the communication abilities of children with Down syndrome.

Conclusion

For your child to succeed in communicating in the classroom setting and in daily living, he needs:

- a reason to communicate,
- strong communication models,

- opportunities to practice communication skills, and
- a system with which to communicate

Your child's classroom setting needs to be designed so that there is a reason to communicate and there are opportunities to communicate with teachers, other children, and school personnel. His IEP should specify how communication skills will be embedded in his school day. For instance, goals in science and social studies should reflect language learning needs in those areas. And there should be specific guide-

lines for how materials such as worksheets, assignments, and subject area tests will be modified, and who will be responsible for making these changes on a daily basis.

Furthermore, it is important that there be consistency in the different communication interactions. Children have many different communication experiences in school. If the occupational therapist is working on motor skills for writing, she can help your child write words that your child is learning in speech sessions and in the classroom curriculum. If the SLP is working with your child on making requests, he should be using these requests in the cafeteria, not just with the SLP. If he is working on retelling events that happened, he can use that skill when he goes to the nurse's office. The goal for all language skills is that they generalize beyond the speech session to interactions in school, at home, and in daily life.

Your child needs strong communication models and communication opportunities both inside and outside the classroom. This is one reason parents often advocate for inclusion, at least for some activities. If inclusion isn't the right option for your child, brainstorm with the IEP team to ensure that your child has regular contact with good peer models—perhaps in after school activities, community-based activities such as Scouting, peer tutoring, a speech-language therapy group, or in a youth group at your place of worship.

Most children with Down syndrome will communicate using speech as their primary communication system. If speech is not a viable system, the speech-language pathologist, teachers, and family need to work together to ensure that your child has an effective communication system, such as sign language, communication board, or computer-based communication device, which can meet his communication needs. See Chapter 10 for information on assistive technology and augmentative and alternative communication systems (AAC).

CHAPTER 8

Communication Skills for Home and Community

Peter is turning six and is so excited about his birthday party. He talks about all of the cousins and friends he wants to invite. He wants a barbe-cue outside with hot dogs and hamburgers. But, when everyone arrives, he doesn't speak to them. He runs back into the house and hides.

Eight-year-old Brittany walks into her house after school. She looks angry. Her mother asks what happened, and Brittany starts talking fast about "hit" and "red" and "not do that again." Her mother can't figure out what happened.

Alex, age 10, is the greeter at his sister's high school graduation party. He greets each person and leads them to the table so they can get a name badge. Every time someone new arrives, he asks their name and introduces them to other people, by saying, "Elliott, this is Josh. Josh, this is Elliott." He remembers everyone's name and is warm and welcoming.

Eleven-year-old Anita is telling her mom about the class trip to the science museum. She is talking about the weather exhibit and how the weather condi-tions are measured. Suddenly, her mom realizes that the topic has changed. Now Anita is talking about the hurricane victims of Katrina, "No house, so sad. We can send clothes and shoes. We help them." Her mother checks with the teacher whether the exhibit was about hurricanes, but it was not.

Sarah, age 12, is getting ready for the school dance. She is dressed and ready three hours early. As she sits impatiently, she continuously says to her dad, "Let's go now!!!"

Denise's sister, Rebecca, comes home from her doctor's appointment with important news. "I have to get glasses," she announces in a matter-of-fact tone. Denise, 14, looks over at her mother and shrugs. "I don't know what to say," she says. She isn't sure how her sister wants her to react, so she doesn't say anything to her. Later, she tells her mother that she had thought of remarking, "That's interesting." She wants to know if that would be the right thing to say.

When speech-language pathologists talk about language for daily living, they call it *pragmatics*. Pragmatics is all about the practical uses of language in real-life communication situations—language for home and community. Pragmatics focuses on the social and interactional use of language. Some pragmatics skills are as basic as making eye contact and smiling or frowning to make your feelings known. These basic skills develop early, often before a child is speaking. Some of these skills have been discussed in the section on nonverbal language, because pragmatics includes both verbal and nonverbal skills. Other pragmatics skills, such as being able to stay on topic during a conversation or even being able to have a conversation, are more advanced and do not develop until children have already mastered many other speech and language skills. Table 8-1 lists the major pragmatics skills.

Table 8-1: What Is Pragmatics

Pragmatics includes:

- **Intent:** the speaker's goal for the communication;
- **Eye contact:** looking directly at the communication partner (also known as reciprocal gaze);
- **Facial expression:** the emotional meaning of the movements of the face such as smiling or frowning;
- **Kinesics:** the use of gestures;
- **Requests:** asking for something through communication;
- **Proxemics:** use of distance and space when interacting with others;
- **Conversational skills:** the social interaction of communication partners, including turn taking;
- **Topicalization:** this includes introducing topics, staying on topic, shifting topics, and ending topics;
- **Stylistic variation:** ability to adapt your speech and language to different conversational partners and audiences;
- **Clarification and repairs:** asking your conversation partner for information that you don't understand, and providing information that the listener needs;
- **Presuppositions:** assumptions a person makes that may influence a conversation;
- **Narrative discourse:** ability to retell a story or to tell what happened.

Pragmatics is a language skill, but in the broader sense, it is also a social skill. Speech is the language system that most children with Down syndrome use to express their thoughts. So, for most children with Down syndrome, speech skills are intertwined with pragmatics skills. In this chapter, we will consider your child's speech and language needs for everyday life, at home, and in the community. Chapter 9 covers more advanced conversational and discourse skills.

Pragmatics Skills in Children with Down Syndrome

There has been a good deal of research on pragmatics and interactional language in typically developing children. There have been fewer studies examining pragmatics in children with Down syndrome, and many of the studies that have been done compare children with Down syndrome to children with autism or fragile X syndrome. These studies show that children with Down syndrome score higher on measures of social interactional language than children with autism and fragile X do. However, study results do not provide information that is useful for developing treatment goals and methods.

The good news is that children with Down syndrome interact very well socially and can and will communicate with others even before they have speech, through gestures and sign language. Most children with Down syndrome have the desire to communicate and often have good social interactional skills. Researchers have found that children with Down syndrome usually show strength in nonverbal social interactional skills. Thus, although we may need to teach "how to" use language in certain situations, children with Down syndrome "want to" interact and to communicate with others. Social communication such as greetings and nonverbal communication are usually the easiest pragmatics skills for children with Down syndrome. Advanced conversational skills such as staying on topic, handling communication breakdowns and repairs, and narrative discourse are the most difficult skills.

The goal for all children with Down syndrome is to develop appropriate social interactive communication skills. For some children, this is a realistic goal during the elementary school years. For many individuals with Down syndrome, this goal will be an ongoing one, with social interactive skills continuing to develop well into adulthood. These skills will be developed and practiced in school, at home, in community activities, in recreational activities, in friendships and relationships, and in job settings. Social interactive communication skills can continue to develop throughout life.

General Methods for Teaching Pragmatics

Although your child's SLP may work on pragmatics skills with her in therapy, these skills need to be practiced in her daily life, because that is what they are all about—using communication skills appropriately in real life. Both parents and SLPs can use the same general methods to help children with Down syndrome improve pragmatics skills. These methods include:

- Using games or role playing activities;
- Having the child watch live or videotaped models of a successful social situation. For older children, films and video can form the

basis for discussions about social situations that involve communication and how to handle them.

- Using books or personalized stories to set the scenario for real-life situations that can be analyzed and practiced in therapy.

Practice can be *skill based*—that is, focused on learning to use specific social skills. For example, children can practice how they would greet different people who are visiting their classroom. Photos can be mounted on tongue depressors or foam core board. One child holds the card, and the other child greets and talks with the visitor. Some possible visitors could include: the president of the United States, Harry Potter, the school principal, an American Idol winner, or a famous actor. Children might also watch videos of themselves or others successfully interacting with others to learn the right way to act. (See section on Video Modeling, below.)

Practice may also be *strategy based*. Using this approach, children are taught to first identify different social situations, then discuss several different solutions and the consequences of each choice, and finally to select the best solution for the situation. This approach may require more language, because it is basically an analysis type approach. Using Social Stories, as discussed immediately below, is perhaps the best known strategy using this approach.

SOCIAL STORIES

Social Stories were first created by Carol Gray as a tool for teaching social skills to children with autism. However, they can be helpful for any child who is having trouble understanding social cues, knowing how to act in a given situation, or other people's reactions and perspectives.

As the name suggests, Social Stories are stories about social interactions. Social Stories can be specifically written for a child, or you can use prepackaged Social Stories that address common issues such as waiting, taking turns, or entering a conversation. Social Stories can be used either proactively (before a child has problems in a situation) or reactively (to help her deal with a known problematic situation). Typically, Social Stories are written on paper, with or without illustrations, but there are also videotaped versions of Social Stories, including Carol Gray's own *Storymovies*.

Reading or watching Social Stories with a child can lead to discussions about:

- Typical situations the child will encounter;
- What the important social cues are;
- How you can tell what other people are thinking or feeling;
- The sequence of events that might occur;
- The appropriate actions to take;
- Appropriate reactions to other people.

The goal of a Social Story is to examine a specific situation that a child is having difficulty with (or might have difficulty with). For example, Haley may be ignoring her classmates' greetings, Chris may be hitting other children when he wants to have a turn on the swings, and Amanda may be sitting alone at lunch because she doesn't know how to ask other students if she can sit with them. To develop a Social Story for Haley, Chris, or Amanda, a teacher or parent would write a story describing the appropriate way for these children to respond in these situations. The parent or teacher would then read the story with the child, and afterwards discuss the right thing to do in the situation. For example, a Social Story for Chris might go like this:

I can do many wonderful things with my hands. I can wave, give a high-five, and throw a ball. But, I should not use my hands for hitting. When I am on the playground, I am excited and I want to go on the swings and the slide. But, if someone is already on the equipment, I have to wait. I can say, "Tell me when you finish" or "My turn next." Then I need to wait. Soon, it will be my turn to swing.

Carol Gray has developed guidelines for writing Social Stories that teachers or parents can use. She has also published several books and DVDs with prewritten stories about common scenarios that present difficulties for children with autism and other disabilities. See her website at www.thegraycenter.org. Also see the Resources for websites that can help you learn how to write Social Stories. For instance, Sandbox Learning has developed a program called Success Stories in which the stories and the illustrations can be customized for a specific child (www.sandbox-learning.com).

VIDEO MODELING

Video modeling is another strategy that is most often used with children on the autism spectrum, but can also benefit children with other disabilities. It is a strategy that can work well with children who are visual learners, as many children with Down syndrome are.

Video modeling involves making a video/DVD (or purchasing a commercially available video/DVD) showing appropriate behavior and then having the child watch the video. For children with autism, a variant of video modeling known as video self-monitoring is increasingly being used. The child herself is filmed performing the skill or behavior, and then the video is edited so that it only shows the child doing the skill correctly. For example, a video might be made of Molly asking for a turn on the swings. To get footage of Molly asking for a turn, an adult may need to prompt her to ask, or may even need to say the words one by one and have the child repeat them after her. The adult prompts would then be edited out of the film, so that on film, Molly looks like she is asking, "May I have a turn?" (or whatever words are chosen) on her own. There would also be footage of the other child giving up the swing, and then scenes of Molly happily swinging after asking appropriately for her turn.

Why is video modeling more effective than live modeling or role playing? Videos enable the child to focus on what is essential for her to learn. By zooming in on certain activities, video cuts down on the distracting or irrelevant environmental features, such as noise and movement of people. In the natural environment, these factors often distract a child.

Recent research has shown that video modeling can result in improvement in social communication skills and in behavior (Bellini & Akullian, 2007). Video modeling has been used to teach conversational skills to children with autism, including turn taking, asking questions, and following through with questions based on what the speaker has said. The method was successful, with the skills generalizing to other conversations, and maintenance of the conversational skills at a fifteen-month follow-up. The Model Me Kids program has been used successfully for children with autism to teach play sequences involving both verbal and motor responses, social skills (e.g., behavior at a birthday party) and conversational skills (www.modelmekids.com). Most of the current research focuses on children with autism (LeBlanc et al., 2003), but it appears that the method could also be used for children with Down syndrome to teach social and conversational skills.

The key is to choose a skill for the child to learn that is not too far above her current abilities. So, if a child is currently using two-word phrases, you might edit a film to show her using three-word phrases. If she can ask for help in one situation, but not all situations, you might film her asking for help in a new situation. You then allow the child to watch the video/DVD whenever she wants, without lecturing her that this is what she *should* be doing.

The Major Areas of Pragmatics

INTENT

Communicative intent is your purpose in the communication or conversation. A younger child might say, "I'm thirsty" right when you pass a fast food restaurant, with her intent being, "Let's stop and get a drink now." An older child might say, "I'm cold," meaning that she wants you to make her some hot chocolate. An adolescent girl might

say to her mom, "That blouse is pretty. I like pink" with the intent that she would like her mom to buy the blouse for her. A boy might say, "That bike is awesome" meaning that he would like a new cool bike like that one. Children with Down syndrome usually reveal their intent; they are not good at hiding it.

People have many different types of intentions when they communicate, including:

- requesting,
- greeting,
- socializing/being friendly,
- protesting,
- regulating the environment, and
- asking for information.

Intents are almost always part of purposeful communication attempts. That is, we usually have an underlying reason for trying to communicate. You want to encourage communicative intent—using communication to get your needs met. When your child is younger, you will want to work on helping her realize she can get her needs met through communication. When your child is older, you can progress to helping her understand "how to" get her message across—how to frame her message to accomplish her purpose.

Linguists use specific terms for the speaker's intent and the listener's interpretation of that intent. The speaker's intent is referred to as the *illocutionary act,* while the listener's perception of that intent is referred to as *perlocutionary act.* What is important is that the speaker's intent and the listener's intent match. When the listener's perception of the speaker's intent is the same message that the speaker intended, we have effective communication. When the listener doesn't accurately receive the message that the speaker intended, there is a mismatch.

When children with Down syndrome have difficulties speaking intelligibly, there is often a mismatch between their intent and the listener's understanding of the mes-

Effective Communication

Speaker's intent matches listener's perception (understanding) of the message

Communication Mismatch/ Ineffective Communication

Speaker's intent does not match the listener's perception of the message.

sage. This results in frustration, and it may be a source for behavior problems at home, in school, and in the community. The child knows what she wants to say, then says it, but finds it frustrating when you don't understand her. Speech intelligibility is closely connected with communication skills, because if the listener cannot understand you, then you haven't been able to communicate your intended message.

If your child is often frustrated by her inability to get her message across due to speech problems, it will be important for you to investigate AAC, while continuing to work with her on speech development. At all ages, children need a system that enables them to effectively communicate. See Chapter 10 on AAC.

HOME ACTIVITIES FOR INTENT

Home activities that lend themselves to practicing intents are role playing or games that simulate real-life activities such as playing grocery store, playing restaurant, or playing gas station (for younger children, use toys; for older children, use props). The goal is to know how to use language appropriately so that you accomplish your intent. Play activities should be followed by practice in real situations in the community. If your child needs more practice between play and the real situation, you can always take digital photos or video footage to highlight what will happen in the real situation. Also, be sure to take photos of everyday activities to use as visual cues to help your child retell the day's events. The ability to retell what happened is known as narrative discourse, and is discussed in the next chapter.

- Comment on your child's verbal and nonverbal intent. For example, "I can see that you're looking in the refrigerator. Do you want to ask me something?" If you get no response, ask, "Are you hungry? I have macaroni and cheese in the refrigerator. Do you want some?" Or, "You really like to listen to that song. Do you want to ask me anything?" If you get no response, ask, "Do you want to add it to your iPod?"

- If you have a pet, try commenting on her communicative intent sometimes. For instance, if your cat meows a certain way, say, "What is she trying to tell us? Does she want to go out?"

- If you can tell that your child wants something but she is not gesturing or speaking to show what she wants, help her express her intent. For example, your child can't get to her lunchbox because it is on a high shelf. You see that she is looking at the shelf, but she is not pointing to it or saying anything. Depending on her skill level, you might point to the shelf or say, "Tell me what you want and I can help you get it." If she still does not say what she wants, try asking, "Do you want your lunchbox?"

- With children who have more advanced pragmatics skills, you can work on the difference between what you think and what is appropriate to say. For example, your child can see her friend opening up a birthday present and think, "I want that. I wish she would give it to me." But, it is inappropriate to say, "I want that. Give it to me." You might draw a cartoon character with two bubbles, one above her head and one coming from her mouth. Use it to role play, what you might think and what you should say. Take turns with your child. This is a good exercise for siblings too.

TEACHING YOUR CHILD ABOUT OTHERS' INTENTS

When Crystal was in fourth grade, a group of girls targeted her for teasing. At recess, they often teased her about liking a boy in their class who couldn't speak much English. They would ask Crystal, "Do you like Eduardo?" Crystal would answer honestly, "yes." Then the girls would escalate to questions such as, "Oh, do you want to go on a date? Do you want to kiss him?" As the questions went on, Crystal would become very uncomfortable and want to stop the questions. She realized the other girls were teasing her, but didn't recognize that she had opened the door to their teasing by engaging in conversation with them in the first place.

As illustrated in the anecdote above, children with Down syndrome can become the unwitting target of teasing when they fail to recognize the other children's intent. They can also easily be led into doing the wrong thing if they do not realize that another child is trying to get them into trouble. They often wrongly assume that everyone is kind and helpful and says what they actually mean. They may have difficulty when the facial expressions or voice do not match the message, so they often have trouble recognizing sarcasm, or deciphering expressions such as eye rolling.

Suggestions for helping your child recognize other people's intents include:

- Watch movies or TV shows together and point out characters' intents. Cartoons and animated TV programs and movies such as *The Simpsons* and *South Park* often have humor based on sarcasm and mismatched channel messages, so these may be good resources.
- Role play real-life situations in which other children have taken advantage of your child. Show her another way to respond. Try role plays in which you say the same thing to your child in a sincere and an insincere tone of voice (e.g., "I like your new shirt" or "Nice going"). Teach her to hear the difference.
- Carol Gray's published Social Stories, discussed above, include situations that involve bullying or taking advantage of children, and provide scenarios for discussion. You can also make your own Social Story about specific situations your child has encountered.

EYE CONTACT

Looking at someone when you talk or listen is considered very important in many, but not all, cultures. In Asian and African-American cultures, it is considered a sign of respect to look away from a teacher or other adult in authority when she is talking to you. But, in most North American and European cultures, if you look away, the speaker will assume that you are not listening. Teachers will say, "Look at me when I talk to you." So, eye contact is considered important.

Many parents of children with Down syndrome tell me that their child looks down or away when someone is speaking to her. To help your child learn to look at the speaker, a prompt to "Look me in the eyes" or "Let me see your beautiful eyes" may be all that is needed. With an older child or adolescent who is self-conscious, you might agree on an unobtrusive sign—such as pointing to your eye with your index finger while holding your hand on your cheek—to remind your child to look at you. This kind of cue can work well in the community. At school when your child is seated, a visual prompt can be used. For example, the teacher might put a Post-it note with a drawing of wide-open eyes on your child's desk, or a small photo of a favorite rock star or movie star in which the eyes have been darkened or colored to make them more prominent.

Older children and teens can also learn and practice eye contact when giving oral reports or doing public speaking. I have noticed that the teenagers and young adults who are self-advocates and who have lots of public speaking opportunities usually have good eye contact. So, it really is about practicing eye contact and developing the habit

Can You Look Me in the Eye?

Many children, with and without Down syndrome, have difficulties with eye contact due to shyness. Younger children may hold onto their mothers or hide behind them. Older children may back up so they are farther away from strangers, and be hesitant to talk with new people. This is typical and not in and of itself a possible sign of autism.

When a child with Down syndrome has a dual diagnosis of autism, lack of eye contact will not be the only sign. Besides not looking you in the eye, he or she may not follow your gaze, either (look at whatever you are looking at). She will also have the signs discussed on page 257.

of looking at the person you are speaking with. Once your child gets into the habit of looking at the speaker, she will continue to maintain eye contact and will not even have to think about it.

HOME ACTIVITIES FOR EYE CONTACT

- Make a pair of hand-decorated eyeglasses or buy cool sunglasses that your child likes. These are the "look at me" glasses. Whenever your child is wearing them, she needs to look at your face. Use the glasses for perhaps five minutes at first. Gradually increase the time that your child wears the glasses so that she develops the habit of looking at people. Dinnertime or anytime when everyone is seated around a table is another good time to practice.

- Bring different types of eye contact into your child's awareness. Discuss the difference between looking, staring, and peeking. Sometimes when several members of your family are sitting together, such as at dinner, play a looking game. One family member starts and either looks, stares, or peeks at another person. Your child needs to say whether that person is looking, staring, or peeking.

- Play a variation of musical chairs with a small group. Sit in a semicircle with one person in the center. When the music starts, the person in the center (the leader) takes turns looking into the eyes of each of the people in the semicircle (either in turn, or randomly). When the music stops, the person the leader is looking at gets a point (or token/poker chip) if he or she is looking into the leader's eyes and not away. The person who receives the most poker chips is the winner.

FACIAL EXPRESSION

Chapter 7 discusses the difficulties that children with Down syndrome can have in expressing their feelings appropriately in words. Children with Down syndrome generally do *not* have trouble expressing emotions nonverbally. They usually use appropriate, accurate facial expressions and nonverbal communication that reflects their feelings and mood. Even when they cannot tell you what is bothering them, you can usually sense through their nonverbal communication that something is bothering them..

In addition, children with Down syndrome are often very adept at reading some emotions. They might know immediately that you're feeling sad. However, children with Down syndrome sometimes have difficulty reading facial expressions, especially

subtle signs related to annoyance or anger. For example, if you are shopping with your child for holiday gifts, and she sees a new backpack that she wants, she may persist in asking you to buy it after you have said no. Even if you look annoyed and raise your eyebrows, she may keeping asking. In a situation like this, it probably would help to tune her into your facial expressions: "Look at my face. I am getting annoyed with you. When I look like this, you know that I am annoyed. I already said no. Please stop asking me again and again."

It is important that a speaker's facial expressions match the message being sent. For example, if I say, "I love camp" and I am smiling and looking happy, it reinforces my verbal message. But, what happens if I look sad and if my voice sounds sad or angry even though I am saying "I love camp?" Research has shown that most listeners will believe the nonverbal message if the verbal and nonverbal messages being sent don't agree. The listener will assume that I really hate camp. Children with Down syndrome, however, sometimes listen to the words instead of keying into the speaker's expression or tone of voice.

It is very important for your child with Down syndrome to be able to understand and decode facial expressions and emotions and to be able to use appropriate facial expressions that will reinforce her verbal message. Facial expressions are really best learned at home through real-life experiences, within the family setting.

HOME ACTIVITIES FOR FACIAL EXPRESSION
- You can practice making different kinds of faces in the mirror and comment on them. Talk about the situations where you might use those faces. So, you might try laughing hysterically in the mirror. Then look disgusted. Talk about what might have happened to make you look that way.

- Look at photos in which family members or friends are showing emotion, and talk about what they were doing at that time. For example: "Thomas looks scared in that picture. That roller coaster he is riding on looks very big. Wow, he must feel scared." Or, "Robin looks annoyed. She is looking at her watch. Do you think she's waiting for Sally? Sally is always late."

- Talk with your child about family members' expressions. For example, your family is waiting in a long line to see a movie or ride on an attraction. Discuss how each person looks and have them talk about how they are feeling. Dad may be annoyed that no one was ready to go earlier. Mom might look upset that they didn't buy tickets in advance. Jeremy might look worried—he really wants to see this movie, he told his friends he was going to see the movie, and now maybe there won't be any tickets left.

- Read a book with your child that explores feelings such as *Alexander and the Horrible, Terrible, No Good, Very Bad Day* by Judith Viorst. Make faces that describe how Alexander is feeling as you read about each situation.

- You may find the *Social Skills Picture Book* by Jed Baker a helpful resource, especially if your child has other difficulties with social skills besides recognizing others' emotions. The book has many clear photos of children in social situations, with thought balloons showing what they're thinking. There are good illustrations of expressions and body language.

EXPRESSING EMOTIONS APPROPRIATELY

Although it's important for all children, verbal or not, to be able to appropriately express frustration, confusion, anger, happiness, etc., this is rarely discussed at school. For the most part, describing feelings and discussing emotions is out of the awareness of many children.

Jennifer Wishart, a British researcher, has found that children with Down syndrome have selective difficulty understanding words relating to fear but not words relating to anger. Perhaps this is because families and teachers discuss anger and controlling your anger more than they discuss fear. Children probably have more experience observing anger and emotional outbursts. Fear is more internal, and many men often don't admit to being afraid.

Since children with Down syndrome can have difficulty articulating how they are feeling, they may show how they feel through their behavior. For example, if your child doesn't know how to tell a friend she is happy to see him, she may hug him when hugging is not appropriate. Or, if she doesn't know how to tell the teacher she is afraid to put leaves into the jar with the class caterpillar, she may cry or hide under her desk instead. Again, role playing and Social Stories are good strategies for helping children learn to express emotions appropriately. You may also want to see the suggestions for teaching about emotions in *Teaching Children with Down Syndrome about Their Bodies, Boundaries, and Sexuality* by Terri Couwenhoven.

If a child is not yet speaking, it is important to make sure she can express her emotions using AAC. For example, if the child is using a VOCA (voice output communication device) with preprogrammed phrases, the phrases relating to anger or frustration would need to be preprogrammed into the communication device. In therapy and at home, the child would need practice in how to use those phrases or words appropriately. For children using alphabetic typing to type in their own words, they would need practice in spelling and typing the appropriate feelings words.

For children who are speaking but having difficulty labeling their emotions, you can work at home by reading books about emotions (both fiction and biographies). Books that describe situations that are emotional are helpful. For example, *Judy Moody* by Megan McDonald is a book about a third grader that talks about her emotions at home and at school.

It's important to remember that your child is learning what's appropriate according to your social and cultural views. Your culture may have views on what are appropriate responses to difficult situations, and those views may differ according to age or gender or social status. Your child can't always learn by watching. Think about what society or the media thinks is an appropriate response for a political candidate, or for a sitcom character. Those may not be the responses that you would feel are appropriate for your child. Be alert to models who are not setting a good example for your child—whether in real life or in the media—and let her know when an emotional response she witnesses is not appropriate.

KINESICS

Kinesics is the use of gestures in communication. Examples of kinesics are shrugging your shoulders for "I don't know" or giving a high-five sign or pointing to the cereal box on the top shelf that you want to reach.

In my work with children with Down syndrome, I have observed that they do not have difficulty with gestures, and usually use them appropriately when they have lots of practice at home and in the community. Researchers have found that children with Down syndrome also respond to gestures very well. Sometimes, however, your child may pick up rude or inappropriate gestures, and use them in situations that can get her into trouble. So, you might need to take some time at home and in the community to talk about and demonstrate what is and is not an appropriate gesture. This is especially difficult because inappropriate gestures, such as giving the finger, are used on television frequently, and often get laughs.

If your child is school-aged and is not using pointing and other gestures, further diagnosis is probably advisable. Children with the dual diagnosis of Down syndrome and autism often do not point and use gestures to communicate. Or, they may use gestures early in development, and then stop using them, especially the pointing gesture, at older ages. See page 257.

🏠 **HOME ACTIVITIES FOR KINESICS**
● Play "Pass the Gesture" with your child and other family members. Stand in a circle so everyone can see everyone else. The first person begins by making a gesture such as waving. The second person waves and then adds a new gesture such as bowing. The third person repeats the first two gestures in sequence and then adds another gesture such as shaking her head no. (Other good gestures: the peace or quiet sign, nodding your head, beckoning with one finger, putting your finger to your lips, the "you're out signal" used by umpires, moving your finger across your throat to indicate "cut.") Play continues until somebody forgets the sequence of gestures. (You're out if you make an inappropriate gesture.)

- Play "Rock, Paper, Scissors." Show your child how to make a rock with her fist, a piece of paper by holding her hand out flat, and scissors with her first two fingers. Show her how the rock "beats" the scissors by crushing them, the paper beats the rock by wrapping around it, and the scissors beats the paper by snipping it. On the count of three, you and your child show either rock, paper, or scissors and see who wins. Repeat as long as you both like.

- If your child is older, you may try teaching her how to play charades the conventional way, where players act out the names of movies, books, songs, etc., word by word (and sometimes syllable by syllable). If so, you'll have to teach her gestures such as pulling on her earlobe to indicate "sounds like" or touching her nose to indicate "on the nose" (as in, that's exactly the right word). If your child is younger, you will likely want to try one of the commercially available charades games, which are easier. For instance, in *Charades for Kids* (Pressman), players draw a card that tells them what to act out without speaking (for instance, act like a frog). *Cranium Cadoo* asks players to act out situations in addition to sculpting things from clay, answering trivia questions, and racing around the house to find things asked for on the playing cards.

If your child needs help learning basic gestures such as waving, shaking her head yes or no, or pointing, see *Early Communication Skills for Children with Down Syndrome* for activity suggestions.

REQUESTS

For your child to get her needs met, she needs to make requests of people in her environment. Requesting may be verbal or nonverbal. It may be simple or complex. We can request help; we can request information; we can request a specific object; we can request permission. Verbal requests follow certain forms. Requests are usually divided into six types:

1. Imperative Ellipsis:

This is a request which names what is wanted without using a verb—for example, "More nachos" or "Right now." Children usually use this type of request earliest. This type of request is used frequently.

2. Imperatives:

This is a request which uses the imperative form or "command" form—for example, "Give me the ball" or "Don't hit your brother." Parents often use these requests to direct their children, but children also need to learn to use this form (with or without a "please" in front of it).

3. Explicit Need or Want Statements:

These types of requests include the phrases "I want" or "I need"—for example, "I want more cheese" or "I need my coat." This kind of request is easier for children with Down syndrome than imperatives because these requests usually include a carrier phrase (a fill-in-the-blanks phrase that can be used for many purposes).

4. Permission Requests:

These are requests for permission to have something or to do something. They are usually directed from the child to the adult—for example, "May I go to Sam's house to play?" or "May I have more butter on my popcorn?" or "Can I get that shirt? It's cute!" Permission requests usually use the words "can" or "may."

5. Imbedded Request:

These are requests that specify the agent, action, and object. In other words, these are requests in which you ask someone else whether she can or will do something for you, and you use the word "you" in your request. For example: "Can you reach the cookies?" or "Would you turn on the water?" This is a difficult form of request for many children with Down syndrome, as it is more complex grammatically.

6. Conventionalized Hints:

Typically developing children don't usually make this type of request until the elementary school years, and it is more commonly used by adults. It is not an explicit direct request, but rather a hidden covert request. It is left to the listener to figure out what the speaker is requesting—for example, "Is there any ice cream left?" or "Do you think I need more money to go to the movies?" The person asking the question wants you to give her ice cream or money, but she is not directly asking for it. This is different from the explicit need or want request, "I need money" or "I want ice cream."

Conventionalized hints are used more in some cultures than others. There is also a gender difference. Women use more conventionalized hints than men. When a woman says, "It's hot in here," she may mean "please open the window." Men sometimes have difficulty decoding conventionalized hints. This may be a source of misunderstanding. A man might say to a woman, "If you wanted me to open the window, why didn't you ask?" These types of hints are difficult for children with Down syndrome to understand and use. If you recall the discussion of intents above, these are very subtle intents. They are actually manipulative, but generally considered acceptably manipulative in our culture.

HELPING YOUR CHILD MAKE REQUESTS

Researchers have found that children with Down syndrome have more difficulty with requesting than with other pragmatic skills, so your child may need additional help to improve requesting skills. If speaking is difficult for your child, you may want to ensure that she can reliably *use* a couple of the types of requests listed above to get her needs met, and gradually work toward *understanding* all of the types. In the later elementary school and middle school years, it will be especially important for your child to understand conventionalized hints since this is the prime age when other children may try to manipulate or lead your child on to do things that she shouldn't do.

Chances are, you already know what forms of requests your child can use. If not, observe your child closely, and set up situations in which she will need to make requests. For example, give her a desired snack in a container she can't open by herself (for example, a closed plastic jar). Watch to see if she asks for help opening the container. For an older child, you might begin a crafts project that involves cutting, such as making a holiday card. Then don't give your child scissors or something else needed to complete the project. How does your child request help? Does she use

gestures or point, or use words to request? Or, does she get frustrated, cry, or bang things on the table? Requests may be used for different purposes.

Usually, children are using requests to get something that they want. At home or in school, they may also need to use requests for information (discussed in Chapter 7). Children also need to be able to respond to requests for clarification from others. This area of pragmatics is known as clarification and repairs. It is discussed in Chapter 9.

Requesting can be taught and practiced. Some home activities lend themselves very well to practicing making requests. Siblings can help serve as models by making requests, as long as they make their own requests and do not make the requests for the child.

Practicing requests can encompass many different kinds of activities appropriate for a wide range of ages and abilities. Some requests, "May I go out now?" or "I need a green marker" can be taught using a pacing board (see the box on the next page). The requests can be: 1) practiced through pattern practice, 2) reinforced through role playing, and then 3) generalized to everyday conversation. For example:

Explicit needs and wants requests, such as "I want a drink" or "I need my coat," can be taught through pattern practice as follows:

> Parent first models, "I want more cheese" or "I want a drink."
> Child imitates.
> Parent: "What do you want?"
> Child: "a drink."
> Parent: "I **want** [emphasize] a drink. What do you want?"
> Child: "I want a drink."

Next, provide support and practice through role playing a real-life situation. So, you might play that you are going on a picnic. Prompt your child by saying, "You are thirsty and you really want a drink. What can you say?" You may even write out a cue card if your child can read, "May I have a drink [picture or word], please?" Or you may say the word "may" or put your lips together to make the "m" sound (the first sound in may) as a visual cue.

Finally, to help your child generalize requests to everyday conversation, try to insist on complete sentences or phrases when she makes requests. One method is simply not to respond until your child makes a request with a full sentence. Or you can cue her with a sign or picture. For example, use the sign for cookie or a picture of a cookie, or a sign for your pet when your child doesn't see her and wants to know where she is. You can use a pacing board and write the words "I want" or "May I have" on top of the dots. But, only demand what your child is able to say. If she can say four word phrases, don't withhold what she wants because she is not telling you in six words.

Remember: if your child has Childhood Apraxia of Speech (CAS) she may not be able to say sounds or words consistently. This is not willful. If you demand that your child say more than she is able to say, it will result in frustration and diminished communication. She may need to use a combination of speech and sign language, or a communication board with signs until the time that she is able to use speech alone.

What Is a Pacing Board?

A pacing board provides a visual and tactile reminder of the number of words your child is able to use. The pacing board may consist of colored dots on a piece of cardboard, stars or hearts put next to each other, squares of material with different textures (velvet, sandpaper) mounted on a board, colorful NASCAR stickers mounted on a piece of cardboard—or anything else that your child likes. The number of dots or stickers should be the number of words that you would like your child to include in her phrases.

Using the pacing board provides multisensory cues—visual and tactile reminders—for your child to use all of the separate words. So, if you want your child to request using the format "I want a _____, please," the pacing board should have five dots. Your child touches the dots as she says the words.

Pacing boards are especially helpful for children with Down syndrome because they make use of the child's visual strengths to remind her to include all of the words. For older children, you can make multiple pacing boards and write the words on each one, or make a sentence strip that you use above the dots so that your child can actually read the words. If you are using pacing boards to help your child lengthen her phrases or sentences, then you can made a two-sided pacing board. On one side, put the number of dots to match the number of words she uses. On the flip side, add one more dot to that number. You would then imitate what your child says; for instance, "I want drink" (pointing to three dots). Then flip the board over and say, "I want a drink" (four dots) or "I want drink please" (four dots).

✳ ✳ ✳ ✳
I   want   a   drink

HOME ACTIVITIES FOR MAKING REQUESTS

Activities to help your child make requests at home are included in this section. See the section on Providing or Requesting Information, on page 245, for suggestions on making requests in the community.

REQUESTING OBJECTS OR ASSISTANCE

Cooking using recipes is an activity that lends itself well to practicing requests for objects or assistance. Start with a simple recipe with two to five ingredients, such as a dip for vegetables or chips. If your child can read, ask her to read the list of ingredients and tell you what you need to take out of the refrigerator. A photo/picture cookbook can be used, as well.

If your child does not know how to phrase a request as "We need _____" you might use a pacing board that has three dots, and the words "We need _____" written over the dots.

Your child can use the pacing board to cue her as to which words to use.

If your child can't make requests, but is able to recognize and take out the ingredients, you can say the requests, providing her with a correct model:

"We need sour cream. We need onion soup mix. We need carrots. We need celery. We need potato chips. We need 2 bowls, a large bowl and a small bowl. We need a tablespoon."

Once the ingredients are lined up, more requests are used: "How much sour cream do we need? We need 2 cups. How much onion soup? We need one package/envelope."

Later, you can work requests for assistance into your cooking activity: "Can you help pour the sour cream into the bowl? Can you shake the soup packet into the sour cream? What do we need to do next? Can you help me mix the onion soup and the sour cream?"

Eventually, you put the vegetables on a plate. Pour the chips into a bowl. Serve. What do we do? Scoop up some dip with the vegetables and the chips. But don't double dip! This presents a good opportunity to discuss what double dip means.

You can also use crafts activities, shopping, using the computer/Internet or DVD player, and activities of daily living such as washing dishes or clothes to help your child practice making and understanding requests.

REQUESTING INFORMATION

Chapter 7 provides suggested activities for teaching information requests at school. Here are additional activities to work on this skill at home:

- Play card games and board games that present good opportunities for practicing requests for information. For example, try Go Fish or Old Maid, which require questions such as, "Do you have any___?" When you are playing board games, ask questions such as "Who spins next?" or "What does your card say?" or "What did you roll?"
- Do crafts activities with your child. Ask and answer questions such as "What color do you want?" and "How big should we make this?"
- Watch television quiz shows with your child such as *Jeopardy!* or *Are You Smarter Than a Fifth Grader?*
- Use cooking activities to focus on requesting information rather than assistance or objects. For instance, ask "What flavor should we make?" or "How does it taste?"

PROXEMICS

Proxemics is how people handle space and distance in communication. There are striking differences among different cultures in the use of space between speaker and listener. In some cultures, people speak standing at a very close distance, even with acquaintances. In other cultures, people stand further apart and do not touch each other, even when they are close family members.

Proxemics is often a difficult issue for children with Down syndrome. Many children are affectionate and enjoy hugging friends and acquaintances. The problem is that people generally find this adorable in a three-year-old, but are apprehensive and uncomfortable if a teenager tries to hug them. Although the stereotype is that children with Down syndrome are overly affectionate and therefore may intrude on others' space, this may be a self-perpetuating stereotype. That is, many people

expect children with Down syndrome to be affectionate and therefore ask them for hugs and other physical signs of affection past the age when they would hug a typically developing child. So, some children with Down syndrome may learn that indiscriminately hugging and getting very close to others is appropriate.

If your child has already learned this lesson, then improving her use of proxemics will involve retraining everyone in her environment, not just her. It is beyond the scope of this book to explain how this is done. I recommend the book *Teaching Children with Down Syndrome about Their Bodies, Boundaries, and Sexuality* by Terri Couwenhoven for guidance. There are also Social Stories available that address appropriate space and distance, or you can write your own.

There is no right and wrong in proxemics. The goal is for proxemics to be appropriate for the situation. Hugs are appropriate in some situations and handshakes are appropriate in other situations. In some cultures, hugs in a public situation are not considered appropriate in any situation. Practice at home and practice in the community to help your child learn what is appropriate. Experience in inclusive settings at school helps children learn what is appropriate and acceptable and what is not.

You need to evaluate what's appropriate in your child's school on a yearly basis. It may be appropriate for two third grade girls to hold hands or stand close, but not for two boys. On a sports team, physical contact, as well as proxemics, will be different than it is in the classroom. It may be appropriate for two guys on the team to jostle each other, or punch each other playfully on the shoulder, but that would probably not be appropriate in class. From grade to grade, there will be changes. If your child is hugging or touching inappropriately, a positive behavioral support plan can be used to address the problem. The classroom teacher and guidance counselor can provide helpful input when writing the IEP relating to proxemics.

We want children to be aware of proxemics and able to be flexible and make adjustments according to the needs of the situation. In school and in the community, the older child and adolescent should have practice so that she can use the correct proxemics for the moment.

What Are the Goals for Social Communication?

If we want to know what the goals for social communication are, we first need to discover what the goals for the future are for children with Down syndrome. When we work with younger children, their parents have a vision for their child's future. Adolescents and young adults have a vision for their own future. Mia Pederson, a self-advocate with Down syndrome, jointly completed a study with Dr. Laura Meyer, in which she asked adults with Down syndrome what goals they have for the future. Among the responses were:

- have my own apartment,
- improve social skills,
- have friends,
- get married,
- have a good job,
- answer the phone myself, and
- go on trips.

Once you and your child have a vision for her future, you, your child's SLP, and her teachers need to figure out how communication skills can be developed that will support those goals. Although those of you with children towards the younger end of the age range for this book may not even have begun to think about these issues, those of you with children who are in middle school probably are thinking more seriously about the communication skills your child will need in adulthood. The next section will therefore delve into some issues related to communicating in the community that will become more important the older and more independent your child becomes.

Communicating in the Community

Realistically, most typically developing children aged 6 to 14 are not out in the community communicating on their own much, if at all. The same is true for children with Down syndrome. When your child or young teen is out in the community, she will usually be with an adult or older sibling who can help her communicate in restaurants, when shopping, at the doctor's office, etc. But children with Down syndrome have been known to get lost and need to communicate with strangers. And, it is important for you to start working with your child on the foundation skills she will eventually need for communicating on her own—especially with strangers such as cashiers and medical professionals who may have difficulty understanding her speech. These skills include:

- Providing or requesting information,
- Requesting assistance (to include repetition of information/instructions),
- Saying "no,"
- Understanding and communicating about danger,
- Knowing what *not* to say (refraining from making inappropriate, but true comments, telling white lies, keeping secrets), and
- Talking on the phone.

PROVIDING OR REQUESTING INFORMATION

As your child progresses through elementary school and into her early teens, there will be many situations when she will want or need to communicate with people providing services in your community. At times, it may be more appropriate or efficient for you to speak for your child—for example, when your child is too agitated to communicate for herself or when you know she is going to ask for an item that you have no intention of buying for her. But there will be many more opportunities when your child can express what she wants for herself, and you should let her do so to the extent possible. The more opportunities your child has to practice exchanging important information with community members as a child, the more independently she will be able to do so as an adult. Here are some common situations where your child can provide or request information:

1. She will want to express preferences—for example, when presented with three sneakers to choose from at the shoe store, when getting her hair cut and washed, or when ordering at a restaurant.
2. She will want to be able to express when something hurts or is uncomfortable—for instance, at the doctor's or dentist's office or when renting skates or bowling shoes.
3. She will want to ask for information—for example, where to find a book in the library, a DVD in the video store, a toy in the toy store; where the restrooms are; how much something costs; what something is or includes (for example, when you order a "combo meal," do you get a drink with it? What is gouda?)
4. She will need to give her name and perhaps her phone number and address, and also realize what information is private and shouldn't be given out.

TALKING THROUGH SITUATIONS IN ADVANCE

If you can anticipate your child's major communication needs before you go into a situation, you can often prepare her so she can participate in interactions. For example, if you are going out to eat or to shop, you can look at the menu or catalog pictures beforehand with your child and talk about what she might want to order to eat or what color of shoes she might like. This is now so much easier because a great deal of material, including menus and on-line catalogues, are available on the web. You can then talk your child through the types of questions and requests she may want to make. For children who are not using much speech or who have intelligibility problems, you can cut out pictures from ads or print them out from the company's website and bring them along so your child can indicate her choices.

Pattern practice and carrier phrases such as "I want," "I need," "Let's go to," and "Let's call" can help your children make requests. For example, if you are going to be ordering at a fast food restaurant, you could practice a script for ordering food.

For example, "I want a burger well-done with no cheese or onions. I want fries and a small Coke with no ice." You could also write out a list as a visual cue when you are practicing with your child. Or, if you are going to the library to look for books on dolphins, you might practice a script such as: "Do you have books about dolphins? Where can I find them?" Depending on your child's language level, you might also practice responses to the librarian's questions such as "What kind of books?" For instance: "I need facts, not stories" (or reference books, not fiction books, depending on your child's language level).

You can use a pacing board at home to help your child learn to make requests when you are practicing. For older children, you would not bring a large pacing board out in the community. If your child needs some cues, you can put dots of glue on a tongue depressor or popsicle stick and your child could carry that in her pocket, and reach in and use the dots as cues. What would probably be more helpful would be a small cue card or Post-it note with words as cues—for example, "burger-fries-drink" or "facts about dolphins." Words can be used for readers and signs or pictures can be used as cues on the card for nonreaders.

If you are taking your child to a setting that has been traumatic or confusing for her in the past, it may help to write a combination script and Social Story. This will let your child know what would be appropriate to say and what she can say or do this time to feel more in control. For example, perhaps you are taking your child to get her hair cut. Many children with Down syndrome are sensitive to touch and temperature. Let's say your child got upset the last time because the water used to wash her hair felt too hot and she didn't like the feel of the razor on her neck. You could write a story talking about the steps involved in getting her hair cut and teaching her to say "Use cool water, please" before the shampoo and "No razor, please" before her hair cut.

TEACH THROUGH SCRIPTS AND ROLE PLAYING

During the day, there are many conversational "scripts" that we use frequently. For example, when answering the phone, many of us tend to use the same greeting. One person may typically say, "Hi, how are you doing?" to a caller, while another will typically say, "Hello, who's this?"

Scripts make it easier for us to converse; we don't have to think about each word every time we need to greet a friend. Scripts can be practiced very effectively at home. What makes it fun for your child is using "props" and making the role playing into "rehearsal time" with a real "show time" or a real field trip to follow.

One script that works well for older children and adolescents is "ordering in a restaurant." Usually, fast food restaurants and family restaurants are willing to give you copies of menus and other props. You can also download menus for many restaurants from the Internet. Plan in advance so that your props are ready. We usually use menus, napkins and utensils, plates, and water glasses when scripting the customer's role, and colored apron and "fast food" hat or cap, and pad and pencil when scripting the waiter's role.

Talk about what goes on in a restaurant. How does the waiter know what you want? What does the waiter say? "May I help you?" What does the customer say? Depending on your child's language and speech ability, that might be, "I'll have a hamburger and fries, please," or "hamburger, fries," or pointing to the items on the menu.

Set up the scene, involving siblings and friends, if appropriate. Once the scene is set, rehearse the lines. What does the waiter say? What does your child say? Then, get

Setting Your Child Up for Success

As your child gets older, she will likely be participating in at least some organized activities out in the community without your supervision. You can help lay the groundwork for her successful communication by providing suggestions and information to the adults who will be in charge of the activity. This may be as simple as verbally telling the adults that the best way to get your child's attention before speaking to her is to say her name and then wait for eye contact. Or you may want to write up a list of suggestions to give the adults in advance. For example, here is a list of strategies that Jessica, mother of Alex (age 12), shared with the Scout leaders to promote his positive behavior at Scouting events:

- **Agenda**—The man loves an agenda or schedule. The more Alex knows what is going to happen ahead of time, the more secure he feels. The more secure he feels, the better his mood and behavior. Whenever possible, give him a visual schedule with times of events (his parents would be more than happy to create this if you give them the schedule).
- **Change**—Whenever there is going to be a change in routine, give him as much notice as possible.
- **Choices**—Give choices whenever possible. But real choices, not threats disguised as choices. An example of a threat disguised as a choice would be, "You can either finish this work or go to time out." An example of a real choice: "You can either gather wood for the campfire or give out the long sticks for toasting marshmallows."
- **Speak and Spin**—If Alex is in "debate" mode, simply state what he needs to do and turn your back to him and walk away. If he is repeating the same statement over and over with a "but. . ." remind him that no matter how many times he repeats something, he will get the same response.
- **Food**—Keep him fed! When Alex is hungry, he is a bear and he will seldom say, "I'm hungry; I need to eat." Try not to let too much time go by between meals or provide a snack if it's going to be a long time between meals
- **Praise**—Positive words go a long way. Every chance you get, catch Alex doing something right. At a minimum, there should be two positive comments for every one negative feedback comment to him.
- **Generosity**—Give him opportunities for responsibility and to give back. Nothing is more rewarding than being a contributing participant and he loves to have responsibilities.
- **Leadership**—Give him opportunities for leadership. You may be surprised at how he will rise to the occasion. He will be happy and very cooperative.
- **Equal Opportunity**—Alex loves to do what his peers are doing and sometimes those activities are not positive or are not desired behaviors! However, sometimes he can't do them as quickly as his peers and he's the only one who gets caught.
- **Boundaries**—Be a person of your word. If you tell him there will be consequences for his behaviors, follow through. If you don't, he won't forget it and he'll push and push and push.
- **Evaluate**—Every behavior is a form of communication. If Alex displays a behavior that is interpreted by others as inappropriate, ask, "What is Alex trying to tell us through this behavior?"
- **Giving instructions**—keep instructions to two or three steps max. If possible, provide a check list.
- **Breaks**—Alex has been so included in his community that sometimes we all forget that most of what he participates in is consistently hard work for him. Provide him breaks. If he is working on a task that may be difficult, ask him to run a chore or if he'd like to get a drink of water.

the props ready and start role playing. When you, the director, feel your child is ready and the "scripts" have been learned, it's time to go out to eat and try out the script. In the real setting, you will be able to see which "scripts" have been learned and what may need revision and more rehearsal.

Other community activities where your child can learn to communicate effectively through scripts and role playing include:

- buying shoes (how can your child indicate that the shoes don't feel right or she would prefer a different style or color?)
- visiting the doctor or dentist
- going to the movies
- visiting a friend's house or attending a party (to include situations that arise when eating a meal or sleeping over). For example, when the chip bowl is empty how do you ask for more?
- getting a haircut
- buying a music CD or DVD
- ordering photos or prints
- ordering an ice cream cone where there are many possible choices and combinations
- ordering food by phone for delivery
- buying tickets for a sports event or concert

REQUESTING ASSISTANCE

Asking for help is a skill that is somewhat related to providing and requesting information. Instead of just asking someone to answer a question for you, though, you are usually asking them to physically do something for you—to make some effort on your behalf—so you need to ask properly if you're going to get the results you want. In addition, to ask for help, you have to be willing to be seen as needing help—which can be difficult for all children at certain stages of development. For instance, a younger child who is in the stage of "I do it myself" often does not want help, and an older child or teen may be self-conscious about asking for help if she thinks this reflects poorly on her competence.

What are the important things to teach your child so she will be able to ask for help when she needs it? First, your child can learn from you that it's OK to ask for help and that everybody needs help sometimes. Bring this into awareness by pointing out when, how, and who to ask for help. Let her see you and other members of the family seeking and accepting help in many situations, and thanking others enthusiastically for their help. For example, take her with you when you are asking the librarian where a book is or when you are asking someone in a grocery store to help you reach something that's up too high.

Talk about situations where your child may need help and explain how to politely indicate that you need help, with or without words. Start with familiar, nonthreatening situations such as when the teacher asks you to help carry the volleyball equipment, your hands are full, and you need someone to open the door for you.

As in teaching other pragmatics skills, some of the best ways to teach your child these skills include:

- Using role play to demonstrate what is appropriate to say and do. Use props to make it real, whenever possible.
- Work on scripts that your child can use to ask for help, such as "Excuse me" and "Could you help me?"

- Use Social Stories to teach your child how to handle specific situations that are difficult for her. For example, if she is going camping with the Girl Scouts and you know she will need assistance putting on sunscreen and getting her air mattress blown up, you could write a Social Story about some of the things she will do at the campsite, and include information about what she can say to get the needed assistance.

TEACHING YOUR CHILD TO ASK FOR ASSISTANCE WHEN SHE IS LOST

How do you help your child learn how to get help when she is lost? Your first consideration relates to your child's ability to recall pertinent information and to her speech intelligibility. Is your child able to recall name, address, cell phone, or home phone number when asked? Can your child's speech be understood when she is giving that information?

If the answer to either of those questions is no, you need to find an alternate way for her to communicate this information and get the help that she needs. Here are some possible solutions:

- Make business cards for your child that include the pertinent information. A young man, at one of the national conventions, handed me his business card with his pertinent information and his title as *future self-advocate*. You can work with your child on when to use the cards, and put the cards in a credit card holder or wallet that is always available for your child.
- ID bracelets are another possibility with important information engraved right on the bracelet. The problem with ID bracelets is that anyone can look at that information at any time. With cards, your child has control over who she gives the card to.
- If your child uses an AAC device, messages that request help or indicate that she is lost could be programmed into the communication device.
- As your child gets older, cell phones with preprogrammed numbers are a good possibility.
- For safety, when speech is not a possibility, GPS technology is becoming more widely available to be able to track where a child is at any time. Parent support groups and the local police department are good sources of information for equipment available.

If your child *can* speak intelligibly and is able to give pertinent information, you still need to teach your child to give the right information if she become lost, and to give it to the right person. Again, scripting and role playing are effective techniques. In addition, it may be helpful to read books to your child about getting lost. Some helpful books include *I'm Lost* by Elizabeth Crary and *Just Lost* by Mercer Mayer (now out of print, but available used or in libraries).

You might also want to make the practice into a game. Take a file folder and draw a game board, as discussed in Chapter 6. Develop a stack of cards with different situations on them. For example, you are on a family trip and you get separated at the zoo. Or, you are at the grocery store or shopping mall and get separated. Write some scenarios where there are likely to be officials (security guards) you can ask for help and some situations where there is no way to know who will be there to ask. Use game pieces and a spinner to make the practice more fun.

After your child draws a card, she needs to tell you who she would approach to ask for help. If she has no ideas, you can give her two or three choices to select from: Should she ask a mother with little children? Or should she ask the teenaged boy talking on his cell phone? After your child decides who to ask, you play the role of that person and respond to the questions she asks you. What should your child ask? What kind of information should she divulge and what is private information? That is your decision as parents. Discuss this with your child and set guidelines for what information is public and what is private.

Practice many times at home or in protected environments. If your child ever does get lost, after reuniting with her, try to find out from the person who found her what information your child was able to give. Then talk to your child about what she did right. Later, perhaps, venture into more public settings and perhaps let your child practice asking for help when you are within earshot, and can monitor and adjust the script, if need be.

SAYING "NO"

All children with Down syndrome, whether verbal or not, need an effective way to say "no" to things they don't want when they are out in the community—whether it is a hug, a push on a swing, or a piece of candy. When children don't have a way of refusing things they don't want, they often resort to what others consider bad behavior to say "no."

If your child is over the age of 4 and cannot express "no" in a way people outside your family can understand, teaching her to express "no" should be a priority. Typically developing children say "no" by about 2 to 3 years of age.

What are some ways to teach saying no to a child who has severe communication delays? The easiest way is to teach the child to shake her head no. That is a nonverbal gesture that will be widely understood and can replace the word. You can deliberately offer your child things that you know she doesn't like or want, and teach her that shaking her head no will make you take it away—almost always. That is sometimes difficult because there are some things, like medicine, that you can't take away no matter how much she shakes her head.

If your child can't say no or shake her head no, you need to find a way to enable her to communicate no with AAC. A card with the word no, or a picture of a stop sign are possibilities. If you are unsuccessful at teaching your child to express "no," by the time she is in school, it should definitely be a high priority goal on her IEP.

If your child can express "no" clearly, she will need to learn to match her response to the situation—for example, to learn when to say "no" vs. "no thank you." Again, scripting, Social Stories, and role playing are most helpful. You hope that the practice will generalize from your scripted situations to all appropriate situations. But in reality, you will probably need to use preteaching and prompting longer than you would with a typically developing child. For example, before you take your child to eat at Grandmother's house, you will likely want to remind her to say "No, thank you" when Grandma offers her a food she doesn't like. And when she forgets and blurts out "No!" or "Yuck!" when Grandma passes the potato salad, you will need to prompt her to say "No, thank you." With an older child, you may want to work out a private cue to remind her discreetly to use her polite words. Also see the suggestions in the section on Knowing What *Not* to Say, below.

COMMUNICATING ABOUT DANGER

Many parents of children with Down syndrome continue to hold their children's hands when out in the community (or even to push them in strollers) past the age that parents of typically developing children do so. This may be because the child is impulsive, or seems unaware of hazards, or because she doesn't seem to understand or heed words such as "Stop!" or "Look out!" This is a greater problem for children with the dual diagnosis of Down syndrome and autism spectrum disorder.

If your child is eventually going to be able to navigate independently or semi-independently in her community, she obviously needs to comprehend and respond to a variety of danger words, spoken and in print. For example, at an early age it is important to understand "Stop!" and "Don't." Later on, she should understand "Danger," "Be careful!" or "Caution!," "Look out!," "Stay out," or "Watch your step." As she learns to read, she also needs to understand warning words that are not often spoken such as "entrance" and "exit." After all, if your child goes through the wrong door, she may be hit in the head by a door opening in a different direction. Still later, it may be appropriate for her to learn "Prohibited" and "Forbidden."

HOME ACTIVITIES FOR TEACHING DANGER WORDS

Here are some suggestions for teaching your child to understand and respond to these words:

- Play a variation of musical chairs in which the players walk around the chairs without music and stop (and sit down) when you say "stop."

- Play a stop and go game in which everyone walks (or dances) around the room and stops and freezes in place when you say "stop." Anyone who doesn't stop is out. To make the game more fun, the person who says "stop" can walk around and look at the frozen players and choose the one who looks like the best statue. Then that person becomes the next one to tell the others when to stop moving.

- Play a Simon Says game where you use the words "stop" and "don't" in your instructions. For example, "Simon says don't look at me," "Simon says don't stand by the chair," "Simon says clap your hands…. Simon says stop." "Simon says march in place…. Stop!"

- Use toy cars and action figures to set up dangerous scenarios and ask your child what to say to warn the people. For example, put an action figure in the path of a car. See if your child knows to say "Watch out!" or "Look out!" to the figure.

- With your child, look at pictures in books, magazines, or online depicting dangerous situation. Ask your child to show you what is *dangerous* in the picture. Usually, local police departments have safety programs in the schools. See if you can attend, and then follow up at home with practice in the situation.

- Post signs in your house to help your child learn new vocabulary words relating to dangerous or prohibited activities. Use written words for children who can read and symbols (e.g., circle with a slash through it) similar to those found in your community for nonreaders. For example, make a sign that says "Danger!" if you are mopping the kitchen floor and it is slippery or if you want to keep children out of the cabinet with cleaning supplies. Or post a sign in the living room that says "Drinking is prohibited (or forbidden)" if you are tired of people spilling their drinks there.

KNOWING WHAT *NOT* TO SAY

Sam, 8, eagerly unwrapped the present his grandparents had brought for his birthday. His face fell when he saw what was inside, a sweater. "I have one already," he said. "I don't like itchy stuff!"

Eleven-year-old Lakeisha was chatting with her doctor before her appointment. "You look like Frankenstein," she told the doctor. Later on in the appointment, she remarked to the nurse, "You remind me of my reading teacher. You both have blonde hair and are a little fat."

All children, with and without Down syndrome, make inappropriate or tactless remarks at times. Sometimes, the comments are funny or whimsical, and make the parents laugh. At other times, the comments may be rude or hurtful.

Sometimes parents of children with Down syndrome may be more indulgent of inappropriate comments and questions. They may just be happy that their child is talking at all, or believe she doesn't know any better, or think that it is cute to hear their child make outrageous remarks. However, when your child is older, you undoubtedly do not want her asking adults how old they are, or why they have so many wrinkles, or why their teeth are so ugly. You would also probably prefer that your child learn to tell white lies or just keep quiet when her honest opinion would hurt someone's feelings—for example, if she thinks her friend's new haircut looks funny or if she doesn't like the cookies her aunt made just for her.

Most children with Down syndrome are kind, and do not mean to say something that will hurt someone's feelings. Once they learn that particular comments could hurt, they try to be more careful.

HOME ACTIVITIES FOR TEACHING TACTFUL LANGUAGE

- Keep a short list of words you do *not* say in your family. This may include words such as *stupid*, *ugly*, *dumb*, and *fat*. Then every time anyone in your family says one of those words about another person, you say something like "We don't say 'stupid.' That hurts people's feelings." Or, "Stupid is a mean word. Please don't say it." When your child is older, the person who says those words could get fined, and have to put a penny in the Mean Words Jar.

- Develop a game called What You Say Counts. First, come up with scenarios where it is important to be tactful—for example, trying something your sister cooked, noticing that your teacher has a new dress, seeing a friend's new eyeglasses, or commenting on a picture that someone painted. Create a card deck of situations. Use role playing, or, for the child who is more advanced in language, talk about what you could say in this situation. For example, your dad got a buzz haircut for the summer, and you think it is ugly. Discuss various comments you could make. Think of something kind to say that won't hurt his feelings, such as "That's a cool haircut." If you want, you can award your child points: for instance, 3 points for a tactful, appropriate comment, 2 points for an appropriate comment that is neutral (e.g., "your hair is short"), 1 point for not making a comment where it would be inappropriate, and lose a point for a tactless or rude comment.

- When a situation is coming up where you know your child might be tempted to say something inappropriate, talk about the situation ahead of time. "You are going to get a lot of presents. You might not like them all. Or you might get something you already have. What should you say if you don't like a present?" For these situations, you can agree on a sign cue or a small written card or picture cue to remind your child that this is a time to think before you talk or maybe not talk at all in this particular situation. For example, you might discreetly make the sign to "zip your lips" or have a picture cue of a light bulb over the head.

- Consider giving your child a Power Card (see page 264, Chapter 9) listing pointers on appropriate behavior in advance of a situation where it is very important for your child to be polite.

- You can't anticipate every situation where your child might make a tactless remark. If your child does say something rude, it is usually better not to comment at that time. Don't laugh or make the comment the center of attention, but don't get angry either. Afterwards, review the incident in privacy with your child. Talk about why she shouldn't have said that (it hurt Aunt Sally's feelings, adults don't like to be asked their age, etc.). Discuss when that particular comment might be appropriate (with a child, but not an adult) and explore some of the reasons why, if your child is interested.

- Play a compliment game with your child and family. Everyone has to find at least two (or more) nice things to say about each member of the family ("Your hair looks pretty today"; "You have a nice smile"; "Those shoes are cool!"). Emphasize that these are the kinds of remarks it's OK to make to other people.

- Be sure you model tactful language yourself. Even though many parents say things to their children such as "Your hair looks like a rat's nest" or "That shirt looks terrible with those pants," it is probably better not to use this kind of language with your child with Down syndrome if you don't want her to imitate you.

- When you are watching TV or movies with your child, comment on rude or impolite things the characters say. "That was an insult!" "That guy is really rude." "Boy, was that impolite!"

USING THE PHONE

Even in today's culture where emailing and text messaging are increasingly popular, it is still important for children to learn how to use a telephone effectively. Many children with Down syndrome in this age range can learn to communicate well by telephone, but they usually have more hurdles to overcome than other children. First, some have hearing loss and therefore may have trouble understanding what others are saying on the phone without the visual cues of someone's lip movements, facial expressions, and gestures. Second, even if a child does not have a hearing loss, she can have difficulties comprehending what she hears on the phone since it is decontextualized; there are no environmental cues that help the child understand what is being said to her. Finally, many children with Down syndrome have speech intel-

ligibility problems that make it difficult for them to make themselves understood when they are speaking into a phone.

It is important to introduce your child to phones from an early age since it's such an important part of adult life. As with any child, you can begin to work on phone skills with your child with a toy phone. If your family owns two cell phones, you can also call up your child and have practice phone conversations on a real phone. To help your child understand what you are saying, it may help if you both sit in the same room. That way your child can watch your lips and gestures if she needs help understanding decontextualized language.

Using a toy phone or cell phones, you can role play situations and help your child learn the basics (saying "hello" when she answers the phone, and "good bye," "bye-bye," or "talk to you later" when she hangs up.

If you are teaching your child to answer the phone, you can practice what to say in advance, first using a toy telephone and then using the real phone with a familiar caller. Let your child practice responding to some of the specific questions that are asked again and again by callers. For example, "How are you?" "What are you doing?" "Is mommy home? Can I speak to her?" You may want to read one of the children's books that focus on phone use with your child. For instance, reading a book such as *Manners on the Telephone* (Flynn, 2007) might serve as a good introduction to telephone scripts, and might also be used to reinforce the telephone skills that your child has learned.

If your child has difficulties making herself understood over the phone, you may want to ask a relative or friend to give your child practice conversing on the phone. You can coach them in advance about specific things to ask your child and even let them know what answers to expect to help them understand your child's speech. For example, you might let them know that your child can answer these questions: "Are you having a good summer?... Did you have fun at Disney World?... What was your favorite ride?" If your child still cannot be understood, you may listen in on another line and translate for your child, if needed. Or you can use the speaker phone and interpret what your child is saying for the caller.

Sometimes, practice will make it easier for your child to say the words, and make the words clearer and easier to understand. Often the rate of speech is the problem. You may be able to slow your child down using a drum beat or a metronome while practicing speaking.

As your child gets older, you should teach her conventional scripts that we all use when answering and initiating calls. For example, when answering the phone, your child can learn to say: "Just a minute. I'll get her" or "She's not here. Can I take a message?" When calling a friend or relative, she can learn to say "Hello. This is …. May I speak to…?" Again, you can teach her these scripts through role playing, using real phones if possible.

As your child gets older, it may be appropriate to include goals related to using the telephone on her IEP. Remember, once she reaches transition age, the school must provide her with services that are needed to help her succeed in a job, postsecondary program, or out in the community. (Under IDEA, transition services must begin by age 16, but in some states they are provided as early as age 14.) If your child's transition team determines that speaking on the phone is an important transition goal for her, then speech-language therapy will need to focus on helping her achieve that goal. In speech-language therapy sessions, we often make calls to request information as practice for language, speech intelligibility, rate, and fluency difficulties.

If, in spite of your best efforts and the efforts of your SLP, your child is unable to speak intelligibly enough to be understood on the phone, it makes sense to look into technological solutions. For instance, if your child can read and write, she may be able to communicate via text messaging or emailing (see Chapter 10). Or it may be possible for her to communicate via webcam with other people who have webcams. For instance, she could use sign or picture cards to communicate with someone who was able to see her on their computer screen via webcam. If she cannot be understood, you may need to prerecord messages for emergency use. The local police department community liaison may be a good person to contact for suggestions.

When Dual Diagnosis Complicates Down Syndrome

Although most children with Down syndrome are delayed in speech skills, they usually find other ways to communicate their wants and needs and seek out others to listen to their message. For example, a six-year-old who has Childhood Apraxia of Speech and great difficulty putting her thoughts into words may get her toy that needs batteries and bring it over to her mom when she says she is going to the supermarket. It's his way of reminding her to buy batteries. An eight-year-old who notices that a page is missing from her favorite book may not be able to verbally explain but will bring the book to her mom, and turn to that page. She may also point to her baby brother to indicate that she thinks he tore the page out.

Self-Talk

Some children, and, more often, adolescents and adults with Down syndrome, try to make sense of events by having conversations with themselves. This is known as self-talk. Dennis McGuire and Brian Chicoine, cofounders of the Adult Down Syndrome Clinic in Park Ridge, Illinois, reviewed their adult patient records and found that 83 percent of them talked to themselves and that many of the other 17 percent were nonverbal. So, self-talk is very common in people with Down syndrome.

Self-talk is more likely to occur at home. Many parents report that the best way for them to find out what happened to their adolescent or young adult during the day is to tune in to the self-talk, when the person reviews the events of the day. McGuire and Chicoine describe five reasons that people with Down syndrome use self-talk:

1. To direct their own behavior,
2. To review the happenings of the day,
3. To try to work through a solution to a problem,
4. To let off steam, and
5. To entertain themselves.

Parents may understandably be concerned that their child's self-talk will interfere with jobs, friendships, housing, and independent living. The best strategy is to talk with your child about where self-talk is and is not appropriate and to try to limit the self-talk to appropriate settings. For detailed information about determining whether your child's self-talk is "normal" and helping her learn where it is OK to use, see *Mental Wellness in Adults with Down Syndrome* by Dennis McGuire and Brian Chicoine (Woodbine House, 2006). (Despite the title, the book also covers behavior in children and teens ages 12 and up.)

It is typical for a young child with Down syndrome to use gestures and pantomime to help get her message across. If a child with Down syndrome does not find alternative ways to interact and communicate with people when she does not have sufficient language and speech skills, then we need to consider whether there is some other complicating condition that is preventing her from communicating.

If your child has difficulty responding to people in the environment and seems to be in her own world, that is a red flag. If she often covers her ears, runs into the corner and rocks, or gives other signs that she finds sensations in the environment painful, that may be another signal that there are other difficulties besides Down syndrome. Also, if your child has begun to develop social or communication skills, but then begins to withdraw or seems to lose her skills, we need to consider other diagnoses. Regression is not typical for young children with Down syndrome.

An evaluation by a physician or psychologist should consider the possibilities of seizure disorders, reactive attachment disorder (especially if your child was adopted), and autism spectrum disorders (including autism, pervasive developmental disability, and childhood disintegrative disorder).

It has been estimated that 5 to 8 percent of children with Down syndrome also have an autism spectrum disorder (ASD) (Kent et al., 1999), and that the dual diagnosis is more common in males (Capone et al., 2005).

SYMPTOMS OF AUTISM

Pediatricians are now required to screen babies for autism twice by 24 months of age. Screenings are usually conducted at 18 and 24 months and conducted with the *Modified Checklist for Autism in Toddlers* (MCHAT), a parent report screening test.

On screening tests, signs that a child may have autism include the *absence* of some or all of these behaviors:

- pointing to indicate that he child wants something,
- following someone else's point or looking at what others are looking at (shared gaze),
- responding to her name,
- showing interest in other children,
- imitating
- responding to smiling with a smile.

If a child is found to have difficulties with these areas during a screening test, she should be referred for an evaluation. In an evaluation, the physician will conduct tests and do observations to look for further evidence that the child does or does not have an autism spectrum disorder.

The symptoms of autism spectrum disorders fall into three major areas: communication impairments, impairments in social skills, and restricted interests. The major signs are:

1. absence or severe delay in using spoken language;
2. lack of communication interaction using speech or gestures (children don't try to compensate for lack of speech by using gestures or other nonverbal means to get their message across);
3. a failure to initiate communication with others;
4. poor social relatedness with adults and peers;
5. a limited repertoire of activities and interests;
6. stereotyped and repetitive use of language (repeating or echoing other people's words or using the same words and phrases over and over, often in situations where they don't make sense);
7. poor receptive language skills, which may give the appearance that the child does not hear; and
8. lack of varied spontaneous imaginative play (Capone, 1999; Capone et al., 2005).

Other behaviors that may be signs of autism include repetitive, stereotyped motor mannerisms such as hand flapping and self-stimulating behavior such as staring at the fingers and moving the hands. Parents may also report that children are preoccupied with nonfunctional routines or rituals, and can't change routines or transition from one activity to another easily.

A child with autism does not seek communication and does not use speech meaningfully to communicate. She may repeat what you say; this is known as echolalia. For example, you say, "What is your name?" and the child says "name." She may not use gestures or pointing to get her needs met. She may appear as if she does not hear or understand you, but may be uncomfortable when sounds in her environment are loud. Shopping trips to stores may be very difficult for her to tolerate due to overstimulation from people, fluorescent lights, and a variety of noises. She may rock back and forth or twirl around repeatedly. She may have strong food preferences and go through periods where she will only eat one or two different foods. She may not like the feel of certain textures in clothing, blankets, or toys. In short, she finds it difficult to respond to the sensory stimulation she receives from the environment.

It can be tricky to diagnose an autism spectrum disorder in a child with Down syndrome. One reason is that delays in spoken language skills—a primary symptom of autism—are also a problem for many children with Down syndrome who do not have any signs of autism spectrum disorder. The diagnosis therefore needs to rely more on other symptoms. According to Dr. George Capone, a developmental pediatrician with a special interest in the dual diagnosis of autism and Down syndrome, these symptoms often include:

- "marked impairment in nonverbal communication and symbolic play beyond that expected for their mental age,"
- frequent and intense stereotypies, and
- severe to profound cognitive impairment (in one study, Capone found that 87 percent of children with autism and Down syndrome had a severe to profound impairment, whereas only 37 percent of children with Down syndrome without a coexisting ASD fell into that range of impairment).

Another difference is that children with Down syndrome and ASD generally do not initiate communication and conversation and do not relate socially to others. In one study of 278 children with Down syndrome who had severe cognitive impairment but did not have coexisting autism, researchers found all but one of the children to be sociable (Wing and Gould, 1979). So, sociability is a differentiating diagnostic characteristic.

Important: Just because your child may be very delayed in speaking or may be developing language skills very slowly does not necessarily mean she has an autism spectrum disorder. Delays in expressive language are common in children with Down syndrome. Repetitive behaviors such as twirling hair, watching one section of a movie over and over, or lining toys up "just so" are not necessarily an indication of autism, either. Many children with Down syndrome who do not have a dual diagnosis have some repetitive behaviors. Your child most likely does not have autism if she interacts with others in many nonverbal ways, such as by maintaining eye contact, taking turns, and seeking out interactions with others.

If you suspect your child may have an autism spectrum disorder, ask your pediatrician for a referral to a developmental pediatrician or psychiatrist who specializes in this area. The combination of Down syndrome and autism is not frequently seen and is difficult to diagnose. The most frequently used diagnostic tools are the Autism Diagnostic Interview (ADI-R) and the Autism Diagnostic Observation Schedule (ADOS). The Differential Abilities Scale (DAS) is often used to test children with ASD. It has teaching items to help children learn to respond, and it has norms for people with intellectual disabilities. Autism occurs early in development, but there is a form of autism spectrum disorder known as childhood disintegrative disorder that occurs later in development (late onset autism) after apparently normal development for the first two years of life. It may become apparent at age 8 or 9, and follow a period of withdrawal in older children with Down syndrome.

The focus of treatment and specific methodologies used for treatment are different when a child has a dual diagnosis, so it is important to determine whether autism is present. Since sensory processing difficulties are an integral part of autism spectrum disorders, co-treatment by the speech-language pathologist or collaboration and consultation will be necessary. If a child has difficulty with maintaining focus and attention, and with processing stimuli and sensory input in treatment, those issues need to be worked on to enable the child to benefit from speech and language treatment.

Most children with a dual diagnosis use an augmentative and alternative communication system. Children with ASD have difficulty initiating communication, and need to be taught how to communicate, not only how to use language or speak. The Picture Exchange Communication System (PECS) is one useful method for teaching children to initiate communication. For more information on AAC and PECS, see Chapter 10, as well as the References and Resources Section Bibliography. See also the Best Practices for Autism, published by the National Academy of Sciences, listed in the Bibliography.

Conclusion

In this chapter, we have discussed the basic skills that your child will need to communicate competently in the community. Typically developing children need to learn these same pragmatics skills. The difference is that they usually pick up the skills just from observing people around them and from having some experience using the skills. Whereas grammar and vocabulary skills are taught at school, pragmatics skills are not taught. Still, society expects children to learn these skills.

For children with Down syndrome, we need to bring the pragmatic language skills into awareness, and teach them how to use these skills. Most children with Down syndrome do very well with these basic pragmatics skills with teaching, guidance, and plenty of practice. If your child is having great difficulty with social interaction and is not using language and speech or an alternative system such as gestures or pantomime to interact, it is important to determine whether she has another condition in addition to Down syndrome. In the next chapter, we will talk about more advanced pragmatic skills—conversational skills & narrative discourse.

CHAPTER 9

Conversational Skills

There are specific skills that you need to know to start a conversation. Typically developing children often learn these skills by observing other people. Some children with Down syndrome will learn conversational skills by watching, but many children will need to be taught conversational skills. How do you approach someone to start a conversation? What do you say? Some children poke the other child or get right in their faces. What happens when they want to join a conversation that is already in progress?

To hold up your end of a conversation, you need to use many different language and speech skills. You need to listen to the other speakers and determine what the topic of the conversation is. You need to think of something relevant to say. Then you need to wait for a logical place to jump into the conversation and make your contribution, formulating your sentences so others can understand them and speaking intelligibly. You may need to move closer or enter the circle in which people are standing. If you are sitting with a group, you may need to lean forward to enter a conversation. You also need to know when to stop talking so that others don't become annoyed at you for monopolizing the conversation.

Not surprisingly, most children and young teens with Down syndrome have trouble with conversational skills. In fact, as you may recall from Chapter 2, complex conversational skills are on the list of communication skills that are the most difficult for people with Down syndrome.

Children with Down syndrome are delayed in acquiring conversational skills. However, in studies matching young children who have Down syndrome with typically developing children based on language level, not chronological age, children with Down syndrome compared favorably in their conversational skills. For instance, if your child's MLU (typical sentence length) is four words, you might expect him to have the conversational skills of a typically developing child with an MLU of four words. So, age and experience helps children with Down syndrome learn conversational skills, as well as learning and practice in speech therapy.

What Are the Major Conversational Skills?

Conversational skills is a very broad category that can include speech and language skills as well as pragmatics. Within the area of conversational skills, we include:

- starting conversations,
- taking turns in the conversation,
- choosing topics and staying on the topic,
- knowing what information the listener brings with him (putting yourself in his shoes),
- understanding how to talk with different people in different roles,
- knowing how to get and give more information if there are communication misunderstandings,
- changing topics, and
- ending conversations.

STARTING CONVERSATIONS

Children and young teens with Down syndrome can have a variety of problems in starting conversations. First, they may not even try to initiate conversations and instead be content not to say anything or to wait until the other person asks them a question. Or they may make an opening gambit that does not make sense to the other listener(s)—perhaps because their comment is unintelligible or garbled grammatically, or because they talk about something or someone the other person is unfamiliar with. For example, a child might say "Mandy is coming today" to someone who doesn't know who Mandy is or where she might be coming. Children with Down syndrome may also make statements about topics that their listeners have no interest in. For example, a child might say "I have all the *Full House* DVDs" to a child who has never watched the series. And some children with Down syndrome just have difficulty starting a conversation because they don't know how to do that. They are not sure what to say.

Many of the techniques that are helpful in teaching children with autism spectrum how to start a conversation can also help children with Down syndrome. For example:

- SLPs may use a therapy program such as *Conversations* that uses a coaching model to teach groups of children how to have conversations.

- You can write a Social Story or a script about how to begin conversations and read it with your child before he goes into a situation where he can practice the skill. For example, if your 8-year-old goes to a daycare program after school, you might write something like: Snack time is a good time to talk to other kids. I can talk to the kids who sit at my table. I can ask Joe and Nick, "Do you like this snack?" ("What TV shows do you like?")

- A Comic Strip Conversation could also be used to help your child understand how to start a conversation. Comic Strip Conversations are similar to Social Stories and were another technique originated by Carol Gray. The difference is that a Comic Strip

Conversation often shows cartoonish stick figures interacting, with speech bubbles showing their actual words (and sometimes with thought bubbles showing characters' thoughts). For example, using the same daycare scenario described above, a Comic Book Conversation would include stick figure drawings of your child, Nick, and Joe. You would write suggested words for your child to say in speech bubbles along with the answers Joe and Nick might give. (See *Comic Strip Conversations* by Carol Gray for more information.)

- Use video modeling to teach conversational skills. See Chapter 8.

- If your child is older and can read, he might benefit from using a Power Card. See the box on the next page.

- You can prompt your child to start a conversation when it is clear that he wants to talk to someone. For instance, you are at a company or support group picnic and your child keeps looking at another child. If your child is older, you might tell him, "Go say 'Hi.' Ask him what grade he is in and where he goes to school." For a younger child, you might suggest something concrete he can do: "Bring the beach ball over and ask if he wants to play ball with you."

TURN TAKING

If you don't know how to take turns in conversation, you cannot be a good conversational partner and other people won't find it rewarding to converse with you. You might interrupt when it is not your turn, fail to keep the conversational ball rolling when it *is* your turn, or take a turn but change the topic in a way that makes no sense to your partner.

James MacDonald, a speech-language pathologist who has worked with many families and children with Down syndrome, feels that learning to take enough turns in conversation is one of the areas that is most important for communication success. The major area that he addresses in treatment is increasing the number of conversational turns, and focusing on engaging the child in conversations frequently and on a regular basis. MacDonald emphasizes the central role that parents should play in helping their child learn to be a communicative partner. He has developed an approach called ACE (for Adult Communicating Effectiveness) to teach parents strategies to help their child gradually progress from being noninteractive to conversational. See his website at www.jamesdmacdonald.org for information.

By early elementary school age, many children with Down syndrome know how to take turns nonverbally—they can take turns with playground equipment or wait for their turn to use the sink or drinking fountain. But, they have difficulty in conversational turn taking. Specifically, they don't continue to take turns. If we think of a conversation as a tennis game, older children with Down syndrome often hit the first ball back, but then don't hit any subsequent balls. As a consequence, children with Down syndrome often have very short conversations.

Conversational length may also be related to difficulties in topicalization (discussed below) and to vocabulary (semantic), grammatical (syntax), and verbal skills. You can help your child build up to longer conversations at home, and can also help practice and reinforce those longer conversations. Often, turn-taking and topicalization must be practiced together because they are so intertwined.

Power Cards

Power Cards™, developed by Elisa Gagnon (2001), use special interests to motivate students with autism. Power Cards are most often used with students who can read, but parents and teachers can adapt them for use with nonreaders, as long as the pictures used clearly represent the concept you are teaching. Power Cards can help an individual increase appropriate conversational topics. In addition, Power Cards can help children understand language related to abstract concepts.

Power Cards can be made in a smaller, business-card size for a child to keep in his pocket or carry in a wallet, or they can be attached to a desk. Adding a photograph or drawing to the card will make it more attractive to the student. The example shown below is designed to help the student remember how to initiate and maintain a conversation. [This example shows "Astro Man" giving advice to the child. If you were designing a Power Card for your child, you would choose a cartoon character, actor, singer, or someone else your child might be motivated to take advice from and use a picture from the Internet, a magazine, TV guide, etc.]

Astro Man likes to talk with different people. He has to keep the conversation interesting and remember not to focus only on his interests. Sometimes he gets nervous, so he follows these tips to get started.

1. Start the conversation by saying "Hello."
2. Then ask, "Would you like to talk?"
3. There are a lot of different topics I can talk about, but pick just one.
4. Some good topics are:
   - What did you do last night?
   - Do you have any plans for the weekend?
   - What kind of music do you like?
   - Do you have any pets?
   - What is you favorite food?

If the person I am talking to says they have to go, I should say, "Thanks for talking to me" and then let them leave.

Reprinted from: Cohen, Marjorie and Sloan, Donna. Visual Supports for People with Autism: A Guide for Parents and Professionals. Bethesda, MD: Woodbine House, 2007.

HOME ACTIVITIES FOR TURN TAKING

- Play movie director and have your children "act" out roles with dialogue that require taking turns. (Write out the dialogue at first or use photos; later try to progress to improvised dialogue.) Get a blackboard or a movie board, and a baseball cap or beret for the "director" as props to make this activity more fun and realistic. Cue cards may also be used to provide suggestions for your child on what to say and to emphasize that each "actor" must wait for his turn to speak. Or have a sibling play movie director and point to the person who needs to talk. This activity can be done whether your child is using two- to three-word phrases or long sentences. He just needs to have something to "say" and be able to take a conversational turn.

- To capitalize on most children's love of technology, play a game where you pass a microphone or portable cassette recorder to the person whose turn it is. At first, the adult can get the conversation going by posing a question and answer ("My favorite kind of ice cream is chocolate chip. What's yours?") and then pass the recorder to the next person to have a turn. Later, you can progress to having more free-form conversations, but still insisting that people not speak unless it is their turn (signified by holding the recorder).

- Pick a topic to discuss that you know your child will be interested in. Choose a visual cue related to that topic. For example, if you are going to talk about an upcoming trip to a baseball game, use a baseball as the visual cue. Use that cue to show whose turn it is and to help keep the conversation going. The person who starts the conversation holds the ball. When he finishes, he passes the ball to the next speaker. This activity can involve two people or even a small group. Don't make the group too large, however, or your child may get bored or distracted waiting for his turn. You may want to let the last speaker keep the ball (or other visual cue). This game may motivate your child and provide practice in longer conversations. This is an exercise in turn-taking and topicalization.

- Use scripts and role playing to teach your child phrases that can keep a conversation going such as: "What about you?"; "Do you agree?"; "What do you think?"; "Why do you say that"?; "Really?"; or "That's interesting—tell me more." At first, you might write the phrases on index cards and put them face up where your child can easily read them.

- You might set a goal for each person to take three or four turns in a conversation. (You can keep track with tally marks or by letting each person take a poker chip or the like each time he takes a turn.) If your child meets the goal, give him some kind of reward if he doesn't find conversing with you intrinsically rewarding. For example, let him go watch TV or play a computer game, or whatever it was he wanted to do when you made him talk with you.

- Use video modeling or video self-modeling, as described in Chapter 8. If you don't want to make your videos, you may want to check into the Model Me Kids videos (www.modelmekids.com). These DVDs use children to model each skill and also narrate.

JOINING A CONVERSATION IN PROGRESS

One of the basic conversational skills, called simply "conversational manners," is knowing when you can interrupt, when not to interrupt, and how to interrupt when it is not your turn in the conversation or when you are not part of the conversation. Role playing and commenting during real situations are the methods usually used to teach conversational manners. Practice through role modeling and in real situations. For a younger child, you may say, "It's not your turn now" or "Wait your turn," as long as it is not a situation that would embarrass him. For an older child, it's better to prearrange a discreet cue to let him know that he needs to wait his turn. For instance, you might cross two fingers to signal him not to interrupt.

There may be benefit to trying video modeling of appropriate conversational manners—that is, to have your child watch a video showing others using good skills. Another possibility is to videotape your own child and then use the tape as you would a Social Story to discuss what went well and what should be changed.

If your child is in inclusive settings at school or in community activities, he will hopefully have many opportunities to learn the right and wrong way to join a conversation. The natural consequences of other children and adults saying, "Don't interrupt; it's not your turn now" or "Knock it off" tends to modify the behavior. Many experiences, high expectations, and lots of practice are the best teachers for conversational manners.

If your child is not using many spoken words or uses AAC to communicate, he still needs to learn conversational manners. Make sure that he has a way to express polite phrases for joining a conversation such as "excuse me"—through sign, PECS, or a recorded phrase.

HOME ACTIVITIES FOR JOINING A CONVERSATION

- Choose a topic of conversation that your family or your child and friends will enjoy. Then play a game in which everyone has to ring a bell or press a buzzer for a turn in the conversation—you "buzz in" for a turn, as in a television game show. When a player buzzes in correctly, without interrupting, he gets a point or token. When he buzzes in while someone else is still talking and interrupts, he loses a point or a token.

- Sometimes when you are watching TV or a movie with your child, comment about characters interrupting each other or not letting others finish their sentences. Use the word *interrupt* to help your child understand this word and concept.

TOPICALIZATION

Topicalization involves skills in introducing topics, maintaining the topic, staying on topic, and changing topics. Maintaining topic and staying on topic are skills that are often difficult for children with Down syndrome. When you have difficulty maintaining the topic, conversations are short. You run out of things to say about the topic. When you have difficulty staying on topic, your conversation may seem rambling. You start talking about things on other topics instead of sticking with the original topic.

Here's an example of a conversation that doesn't maintain topic:

Rory: Do you want to come shopping?

Kim: Yeah.

Rory: Do you want to go to the mall?

Kim: Yeah.

Rory: Terry's birthday is soon. Should we buy her a gift? She likes music boxes. Should we look for that?

Kim: Don't know.

Rory: What's her favorite song?

Kim: (No answer.)

Rory is trying to have an organized conversation, but Kim is not maintaining and adding to the topic. She is not contributing to the conversation.

Here is an example of a similar conversation demonstrating difficulty staying on topic.

Rory: Do you want to come shopping?

Kim: Yeah.

Rory: Do you want to go to the mall?

Kim: Yeah. I go to mall near Grandma's. Big mall. Walk all over mall. Love KFC at mall. Let's have chicken.

Rory: Terry's birthday is soon. Should we buy her a gift? She likes music boxes. Should we look for that?

Kim: I'm hungry. Let's go have chicken. I like mashed potatoes and gravy. Yum!

Rory: What's Terry's favorite song?

Kim: (No answer.)

This time, Rory is trying to stay on the topic, but Kim is going off topic.

In the third example, Kim again changes the topic by talking about chicken, but this time Rory goes along with the change of topic.

Rory: Do you want to come shopping?

Kim: Yeah.

Rory: Do you want to go to the mall?

Kim: Yeah. KFC at mall. I like KFC.

Rory: I like KFC too. Do you want to have lunch at KFC?

Kim: Yes, chicken and mash potato. I like the biscuit too.

Rory: OK. There's a music box store in the mall. Maybe, we can buy Terry a birthday gift after lunch.

In everyday conversations at home with your child, you can help him improve his topicalization by gently pointing out times when he strays off topic and then trying to coax another appropriate response from him. For example, you might say, "I wasn't quite done talking about the snow. Let's finish that topic and then we can talk about bowling....What else can we say about snow? .... Do you like the big slow flakes or the fast little ones?"

Try to work with your child in private, but be discreet when correcting him in public. When your child can stay on topic more than half of the time, then you can develop a private signal to let him know when he is off topic, but don't try this while you are still teaching him how to stay on topic. Practice the skill, but also maintain your sense of humor. Don't expect perfection. Every child makes some comments that are off the topic, but may be delightful comments on life.

HOME ACTIVITIES FOR TOPICALIZATION

- Vocabulary words that are associated are words on the same topic, so association games are good ways to learn which words go together. For young children, picture games such as Lotto can be used. Lotto games that are personalized to your child's interests and people in his life can be made by scanning in pictures and making two copies, one for the board and one for matching. For example, you can make boards show- ing people and things associated with going to the beach, the movie theater, or the county fair. You may want to refer to the book *Teaching by Design* by Kimberly S. Voss (Wood- bine House, 2005) for tips on making lotto boards. For older children and teens, games such as *Password*, *Scattergories*, and *Pictionary Jr.* are fun to play and ad- dress topicalization skills.

- *Cranium Whoonu* (Cranium, Inc.) is a good game for practicing having conversations on the topic of favorites. The game focuses on guessing the other players' fa- vorite things. Players ask, "What's your favorite thing?" (e.g., burgers or bubble gum, sand castles or snow- men). The game can be adapted by adding the follow- up question "Why?" See the Resource Guide for more games that help children practice language skills.

- Keep a record of an event in a photo album to form the basis for a conversation. Go to a sports game, a zoo or aquarium, or to an amuse- ment park. Take many photographs. Mount them in the photo album in sequential order, print them out, and staple together in a book, or have them printed in a "photo flip book" at an online photo developing website such as Snapfish or Kodak.com. Then ask your child about the excur- sion. Ask questions about the book that can't be answered with just "yes," "no," or one word, such as, "What did we do at the aquarium?" Using the photos as cues, encourage him to talk about everything that "goes with" the excursion. After several "conversations" about the excursion, when the topics are familiar, do the same activity without the photos.

    If your child is less verbal, you can still use photos to practice topi- calization. You can take photos of several family trips (e.g., one to an aquarium and one to a baseball game). Mix photos from the two trips together and ask your child, "What did we do at the baseball game?" Your child can then sort through the photos to show you various things that you did at the baseball game.

● Read books together and discuss what the book is talking about (what topics go with the book). For example, after you read a book about aquariums, ask "What was the topic of this book?" Try to get your child to respond "It was about fish" (prompt if necessary). Keep the conversation going with a question such as "Do you prefer going to the aquarium or the zoo?" Then, discuss either the aquarium or the zoo, or, if your child is proficient on staying on topic, you can discuss both, and how they are different.

● Make a game board related to your child's activities or interests. For example, you could make a board about shopping for your middle school daughter, or a board about your recent trip to the beach for your son. Open up a manila folder and draw squares with markers, or use a piece of tag board that can be rolled up. On the spaces for the shopping game board, you might write (or attach pictures of) "new dress," the names of several stores your daughter likes, "food court," "gift cards," or "escalators." Use a spinner and game pieces. Whatever space you land on, you have to say two things about that topic. When your child can say two things, up the ante to three. Use cues, such as "What else could you tell Aunt Mimi about your new dress?" or "What did you build in the sand? What did you do with the seashells you collected?" "Did you use a metal detector this time? What did you find?"

● Create topic totes. Fill a decorated box, basket, or plastic tote with objects and books that relate to a single topic area. For example, make a beach tote for a younger child by filling a plastic pail or a beach bag with books about the beach and swimming, sunglasses, flip flops, a bathing suit, beach towel, a doll dressed for the beach, shovel, and shells or a little jar of sand. For an adolescent, you might fill the tote with tour guides or maps of a beach resort you will visit, and books about different varieties of shells, with samples of shells, a sun hat, and sunglasses.

Depending on your child's age and interests, there are many possible theme totes. How about using a jewelry box for a tote and filling it with beads, yarn, and other makings for a necklace? Or fill a greeting cards tote with felt pens, paper, rubber stamps, envelopes, and postage stamps? Or make a picnic planning tote with checklists of food to be served, people to be invited, recreational activities? In addition to objects and books, you might include appropriate CDs or DVDs. Use the materials in the theme totes to plan an activity (picnic or trip) or complete an activity (crafts). Talk about the activity, read the books about the activity, or simulate the activity in play (have a picnic with dolls).

● Practice routines with your child through role playing. For example, for a younger child, discuss going to McDonald's, and point out what is and is not on the topic. Use props to make the situation more realistic, such as a McDonald's French Fry container, placemat, and tray. You can use a picture menu from McDonald's to visually prompt what is on the topic. For instance, can we buy popcorn at McDonald's? You are pointing out what "goes with" McDonald's and what does not. For an older child or teen, you might talk about going to buy tickets for a concert. What do you need to ask for? It is appropriate to talk about who will be singing or what band will be playing, when you are in line, or while waiting with your family or friends. Then discuss what is appropriate when you get to the ticket window—for instance, that it isn't appropriate to have long conversations with the ticket person when there is a line behind you. What is the pertinent information that the ticket person needs? Practice that as a script routine. Or if your teen's speech is very clear, try letting him order tickets by phone.

● Ask questions about experiences your child has had. "What did you do at Jennifer's birthday party?" Ask for details, such as, "What did you eat? Who did you see? What games did you play? What gifts did Matthew get?" Or create a visual organizer with on-topic questions or with visual icons to help him organize his thoughts. Coach your child to help him stay on topic.

● To help an older child or teen understand how to draw out more information on a topic when talking with others, consider giving him a graphic organizer or written list of questions to ask about any activity people are talking about. For example: WHO did you do it with, WHAT did you do, WHEN, HOW did you get there, WHAT did you like about it? At home, when you or another family member is talking about something you did, have your child practice asking you these questions. If your child cannot read yet, you can use pictures to remind him of the questions to ask.

● Play "Guess the Topic." With another family member, privately agree on a topic of conversation, such as "animals at the zoo," "good picnic food," "what we did last summer" or "what I'd buy if I were rich." Then start talking about that topic: "I like to bring turkey sandwiches or maybe sub sandwiches from the grocery store…. I need some chips and dips, too…." See if your child can figure out the topic of your conversation. If he is stumped, give him a list of a few choices to pick from. This is a good game to play when you are waiting at a restaurant, driving in a car, etc.

● If your child enjoys writing lists, capitalize on this interest to help him improve his topicalization skills. Drs. Dennis McGuire and Brian Chicoine, among others, have noted that some older children and teens with Down syndrome enjoy making lists of things in their free time. For instance, they might make lists of their favorite songs, TV shows, or favorite foods, or lists of people they want to invite to their next party. Clearly, they have categorization skills and enjoy using them. To have a real conversation, though, you have to be able to do more than list things in a category. You have to be able to explore different aspects of the topic—what you like and don't like about it, what the other person thinks about it, etc. Lists, however, are a good way to begin.

When your child has a list of favorite songs, talk about what other lists he could compile that are related to those songs. For example, who sings the songs? Are they all country or all gospel or are the songs from different categories? Role play a conversation about songs. Discuss that, in addition to telling which songs and recording artists *you* like, you also want to ask the other person what songs *he* likes. In a conversation, you need to find out about the other person's views on the topic. Also discuss that some people are shy and don't want to take a turn and other people are very talkative and want to take all of the turns, and not give anyone else a chance.

Theme Parties

Planning a theme party is a wonderful way to practice topicalization skills, as well as language, organizational skills, reading directions, and measuring, and results in a wonderful event that can be shared by all.

The first question to ask your child is what should we choose as the theme? How about a sport such as soccer or baseball? Or a hobby such as CD collecting? Or a pet party? Or a theme party based on a favorite TV show or movie?

To plan the party, you will need to practice topic skills. What goes with your theme? For sports, maybe the teams or sports equipment. For pets, different types of dogs and cats.

What will you do at the party? Again, the discussion will involve topical skills—what is appropriate at parties? Should you play games, do crafts, eat? Which games or crafts? If you are having a pet party, should you watch DVDs that involve pets? Should the partygoers bring photos of their pets or should they bring their pets?

Developing a menu based on a theme also involves research. What food goes with baseball games? Perhaps hot dogs, nachos, soda, lemonade? Can you make a cake shaped like a baseball mitt? Can you find napkins and paper plates in the colors of your favorite team? What music would be appropriate to play? *Take Me Out to the Ballgame*? If you have decided on a pet theme, what food goes with pets? Cookies shaped like various pets, goldfish crackers, animal crackers?

Once you have made the decisions, there is a lot to do to organize the event. Make a list of people to invite. Design or buy invitations. Send out invitations. Buy or make decorations. Buy ingredients for food to be served. Buy materials for games or activities.

Prepare the food. Decorate the room or outside area with pictures or objects that relate to the theme. Have you asked people to dress for the theme? If so, you will need to plan your own outfit.

At the party, your child gains practical experience in welcoming guests, organizing and replenishing food and refreshments, actually playing the games, doing the crafts, etc. This provides practice in pragmatics—language in use in real life. Planning the party can also be a group project, where everyone plans together, but individuals or subgroups take on the responsibility for one phase of the party.

STYLISTIC VARIATIONS

Stylistic variations is the term used to describe an individual's ability to modify and adapt his communication to both the audience and the situation. Sometimes, the variations are known as registers.

To modify how we communicate to a particular audience, we modify how we talk to people, not necessarily what we actually say. As children grow, they learn a variety of different rules or formats to use when talking with people in different social roles. This might include knowing how to use polite, formal, and colloquial language. It also includes knowing when to modify our vocabulary, loudness, rate, and even gestures, depending on where we are and what is happening. For example, when your child goes to a family owned pizza place where everyone knows him, it is okay to be very informal and to speak in a louder voice. But, when your child is attending a religious service, he needs to speak formally and in a quiet voice. And when your child is talking to the school principal, he needs to use a different tone of voice and different words than when he is talking to his six-month-old cousin.

Stylistic variations are difficult to learn because there are so many possible permutations and different situations and because children and teens with Down syndrome often have trouble generalizing communication skills. In addition, sometimes children with Down syndrome may generalize the *wrong* skills. For instance, they may want to model the behavior of television or movie characters who make smart aleck comments to teachers or other adults. Furthermore, children with Down syndrome often have trouble judging the loudness of their own voices, so even though they may realize they should use a quiet voice in a given situation, they may still speak too loudly.

Children with Down syndrome benefit from extra help and practice in this area. Parents are usually the best teachers of this skill. Usually, it is best to talk to your child about adjusting the way he interacts with someone prior to encountering them or as the situation presents itself. It may help to connect appropriate talk with something tangible your child is aware of. For example, you might tell your daughter, "You're wearing a fancy dress today. It's a special day and we need to use good manners. We can't say 'What's up, man' today." Of course, you can't always plan ahead for everything your child might say, and planning doesn't always work.

HOME ACTIVITIES FOR STYLISTIC VARIATIONS

● Role play with your child in advance of a novel activity or one where he has experienced difficulties in the past. Practice in the most "natural" setting possible. Set up the situation clearly, and use props and costumes to make the role playing as realistic as possible. For example, if you want your child to practice going to a friend's house for a sleepover, have him pack his pajamas, bring his sleeping bag, and take clothes for the next morning. Then set up a part of the room that is "your friend's house" and play out various scenarios to practice what is and is not appropriate communication. For example, how do you ask your friend's mother for a drink, or what would be appropriate to say if your friend's younger brother is annoying you?

● Use verbal coaching or provide specific instructions to help your child give appropriate responses while you are role playing. You might whisper in his ear to provide suggestions, such as "talk softly" or "call her Mrs. Ranie, not Sally." Don't assume that your child is going to figure out the rules; teach him the rules of conversation. After the event or activity is over, praise your child for his successes: "You spoke so nicely to Mrs. Ranie" or "You used your quiet voice and were so polite when you told Joe's girlfriend how pretty she looked." If you can find a book about a similar situation, read the book together and talk about it. Practice is needed, and experience is very important in teaching this skill.

● Consider using holiday celebrations as opportunities to teach your child about stylistic variations. Many families have large dinners centered around holidays such as Thanksgiving. Some adults and children attending are people your child is close with and sees very often. Other people at dinner may be new to your child, or may be less familiar. Some older adults may have hearing loss, and your child may need to speak louder. Some folks are huggers and others are not. Before the holiday would be a good time to talk about how we sometimes talk differently to different people.

● If your child enjoys playing with action figures or dolls, retell the plot of a favorite video or story using the figures. Change voices, loudness, etc., as appropriate. Act out some loud scenes and some quieter ones. Talk about the characters and how they would sound.

● Watch TV or movies with your child and check during the commercials that he understands that the way the characters are talking would not be appropriate in real life. For example, "That was sure funny when Justin said 'You talking to ME' to the teacher, wasn't it? Do you think kids should talk to a teacher like that in real life?"

● This is a good activity for a group at Scouts or other social groups. Set up a room with study carrels, screens, or dividers. In each section, have a large tagboard or presentation board. One board might have a scene of a camping trip with tent and campfire in the background. Another might show a library with pictures of books on shelves and people working at computers. A third might depict people at a football stadium watching a game and cheering. The scenes can be drawn, enlarged from a digital photo, or projected on a screen with an overhead projector. Set up a scenario, and role play with the group. If necessary, make comments pointing out the differences in appropriate conversation for the different scenarios— e.g., "he was using a lot of slang when he was on the camping trip" or "he was using a loud voice and cheering at the football game." Then discuss the differences in the way they communicated during the role playing.

- Play a loudness game when you are watching television. Turn the TV to a talk show or a news show where people are talking constantly at an even level. Then give your child the remote, and ask him how loudly these people should talk if they were in the library ... at a party ... having a group discussion at school ... at a rock concert ... at the dinner table, etc. Let him adjust the volume to what he considers appropriate, then you can let him know if you think he needs to make it louder or softer.

- You might want to look into getting software or videos designed to help kids with autism spectrum disorders master conversational skills (or see if your local Down syndrome group will buy the software or DVDs for their libraries). Some examples:
  - *My Community* software, available from Silver Lining at www.silverliningmm.com
  - *Fitting In and Having Fun* DVD, available from Different Roads to Learning at www.difflearn.com
  - *Manners for the Real World*, a DVD for young people with Asperger syndrome, available from Coulter Video at www.coulter-video.com/manners.htm
  - *Model Me Conversation Cues* DVD, available from Model Me Kids at www.modelmekids.com

CLARIFICATION AND REPAIRS

Two children are sitting on an airplane on the runway:
> *Child 1:* We're moving.
> *Child 2:* Where are you moving to?
> *Child 1:* No, the plane is moving.

These children have just demonstrated their skills in clarifications and repairs. Clarifications and repairs are skills that fit with each other. They are both skills involved when there are misunderstandings in communication, known as communication breakdowns. Clarification is the ability to ask for more information when there is something that you missed or did not understand. Clarifications are also known as *contingent queries* or *requests for repair*. Using clarifications helps signal that you are paying attention to the conversation and also keeps the conversation moving along. This is a skill that is needed in school settings.

The listener may ask for repairs in three ways:
1. clarification ("What did you say"?)
2. specification ("Can you tell me what you mean?")
3. confirmation ("Is this what you are saying?")

Repairs refers to the ability: 1) to recognize that a misunderstanding has occurred or that your listener did not understand or hear something that was said, and 2) to follow-up by providing the information needed to "repair" the misunderstanding. Usually, in a conversation, the listener asks for clarifications and the speaker makes repairs. There are many different types of repairs. Repairs are very specific to the situation.

The speech-language pathologist can work with your child to increase his awareness of different types of communication breakdown, and help him learn how to make various types of repairs. For example, an unintelligible word may be the source of the communication misunderstanding. The contingent query might be "I didn't understand what you said; can you repeat it?" and some possible repairs may be repeating the word, pointing to the object or person that you were naming, or spelling the word. Other possible misunderstandings might arise if the speaker gives an impossible command, uses unfamiliar words, or isn't specific enough. For example, you might ask, "Do you want to come with me to the store?" Since your child likes to go to the sporting goods store but hates to go to the hardware store, he needs to ask for clarification such as "Which store?" Or you might ask your child, "Did you see the badger by the lake?" But your child doesn't know what a badger is so he needs to ask you what the word means.

If your child with Down syndrome has a younger sibling or cousin, you might point out when the younger child gets frustrated because you don't understand him and don't give him what he wants. An example might be when he points to the refrigerator and you give him apple juice, but he wanted orange juice. You can comment, "I didn't know you wanted orange juice. Next time, tell me which (or what kind of) juice you want."

HOME ACTIVITIES FOR CLARIFICATION AND REPAIRS

- Play *Simon Says* and have Simon sometimes give instructions that need clarification such as: "Give me that"; "Sit on it"; "Touch it"; or "Walk over there;" "Put it on the table." If your child tries to do the action without enough information, stop him. Say, "I didn't tell you what to sit on. You need to ask me 'Where should I sit?' (or 'Which one?')."

- Play *Twister* and give incomplete instructions. For instance, just say "blue," or "right foot," or "put your foot on blue" without specifying "right foot on blue." If other, more verbal children are playing, make sure they give your child a chance to ask for clarification himself.

- Play a variation of *Twister*. This game can be used once your child knows some colors and shapes (and possibly also large and small concepts). Cut out different shapes in different colors (may include big or large and small). Spread these out on the floor. You can use two shapes and one color or two colors and one shape to start (blue circle and blue square or blue circle and red circle). Ask your child to bring you the "blue one." Cue your child (whisper in his ear) or use a sibling as a model, to ask the question, "Which blue one?" or "The blue circle or the blue square?" Increase the complexity as your child's skill increases.

- Cook together. When two or more people work as a team—for example, using a recipe to make a snack—clarifications and repairs need to be used. So, food activities using recipes are good ways to practice clarification and repairs.

- Get a long roll of paper. Draw or trace (for a 6 or 7 year old) the full size outline of your child. Tape the outline to the wall and give your child colored markers, stickers, stars, feathers of different colors, etc. Give instructions for decorating that are not clear. Put stars (don't say which color), or draw red mittens on one hand (don't say which one). Keep prompting the child, "What do you need to ask?"

- Sometimes deliberately give instructions that are vague. For example, say, "Bring me that thing." When your child looks confused, ask him, "What do you need to know? Say, 'What do you want?'" Provide models and examples, and teach him what kinds of information he needs to ask. For example, "Do I want the telephone?" Name objects that are visible that you might be asking for.

- Sometimes ask your child to bring you things that he is unfamiliar with. For example, in the kitchen ask him to bring you a utensil that he doesn't know the name of. "Please give me the spatula (garlic press, colander, egg separator, etc.)." Or when you are working with tools in the garage or basement, ask him for an unfamiliar tool such as a wrench or ratchet. If your child doesn't say anything to clarify your request, prompt him (e.g., "Wrench? What's that?").

- Make a *Go Fish* or *Old Maid* card game using index cards and photographs or pictures of unfamiliar objects. For instance, make pairs of aardvark, ferret, and prairie dog cards, as well as cards depicting animals your child already knows. Deal out a hand of five cards per player and then take turns asking, "Do you have a ferret (or other animal)?" If your child doesn't know what the animal is, he needs to ask for clarification. And, before he can ask whether you have a ferret card, he will need to ask what the picture on his card is. The idea is to teach your child that it is OK to ask, "What's that?" or "What's this called?"

- Sometimes deliberately misunderstand your child if you know he can make repairs. For instance, if he asks simply for "more, please" and you are pretty sure that he wants more gravy, give him more of something else instead, like peas, and see if he will make the repair and ask for more gravy. Or say, "Oh, you didn't want peas? If you want more gravy, tell me, 'I want more gravy.'"

One Step at a Time

Agood way to teach and practice clarification and repair skills is through the use of barrier activities. In a barrier game, there is a physical barrier—a piece of folded cardboard, a manila folder, a screen, or a stack of magazines between the two participants. Anything that will prevent each player from seeing what the other person is doing is fine.

A barrier game sets up a situation where the child with Down syndrome can't use a visual model. In the barrier game activity, one person gives the instructions and the other person follows the instructions. The person who is listening needs to try to follow the instructions and ask questions when he doesn't understand the instructions. The person giving the instructions needs to make repairs when his communication is not clear to the listener. You can use a series of barrier game activities, and the listener and speaker can change roles.

The activity can be a food activity, such as making an ice cream sundae, decorated cookies, or a sub sandwich. An art activity, such as making a sports poster or a greeting card, would also lend itself to a barrier activity. The important thing is that you (or a brother, sister, grandparent, babysitter) and your child communicate by speaking, listening, and asking questions. No peeking to see what the other one is doing!

Let's say you are going to make the perfect sundae. First you put the barrier up. Then your child needs to describe to you what to do. For example, "Put vanilla ice cream in the dish." "Put chocolate syrup on." The first couple of times you try a barrier game, you can ask questions to clarify: "How many scoops of ice cream?" "Lots of syrup or a little?" On the first or second tries, you may need to teach your child how to ask questions or what questions to ask.

Once you've done this several times, try to get your child to include the details. At the end of the sundae construction, you remove the barrier. Ask your child, "Is this the sundae you wanted?" If not, find out how it doesn't match your child's ideal. More syrup? No cherries? Discuss giving instructions. What should he ask for the next time if he wants more syrup?

Once your child can give the directions, change roles. You give the directions and your child asks the questions and makes the sundae. The bonus to this activity is each time you practice, you get to make a sundae!

Other ideas for barrier games include:

- Make tacos
- Build with Legos or other blocks
- Make a picture or design with Colorforms or construction paper shapes
- String a necklace with different colors and shapes of beads
- Decorate a cupcake
- Color a map with markers
- Draw a face on a pumpkin with markers

If you're making a craft or building with blocks, it is helpful for both the speaker and the listener to do the activity. That is, both players sit on opposite sides of the barrier with a matching set of ingredients or supplies. In this scenario, the players can compare the finished products when they are done and see where they went wrong.

What is important is that there are lots of pieces with lots of choices, so that the speaker has to be specific in describing how to use the materials, and the listener has to choose from the materials and use them based on the instructions given. The idea is to have items that can be confused if detailed instructions are not given, and items that lend themselves to simple questions to clarify the instructions.

Barrier games can be used for children and teens with a wide range of language and speech expertise (three-word phrases to sentences).

Presuppositions encompass the background information and prior experience that the listener brings to a situation. When we talk about considering your listener's needs or audience analysis (in public speaking), we are talking about presuppositions. Presuppositions involve walking in your listener's shoes, or taking the attitude of your listener. What does your listener know? What do you need to tell your listener?

Before a child can use presuppositions, he needs to develop a "theory of mind." This is the sense that other people have their own thoughts and beliefs and do not necessarily know or feel what we know or feel.

One way to determine whether a child has developed a theory of mind is to set up a scenario for him to watch and then ask him questions to determine whether he can put himself into someone else's shoes. A classic test of theory of mind involves showing the child two characters (perhaps enacted by puppets), one of whom hides something while the other isn't looking. For instance, Mary puts a marble in a basket while Jane is watching. Then Mary leaves the room. While Mary is gone, Jane takes the marble from the basket and hides it under a chair. The child is then asked where Mary will look for her marble when she comes back into the room. A child with a mature theory of mind will realize that Mary will look for the marble where she left it—in the basket. A child who hasn't yet developed theory of mind will assume Mary will look for the marble where he himself knows it to be—under the chair.

Researchers have found that children with Down syndrome have more delays in developing a theory of mind than would be expected based on their nonverbal intelligence. Specifically, one study found that a group of children and young adults with Down syndrome, aged 11.5 to 23, had more difficulties with theory of mind than both typically developing children and individuals with fragile X syndrome with similar mental ages (L. Abbeduto et al., 2004).

How do problems with theory of mind translate into problems with conversational skills? All young children are egocentric, and will assume that you understand their references when they are telling about events that another person has not directly experienced. Children with Down syndrome, however, linger in this stage for a longer time. So, for example, a child with Down syndrome might start talking to a new teacher about Evan, without clarifying that Evan is his older brother. An older child might start talking about a family vacation, who was there, and what they did without indicating who the members of the family are or where they went. Whenever a child talks about an event or a place that the listener is unfamiliar with, skills in using presuppositions come into play. We need to convey to the child who is speaking that the listener needs more information.

Presuppositions are an advanced pragmatic skill, but you can work on them at home. One way is to let your child know what you (the listener) need to know. Stop your child, and ask, "Who's Sunita? Is she a girl in your class?" or, "When did you have a spelling test? Was that today in school?" "You need to tell me, because I don't know that." Children with Down syndrome have difficulty with presuppositions, and need more practice, coaching, and reminders to learn about what the listener needs to know. This important skill continues to develop throughout childhood and can continue to develop into adulthood.

HOME ACTIVITIES FOR PRESUPPOSITIONS

- Giving directions is one way to practice presuppositions. Children with Down syndrome are generally able to learn a board game, and then teach the rules to another person well. This provides good practice for presuppositions. The person teaching needs to figure out what the learner needs to know in order to play the game. When they haven't figured it out, they use repairs and requests for clarification such as "No, that's not what you do. You need to spin again."

- Play barrier games, as described above. When your child gives you a direction you don't understand, emphasize why he needs to clarify. For instance, "I can't see what you're looking at. You have to tell me where to put it."

- Use Comic Strip Conversations, as discussed above, to help your child understand that other people don't all think and know the same things he does. You may also want to read *Teaching Children with Autism to Mind-Read: A Practical Guide* (Howlin, Baron-Cohen, Hadwin), which goes into detail about helping a child with autism develop theory of mind.

- Make a deliberate effort to use words such as *think, wonder, guess, believe, know, hope, doubt,* and *remember* with your child to increase his awareness of other people's differing thoughts and perspectives. Especially point out instances when you think, feel, believe, or guess something different than your child does. You can also invite him to guess what you're thinking. For example, you might sometimes say to your child, "I'll give you three guesses what I'm thinking" when there is some context that might help him guess. For instance, perhaps you've both been walking around in the hot sun and what you're thinking is that you need a cold drink.

- For older children, take turns describing something where one of you cannot see what the other is looking at. For example, one of you might be looking at photos on the screen of a digital camera, a movie on a camcorder, or pictures using a Viewmaster toy. When your child is describing what he is looking at, ask questions to help him understand that you don't see what he sees.

NARRATIVE DISCOURSE

It is often difficult for children and adolescents with Down syndrome to tell their parents what happened at school or at a community event. They have difficulty remembering the parts of the story or event, keeping them in order, and organizing and retelling the story. The ability to retell a story you have heard or retell about an event is known as *narrative discourse*.

USING A CUEING BOARD

To help your child retell a story, a cueing board can be developed to establish the categories of information that he needs to include in the retelling. For example:

- Who?
- What happened? (What happened first? second? last?)
- Where did it happen?
- When did it happen?

How you physically design your child's cueing board will depend on his age and reading abilities. For a younger child who can't read and who isn't concerned about appearances, you might use colored symbols or photos attached to tag board or laminated on a piece of paper so it will be durable. For instance, a person can stand for who, a clock for when, a road sign with arrows for where (or a house graphic), and a questions mark for what. For older children, a smaller, bookmark-sized cueing system or even a Post-it size note can be designed.

A bonus to using a cueing board is that your child gets practice in organizing information, not just in re-telling stories. A ten-year-old boy, Sean, had difficulty telling about events that happened during the day at school. I developed an organizer for him similar to the one to the left. Now, at age eleven, he can retell what happened in school and he no longer needs to use the organizer to structure the information. He has internalized the framework for retelling a story.

When your child is used to using the visual organizer, it can help him when he is telling you about something novel that happened, or when he is upset and trying to recount what happened. When your child is trying to relay a new situation or situation using new vocabulary, you may want to encourage him to use pantomime to show names, objects, or situations he does not have the vocabulary to describe. For example, if he is talking about electric hedge clippers, but doesn't know the word, he may use gestures like scissors and make a loud whirring sound.

Recounting an emotionally charged situation is the most difficult, but this is difficult for everyone. When your child is upset, he may be sobbing and shaking at the same time that he is trying to speak. First, try to get him to calm down and then to think through what he is trying to tell you, using his *wh-* organizer to help him organize his thoughts.

Your child's speech-language pathologist can use published therapy materials such as *Narrative Toolbox* (Hutson-Nechkash, 2001) and *Conversations* (Hoskins, 1996) in treatment to help your child master narrative skills.

SEQUENCING WORDS WITH PHOTO CUE CARDS

Using sequencing words such as *first, next, then, last* to describe a sequence of activities is sometimes difficult for older children and adolescents. It is a skill needed when you tell a story, or tell what happened. It is easier to sequence when you have photo "cue cards." Take photos of activities that your child does that involve sequences of actions, such as making popcorn, making a sandwich, going to the video store, buying and wrapping a gift, doing a dance such as *YMCA* or *Macarena,* swimming, diving, track, or other sports activities. Most cooking and crafts activities involve sequences.

In the beginning, use only three photos to represent different stages of the activity sequence. Mount the photos on poster board or colored paper. Then glue the pictures in sequence to a larger black poster board or tack them to a bulletin board. Model for your child how to describe the activity using the pictures as cues. Emphasize the sequencing words. For example: "FIRST you spread the peanut butter. NEXT you spread the jelly. LAST, you put the two pieces of bread together." You can leave the photos on the bulletin board, and let your child use the photos to tell other people about the activity. Change the photos frequently to maintain interest. Keep the photos in a conspicuous place so that family and friends will ask about them.

Another variation is to mount the sequence pictures in a photo album. You or your child can then write a description of each photo under it in the album. Memory books are very popular now, and these sequence pictures can become part of a memory book.

Family Conversations

Conversations begin at home. I can't emphasize enough the importance of having frequent conversations at home. Dinner time is a good time for conversations. But, with the frantic pace of our days, dinner is sometimes eaten on the go, in the car. Dinner at home is a better time for conversations than dinner in the car, because it is important to make eye contact and turn your full attention to interactions and attention to each. So, if your family does not often sit down together to eat dinner, look for another time when most family members usually are around and feeling relatively relaxed.

Here are some suggestions for helping your child improve his conversational skills simply by including him in family conversations:

- Make sure your family conversations are on topics and at a level where your child can join in. From an early age, you want your child to learn that he can contribute to conversations and that other people want to know what he has to say.
- How about a weekly joke that each family member shares? Or a word of the day?
- Make a habit of asking open-ended questions that your child can't answer with one word (unless he's at the one-word stage). How about asking about the best thing that happened all day, the funniest thing the dog did, or what everyone wants to do on the weekend? Be sure to vary your questions so others really listen to what you're asking and vary their answers.

- Let your child choose the topic for the conversation some days.
- If something funny or unusual or sad happened right before dinner, talk about it at the table.
- If your family is having a conversation and your child is tuned out, make an effort to draw him in by asking things like "what do you think" or "do you agree?"
- Sometimes use fill-in sentences to start the conversations. For example: "My favorite time of the day is _____." "If I could have dinner with anyone in the world, I would choose _____."

Conclusion

During the time period that this book covers (approximately ages 6 to 14) most children with Down syndrome make significant strides in conversational skills. At age 6, many children are having very short conversations. For example, they might

be able to ask one question or respond to questions. By age 14, many children with Down syndrome are having long conversations with their families, although they may be shy around unfamiliar people, and converse very little with those outside their immediate circle of family and friends.

Conversational skills are important and they can be developed over time, into adulthood. I know many teenagers with Down syndrome who are excellent conversationalists. They are engaging and fun to talk with. They are interested in many topics. They enjoy hobbies and traveling, music and shows. Although your child's SLP may work on conversational skills, you and your family will play the biggest role in teaching your child these skills. Remember, it takes time and practice to learn to be an active participant in conversations. You are in a perfect position to provide that practice over time.

CHAPTER 10

Assistive Technology for Communication

Most children and adults with Down syndrome use speech as their primary communication system. But, they may need an assistive technology system as a support to communication in some situations. For example, your child may be able to communicate well socially when she can help clarify her message with gestures, facial expressions, and repetitive expressions ("Hi! How're you doing? See ya!"). But when your child has to give her name and address or communicate with nonfamily members on the telephone, she may have difficulty getting her message across. A card with written information or a tape recorded message on a communication system may be needed as a back-up because, in these situations, the information given needs to be clearly understood and your child can't use gestures, facial expressions, and repetition to help clarify the message.

Other children and adults with Down syndrome cannot use speech to communicate effectively in most situations. Their speech may be unintelligible, or they may have difficulty with language and be unable to formulate verbal messages. They may use vocalizations but not be able to produce understandable words. (Vocalizations are any sounds made, such as a grunt, laugh, shout, or groan, that are not recognizable words.) These individuals need to use another system such as signs or a communication board to communicate because they do not have sufficient speech to say the message that they want to convey.

Finally, some individuals have a dual diagnosis, such as Down syndrome and autism, that makes it difficult to communicate verbally. For them, augmentative and alternative communication (AAC) can be designed to serve as their main communication system. AAC is any method that assists with or supplements speech and language, or that replaces speech as the primary communication system.

In this chapter, I will discuss the reasons that children and teens with Down syndrome may need to use AAC to help them communicate, the types of communication strategies and devices that are most often used, and how to obtain an evaluation and treatment services for AAC.

How Many Children with Down Syndrome Need Alternatives to Speech?

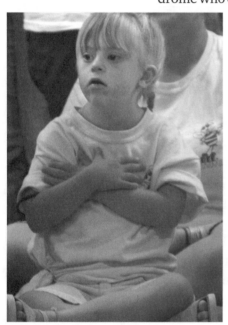

Research suggests that only about 5 percent of children and adults with Down syndrome will be unable to use speech to communicate. Some of these individuals are able to say a few words or vocalizations but they usually can't get their message across with speech alone. In my experience, however, the number of people with Down syndrome who can use speech, but have difficulty communicating so that people outside of their families can understand them, is higher. In the intelligibility survey that we conducted, only 5 percent of parents said that their child *never* has difficulty making herself understood to unfamiliar people.

Many children with Down syndrome can make themselves understood at home and with their circle of family and friends. They encounter more difficulty when they are communicating with unfamiliar people, or when the message gets more complex. They may speak too quickly or their words may not be clear to listeners. Or, they may be capable of understanding and using more complex language, but since they are unable to "speak" those complex phrases and sentences, they are forced to use short, simple sentences.

When your child can't make herself understood, interactions at school, with friends, and in the community are more difficult. AAC methods should be considered for anyone who is having trouble making herself understood. Each individual, whether or not she can use speech effectively, wants, needs, and has the right to communicate with the people in her world.

What Is AAC?

Augmentative and alternative communication (AAC) is any method that assists or supplements speech and language (augmentative communication), or, in some cases, replaces speech as the primary communication system (alternative communication). AAC is generally divided into aided and unaided systems. Unaided systems include natural gestures and sign language, and aided systems (using something external to the body) include photo and picture cards, communication boards, and electronic or nonelectronic communication devices.

If your child is elementary school aged or older, the chances are that she has already used one or more types of AAC. Currently, to help with the transition to speech, one or more of the following systems is recommended for most young children with Down syndrome: 1) Total Communication (a type of AAC); 2) sign language; or 3) picture communication (communication boards or the Picture Exchange Communication System).

Once children with Down syndrome begin to use speech to communicate, they still use gestures, facial expressions, and pointing to help get their messages across. Often when their speech is difficult to understand or produce, people with Down syndrome are very creative at using alternative methods of communicating. For instance, if a child wants the newest version of a video game, she may show her parents the older version and say or sign "new" or put up two fingers if the new edition is volume 2.

We all use gestures and facial expressions as an assist to get our message across. In conversations, we use our hands and arms to make gestures; we change our facial expressions or move our heads; we point to objects, photos, or people to illustrate our point. All of these things are AAC. We use every possible channel to communicate: sound, sight, smell, touch, and even taste. Children and adults with Down syndrome are no different. Studies have shown that people with Down syndrome use gestures and facial expressions appropriately, and that these modes help them get their messages across. Their gestures and facial expressions match this message and are usually accurate reflections of how they are feeling.

Augmentative and alternative communication merely changes the options of communication methods available, expanding the messages a child can send and making it easier to understand her messages. Let's say your child wants to listen to music but can't use speech to tell you. The easiest way for her to accomplish her goal is to go over and turn on the CD player. But, what happens if someone has moved it to a high shelf and she can't reach it, or if the batteries are dead and there are no more left in the drawer? How can she let you know that?

One way your child can communicate about her needs is through actions and gestures. She can bring the player over to you, open it up, and show you that she has taken out the batteries. Or, she can pull you over to the shelf and point to the player. She could also use signs for "want music." She could use a picture card or picture board that has a drawing or photo of her player. Or she may have a voice output communication device with recreation choices programmed on it. With this device, she could tell you, "I want to play music now, please," in a recorded voice from the device. She may have options that she knows how to use on her communication device so she can ask you, "Where is my music player?" or tell you, "I need new batteries" using the voice output. Her message is the same, but using the AAC device enabled her to build a sentence using "I want" and "please" and enabled you to understand what she wanted.

With AAC, your child does not need to get frustrated and have a behavior outburst. She does not have to limit herself to communicating with single words because that is what she is able to say. She is able to build her language skills and use language effectively, and she is able to get her needs met. With any of these methods, she may or may not also use her own voice at the same time. All of these methods of communicating, with or without speech, are called augmentative and alternative communication (AAC).

How Is AAC Related to Assistive Technology?

Technically speaking, AAC is a form of assistive technology. This is important for you to understand because, in the United States, children who are eligible for special education are also eligible to receive assistive technology services. The Indi-

viduals with Disabilities Education Act (IDEA) requires that each time an IEP is developed for your child, her team must consider whether she would benefit from assistive technology.

"Assistive Technology Device" is defined in the IDEA Improvement Act of 2004 as "any item, piece of equipment, or product system, whether acquired commercially off the shelf, modified, or customized, that is used to increase, maintain, or improve functional capabilities of a child with a disability" (H. R. 1350; 602). Since AAC is a type of assistive technology, this means that your child's needs for AAC must be addressed at least once a year. See the section on "AAC Evaluation" later in this chapter for information on requesting that your child be evaluated for AAC during the IEP process.

Who Needs AAC?

Whatever a child's age, it is important to ensure that she has an effective method for communicating. When a child can't get her message across, she usually becomes frustrated. She may stop trying to communicate or may find alternative ways of getting her message to you. Sometimes, she will use pantomime or drag you over to show you what she wants. That may work for young children. For older children and adolescents, messages are often more complex and can't be easily pantomimed or shown. In school or at community events, the child cannot drag someone over to show what she wants. That is not considered appropriate behavior, in most situations. It also isn't considered appropriate behavior if the child vents her frustration through behavior such as kicking, biting, screaming, hiding under the table, or running out of the room to get what she cannot get through communication.

In these situations, it is important to provide an *additional method of communicating* or *alternate method of communicating*. This gives your child a way to share her message, promotes communication, and often reduces problem behavior resulting from communication frustration. Some children who are not communicating do not get to that level of communication frustration for a long time. Instead, they passively let the world go by and do not interact with others because they do not understand how they can successfully engage other people. This is just as serious a situation as if the child *is* venting her frustration. If a child has no way to interact with others in her world, the lack of social interaction can lead to depression later on.

**GENERAL
REASONS TO
CONSIDER AAC**

The sections below discuss the major reasons that a child or young teen with Down syndrome might benefit from AAC. In general, AAC systems are used as transitional, supplementary, or alternative means of communication.

USING AAC AS A TRANSITION TO SPEECH

A transitional system is typically used as a bridge between language and speech. Most children with Down syndrome are ready to use a language system by eight to twelve months of age, but often don't have the neurological and muscular development to be able to speak until they are three to four years old. If the child has Childhood Apraxia of Speech or a dual diagnosis such as autism, she may not begin to speak until even later.

Transitional augmentative systems such as sign language, the Picture Exchange Communication System (PECS), and communication boards are used to help children communicate until they are able to use speech. For detailed information on using AAC to help young children with Down syndrome make the transition to speech, see *Early Communication Skills for Children with Down Syndrome* (Kumin, 2003).

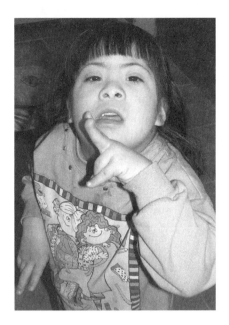

USING AAC TO SUPPLEMENT SPEECH

A supplementary system adds to a child's communication abilities by providing vocabulary, sentence structure, and comments that are new or too difficult for her to say. Sometimes signs, communication boards, or electronic devices are also used to supplement speech when intelligibility is a problem for the older child or adolescent who has a lot to say, but is hard to understand. In particular, AAC can be used to help a child respond in class, so that she can be an integral part of the learning community. AAC can also be used as a supplementary system in any situation where a child cannot communicate effectively through speech.

Any supplementary AAC system must be individually developed for the child and the child must then learn to use the system. The IEP team, including the family and the child (if able), needs to determine when and how AAC is needed to supplement speech attempts. You and your child's IEP team need to determine whether the effort in learning will have sufficient rewards for your child, helping her communicate more clearly and with less frustration.

USING AAC INSTEAD OF SPEECH

When AAC is used as an alternative communication system, it serves as a child's primary method of communicating. Alternative systems are used when a child is unable to use speech to get her messages across in many or all situations. These systems are often the most complex and time consuming to design, because they need to meet all of the child's needs for communication and learning at school, at home, and in the community.

DOES YOUR CHILD NEED AAC?

As soon as Ian, age 7, got off the school bus, his mother could tell that he had had a bad day. His mouth was turned down at the corners and he pulled away when she tried to give him a hug. "Ian, what happened?" she asked. But all Ian could say was "Bad day!" His mother began to ask questions. "What happened at school? Did something happen on the bus?" Ian kept saying "Bad day, bad day."

Lou Ann, a 12-year-old, is a very friendly, outgoing girl. When something exciting is going on in her life, she wants to tell everyone. She just came back from a trip to Chicago. She loved the parks and the interactive water features. She tries to tell her friends in Girl Scouts about how you jump around and the water comes out of the ground and you get wet and cool off. When they can't understand, she walks away. It's hard for her when she cannot share her excitement. This has been happening more and more lately.

Dante likes to be first in line. He always gets to school early so he can be the first in line on the playground when they line up to go into school. On Thursday, his mom was running late and Frank was already first in line when Dante arrived. Dante tried to explain that he likes to be first, and that his mother was late. Frank couldn't understand him, and did not move aside. Dante pushed Frank, and Frank pushed back. Dante wound up with a scraped knee and Frank with a bloody nose. The teacher called Dante's mother at work to discuss the incident.

Josh is having a hard time at school. When the teacher calls on him, he tries to give the answer, but often he begins to stutter. His blocks are so severe that it looks as if he is choking. He knows the answer but he can't say it.

Carmen always had difficulty with activities involving her mouth. As a baby, she had trouble feeding, sucking slowly and losing a lot of milk out of the side of her mouth. She was on a soft diet for a long time because chewing was so hard for her. Her mouth is always open and she breathes through her mouth. She did well with sign language but didn't begin to speak single words until age 7. Her speech is very limited, and she becomes very frustrated because no one understands what she is trying to say.

Ethan had sensory issues from birth. He didn't like to be touched near his mouth, and startled at any loud sounds, although he did not appear to tune in to sounds and people around him. He appeared more interested in looking at his mobile than at his parents' faces. At 5, he was not yet speaking, but was fascinated with tops and trains. He liked to spin his top for hours. Around this time, he was given the dual diagnosis of autism and Down syndrome. Now, at the age of 8, he uses an electronic communication device that "speaks" for him with a synthesized voice.

All of the children in the vignettes above could benefit from some form of AAC. Most of them need a supplementary system to help them communicate in only certain situations. The majority of children with Down syndrome do not rely on AAC as their only communication system. Most learn to speak and can communicate through speech in at least some situations by the time they are in first or second grade. A few children like Ethan and Carmen may need to use an AAC system as an alternative system—not because they can't speak, but because their speech cannot be understood. Children who have Childhood Apraxia of Speech or autism in addition to Down syndrome may need AAC for a period of time while they are working on their speech, or as a long-term communication system.

In general, if your child has reached kindergarten age, and speech and/or sign are not meeting her needs to communicate effectively, other alternative communication systems should be considered. AAC should also be considered at any time when your child is frustrated and unable to communicate to meet her needs on a regular basis. All children have moments when they cannot be understood or can't get their message across, but if this is occurring on a daily or very frequent basis, AAC support may be needed. When children do not have a communication system that is adequate to meet their daily needs, they sometimes just give up and stop trying to communicate. We certainly don't want that to happen!

In addition, it may be appropriate to consider AAC support at an earlier age if:

1. Your child has a dual diagnosis of autism and Down syndrome. Having autism in addition to Down syndrome usually compounds communication delays, and learning a system other than speech to communicate can help a great deal.
2. Your child has been diagnosed with Childhood Apraxia of Speech. Children who have difficulties in motor planning for speech (apraxia) may be more delayed in developing speech and more difficult to understand when they speak, so they may need assistive or alternative communication systems to communicate.
3. Your child has other diagnoses such as significant cognitive, motor, or hearing difficulties that are making learning to speak very difficult.

Children with severe speech intelligibility problems may need an alternative communication system at all times for daily communication, or they may need it only when they are interacting with people outside of their immediate circle. They may need AAC in the classroom in learning situations but may not need to use AAC for social situations.

Many parents worry that if their child is given an AAC system, it will prevent her from improving her speech or even developing speech at all. They are concerned that their child will learn to rely on AAC. This fear is understandable, but the truth is actually the opposite. Although studies have not been done specifically on children with Down syndrome who use AAC, research on children with developmental disabilities which have included children with Down syndrome in the sample has shown that AAC generally stimulates speech, rather than reducing it. Studies have shown that speech production increases following the use of both aided and unaided AAC (Romski & Sevcik, 1993; Sigafoos, Didden & O'Reilly, 2003).

Communication Bill of Rights

The National Joint Committee for the Communication Needs of persons with Severe Disabilities published a communication bill of rights for all people, including those who cannot speak.

All persons should have the right:

- to be communicated with in ways that are meaningful, understandable, and culturally and linguistically appropriate
- to be communicated with in a manner that recognizes the individual's dignity
- to be given attention from and the ability to interact with other people
- to request objects, actions, and events
- to be offered choices and to participate in decision making
- to express feelings
- to refuse objects, actions, and events
- to have access to environmental context, interactions, and opportunities that expect and encourage participation as a full communication partner
- to be informed about people, things, and events in my environment

(The National Joint Committee for the Communication Needs of Persons with Severe Disabilities, 1992)

What Types of AAC Systems Are Available?

There are a wide variety of options for AAC systems. They include:

- Gestures/sign language systems;
- Communication boards;
- Communication books, including portable books and notebooks or large books;
- The Picture Exchange Communication System (PECS); and
- Electronic devices.

GESTURES/SIGN LANGUAGE SYSTEMS

Sign language is an excellent transitional communication system as children are developing speech. Information on using Total Communication to help a child make the transition to using spoken language can be found in *Early Communication Skills for Children with Down Syndrome*.

By the age of five years, most children with Down syndrome are speaking and have outgrown the need to use signs as their primary communication system. Signs may continue to be helpful for older children as an augmentative system when:

1. A new language concept is introduced. For example, signs for prepositions such as *in, between,* or *through* are very visual and help children learn the concepts.
2. It is hard for your child to get her message across verbally, such as when she is angry or tired.
3. You or teachers want to cue your child to use a word or perform an action. For example, the teacher may want to give a sign language cue to your child to use eye contact.

4. Signs may also be used when your child really wants to be understood clearly. Children with Childhood Apraxia of Speech or low oral muscle tone may therefore find it helpful to continue to use signs for a longer period of time.

Sign language should always be used in the context of Total Communication. That is, the child may sign her message but her communication partner should repeat the message using words. That shows that the listener has understood the message. Then the listener should reply using speech and sign, never only in sign. That way, she is teaching language and providing models of spoken language.

Again, the expectation for most children with Down syndrome is that they will speak. Signs are not usually the primary communication system for older children and adults with Down syndrome unless they have a significant hearing loss and are using signs the way any deaf person might. In this case, it is important for parents to understand the communication options for deaf people and carefully choose the sign language system that will best meet the child's and family's needs, whether that is American Sign Language (ASL), cued speech, or some other method. (You can read detailed descriptions of the communication options for deaf people in *Choices in Deafness: A Parents' Guide to Communication Options* by Sue Schwartz (Woodbine House, 2007)). I have worked with elementary and middle school children with Down syndrome who have significant hearing loss and wear hearing aids. Generally, they have been able to use speech. Teaching them language and teaching them to speak has always included visual methods, such as signing and reading. Cued speech can be used to help them understand distinctions between sounds, and learn how to make sounds.

By first grade, the messages that children want to send are complex. Even if they use the appropriate signed messages, very few people will be able to understand the messages. That will limit the number of people with whom they can communicate. Simple signs such as "eat," "drink," and "come here" are easy for the listener to decode. But, more complex sign language would not be understood by most people in the child's environment. So, sign language may not be the best choice for an alternative communication system for older children with Down syndrome—unless they have a significant hearing impairment and that is the communication option chosen for the child.

COMMUNICATION BOARDS

Communication boards are individually designed communication systems that may involve the use of pictures, photographs, rebus symbols or pictographs, alphabet letters, or words. The pictures may be mounted on paper, tag board, foam core board, flannel board, magnetic board, or other surfaces. The child communicates by pointing to the pictures or words. Although the child is using the communication board to communicate, the communication partner should use speech and should provide a verbal equivalent for what the child is saying. ("You want pizza and a glass of milk. OK!")

A communication board may be used as a supplement to speech or more extensively. For instance, if your child's speech can be understood by family but not others, she might use speech at home and a communication board at school. If she frequently communicates with people in the community, such as daycare workers or bus drivers who do not know sign language, or if she has difficulty with the motor skills needed to sign, communication boards offer another channel for communication.

Communication boards are inexpensive, low tech, adaptable, and easy to change and update. They are also easy for the communication partner to decode. You can develop separate communication boards for different situations. For example, you might have a different communication board (related to music, TV, and other recreational activities) in the family room than you have in the kitchen (where you need to communicate about food and drink).

Communication boards may range from the simple to the complex, and the system may not even involve a "board." Some examples of communication boards are:

- photos of pizza, grilled cheese, orange juice, cola, and milk, or a card that says "today's special" mounted on cards on a keychain so your child can order lunch in the school cafeteria;
- small photos of friends and relatives and line drawings of basic needs (bathroom, glass of water) inserted in the plastic pockets of a board book so that your child can call to ask someone for help;
- symbols or alphabet letters written on a masonite board;
- topic boards in specialized areas at home such as the bedroom (clothing) or bathroom with vocabulary and requests appropriate for the area. Topic boards are usually not used in the older elementary school grades.

The best communication boards are developed to meet the unique needs of a specific user. Pictures included on your child's board should be geared to her interests and vocabulary and should be updated frequently as her needs change. As a parent, you may develop a communication board for your child to use at home, or you may serve as a major source of information for the speech-language pathologist when he or she designs communication boards for school.

There are many materials available commercially that simplify the actual production of communication boards. These range from laminated folders to albums to plastic keychain tabs. There are photos, line drawings, and symbols that can be purchased in different sizes, shapes, and colors. You can also use digital photos of specific people, things, and places in your child's environment. The wide variety of pictures available makes it possible to meet the specific needs of any communication board user. You and the speech-language pathologist can work together to design the best system for your child. The Picture Communication Symbols© made with Boardmaker™ software (Mayer-Johnson, Inc.) are the most widely used pictures for developing communication boards. Sources for pictures and symbols that may be used on communication boards are provided in the Resource Guide at the back of the book.

COMMUNICATION BOOKS

Older children may find notepad- or pocket-sized books that have pictures, symbols, or words on the pages more useful than a communication board. Portable books may also be wallet type, credit card case, mini photo album, or plastic cards on a keychain. Any of these systems can serve as the venue for communication systems for a child or adult.

Sometimes, separate books, albums, or keychains are used for different domains and situations. For example, a child may use one book for lunch, and a separate book for reading and science. She may have one book for school, one for home, and one for visits to grandma's apartment. Older children may have topic pages specific to each academic subject in a notebook and put them on their desk for each subject, as appropriate. Portable books or cards may be attached to belt loops using a coiled, phone-cord-like key chain, or hung around the neck on a lanyard.

Notebooks or photo albums are larger-sized communication books. These are often used in specific situations, where they can stay in one place. For example, a communication notebook can be available in the kitchen, in the bedroom, or in the playroom at home, or in the classroom at school. Since these books are larger, they are a bit less portable, but they can hold more pictures, photos, symbols, or words.

Whatever format communication books take, they often include the words for the objects in addition to pictures. At first, pictures may need to be very realistic. As children grow older and begin to read, they are often able to use less realistic pictures (such as line drawings). When they become better readers, the words alone may be sufficient.

PICTURE EXCHANGE COMMUNICATION SYSTEM (PECS)

The Picture Exchange Communication System was originally developed by Andy Bondy and Lori Frost to help children with autism learn how to *initiate* communication, but it can also serve as a child's means of communication. PECS is especially useful for children who are having difficulty communicating—for example, children who do not use sign, gestures, or pantomime to try to get their message across. It is also a good system to use for children with the dual diagnosis of autism and Down syndrome. It actually teaches children how to communicate, including how to initiate communication and how to persist until their message is understood.

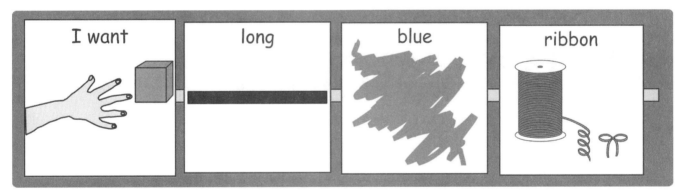

Example of PECS sentence strip.

Reproduced with permission of Pyramid Educational Consultants.

Using the system, communication partners physically "exchange" (hand to one another) communication symbols such as photographs or line drawings. When the child is first learning to use PECS, pictures are chosen that will help the child get her immediate and most desired needs met—for instance, by requesting orange juice or a favorite DVD. PECS initially helps teach communicative intent and turn-taking. As the child becomes more skilled at communicating, she learns to build sentences using a combination of picture symbol or photo cards to express desires, make comments, and answer questions.

Studies have shown that PECS does not discourage children from going on to develop speech, and may actually encourage speech. As with Total Communication, the communication partner models correct speech when responding to the child. For example, if the child hands her mother the "I want" and "banana" symbols, the mother reads the child's message aloud ("I want banana") before responding to the message. The strength of PECS is that it teaches the process of communication in a way that actively involves a communication partner. It teaches communication in the context of two people interacting with each other, sending and receiving messages.

Because PECS is a specific method of using objects or symbols, it is essential that it be taught in a specific manner, preferably led by someone who has been trained to teach PECS. For further information on PECS, see the Resources and Reading List.

ELECTRONIC DEVICES

A variety of high tech electronic communication systems can enable children to communicate through speech, pictures, or writing. These devices may be large and computer-based or smaller and more portable. There are many good choices available from a variety of companies.

Computer-based communication devices are expensive and are more likely to be used by older children who cannot use speech to communicate. For children who have a great deal to communicate, but have difficulty learning sign language, a computer-based communication system that uses synthesized speech can enable them to communicate by "speaking electronically." These are known as Voice Output Communication Aids or VOCAs.

For older children, electronic communication devices can be used to supplement speech or to substitute for speech. A child might use the device in all settings, or only in selected settings such as school where the language demands are more difficult. Note, however, that a child should have access to the device whenever she needs to use it.

Research has shown that speech synthesizers stimulate children's language and speech growth. Parents often fear that their child will not want to speak if she can use a

Benefits of Synthesized Speech

Computer learning and communication devices using synthesized speech (VOCAs) can be helpful because:

1. They can provide a voice when the child is not able to speak.
2. They can provide consistent stimulation for speech. That is, when your child accesses a word or phrase, the computer produces it the same way each time. So, your child hears it said the same way each time.
3. Synthesized speech is slower than natural speech. For children with auditory processing difficulties or with speech production difficulties such as apraxia, slower speech is easier to process.
4. Synthesized speech can be repeated as many times as needed.
5. The computer gives the child control.
6. Using synthesized speech and text writing can help children develop literacy skills. Written language can also help children learn meaning directly without speech. Children can learn concepts and the label for the concept (word) without saying the word.

Reprinted from **Early Communication Skills for Children with Down Syndrome** *(Kumin, 2003).*

device that speaks for her, but that is not the case. The "talking" communication device not only provides a voice for the child and models for the child to imitate, but also increases her motivation to speak by demonstrating that speaking gets the desired results.

Not all high tech devices use synthesized speech. Smaller, less expensive, and more portable devices are often tried before a computer with a speech synthesizer is used. There are many choices of portable high tech devices that can be used to help children communicate. For example, parents can use "talking" picture frames or "talking" photo albums to record messages appropriate for a specific place or activity, similar to the way topic boards are used.

Along the same lines, the BigMack Communication Aid (Mayer-Johnson and AbleNet) is a small electronic recording device that can record and play back messages that are from twenty seconds to one minute long. You can record messages that your child frequently needs to use at home. At school, a classroom aide can record messages for your child right before she needs to use them. For instance, the aide might record morning greetings for your child to play back when she sees her friends, or a repetitive line from a book the teacher is reading to the class. For an older child studying the civil rights movement in social studies, the aide might record "I have a dream" for the child to participate in a discussion about Martin Luther King, Jr.'s famous speech.

Examples of other devices available in the U.S. at the time of this writing include:

- Mayer-Johnson Company: Big Mack (M3, Tech Scan 8) and Tech Scan 32 Plus (for scanning or direct selection)
- Dynavox: Dynavox V; M3; Dynamo, iChat 3; Palmtop 3; asVOCAte
- Prentke Romich: Vanguard Plus; Chat Box; Pathfinder Plus; ECO-14; Spring Board
- AbleNet: One by Four Talker; SuperTalker; Tech/Talk; Tech/Scan; tech/Speak; MACAW; Talara; Gus
- Attainment Company: Go talk 4+; Go Talk 9+; Go Talk 20+
- Great Talking Box Company: Touch Speak; e-Talk; The Q 1 Ultra Solution

The devices are upgraded frequently and change often as more advanced technology becomes available to improve the devices. Your best bet is to work with an AAC center, which will have up-to-date equipment as well as expert professionals who can develop a customized system to match your child's needs. See "Who Should Evaluate Your Child," on page 303.

Designing an AAC System

Any AAC system can and should be customized to meet the needs of the child who is using it, as well as to capitalize on her strengths. That is why we refer to *designing* an AAC system, rather than choosing one.

The first step in designing an appropriate and effective communication system for your child is the completion of an augmentative and alternative communication (AAC) evaluation. In some school systems, the evaluation is conducted by an augmentative communication team; in other school systems, by a speech-language pathologist. Augmentative communication teams are more commonly found in larger school systems or consortia composed of several school systems working together.

An augmentative communication team can:
- evaluate whether your child is eligible to receive AAC equipment and services through the school,
- evaluate which systems will meet your child's needs, and
- order, program, and service the equipment.

Regardless of whether your school uses a team or a speech-language pathologist to conduct AAC evaluations, you, as a parent, should be involved by providing information on your child's communication needs at home and in different settings. And, once your child is using the system, you can provide important feedback on its effectiveness. See pages 301-304 for more information on the evaluation and eligibility process.

The most important considerations in designing a system for your child are that:
1. The system matches your child's language skills and needs;
2. The system matches your child's motor skills and needs, so it is usable by your child;
3. The system is available to your child whenever she wants to communicate.

A system that sits on a shelf is useless. The only valuable communication device is one that is used constantly and meets your child's communication needs. The device should be as usable and available as your child's speech would be.

A parent of an eight-year-old told me that he was using his communication device successfully in school, but that the school would not allow him to bring it home. As a result, her son was frustrated when he could not make himself understood at home. Similarly, a parent of a ten-year-old complained that her child's elementary school had informed her that the AAC device needed to stay in the speech room because it was expensive and could get broken in class. I have also heard of instances where the communication device is taken away from the child when she leaves elementary school to go on to middle school. Doesn't she need to communicate in middle school? In addition it seems to be common practice for the communication device to be used only in speech therapy sessions or only in school. Many times, the communication device is not sent home over the summer.

To be effective, *the AAC system needs to be available whenever your child wants to communicate.* If she uses the system as her primary communication system and it is not available, she can't "talk." It would be the same as tying the hands of someone who uses sign language. The person would not be able to communicate. In short, to be an effective communication system, any system needs to be available 24/7, just as speech would be available 24/7 for the child who uses speech to communicate.

ISSUES TO CONSIDER

In designing your child's AAC system, there are a number of issues the members of the communication team, including you, should consider. The team should revisit these issues regularly so that your child's system can be altered to reflect your child's changing needs and abilities. Each time, you should consider the following issues discussed below:
- your child's current communication system,
- access (how your child operates the system),
- environments where the system will be used,
- portability,

- availability and usability,
- content,
- types of symbols,
- layout and design,
- communication partners, and
- your child's training needs

CURRENT COMMUNICATION SYSTEM

In designing your child's AAC system, the team should consider the current methods of communication your child uses, as well as her movement abilities. This means the team should consider any gestures, signs, speech, or vocalizations your child uses successfully. These include facial expressions, head nodding or shaking, pointing, and word approximations ("yah" or "nah"). The team will use this information in making decisions about purpose, content, and the way your child uses the system or makes it work, often called "accessing the system."

ACCESSIBILITY

Access refers to the method your child will use to create messages with her AAC system when she wants to communicate. For example, she might use a keyboard to type a message, her finger to point to a picture, or a switch or button to activate an electronic device.

Your child's fine and gross motor skills will determine what types of systems she can use effectively. For instance, if your child points to things using her entire hand rather than one finger, then there must be enough room on the communication board, switch, or keyboard for her to use her whole hand to access the message. Alternately, she could learn to use a communication system that requires less fine motor control—for example, by handing cards to her communication partner.

If your child is able to use a mouse or keyboard successfully, then computer programs may be considered. In an online survey of computer usage among children with Down syndrome, parents reported that children with Down syndrome often are able to use the mouse successfully, but may have difficulty with a keyboard due to difficulties with fine motor coordination or spelling skills (Feng, Lazar, Kumin & Ozok, 2008). If your child has difficulty using a single finger at a time, she may need an adaptive keyboard protector, to keep her from hitting several keys at once. If she cannot point or hit a key with her finger, she may need a scanning system that will scan all of the choices. She can then stop the machine at her choice by hitting a switch, paddle, or other device.

ENVIRONMENT

In designing your child's AAC system, the team should also keep in mind where your child will be using it. This is especially important to consider when selecting vocabulary for the system. For instance, if the goal of the system is to improve your child's vocabulary use or sentence structure in the classroom, the type of language selected will reflect appropriate messages for school. These might include, "I don't understand," "I need a break," or "When is recess?" If your child will mostly use the system at home, the messages may include, "I want to watch a DVD," "When will dinner be ready?" or "I need help with this homework." If your child will use the system in any or all environments, then the system must be able to accommodate the different messages and vocabulary needed for those environments. Systems can be designed with separate overlays for each environment.

PORTABILITY

The portability of an AAC system—how easily it can be moved from one place to another—must also be taken into consideration. Would your child be able to carry the system with her if she needs or wants to? Even if the system is otherwise appropriate for your child, if your child can't carry it where she needs it, it will be useless.

Sometimes, a system may not need to be very portable—for example, if it is designed only to be used at home or in the classroom. However, if the purpose of designing an AAC system is so your child can use it all day long in all environments, then it must be easy for your child to carry from place to place and use. It must also be sturdy enough to withstand usage in different environments. For instance, even though a laptop computer is easy to carry between classrooms, it might get broken or stolen if your child takes it to recess while she is playing with friends.

Once your child is old enough to be assigned a locker at school, the team should make sure the device will fit in a locker if she needs to stow it there during physical education or another activity. If not, other arrangements should be made to keep the system safe when it is not in your child's possession.

AVAILABILITY AND USABILITY

As mentioned above, the communication system must be available to your child and her communication partners at all times, in order to be useful. This may seem obvious, but I have observed many situations in which this was not happening. In one case, the classroom aide kept the communication cards zipped inside her fanny pack. The child could not get to the cards. Even when she pointed to the pack and tried to open the zipper, the aide did not take the cards out. In another case, the high tech communication device was in a classroom closet, and was only taken off the shelf for one hour each week when the SLP came into the classroom for speech therapy. I have seen many instances where the communication device is used in the classroom and by the speech-language pathologist, but is not sent home.

Recently, the mother of a twelve-year-old told me, "My son was talking all year, but now he has stopped talking to us." After asking her many questions to try to determine what might be causing a loss of speech, I found out that the child was relying on a communication device with a speech synthesizer to "talk" with his family. During the year, the elementary school sent the device home with the child over the weekend. But, now the child was entering middle school. The parents were told that the communication device belonged to the elementary school, and that the child could not take the device with him. So, he had stopped "talking" because he had no way to talk.

In addition to being available to the child, the AAC system needs to be usable by the child. If a notebook has hundreds of pictures that are not organized, it will not be usable. If the child cannot hit one discrete key on a communication device to activate individual messages, it will not be usable. If the child is not sure what the abstract symbols used to represent verbs or prepositions mean, the system will not be usable. The bottom line is, your child's individual strengths and challenges need to be considered and the device must be individually designed to be really usable.

CONTENT AND LANGUAGE

Content. The content of the system is basically what your child will be able to "say" when she uses it. It is essential to include messages that are important to your child, the person who is using the system. It is equally important for messages to reflect age-appropriate vocabulary, as well as family values. For instance, when someone is bothering a typical teenager, does she say, "Please leave me alone," or would she say, "Stop it!" or "Knock it off!" Your child needs to be able to use the system to say what would be appropriate for her age and for the situation.

Visit your child's school during recess or lunch and notice how children are speaking to each other. What words and phrases are they using? What are the "in" terms? Not only does age-appropriate language make sense, it is more inviting to the user and the listening partners.

Parents must be included in determining the content that will be programmed into the device. The AAC team has no way of knowing what words and phrases would be useful and appropriate for scouting or a crafts group or religious school activities. If the device is to be useful for communication at home and in the community, parents must help choose the vocabulary, and the equipment must be available to the child at all times.

Language. When designing AAC systems, "language" means the type of symbol used for the system. For instance, some students use written words or spell with letters to create their messages. They encode or formulate the message the same as if they were speaking, but the synthesized voice speaks for them. Some children choose phrases to combine (e.g., "I want," "I need," "May I"). Other students use drawings or photographs to represent an entire message or to build sentences—for example, they might use a picture of a drink in a glass to access the phrase "I'm thirsty." The types of symbols and language chosen will reflect your child's language, spelling, writing, and cognitive abilities.

LAYOUT AND DESIGN

The layout and design is the way the components used to make messages are organized and displayed on the AAC device. For example, words might be arranged

Symbol Systems

What types of symbols can be used to enable your child to communicate? Some may represent individual words such as "dog," and some may represent concepts or ideas such as angry, frustrated, or not to my liking. The speech-language pathologist will choose symbols for language that will be most appropriate for your child's needs. They can range from photos that you take to represent Mom and Dad, to alphabet letters that the child uses to spell out her messages, to a picture that activates an entire phrase that has been preprogrammed—such as a sun representing "Can we go outside now?" The hierarchy of difficulty is:

- Objects such as a miniature car or dog (usually used for younger children)
- Photographs
- Colored pictures
- Black and white line drawings
- Abstract symbols (such as Bliss symbols)
- Alphabet letters (for older children)
- Written words
- Written phrases
- Written sentences or conversational comments

in alphabetical order. Or, the symbols or words for specific types of activities might be grouped together (for instance, those related to mealtime in one place and those related to school routines in another). Or, the symbols your child uses most often might be grouped in one place, with less frequently used symbols somewhere else.

Another issue to consider when determining the layout and design of an AAC device is the types of messages your child will need to create. For example, if your child will be putting individual words together to form complete sentences, the layout would need to enable her to quickly type in or access a variety of words. With electronic devices, the layout and design is often determined by the design of the computer keyboard. However, even in this instance, a specialized computer keyboard such as Intellikeys could be used so the layout and design can be customized to your child's needs. The success of AAC systems that use symbolic representations for words or phrases is greatly affected by the layout and design of the system.

COMMUNICATION PARTNERS

Who your child will communicate with using her AAC system is another important consideration when designing an AAC system. Not only must she learn to be a competent communication partner, but the people communicating with her must also be able to use the system effectively. For instance, if you are considering using sign language as the AAC system, how well will others understand your child? In general, as children become more sophisticated in their use of sign language, fewer people at school and in the community are able to understand them. It may be more appropriate to use pictures or words in a notebook or a simple voice output device. This helps

others who do not have specific training understand your child's attempts to communicate.

Most of us have not had an opportunity to be around other people who use AAC systems. People may be uncomfortable or unsure of how to respond to your child's attempts to use her new system. However, with familiarity, other people (and especially children) become very comfortable with the sound of a synthesized electronic voice, and are readily able to "talk" with a child using the voice.

Training for communication partners (classmates, teachers, librarians, parents, siblings, friends, and related service providers) should be included as a part of the AAC implementation process. Training should include information about how to respond to the child and the need to wait for her message, as well as opportunities for practice.

There are many ways to train communication partners. In some cases, little training is needed for a communication partner. Children often adapt easily to communicating with a person using AAC. They may just need some hints such as: "Don't jump in and finish the sentence." Or, "wait until Kaitlyn has finished typing in her message." In other cases, parents, teachers, and others may need specific training provided by the speech-language pathologist or another qualified person. See the section on "Learning to Use AAC Systems," below.

AAC and Assistive Technology Evaluations

As explained above, your child's needs for assistive technology, including an AAC system, must be considered at each and every IEP meeting. If your child is not

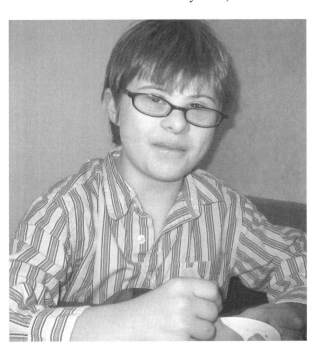

currently using AAC, an AAC evaluation can determine whether she could benefit from an AAC system. Likewise, if your child has other needs (such as fine motor or gross motor delays or a visual or hearing impairment) an Assistive Technology evaluation can determine what devices or adaptations could help your child succeed at school. See the Assistive Technology Report for Alex at the end of this chapter for an idea of how assistive technology in general can help students with Down syndrome.

An AAC evaluation can be requested by your family, the IEP team (especially the special educator, classroom teacher, or SLP), or a developmental pediatrician or another specialist at a comprehensive Down syndrome center who follows your child on a regular basis.

If the school does not have a team with sufficient experience or sufficient equipment to evaluate your child and prescribe and develop an AAC system for her, you can request an outside evaluation. SLPs do not work under a

Questions to Answer When Designing an AAC System

Some of the questions that you and the communication team should answer when your child's AAC system is being designed include:

1. How can your child best respond or activate the system (pointing, pushing a switch)?
2. What methods does your child currently use to communicate?
3. What should the content of the communication system be? What does your child want to "say?" This will entail determining your child's favorite activities, what settings she needs to communicate in, why she needs to communicate, what expressions are appropriate for her age and gender, what words and phrases will help her participate with peers, etc.
4. Where will your child use the communication system—in one setting, such as in school, or in many settings? Needs may be different in different settings (school, home, or community activities such as scouting).
5. Will the system or device be moved from place to place? Will it be used outdoors as well as indoors?
6. With whom will your child use the communication system? Will she use the system with the same few people or many different people (parents, sitters, teachers, scout leaders, bus driver, siblings, friends)?
7. What type of symbols will be used—pictures, photos, line drawings, words? (See "Symbol Systems," above.)
8. How many symbols will be used? Can your child choose from three symbols or can she choose among twenty symbols? Fifty symbols?
9. How will the system be organized? For instance, how many symbols will there be per page and how will they be arranged on the page?
10. Will all of the symbols be grouped together or will they be arranged in domains (home, school, scouts, religious activities)?
11. How will your child select the language components to use them for communication? Will she use direct selection (see below) or will a light scan all choices until she stops the system at the choice she desires?
12. How simple or complex are your child's language needs and language capabilities?
13. Does your child use speech (i.e., is this an augmentative system), or will the system need to provide all communication needs (i.e., is this an alternative system)?
14. How will the "listener" receive the message? What kind of output system (synthesized voice, printout on screen, typed message on paper) will be used?
15. What considerations are there relative to the size, portability, and durability of the communication board or device?
16. Will there need to be different communication boards for different settings? Or can different overlays be used for different settings, with your child carrying the system from place to place?
17. How much training does your child need to effectively use the system?
18. How much training is needed for significant people who interact with your child to learn to interact with the system?
19. Who will provide the training for the child? the teachers? the family?
20. When and where will the training occur?
21. What is the plan for follow-up to determine whether the communication system is working effectively?
22. What is the plan for updating the information to keep it current?
23. What is the plan for maintenance of the system? What if the system breaks down? Who will be responsible for maintaining the system?

See the end of this chapter for an expanded version of this form that you can fill out and share with your child's AAC team.

Adapted from **Early Communication Skills for Children with Down Syndrome** *(Kumin, 2003).*

physician's prescription, so you do not need a referral from a physician or from the school system to schedule an evaluation. You do need to work with the IEP team or with your health insurance company to determine eligibility for payment for an evaluation.

WHO SHOULD EVALUATE YOUR CHILD?

Designing AAC systems and prescribing other assistive technology requires expertise and daily experience. The technology changes rapidly and there are frequent upgrades in products. The professional evaluating your child not only needs up-to-date knowledge, but also must have a variety of equipment to "try" with your child to determine which system is most effective. If the equipment is not available, it is difficult to evaluate your child's needs and determine what will work best. If the equipment is limited, there is a tendency to try to prescribe the available equipment, instead of looking for the equipment that meets your child's needs.

There are specialized AAC Centers in most states that can conduct in-depth evaluations to develop an appropriate communication system, as well as to determine what other assistive technology could benefit your child. Under the mandates of The Technology Related Assistance to Individuals with Disabilities Act of 1988 and the subsequent bills adding new amendments to the program (PL 100-407; PL 103-218; PL 108-364), technology centers have been developed throughout the United States. For a complete listing of centers, contact RESNA (www.resna.org) or see the Resource Guide at the end of the book. There is also a network of augmentative communication provider centers known as The Alliance for Technology Access (ATA). For a complete listing of ATA centers, contact ATA (www.ataccess.org) or see the Resource Guide.

These specialized centers can provide a variety of assessment services. Some centers help to develop personal communication systems for children, but you or the school are then responsible for purchasing the system. Other centers have equipment available to lend to families. Many have staff who can help you learn more about funding the devices. The services vary, so be sure to check the websites for RESNA and ATA. Although there are one or more centers in each state, you are generally not limited to seeking help from the center in your state. The centers do not offer exactly the same services, so contact several centers to determine which center can best meet your child's needs.

QUALIFYING FOR ASSISTIVE TECHNOLOGY SERVICES

Based on the evaluation results, the IEP team should consider whether your child would benefit from AAC, and if so, whether she needs AAC as a transitional, supplementary, or alternative system. They should also consider whether your child would benefit from other assistive technology, such as special software or an adapted keyboard, if that was recommended in your child's evaluation.

If the team determines that your child might benefit from AAC or another kind of assistive technology, she will qualify for *Assistive Technology Service* on her IEP. This is defined as any service that directly assists a child with a disability in the selection, acquisition, or use of an assistive technology device. This definition includes:

(A) The evaluation of the needs of such child, including a functional evaluation of the child in the child's customary environment. [This should include an assessment of your child's needs at school, and an evaluation of your child's ability to use a variety of communication aids and access devices.]

(B) Purchasing, leasing, or otherwise providing for the acquisition of assistive technology devices by such child. [That is, your child's AAC system must be provided at no charge to you, the parents, if the IEP team determines he needs it.]

(C) Selecting, designing, fitting, customizing, adapting, applying, maintaining, repairing, or replacing assistive technology devices.

(D) Coordinating and using other therapies, interventions, or services with assistive technology devices, such as those associated with existing education and rehabilitation plans and programs.

(E) Training or technical assistance for such child, or where appropriate, the family of such child. [That is, the school must teach your child and your family to use his AAC device.]

(F) Training or technical assistance for professionals (including individuals providing education and rehabilitation services), employers, or other individuals who provide services to, employ, or are otherwise substantially involved in the major life functions of such child.

If your child is not found eligible for AAC or you are otherwise dissatisfied with the results, you can request an independent evaluation at the school district's expense. It would be wise to request that the new evaluation be completed by an AAC specialist, if your child has not previously been seen by one.

Again, your child's IEP team should discuss your child's need for augmentative, alternative, and assistive devices on a regular basis—at least once a year, during IEP development. And if she is using such devices, their effectiveness should be formally evaluated at least once a year. AAC systems are dynamic: they change as your child's needs and environments change. This means that many times over the course of your child's school years, you and the other members of her communication team may need to reevaluate her AAC system. Do not hesitate to ask for, and provide feedback to, your child's SLP whenever you have questions and concerns about her AAC system.

AAC Systems and Speech and Language Services

Children with Down syndrome who use AAC systems need speech-language therapy!

This may seem very obvious, but I have heard of too many instances where children with Down syndrome lost their therapy services as soon as they were provided with an AAC system. The fact is the system should be used *in* therapy, not *instead of* therapy. The AAC system is a tool, not a substitute for language therapy.

Once your child receives her AAC system, she needs speech-language therapy services to:

- learn to use the system;
- learn vocabulary with the system;
- learn to make sentences (or longer sentences) and converse using the system.

Your child may also need speech-language therapy to continue to build her receptive language skills. And, if the system is supposed to be a transitional or supplemental one, she needs therapy to help her continue to work on her speech skills.

The bottom line is your child will continue to have goals for speech and language skill development, and these should be written into her IEP. (See the next section.) Just as for any child who is receiving speech-language therapy, it will be important to consider where she should receive those services. For example, when your child is first introduced to the system, it may be helpful for her to work one-on-one in the therapy room with the SLP to learn how to use the system. Once she has the hang of it, though, she needs practice using it in the classroom with her peers and teachers (and they may also need to be trained to communicate with her).

Research has shown that students who have intellectual disabilities and are using an AAC system learn speech and language skills best when therapy is provided in the classroom or during an activity as it is happening. In other words, the most effective instruction will be done in the classroom at the time your child will be using the AAC system. Ideally, your child's speech-language pathologist will vary the time he or she provides therapy throughout the day in order to work on using the system for different situations between your child and her classmates.

IEP Goals for School-Aged Students Using AAC Systems

If your child has an AAC system, her IEP should address three broad issues:

1. How will she and the people in her environment learn to communicate with the system?
2. What language and communication skills will be targeted when your child is using the system?
3. How can AAC be used to help your child participate in and progress in the general education curriculum (and when she is older, to make the transition to adult life)?

LEARNING TO USE THE SYSTEM

To help your child and others learn to use her system effectively, your child's IEP should spell out:

- How your child will be trained to use the AAC system;
- How the classroom teacher and others who interact with your child will be trained to "listen" to her;
- How AAC will be introduced to other children in the class to ensure that they will interact with your child when she is using her AAC device;
- The follow-up that will ensure the AAC is an effective communication system in all settings where it is needed;
- Who will be responsible for keeping the system current;
- Who is responsible for maintaining the equipment in good working order.

Training for staff, family, and classmates also needs to be defined in the IEP. In some cases, this is included with accommodations and modifications. It might also be included in Related Services, especially if staff need to attend workshops or classes to learn to use and operate the system. You can also suggest language within your child's IEP goals to highlight the importance of this training and measure progress. For example, a goal related to training classmates might be:

- Lily will sustain a 5-minute conversation with at least 3 turns using her AAC system at lunch with friends who are trained communication partners.

A goal related to training family members might be:

- Lily will answer questions on her reading homework by using her VOCA, and working with her parent, who will write the answers on the homework sheet.

When writing your child's IEP, it is also important to include time for teachers and related services personnel to share information and ask questions regarding the AAC system. AAC is being used to help your child communicate, as well as for learning in the classroom. Using AAC is an ongoing process and there needs to be ongoing communication between general education teachers, special education teachers, the SLP, aides, and the AAC team.

IMPROVING COMMUNICATION SKILLS

Your child will probably have speech-language goals in many areas, including receptive language skills, pragmatic language, syntax, and perhaps articulation and phonology, if she is expected to use speech to communicate at least some of the time. But she also needs goals focused on helping her learn to use her new system initially and then helping her to expand her communication abilities with the equipment as her skills develop and grow.

When goals are written for communication skills, it is important that they be geared to your child's proficiency using the system rather than her level of language development. Once she is proficient and understands *how* to use the system, she can make progress on the targeted language goals. This can be accomplished by using graduating steps toward the overall communication goal. Common topics to consider for IEP goals and objectives related to your child's AAC system include:

- Expressing basic needs
- Expressing feelings
- Using carrier phrases such as *I want to* or *Let's go*
- Starting a conversation
- Sustaining a conversation
  - Asking questions
  - Asking for help
- Making appropriate requests (academically and socially)
- Making socially and age appropriate comments ("awesome," "no way")
- Making individual and small group presentations in the classroom

SAMPLE ANNUAL GOALS AND OBJECTIVES

Here are examples of goals related to using AAC to improve language skills:

- Shannon will learn to use the TouchTalker for classroom communication activities including using greetings with classmates and teachers at least 5 times a day, and asking for help on classroom assignments at least 2 times a day.
- James will use a communication board to answer yes/no/maybe/I don't know questions with 80% accuracy.
- Ivan will use a communication board with 6 picture symbols to make requests in the classroom at least 5 times daily.
- Bonnie will communicate using 4-word phrases 80% of the time in class, using the Dynomax.

And here are examples of goals related to making progress in the general education curriculum:

- Henry will participate in small group learning activities using his speech synthesizer.
- Jordan will write and deliver a 4-sentence speech for her book report assignment using the Cheap Talk electronic device.
- Briana will answer questions on her science worksheets using word processing [which is an assistive technology when the child cannot use handwriting].

Although IDEA 2004 requires only annual measurable goals for most students with disabilities, many school systems are choosing to also include objectives (short-term, measurable goals) and benchmarks (time that the skill will be mastered by). For example, for the goal "Steven will use sign language to communicate in class and at home," these objective and benchmarks might be included:

- Steven will use Signed Exact English (SEE) signs for the phrase "I need to" with 6 verbs 80% of the time in class by May 30.
- Steven will use Signed Exact English (SEE) to ask for help with class assignments at least twice daily by the end of the first marking period.

Learning to Use AAC Systems: Issues at Home

As this chapter has emphasized, children who use AAC systems need to be able to use those systems wherever they are. Your child's AAC system is her voice. It goes without saying that your child should use her AAC system at home. First, she should use it at home to complete homework. For example, if your child uses symbols to answer questions on worksheets at school, she needs to do this with her homework, too. But second, and perhaps more importantly, she should use her AAC system around your house and in your community to communicate her desires, thoughts, and questions about daily routines, recreational activities, and community events.

You will need to learn to plan ahead when your child will be doing things in community settings where it might be difficult to use her system. For example, if you are going to the movies and it will be hard for you to see your child's communication book in the dark, bring a flashlight so she will be able to communicate with you. Or, if she uses a system with a synthesized voice and you will be somewhere where it is appropriate to whisper, figure out how to turn down the volume of her device before you are in the situation (or use headphones to listen, if that's possible). If you are going somewhere where the AAC system might get wet or damaged (such as on a boat ride), figure out a way to protect the system from damage (or work out an alternative way your child can communicate for a short time). And by all means, always carry extra batteries if the system is battery operated!

You and your child's AAC team also need to work out ways that your child can communicate by phone. If she doesn't use a voice output device, what are some of the options? Some children may be willing to allow you (or someone else) to act as her interpreter. She might formulate her message using a communication book while you relay the message to a listener on the other end of the phone. An older child might be able to use a TDD device (or another high tech device for the deaf) to type out her own messages. Some children may be able to send text messages via conventional cell phones or cell phones with keyboards. Work with the IEP and AAC teams to plan for any situation that your child may encounter where she will need to communicate.

To support your child's use of any AAC system you need training, encouragement, creativity, and patience. Training for you and other family members should be included in the process of creating an AAC system. This needs to go beyond training in how to use the actual device, software, or symbol system. It must also include training to be an effective communication partner.

Once you begin to use the AAC system at home, there are some key elements to success:

- Ask everyone to use the system with your child. This includes babysitters, relatives, and others who do not see your child very often. Make sure you give them a brief tutorial on using the AAC system before you leave them alone with your child.
- Be responsive. If your child uses an AAC system to augment her speech, respond to sentences created on a board or by a voice output device just as you would to speech. Don't be afraid to say, "What? I wasn't listening carefully. Can you tell me again?" Try to avoid asking for too many repetitions, but it's important to understand your child's message rather than guessing.
- Be honest. If your child is just learning to communicate and asks for something you don't have, don't ignore her to avoid the issue. Tell her the truth. "I'm sorry, we're out of orange juice. Can I get you something else?
- Reward your child's communication attempts *after* the conversation has ended. Answer her question or respond to her comment first. Wait until the conversation has ended and then praise her for how well she is using her AAC system. Tell her how much you enjoy communicating with her.
- Include the AAC system in games. This means teaching siblings and friends to be patient while your child communicates her message, "I want to buy Park Place."

- Include the AAC when your child is out with friends. Figure out a good way to carry it, so that it is available when needed. Sometimes a backpack doesn't work well, because it is too hard to take the device out and put it back.
- Be consistent. Do not use the AAC system only when it is convenient. You will be rewarded for your hard work over time.
- Wait. No one likes to be second-guessed or interrupted. Remember that it takes longer to create a message when using any AAC system. Give your child time to respond. Avoid guessing what word she is going to choose. Wait for her to choose it before you repeat it or respond. And always let her finish her sentence!
- Help all significant others (including siblings, friends, grandparents, and other extended family) learn about how to be a good communication partner.
- Make sure your child has access to the system all day long, everywhere she goes.
- Provide feedback to the SLP or the augmentative communication team regarding how well the system is working with different people in different settings as a communication system. See the box below on monitoring effectiveness.

It takes time to integrate an AAC system into the everyday life of a family. Be patient with yourself, your family, and friends. Begin by implementing the system in parts of the day your child seems most motivated to communicate. Remember that communication and AAC system design is ever-changing. Share what is working and what is not working with the team working with your child and listen to what is working at school. You can build on each other's successes, which will help your child generalize the use of her AAC system across environments and into the community.

Monitoring the Effectiveness of Your Child's AAC System

Your communication system is available to you at all times. Your child's communication system (AAC) also needs to be working and available at all times. Provide feedback to the AAC support team to let them know how the system is working. Let them know:

- Is the system portable enough?
- What problems does your child have in using the system?
- Are there changes needed in the:
  - Content (vocabulary, sentences)
  - Input mode (how the messages are programmed into the system; how they are changed and added to the system; how the child receives messages)
  - Response mode (how the child creates and sends messages and responses)
  - Layout (how information is arranged)
- Is the system available all of the time, as needed?
- Do you need more support or training in keeping the system operational?

Updating, Maintaining, and Storing the AAC System

There must be someone who is readily available to update, maintain, or create new messages for your child's AAC system. Communication is a dynamic process: lesson plans change, classrooms change, friends change, hobbies change, community group memberships change, and so on. Some information changes frequently—for example, names of movies your child has seen and daily class assignments—and other information changes less frequently—for example, teachers' names. The list is endless.

Someone on the team must be ready and able to anticipate and respond to changes in the messages your child needs. That person may be the classroom aide, a member of the AAC team, the SLP, or the parent. It is best if more than one person knows how to update the system, but one person is considered responsible for the changes on a regular basis.

In addition, for the AAC system to be successful, the team must meet regularly to discuss what is working and what is not working. Open and frequent communication regarding the AAC system reduces frustration for your child, the person updating the system, and everyone involved in communicating with your child. If the person responsible for updating the system is a school-based member of the team, parents need to consider how changes will be made over the summer or during school vacations.

Some systems also require maintenance to ensure they are working correctly. This means that someone on the team needs to be able to check the system regularly, as well as fix it if there are unexpected problems. For instance, if your child is using a communication notebook in a three-ring binder, someone needs to be responsible for putting the pages back in order if your child drops it getting off her bus and the pages fall out and blow away. If your child is using a voice output communication device, someone needs to be responsible for replacing batteries or fixing the system if the voice mechanism begins to sound unclear. An AAC system will not be an effective language support for your child if it does not work.

It is important to agree where the AAC system will be kept. If it is for use at school only, everyone needs to know where it will be so they can use it. For instance, if your child will be using text-to-speech software for writing projects, will the program be on the computer in the computer lab, in the classroom, in the library, or in the resource room? If your child needs to use the program during an unexpected time, will she be able to or will it be disruptive to another class? Will the system be available to her throughout the day? At school? At home? Or is it stored on a shelf and only brought out when she has speech therapy? As I've discussed throughout the chapter, this option would be completely unacceptable—unless the system is just being used for curriculum purposes in the classroom only. Then, use could be limited to the classroom.

If your child's team suggests that her system should be stored away unless she is having speech therapy, try these steps:

- Insist that goals be added to your child's IEP that require her to use the device all through the school day.
- Point out the reasons your child needs her system to access the general education curriculum.
- If necessary, observe your child in school to get ideas of ways she could use the system to access the curriculum throughout the day.

● Work with an advocate to convince the IEP team that the AAC
   system be available to your child outside of school. (IDEA does
   not require this, however, so this may be a difficult battle to win.)

If you cannot convince the IEP team to allow your child to take the system home, one possibility is to purchase a duplicate system for home use (and possibly vacation and summer use, as well). Include an IEP goal and a home-school communication program to ensure that the school will provide information about anything added or deleted from the system at school so that you can determine whether to make the same changes at home. You may want to do so to ensure that the communication device will be usable for homework. Or, you may want to customize the content for home and community, and it may be acceptable if the content is different for the different environments and situations.

Technology and People with Down Syndrome

Technology has an impact on all of our lives, including the lives of people with Down syndrome. Technology can be used for learning during the school years and beyond. There is a vast array of educational and language software available that can be helpful to all children with Down syndrome, not just those who use AAC. This software can help children learn to generate grammatical sentences, and to write paragraphs, letters,

compositions, and book reports. The SLP, educators, and other parents can advise you on which programs are most appropriate for your child's learning needs and capable of engaging her interest. Also see the Resource Guide for information on companies that develop and sell software that can help your child with language and communication.

There are also centers dedicated specifically to the use of computers to enhance learning. These centers are part of a national network of centers that specialize in computers and learning and computers and communication. One example is the LINC center in Baltimore, Maryland, which is part of the Alliance for Technology Access network. (See Resource Guide.) These centers typically have a variety of computer-based communication devices on hand, and can provide evaluation services for children with disabilities. Some centers will prescribe software that will meet your child's needs or lend software and computers. Some of the centers are directly funded by the Tech Act. A list of these centers can be found on the RESNA website. Other centers are members of a national network known as the Alliance for Technology Access. Information on contacting both agencies is provided earlier in the chapter and is also listed in the Resource Guide.

Voice mail and email are other applications of technology that can promote communication for children with Down syndrome. Older children who see each other rarely—for example, at national conferences annually—may keep in touch using email. They may also enjoy emailing with friends and relatives, as well as using "instant messaging" to communicate in real time (if their communication partner is willing to wait for a response).

Although I know many people with Down syndrome who use email, results of a recent study show that children and teens with Down syndrome are only rarely avid email users. In fact, 40 percent of the individuals in the study never use it, according to their parents. (See the next section.) It seems safe to assume, however, that using email can help children with Down syndrome improve their reading, writing, and keyboarding skills, and may be more motivating to some children than paper and pencil writing. Like other children, children with Down syndrome can learn to use email and IM shorthand such as CUL8R and GTG, thereby keeping up with popular teen culture.

Again, if your child has trouble using a standard keyboard, there are adapted keyboards available such as Intellikeys that are easier for children with fine motor difficulties to use. Keyguards that allow only one key to be depressed at a time can also be helpful.

Some children and teens with Down syndrome may be able to use the same email programs that their parents, friends, and siblings use. Others may do better with a program developed specifically for children or people with disabilities. Examples include:

- MultiMail (http://mis.deakin.edu.au)
- Kids Online (www.kids.aol.com)
- ZooBuh! (www..zoobuh.com)
- CogLink (www.coglink.com)

Some people with Down syndrome use voice mail, but the ability to use it well is dependent on whether the person has understandable speech (for leaving messages) and whether she can listen and write down information accurately (for receiving messages).

RESEARCH ABOUT TECHNOLOGY USE BY CHILDREN AND TEENS

To date there has been some research into computer usage by individuals with Down syndrome, but very little research about their use of other forms of technology. Recently, however, Heidi Feng, Jonathan Lazar, Ant Ozok, and I completed an online survey of 561 parents of individuals with Down syndrome. In this survey we wanted to document how people with Down syndrome from ages 5 to 21 were using computers. The purpose was to try to improve computer interfaces and computer usability for people with Down syndrome. Here is what we found about the use of technology in people with Down syndrome ages 5 to 21 who are computer users (Feng, Kumin, Lazar& Ozok, 2008):

COMPUTER USAGE

Over 72 percent of the survey respondents reported that their children had started using computers by the age of 5. Most of the children involved in the survey use computers for learning and entertainment.The applications used most often by children and young adults with Down syndrome were educational software, computer games, and the web. Word processing, presentation software, and e-mail were used far less frequently.

Only 3 percent of parents reported that their children frequently use email and over 40 percent reported that their children never use email. It would seem that email should be encouraged because it enables older children and adolescents to have a larger social network. Many times, a child with Down syndrome is the only person in

their school or community with Down syndrome. They meet friends with Down syndrome at conferences, Buddy Walks, and other social events and want to keep those friendships in addition to their local friendships. Email also helps children practice writing, spelling, and keyboarding skills.

Regarding input devices, 86.6 percent reported using a keyboard, 93.2 percent reported using a mouse, and fewer children and adolescents used a touch screen (12.3 percent), joystick (7.5 percent), touchpad (5.5 percent), or trackball (4.9 percent). Almost half of the parents (49.6 percent) reported that their children type using one index finger, 27.9 percent reported that their children type using two index fingers, 11.7 percent of the children type using two or more fingers on one hand, and 10.8 percent report that children type using multiple fingers on both hands. With output devices, parents reported that 89.5 percent of children used the monitor, and 64.7 percent used the printer. Only 7 percent used synthesized speech output.

Children with Down Syndrome can access computers in different locations. Survey results indicated that 99.3 percent have access to computers at home, 86.6 percent have access to computers at school, and 37.4 percent have access to computers at the library.

Laura Myers has written about the writing strengths that children with Down syndrome demonstrate when using the computer. From our study, it appears that the motor skills, *not* the cognitive and spatial skills, may be contributing to the difficulties people with Down syndrome face using the computer. And those difficulties can be overcome through improved computer usability.

USAGE OF OTHER ELECTRONIC TECHNOLOGY

A child's interest in computers may be related to her interest in other digital devices. For instance, survey results indicated that 33 percent use a cell phone, 41.7 percent use a calculator, 37.3 percent use a game system (non-portable, such as PS2 or Xbox), 32.6 percent use a portable game system (such as PSP or GameBoy), 12.3 percent use an iPod, and 8.6 percent use an AAC device (such as Alpha Talker or Blackhawk) to communicate.

Conclusion

Augmentative and alternative communication can be used to assist children in communicating at times, or to provide an alternative communication mode at all times for children who cannot speak. For children with Down syndrome, AAC can be very empowering, making communication possible that was previously blocked by difficulties with speech. Professional expertise to evaluate your child, design a system, and help your child learn to use the system is available through your speech-language pathologist, assistive technology specialists in the schools, and at local, state, and regional technology centers. There is a rich resource network.

Low tech AAC systems such as communication books are inexpensive to make and may or may not require special expertise to put together. High tech communication devices, on the other hand, are expensive and school systems are often hesitant to provide them, especially for full time use by your child. Remember: Regardless of whether your child's AAC system is low tech or high tech, it should be available to your child all of the time.

At the back of the book, you will find organizations, companies that specialize in AAC, sources for picture symbols, and selected references and resources to help you find the information needed to maximize the communication skills of your child with Down syndrome through using AAC and technology.

We all live with technology around us. Learning to use and be comfortable with technology is just as important for people with Down syndrome as it is for other people. Every year, more and more technology is used in the classroom. Furthermore, many jobs that people with Down syndrome may hold as adults require the ability to use technology, including copiers, computers, postage machines, scanners, etc. Encouraging your child to learn how to use technology effectively is to your child's advantage now and for the future.

WORKSHEET FOR DESIGNING AN AUGMENTATIVE & ALTERNATIVE COMMUNICATION SYSTEM

Name: _____ **Age:** _____

Class Placement: _____

Current Needs:

❑ Transitional Pre-Speech System   ❑ Supplementary Communication System

❑ Supplementary Learning System   ❑ Alternative Communication System

Team Members: _____   _____

_____   _____

_____   _____

Type of System:

Unaided: *Sign Language*   Aided: Communication board ❑

SEE (Signed Exact English) ❑   Communication notebook ❑

ASL (American Sign Language) ❑   Picture Exchange System (PECS) ❑

Cued Speech ❑   Electronic device (specify) ❑ _____

Cued Language ❑   Other ❑ _____

Other ❑ _____

Symbols

Type of System:

Objects ❑   Photographs ❑   Pictures ❑   Line drawings ❑   Letters ❑

Words ❑   Phrases ❑   Sentences ❑   Other ❑ _____

Number of Symbols Used: _____

Content of System (vocabulary to include):

School ❑   Home ❑   Community ❑   Other ❑ _____

Sources for Pictures (if used): _____

Settings:

Speech/language therapy sessions ❑   Classroom ❑   Home ❑   Community ❑

Before/after-school care ❑   Other ❑ _____

Purposes:

Communication assisting speech ❑   Communication replacing speech ❑

Language and classroom learning ❑   Behavior prompts (cues that serve as reminders) ❑

Other ❑ _____

Organization of Information (layout and design): _____

_____

Frequent Communication Partners:

_____	_____
_____	_____
_____	_____

Training Needed:

    Child ❏   Parent ❏   Day care ❏   Teacher ❏

    Classroom Aide ❏   Other school personnel (specify) ❏ _____

    Other ❏ _____

Updating the System:

    Person responsible: _____   Intervals (every 6 months or annually):____

    Dates: _____   As Needed: _____

Maintenance/Monitoring of System:

    Person responsible in: School: _____

                         Home: _____

                         Community: _____

Servicing the System:

    Person responsible: _____   Intervals (every 6 months or annually):____

    Dates: _____   As Needed: _____

Transporting the system:

    Where will the system be used?

        Speech class ❏   Classroom ❏   School (all activities) ❏   Bus ❏

        Home (during school year) ❏   Home (during summer vacations) ❏

        All of the above ❏

Person responsible for system at school: _____

Person responsible for system at home: _____

Funding the System: _____

_____

ASSISTIVE TECHNOLOGY REPORT FOR ALEX

Reason for Consultation:

Mother requested Assistive Technology consultation services to support 11-year-old son in his home with completion of homework and strategies for studying. The SETT Framework was utilized in order to explore Alex's strengths and needs, the supports currently in place for him, and the expectations for tasks he needs to complete. The SETT (Student, Environment, Tasks, Tools) Framework provides a means to consider and establish the need (or lack of need) of an individual student for assistive technology and work toward developing a system of tools with which a student can use to address identified needs.

The initial observation used to begin this process was done at the child's middle school, where he is fully included in general education classes. While his mother is interested in Assistive Technology supports that she can implement at home, it was important to see the child in his school setting to gain an understanding of the school environment and the expectations for him at school in his classes.

Student:

Alex is an 11-year-old young man who receives special education services in the context of general education classes at his local middle school. He is talkative and self-confident. He engages peers and adults in conversation easily and with no apparent shyness. He was quite independent in the school building and was able to walk from one class to another without any assistance. In his classroom he knew where to sit and was able to follow classroom routines with minimal assistance from the para-educators in the classroom. He complied with directions to locate his homework but was deterred by the disorganization in his notebook. When observed in English and Science classes, Alex was able to work cooperatively with peers. He needed a few prompts to maintain his attention to independent work and at times looking for needed materials in his notebook took his attention away from the tasks at hand.

Alex is diagnosed with Down syndrome; however, he demonstrates strong cognitive skills and is reading at least at an early elementary school level. As mentioned previously, he has strong oral com-munication skills and good intelligibility, although some dysfluencies were noted in conversation. His fine motor skills for writing appear to be the weakness most affecting him with his school work. His print is very light, oversized, and the letters are quite difficult to read. Alex has difficulty reading his own writing.

Environment:

Alex is a 6th grader at his local middle school. He takes typical 6th grade classes with grade level peers, including Science, English, Social Studies, and Math. Alex's teachers appeared to be provid-ing some scaffolded assignments for Alex in the classroom. There are para-educators in his classes providing support for students with IEP's in the classroom, including Alex. At school, Alex has access to a laptop computer for some note taking, particularly writing down his homework assignments. His notes are then saved to a flash drive which travels home with him so that he can use these notes to complete his homework. Alex has access to a computer at home for homework. He currently uses MS Word and Co-Writer, a word prediction program to help him with his spelling on the computers at both home and at school.

Tasks:

As Alex is included in general education classes, the pace of his classes is quite fast and the workload is significant. As do most middle school students, Alex has a great deal of homework each night. Alex's poor handwriting presents a challenge in doing much of his homework, because even though he has access to a computer, a large percentage of his homework (and school work) are forms and preprinted worksheets. Even when the degree of difficulty of the work is scaled down for Alex, usually a written response is needed to complete assignments.

In addition to written tasks being difficult for Alex to complete in a legible manner, organization of materials presents a challenge to Alex and his lack of organization in his notebook impacts on his ability to successfully complete homework and get it turned in to his teachers.

Tools:

Many of the barriers that written work, both at home and at school, presents can be overcome by an increased use of flexible, digital materials and scaffolds that his teachers can easily produce using word processing tools or low tech/no tech solutions. Some of his teachers are already presenting tasks for Alex integrating these strategies and this just needs to be expanded to more tasks in more settings. In addition, it appeared that many of the materials for studying and work in Alex's notebook were printed word processing documents that can easily be made accessible to Alex digitally.

The following list is an outline of *ways that school and homework tasks can be made more accessible* for Alex.

1. Provide Alex with any teacher-made documents on his flash drive for completion on the computer rather than as pencil and paper tasks. Teachers could also email documents to his mother for downloading at home, if they do not have access to the flash drive at a convenient time.

2. Rather than requiring short answer responses to questions, create fill-in-the-blank worksheet activities with a bank of answers at the bottom. This can then be completed on the computer, where Alex can either copy and paste answers from the word bank into the answer fields, or can be printed out and Alex can use scissors and a glue stick to cut and paste. Word bank answers could also be created as a separate page and printed on labels for easy removal and sticking or on Post-it printer paper so that the answers can easily be moved around for repeated practice with a printed worksheet. Digital word banks can also be created for commercially available Xeroxed worksheets and printed on labels/Post-it paper.
    a. Fill-in-the blank worksheets can easily be made by taking an existing digitally available text (from the Internet, from an already created document, etc.) and replacing key words with an underline. The text removed can then be copied into a table that can serve as a word bank.
    b. ClozePro is commercially available software from Crick that will do this very easily and quickly. ClozePro also provides text-to-speech support for any curriculum-based text that may be above Alex's reading level.

c. WordBar is another software tool, also from Crick, that provides talking word banks that can be used along with any application, including Word and PowerPoint, allowing Alex to quickly insert words into fill-in-the blank assignments or longer written work including short answer and Brief Constructed Response (short essays).

3. When answering questions or writing Brief Constructed Responses on printed papers, if Alex needs to provide support from the text, allow him to highlight the referenced text (on the paper, not in a book) and draw a line connecting the reference to the questions, rather than having to copy the text into the question he is answering. This will allow him to demonstrate his knowledge and understanding even if he is not writing out a full response. Different color highlighters can be used for different questions.

4. For subjects that require an ongoing notebook of class notes and handouts (Social Studies appears to have this), allow Alex to keep a notebook using PowerPoint. Documents for the notebook can be copied and pasted into a PowerPoint slide. If documents are not already available digitally, then they can be scanned as a text and then copied into a slide. Pictures and images can easily be included via digital images or as scanned pictures, as well. Text boxes within each slide can be used for additional notes that Alex needs to take. Alex can then view the slides on the computer for review or print them out.

5. Long-term projects, such as the subject/predicate project from Reading can also be provided digitally by Alex's teachers or scanned in at home (in a text-based format). Any OCR (optical character recognition) software that typically comes with a scanner will allow text to be saved as a Word document, but to preserve the look of a scanned text-based document (so that it looks just like the original document) Kurzweil software can be used. Kurzweil would also provide text to speech support for curriculum-based text that is above Alex's reading level.

6. Alex may benefit from using either the computer with Co:Writer on it for note taking in classes or if the computer is too cumbersome or if the screen is too much of a barrier, he could use a portable word processor such as the Neo from Alphasmart. Notes can then be transferred to his computer or printed out. Alex would need to demonstrate that he is able to maintain his attention to the lecture while taking notes, in order for this to be a viable solution for him.

7. Another solution for notes for Alex (but more time-consuming for his teachers) is for them to provide Alex with scaffolded notes from their lectures. If they present their lectures/interactive discussions using PowerPoint or Word projected up on a screen for the class, providing Alex with a copy of these files would be an excellent way for him to have access to quality notes to study and use for completing homework.

In addition to these strategies for supporting Alex's written work, Alex would also benefit from better organization of his notebook for school. He was observed spending a great deal of time in his classes looking for materials he needed in class. The following is a list of **strategies to keep his notebook better organized**.

1. Provide clear page protectors to put papers in that Alex will need to refer to over time. This will prevent the papers from tearing at the holes and becoming misplaced in his notebook. Use flags or tabs to clearly label the page protectors and contents and organize by subject.

2. Have a clearly labeled Homework folder for each subject. This will minimize the time Alex spends searching through his homework folder looking for each subject's papers.

3. Directly teach Alex how to use tabs in his notebook to find information. He was observed paging through his entire notebook from the beginning to find materials, even though they were located in a specific subject area marked by a tabbed separator.

While many of these suggestions may take some advanced preparation and additional time on the part of both Alex's parents and his teachers, ultimately these strategies will provide more opportunities for success and more independence for Alex in school and during studying/homework time. Certainly the strategies can be approached one at a time to make it more manageable to tackle them.

CHAPTER 11

Keep on Moving Forward

The years between ages 6 and 14 are years of tremendous growth and development. Your child moves from being a beginning student in elementary school to adolescence and middle school. By age 14, your child is navigating the school building, adapting to multiple teachers, and interacting with peers, younger children, and adults

in the community. The communication circle widens a great deal during these years. For many children, communication skills progress from speaking in phrases or short sentences to carrying on complex conversations, and to using language for learning, following complex instructions in school and the community, being able to say what they want to get what they need, and speaking clearly so they can be understood.

People with Down syndrome can keep improving their communication skills all through their lives. They do not "plateau" and there is no fixed end point to what they may eventually learn. Because of anatomical, physiological, sensory, motor, and cognitive differences, however, learning speech and language skills is more difficult for people with Down syndrome. Therefore, parents, other family members, and people close to them need to actively intervene to keep their skills moving forward.

At this stage in your child's life, you may have boundless energy and desire to help your child improve his communication (and other) skills. Or you may have the desire, but don't see how you can fit one more thing into your day. Than again, perhaps you are feeling burned out after years of working on early intervention and/or special education goals and are tired of doing "therapy" with your child at home. Maybe you are tired of being your child's teacher, and want some time to have fun with your child.

Regardless of your present outlook about doing therapy at home, you should know that helping your child to progress in speech and language skills doesn't need to take a lot of your time and energy. Communication is a part of daily life. Once you understand your role in helping your child, you can accomplish a great deal without adding a lot of special "therapy time" to your day, by teaching and practicing as the natural opportunities arise.

10 Tips for Nurturing Your Child's Communication Skills

Here are some tips to help your child's communication skills moving forward. Don't feel as if you need to follow all of these suggestions if you are feeling overwhelmed or burned out right now. The idea is that if you are able to take even a few of these suggestions, you will be helping your child make progress. Later, if you have more time and energy to devote to working with your child, you can revisit this list and see if you can try other suggestions.

1. *Make sure your child has a way to communicate everything that is on his mind.* If he is age 6 or older and can't use speech well enough to communicate his thoughts with familiar people, speak to your SLP about evaluating him for AAC (see Chapter 10). Your child needs a communication system that meets his needs at every age, in every stage, and for every situation. You need to consciously monitor whether your child's current communication system is working for him. When it is not effective, you need to be your child's advocate to ensure that he always has an effective communication system.

2. *If your child is receiving speech-language therapy, make sure you establish two-way communication with the SLP.* Your SLP needs to hear how your child is communicating at home and what your concerns are, and you need to know what to do at home to support what's going on in therapy. You need to know what your child is ready to practice at home, and what may be too frustrating to work on at the moment. If you are getting no communications from your child's SLP except in relation to the IEP meetings, call or email her and request a meeting to come up with a way to communicate on a regular basis. A home-school communication program is a necessity. (See Chapters 5 and 6.)

3. *Find ways to work with your child on speech and language skills naturally, throughout the day.*
    - This could be as simple as choosing one new word to teach your child this week or month. One good way to do this is to think

about your daily routines and the interactions that you have with your child over and over again. For example, at dinner time do you often ask your child, "How was your day?" using exactly the same words? Try thinking of phrasing that another way, introducing a word your child doesn't know—e.g., "What was the *highlight* of your day?" Or, "Did anything *unusual/noteworthy/enjoyable* happen at school today?" Or even "What was your most *monotonous* class today?"

Another example: if you frequently say "Stop fighting!" to your child and his brother, switch to saying "Stop arguing!" or "Stop quarreling!" or "Stop squabbling!" Likewise, if you frequently use the word *very* with your child, make a conscious effort to use a synonym for *very* throughout the day ("That's *extremely* hot!" or "It's *excessively* loud in here!") Remember, you don't want to suddenly use new vocabulary words in every exchange with your child—just choose *one* new word and use it repeatedly over the course of as many days as it takes him to learn it.

- A very easy way to incorporate speech and language learning into your day is to read with your child or encourage him to read. If you still read with your child at bedtime, choose books at his language and interest level. If your child reads independently, help him choose books at his reading level that are of interest to him. Get to know the children's librarian at your local library. They are an invaluable source of information. They love children's literature and will delight in introducing your child to new books.

- Try having a Family Game Night and play some of the games listed in the Resources section. Really, any board game or card game can be a great opportunity for expanding communication skills in a fun way. When you know that new words will be part of the game, try to use them before so that the words will be familiar to your child. Or play the game with just the two of you before you try it with the entire family, so that your child will not get lost when the larger group plays the game.

4. *Make sure your child knows that you value and welcome his communication.* Express your interest and pleasure in what he communicates with you. Make eye contact and use an animated tone of voice in responding. Make yourself a rewarding communication partner. When communication becomes a chore for your child, he will not want to communicate. Stay with him when he is hard to understand. Be an active listener, and ask questions. Let him know that you hear him. For example: "I am so glad that you told me about the science walk to the lake. Maybe we can go over there soon, and you can show me some of the things that your class observed."

5. *Work on technical skills,* such as making speech sounds correctly or using correct grammar, ***only when it does not interfere with communication.*** If your child is really excited about the snow coming down, share his wonder. Don't correct him

because he is saying "no" instead of "snow." If your child says something ungrammatical or leaves out words, repeat back what he said correctly. Then, you might try to get him to repeat your model.

6. ***Ask the SLP to develop a home practice program.*** You want to reinforce what is being worked on in therapy, but you don't want to correct your child unless he is able to make the correct sound or use the correct structure. Until he is able to do it correctly, it will be frustrating when you correct him. But, when he is able to say a sound or use a word ending or a verb tense correctly, it will be very helpful to correct him and help him practice the correct way of saying it. Therefore, the SLP needs to keep you updated about your child's emerging skills so you will know when to reinforce them.

7. ***Try to experience life through your child's eyes, and help him learn how others experience life.*** Let him know that you understand his feelings, attitudes, interests, and opinions, but also help him learn that others may have different perspectives. This can help a lot with conversational skills, and if other children try to mislead him or bully him.

8. ***Remember that speech is difficult for people with Down syndrome.*** Don't confuse your child's communication skills with his overall abilities. Don't think he can't do something because he is hard to understand or cannot express clearly what he wants. Provide the opportunities for him to try many new activities and learn many skills. Don't underestimate his abilities based on his speech.

9. ***Work on social communication skills at home and in the community*** (Chapters 8 and 9). The ability to use greetings, have conversations, or introduce people at a get-together has immediate rewards for a person. For instance, my 12-year-old friend Alex is terrific at introducing people to each other. This has tremendous benefits for him at parties and in church, where he becomes the greeter and gets to meet people as they are arriving.

10. ***Look for resources, both informational resources and people.*** You can use the resources listed at the end of this book as a jumping off point. Local, national, and international organizations provide many informational resources. They also can link you to other people. They have information on family support groups, both in-person and on-line, as well as events. Person-to-person groups with similar cultural or ethnic backgrounds are emerging because of diversity outreach efforts by the organizations. For example, the National Down Syndrome Congress now has a Diversity Outreach coordinator and has sponsored meetings and development of materials for Latino and African-American families. Global Connections is a support group for Asian and Asian-American families. If you have access to the Internet, you can also find many online Down syndrome support groups with specific areas of interest by going to www.yahoogroups.com and typing "Down syndrome" in the search box.

Keep Your Goal in Mind

There's an expression to the effect that you need to know where you are going before you can figure out how to get there. This goes for helping your child to progress in communication skills, as well. If you want to help your child to reach the next speech or language goal that is in his reach, it helps a great deal to know what those next goals are.

As this book has emphasized, having your child's speech and language skills periodically evaluated by a speech-language pathologist is key to setting appropriate goals for therapy. But if your child is not receiving therapy or if you are in between evaluations, it can also be helpful to assess where your child's skills are more informally, and to look at the next skills he can work towards.

To help you keep track of how your child's skills are progressing, you will find comprehensive language and speech treatment plans in the Appendix. You can use these as you plan with your child's communication team and also use them to get an idea of long-range goals you may want to aim for with your child. From ages 6-14, there are a wide variety of communication skills that develop and improve over time, and different skills are needed at school and at home. For this reason, the plans in the Appendix are divided by school age (elementary, middle school, and high school). These age ranges are only a guide, however. Do not worry if your child has not mastered all the area for a given age range as long as he is making progress.

Developing speech and language skills is a journey that you take with your child. The goal is for your child to have an effective communication system that will enable him to engage with the world. For young children, the communication system may be sign or PECS or another visual system until they can learn to use speech. For most children from ages 6 to 14, speech will be an effective communication system. For some children, or at some stages, supplementary systems will need to be used in order for communication to be effective.

I have worked with several thousand children and their families over the past 30 years. The families worked with their children at home and in the community, and all the children made progress. My professional life has been devoted to sharing information with families so they can help their children develop speech and language skills. When I see the young adult self-advocates at conferences communicating effectively, and eloquently talking about their lives, hopes, and dreams, I feel a deep sense of pride. When I work with children and learn something new that can be useful for families, I want to share that knowledge. I communicate through my books and my talks because the information empowers families. Working together, we can make a difference in the communication effectiveness of children and adolescents with Down syndrome.

References & Suggested Reading

CHAPTER 1

Kumin, L. (2007). Basis for speech, language, and communication. Resource guide found at www.ndsccenter.org. Go to "Parent Resources," then "in-depth resources," then "speech and language articles."

CHAPTER 2

Abbeduto, L & Murphy, M. (2004). Language, social cognition, maladaptive behavior, and communication in Down syndrome and fragile X syndrome, In M.L. Rice & S.F. Warren (Eds.). *Developmental language disorders: From phenotypes to etiologies.* Mahwah, NJ: Erlbaum.

Abbeduto, L. et al. (2003). Receptive language skills of adolescents and young adults with Down or Fragile X syndrome. *American Journal on Mental Retardation 108,* 149-160.

Ayres, A. J. (2005). *Sensory Integration and the Child: Understanding Hidden Sensory Challenges.* Los Angeles, CA: Western Psychological Publishers.

Ayres, J. & Mailloux, Z. (1981). Influence of sensory integration procedures on language development. *The American Journal of Occupational Therapy 35,* 383-390.

Berglund, E., Eriksson, M. & Johansson (2001). Parental reports of spoken language skills in children with Down syndrome. *Journal of Speech, Language and Hearing Research 44,* 179-191.

Biel, L. & Peske, N. (2005). *Raising a Sensory Smart Child.* New York, NY: Penguin.

Bird, E. K.-R. & Chapman, R. S. (1994). Sequential recall in individuals with Down syndrome. *Journal of Speech and Hearing Research 37,* 1369-1381.

Bondy, A. & Frost, L. (2001). *A Picture's Worth: PECS and Other Visual Communication Strategies in Autism.* Bethesda, MD: Woodbine House.

Bruni, Maryanne. (2006). *Fine Motor Skills for Children with Down Syndrome: A Guide for Parents and Professionals.* Bethesda, MD: Woodbine House.

Buckley, S. (1996). Reading before talking: Learning about mental abilities from children with Down's syndrome. University of Portsmouth Inaugural Lecture, Portsmouth, England.

Buckley, S. & Bird, G. (2001). *Speech & Language Development in Individuals with Down syndrome (5-11 years): An Overview*. Portsmouth, England: Down Syndrome Educational Trust.

Chapman, R. S. & Hesketh, L. J. (2000). Behavioral phenotype of individuals with Down syndrome. *Mental Retardation and Developmental Disabilities Research Reviews 6*, 84-95.

Chapman, R., Seung, J., Schwartz, S. & Bird, E.R. (1998). Language skills of children and adolescents with Down syndrome II: Production deficits. *Journal of Speech, Language and Hearing Research 41*, 861-873.

Cohen, W. et al. (1999). Health care guidelines for individuals with Down syndrome (Down syndrome preventive medical check list). *Down Syndrome Quarterly, 4,* 1-26. Available online at www.ds-health.com.

Fowler, A. (1995). Linguistic variability in persons with Down syndrome. In Nadel, L. & Rosenthal, D., *Down Syndrome: Living and Learning in the Community.* New York, NY: Wiley-Liss, 121-31.

Grela, B. G. (2002). Lexical verb diversity in children with Down syndrome. *Clinical Linguistics and Phonetics 16*, 251-63.

Horstmeier, D. (1988). But I don't understand you—The communication interaction of youths and adults with Down syndrome. In Pueschel, S., *The Young Person with Down Syndrome*. Baltimore: Paul Brookes Publishers.

Jarrold, C. & Baddeley, A. D. (2002). Verbal short-term memory in Down syndrome. *Journal of Speech, Language and Hearing Research 45*, 531-544.

Kranowitz, C. S. (2006). *The Out-of-Sync Child: Recognizing and Coping with Sensory Processing Disorder.* New York, NY: Perigree.

Kranowitz, C. S. (2006). *The Out-of-Sync Child Has Fun: Activities for Kids with Sensory Processing Disorder.* New York, NY: Perigree.

Kumin, L. (2003). *Early Communication Skills for Children with Down Syndrome: A Guide for Parents and Teachers*. Bethesda, MD: Woodbine House.

Kumin, L. (2002a). Maximizing speech and language in children and adolescents with Down syndrome. In Cohen, W., Nadel, L. & Madnick, M. (Eds.), *Down Syndrome: Visions for the 21st Century,* 403-15. New York, NY: Wiley-Liss.

Kumin, L. (2002b). Why can't you understand what I am saying: Speech intelligibility in daily life. *Disability Solutions 5* (1),1-15.

Kumin, L. (2002c). You said it just yesterday, why not now? Developmental apraxia of speech in children and adults with Down syndrome. *Disability Solutions 5* (2),1-16.

Kumin, L. (2001). Speech intelligibility in individuals with Down syndrome: A framework for targeting specific factors in assessment and treatment. *Down Syndrome Quarterly 6*, 1-6.

Kumin, L. (1996). Speech and language skills in children with Down syndrome. *Mental Retardation and Developmental Disabilities Research Reviews 2*, 109-16.

Kumin, L. (1994). Intelligibility of speech in children with Down syndrome in natural settings: Parents' perspective. *Perceptual and Motor Skills 78*, 307-13.

Kumin, L., Councill, C. & Goodman, M. (1998). Expressive vocabulary development in children with Down syndrome. *Down Syndrome Quarterly 3, 1-7.*

Laws, G. & Bishop, D. (2004). Pragmatic language impairment and social deficits in Williams syndrome: A comparison with Down's syndrome and specific language impairment. *International Journal of Language and Communication Disorders 39*, 45-64.

Laws, G., Byrne, A. & Buckley, S. (2000). Language and memory development in children with Down syndrome at mainstream schools and special schools: A comparison. *Educational Psychology 20,* 447-57.

Leddy, M. (1999). The biological bases of speech in people with Down syndrome. In J. Miller, M. Leddy & L. A. Leavitt (Eds.), *Improving the Communication of People with Down Syndrome,* 61-80. Baltimore, MD: Paul Brookes.

MacDonald, J. (1989). *Becoming Partners with Children: From Play to Conversation.* Chicago: Riverside.

Miller, J. F. (1995). Individual differences in vocabulary acquisition in children with Down syndrome. *Progress in Clinical and Biological Research* 393, 93-103.

Miller, J. F. (1988). Developmental asynchrony of language development in children with Down syndrome. In Nadel, L. (Ed.), *Psychobiology of Down Syndrome*. New York, NY: Academic Press.

Miller, J. & Leddy, M. (1999). Verbal fluency, speech intelligibility, and communicative effectiveness. In J. Miller, M. Leady & L. A. Leavitt. *Improving the Communication of People with Down syndrome*. Baltimore, MD: Paul Brookes.

Miller, L. J. (2006). *Sensational Kids: Hope and Help for Children with Sensory Processing Disorder.* New York, NY: Putnam.

Miolo, G., Chapman, R. S. & Sindberg, H. A. (2005). Sentence comprehension in adolescents with Down syndrome and typically developing children: Role of sentence voice, visual context, and auditory-verbal short-term memory. *Journal of Speech Language Hearing Research 48.*

Roizen, N. (1997). Hearing loss in children with Down syndrome: A review. *Down Syndrome Quarterly, 2,* 1-4.

Rosin, P. & Swift, E. (1999). Communication intervention: Improving the speech intelligibility of children with Down syndrome. In J. Miller, M. Leady & L. A. Leavitt, *Improving the Communication of People with Down Syndrome.* Baltimore, MD: Paul Brookes.

Schwartz, Sue. *Choices in Deafness: A Parent's Guide to Communication Options.* 3rd ed. Bethesda, MD: Woodbine House, 2007.

Shott, S. R. (2000). Down syndrome: Common pediatric ear, nose, and throat problems. *Down Syndrome Quarterly, 5,* 1-6.

Shott, S.R., Joseph, A. and Heithaus, D. (2001). Hearing loss in children with Down syndrome. *International Journal of Pediatric Otolaryngology 1:61 (3):* 199-205.

Vicari, S., Marotta, L. & Carlesimo, G. (2004). Verbal short-term memory in Down's syndrome: An articulatory loop deficit? *Journal of Intellectual Disability Research 48,* 80-92.

CHAPTER 3

Anderson, W., Chitwood, S., Hayden, D. & Takemoto, C. (2008). *Negotiating the Special Education Maze.* 4th ed. Bethesda, MD: Woodbine House.

Kingsley, J. & Levitz, M. (2007). *Count Us In: Growing Up with Down Syndrome.* 2nd ed. Orlando, FL: Harcourt Brace.

Kliewer, C. & Biklen, D. Labeling: Who wants to be called retarded? In Stainback, W. & Stainback, S. (1996). *Controversial Issues Confronting Special Education: Divergent Perspectives.* Boston, MA: Allyn & Bacon, 83-95.

CHAPTER 4

Brown-Sweeney, S. & Smith, B. (1997). The development of speech production abilities in children with Down syndrome. *Clinical Linguistics & Phonetics 11,* 345-62.

Fuchs, D., Fuchs, L., Powers, M., & Dailey, A. (1985). Bias in the assessment of handicapped children. *American Educational Research Journal 22,* 185-97.

Kumin, L. (1994). Intelligibility of speech in children with Down syndrome in natural settings: Parents' perspective. *Perceptual and Motor Skills 78,* 307-13.

Kumin, L. (2004). Mental retardation. In L. Schoenbrodt (Ed.), *Childhood Communication Disorders: Organic Bases.* Clifton Park, NY: Thomson/Delmar Learning, 151-86.

Kumin, L. (2006). Speech intelligibility and childhood verbal apraxia in children with Down syndrome. *Down Syndrome Research and Practice 10,* 10-22.

Kumin, L. & Adams, J. (2000). Developmental apraxia of speech and intelligibility in children with Down syndrome. *Down Syndrome Quarterly 5,* 1-6.

Leddy, M. (1999). The biological bases of speech in people with Down syndrome. In J. Miller, M. Leddy & L. A. Leavitt (Eds.), *Improving the Communication of People with Down Syndrome,* 61-80. Baltimore, MD: Paul Brookes.

Stoel-Gammon, C. (1980). Phonological analysis of four Down's syndrome children. *Applied Psycholinguistics 1,* 31-48.

Stoel-Gammon, C. (2001). Down syndrome phonology: Developmental patterns and intervention strategies. *Down Syndrome Research and Practice 7,* 93-100.

Van Borsal, J. (1996). Articulation in Down's syndrome adolescents and adults. *European Journal of Disorders of Communication 31,* 425-444.

Velleman, S.L. (2002). *Childhood Apraxia of Speech Resource Guide.* New York, NY: Singular Publishing.

CHAPTER 5

Bochner, S., Outhred, L. & Pieterse, M. (2001). A study of functional literacy skills in young adults with Down syndrome. *International Journal of Disability, Development, and Education 48,* 67-90.

Buckley, S. (2001). *Reading and Writing for Individuals with Down Syndrome: An Overview.* Portsmouth, England: The Down Syndrome Educational Trust.

Buckley, S. (1996). Reading before talking: Learning about mental abilities from children with Down's syndrome. University of Portsmouth Inaugural Lecture, Portsmouth, England.

Buckley, S. (1995). Teaching children with Down syndrome to read and write. In Nadel, L. & Rosenthal, D. (Eds.), *Down Syndrome: Living and Learning in the Community.* New York: Wiley-Liss, 158-69.

Buckley, S. & Bird, G. (1993). Teaching children with Down's syndrome to read. *Down's Syndrome: Research and Practice 1,* 34-41.
Available online at www.down-syndrome.net/library/periodicals/dsrp/01/1/034.

Buckley, S., Bird, G. & Byrne, A. (1996). The practical and theoretical significance of teaching literacy skills to children with Down syndrome. In Jean Rondal and Juan Perera (Eds.), *Down Syndrome: Psychological, Psychobiological and Socioeducational Perspectives,* 119-128). London: Whurr Publishers.

Buckley, S. & Johnson-Glenberg, M. (2008). Increasing literacy learning for individuals with Down syndrome and fragile X syndrome. In Roberts, J., Chapman, R. & Warren, S. *Speech and Language Development and Intervention in Down Syndrome and Fragile X Syndrome.* Baltimore, MD: Paul Brookes, 233-54.

Cleary, B. & Gable, B. *Words are CATegorical* (series of books about grammar). Minneapolis: Millbrook Press/Lerner.

Elkins, J. & Farrell, M. (1994). Literacy for all? The case of Down syndrome. *Journal of Reading 38,* 270-80.

Fowler, A. E., Doherty, B. J. & Boynton, L. (1995). Basis of reading skill in young adults with Down syndrome. In Nadel, L. & Rosenthal, D. (Eds.), *Down Syndrome: Living and Learning in the Community.* New York: Wiley-Liss, 121-31.

Fowler, A. (1990). Language abilities in children with Down syndrome: Evidence for a specific syntactic delay. In Cichetti, D. & Beeghley, M. (Eds.), *Children with Down Syndrome: A Developmental Perspective.* Cambridge: Cambridge University Press, 302-28.

Fowler, A. E. (1995). Linguistic variability in persons with Down syndrome: Research and implications. In Nadel, L. & Rosenthal, D. (Eds.), *Down Syndrome: Living and Learning in the Community.* New York: Wiley-Liss, 121-131.

Kumin, L. (2001). *Classroom Language Skills for Children with Down Syndrome: A Guide for Parents and Teachers.* Bethesda, MD: Woodbine House.

Kumin, L., Councill, C. & Goodman, M. (1995). The pacing board: A technique to assist the transition from single word to multiword utterances. *Infant-Toddler Intervention 5,* 23-29

Laws, G., Byrne, A. & Buckley, S. (2000). Language and memory development in children with Down syndrome at mainstream schools and special schools: A comparison. *Educational Psychology 20,* 447-57.

Laws, G., Buckley, S., Bird, G., MacDonald, J. & Broadley, I. (1995). The influence of reading instruction on language and memory development in children with Down's syndrome. *Down's Syndrome Research and Practice 3,* 59-64.

McVay, P., Wilson, H. & Chiotti, L. (2003). "I see what you mean!" Using visual tools to support student learning. *Disability Solutions 5,* 1-15.

Meyers, L. (1988). Using computers to teach children with Down syndrome spoken and written language skills. In L. Nadel (Ed.), *The Neurobiology of Language.* Cambridge, MA: M.I.T. Press.

Meyers, L. (1994). Access and meaning: The keys to effective computer use by children with language disabilities. *Journal of Special Education Technology 12,* 257-75.

Miller, J. F. (1995). Individual differences in vocabulary acquisition in children with Down syndrome. *Progress in Clinical and Biological Research*, 393, 93-103.

Oelwein, P. (1995). *Teaching Reading to Children with Down Syndrome: A Guide for Parents and Tteachers*. Bethesda, MD: Woodbine House.

Pleura, R.E. & DeBoer, C.J. (1995). *Story Making: Using Predictable Literature to Develop Communication*. Eau Claire, WI: Thinking Publications.

Voss. K. (2005). *Teaching by Design: Using Your Computer to Create Materials for Students with Learning Differences*. Bethesda, MD: Woodbine House.

CHAPTER 6

Gibbon, F., McNeill, A., Wood, S. & Watson, J. (2003). Changes in linguapalatal contact patterns during therapy for velar fronting in a 10-year-old with Down's syndrome. *International Journal of Language and Communication Disorders 38*, 47-64.

Hodson, B. & Paden, E. (1991). *Targeting Intelligible Speech: A Phonological Approach to Remediation*. 2nd ed. Austin, TX: PRO-ED.

Kaufman, N. (2001). *Kaufman Speech Praxis Treatment Kits (Basic and Advanced)*. Gaylord, MI: Northern Speech Services.

Kumin, L. (2007). Resource Guides for Speech and Language (on 9 topic areas). Guides on Childhood Apraxia of Speech and Oral Motor Skill Difficulties are available to download at www.ndsccenter.org.

Kumin, L. (2006). Differential diagnosis and treatment of speech sound production problems in individuals with Down syndrome. *Down Syndrome Quarterly, 8*, 7-18.

Kumin, L. (2006). Speech intelligibility and childhood verbal apraxia in children with Down syndrome. *Down Syndrome Research and Practice 10*, 10-22.

Kumin, L. (2006). *What Did You Say? A Guide to Speech Intelligibility in Children with Down Syndrome (DVD)*. Bethesda, MD: Woodbine House.

Kumin, L. (2002). Why can't you understand what I am saying: Speech intelligibility in Daily Life. *Disability Solutions 5* (1),1-15.

Kumin, L. (2002). You said it just yesterday, why not now? Developmental apraxia of speech in children and adults with Down syndrome. *Disability Solutions 5* (2),1-16.

Kumin, L. (2001). Speech intelligibility in individuals with Down syndrome: A framework for targeting specific factors for assessment and treatment. *Down Syndrome Quarterly, 6*, 1-8.

Kumin, L. (1994). Intelligibility of speech in children with Down syndrome in natural settings: Parents' perspective. *Perceptual and Motor Skills, 78*, 307-13.

Kumin, L. & Adams, J. (2000). Developmental apraxia of speech and intelligibility in children with Down syndrome. *Down Syndrome Quarterly, 5*, 1-6.

Mackie, E. (1996). *Oral-motor activities for young children*. Moline, IL: LinguiSystems.

Mackie, E. (1996). *Oral-motor activities for school-aged children*. Moline, IL: LinguiSystems.

Oetter, P. & Richter, E. (1995). *Motor Oral Respiration Eyes (MORE) - Integrating the Mouth with Sensory and Postural Functions.* 2nd ed. Hugo, MN: PDP Products.

Pehde, H., Geller, A. & Lechner, B. (1997). *The Complete Oral Motor Program for Articulation.* Moline, IL: LinguiSystems.

Rosenfeld-Johnson, S. (1999). *Oral-motor Exercises for Speech Clarity.* Tucson, AZ: Innovative Therapists International.

Rosenfeld-Johnson, S. & Money, S. (1999). *The Homework Book.* Tucson, AZ: Innovative Therapists International.

Rosin, P. & Swift, E. (1999). Communication intervention: Improving the speech intelligibility of children with Down syndrome. In J. Miller, M. Leddy & L. A. Leavitt, *Improving the Communication of People with Down Syndrome.* Baltimore, MD: Paul Brookes.

Smit, A., Hand, L., Freilinger, J., Bernthal, J. and Bird, A. (1990).The Iowa Articulation Norms Project and its Nebraska replication. *Journal of Speech and Hearing Disorders 55,* 795.

Stoel-Gammon, C. (1997). Phonological development in Down syndrome. *Mental Retardation and Developmental Disabilities Research Reviews 3,* 300-306.

Strode, R. & Chamberlain, C. (1995). *Easy Does It for Apraxia and Motor Planning: Preschool.* Moline, IL: LinguiSystems.

Strode, R. & Chamberlain, C. (1993). *Easy Does It for Apraxia and Motor Planning.* Moline, IL: LinguiSystems.

Strode, R. & Chamberlain, C. (1997). *Easy Does It for Articulation: An Oral Motor Approach.* Moline, IL: LinguiSystems.

Time to Sing (CD of familiar children's songs played and sung more slowly; helpful for children with Childhood Apraxia). Available from the Pittsburgh Symphony 412-392-3313 and Super Duper Publications 800-277-8737.

Van Borsal, J. (1996). Articulation in Down's syndrome adolescents and adults. *European Journal of Disorders of Communication, 31,* 425-444.

Velleman, S.L. (2002). *Childhood Apraxia of Speech Resource Guide.* New York: Singular Publishing.

Voss, K. (2005). *Teaching by Design.* Bethesda, MD: Woodbine House.

CHAPTER 7

Crimmins, D. B. (1999). Positive behavioral support: Analyzing, preventing, and replacing problem behaviors. In Hassold, T. & Patterson, D., *Down Syndrome: A Promising Future, Together.* New York: Wiley-Liss, 127-32.

Gardner, H. (1993). *Frames of Mind: The Theory of Multiple Intelligences.* New York: Basic Books.

Glasberg, B. (2005). *Functional Behavior Assessment for People with Autism: Making Sense of Seemingly Senseless Behavior.* Bethesda, MD: Woodbine House.

Kumin, L. (2007). *Resource Guide for Parents of School Age Children with Down Syndrome; Resource Guide for Parents of Adolescents with Down Syndrome.* Available online at www.ndsccenter.org.

Kumin, L. (2001). *Classroom Language Skills for Children with Down Syndrome: A Guide for Parents and Teachers*. Bethesda, MD: Woodbine House.

Tashie, C. (1993). *From Special to Regular, from Ordinary to Extraordinary*. Concord, NH: NH State Dept. of Education (ERIC document ED 387063).

Voss, K. (2005). *Teaching by Design: Using Your Computer to Create Materials for Students with Learning Differences*. Bethesda, MD: Woodbine House.

Wolpert, G. (1996). The educational challenges inclusion study. New York, NY: National Down Syndrome Society.

CHAPTERS 8 & 9

Abbeduto, L., Short-Meyerson, K. Benson, G. & Dolish, J. (2004). Relationship between theory of mind and language ability in children and adolescents with intellectual disability. *Journal of Intellectual Disability Research 48,* 150-59.

Baker, J. (2001). *Social Skills Picture Book*. Arlington, TX: Future Horizons.

Bellini, S., & Akullian, J. (2007). Video modeling and video self-modeling. In B. S. Myles, T. C. Swanson & J. Holverstott (Eds.), *Autism Spectrum Disorders: A Handbook for Parents and Professionals*. Westport, CT: Greenwood Publishing.

Capone, G. T. (1999). Down syndrome and autism spectrum disorders: A look at what we know. *Disability Solutions 3:*8-15, 1999. (Can be downloaded from the website: www.disabilitysolutions.org.)

Capone, G. T., Goyal, P., Ares, W., et al. (2006). Neurobehavioral disorders in children, adolescents, and young adults with Down syndrome. *American Journal of Medical Genetics, Part C - Seminars in Medical Genetics 142c* (3): 158-72.

Capone, G. T., Grados, M. A., Kaufmann, W. E., et al. (2005). Down syndrome and comorbid autism-spectrum disorder: Characterization using the aberrant behavior checklist. *American Journal of Medical Genetics, Part A 134A* (4): 373-80.

Carter, J. C., Capone, G. T., Gray, R. M., et al. (2007). Autistic-spectrum disorders in Down syndrome: Further delineation and distinction from other behavioral abnormalities. *American Journal of Medical Genetics, Part B - Neuropsychiatric Genetics 144B* (1): 87-94.

Cohen, M. & Sloan, D. (2007). *Visual Supports for People with Autism: A Guide for Parents and Professionals*. Bethesda, MD: Woodbine House.

Couwenhoven, T. (2007). *Teaching Children with Down Syndrome about Their Bodies, Boundaries, and Sexuality: A Guide for Parents and Professionals*. Bethesda, MD: Woodbine House.

Gagnon, E. (2001). *Power Cards: Using Special Interests to Motivate Children and Youth with Asperger Syndrome and Autism*. Shawnee Mission, KS: Autism Asperger Publishing Company.

Gardner, H. (1993). *Frames of Mind: The Theory of Multiple Intelligences*. New York: Basic Books.

Gray, C. (1994). *Comic Strip Conversations*. Arlington, TX: Future Horizons.

Gray, C. (!994). *The New Social Story Book*. Arlington, TX: Future Horizons.

Gray, C. *Storymovies*. Kentwood, MI: Carol Gray.

Kent, L., Evans, J., Paul, M. & Sharp, M. (1999). Co-morbidity of autistic spectrum disorders in children with Down syndrome. *Developmental Medicine & Child Neurology 41* (3), 153-58.

Kumin, L. (2003). *Early Communication Skills for Children with Down Syndrome: A Guide for Parents and Teachers.* Bethesda, MD: Woodbine House.

Kumin, L., Councill, C. & Goodman, M. (1995). The pacing board: A technique to assist the transition from single word to multiword utterances. *Infant-Toddler Intervention 5*, 23-29

LeBlanc, L., Coates, A., Daneshvar, S., Charlop-Christy, M., Morris, C. & Lancaster, B. (2003). Using video modeling and reinforcement to teach perspective taking skills to children with autism. *Journal of Applied Behavior Analysis 36,* 253-57.

MacDonald, James. (1989). *Becoming Partners with Children: From Play to Conversation.* Chicago: Riverside.

McGuire, D. & Chicoine, B. (2006). *Mental Wellness in Adults with Down Syndrome: A Guide to Emotional and Behavioral Strengths and Challenges.* Bethesda, MD: Woodbine House.

Voss, K. (2005). *Teaching by Design: Using Your Computer to Create Learning Materials for Students with Learning Differences.* Bethesda, MD: Woodbine House.

Wing, L. & Gould, J. (1979). Severe impairments of social interaction and associated abnormalities in children: Epidemiology and classification. *Journal of Autism and Development Disorders 1,* 11-29.

Wishart, J. G., Cebula, K. R., Willis, D. S. & Pitcairn, T.K. (2007). Understanding of facial expressions of emotion by children with intellectual disabilities of differing aetiology. *Journal of Intellectual Disability Research 51,* 551-63.

CHAPTER 10

Alliance for Technology Access. *Computer Resources for People with Disabilities: A Guide to Assistive Technologies, Tools and Resources for People of All Ages.* 4th edition (2004). Alameda, CA: Hunter House Publishers.

Beukelman, D. & Mirenda, P. (2006). *Augmentative and Alternative Communication: Supporting Children and Adults with Complex Communication Needs.* 3rd ed. Baltimore: Paul Brookes.

Bondy, A. & Frost, L. (2002). *A Picture's Worth: PECS and Other Visual Communication Strategies in Autism.* Bethesda, MD: Woodbine House.

Bornstein, H., Saulnier, K. & Hamilton, L. (1983). *The Comprehensive Signed English Dictionary.* Washington, DC: Gallaudet University Press.

Bornstein, H. & Saulnier, K. (1984). *The Signed English Starter.* Washington, DC: Gallaudet University Press.

Bornstein, H. & Saulnier, K. (1988). *Signing: Signed English Basic Guide.* New York: Crown Publishing.

Feng, J., Lazar, J., Kumin, L. & Ozok. A. (2008). *Computer usage by young individuals with Down syndrome: An exploratory study.* Halifax, Nova Scotia: The Tenth International ACM SIGACCESS Conference on Computers and Accessibility.

Kumin, L. (2003). *Early Communication Skills in Children with Down Syndrome: A Guide for Parents and Teachers.* Bethesda, MD: Woodbine House.

Light, J. & Binger, C. (1998). *Building Communicative Competence with Individuals Who Use Augmentative and Alternative Communication.* Baltimore, MD: Paul Brookes.

Meyers, L. (1988). Using computers to teach children with Down syndrome spoken and written language skills. In L. Nadel (ed.). *The Neurobiology of Language*. Cambridge, MA: M.I.T. Press.

Meyers, L. (1994). Access and meaning: The keys to effective computer use by children with language disabilities. *Journal of Special Education Technology 12,* 257-75.

National Joint Committee for the Communication Needs of Persons with Severe Disabilities (1992). *Communication Bill of Rights.* Available at www.asha.org/NJC/bill_of_rights.htm.

Romski, M.A. & Sevcik, R.A. (1996). Breaking the Speech Barrier: Language Development through Augmented Means. Baltimore, MD: Paul Brookes.

Schwartz, S. (2007). *Choices in Deafness: A Parents' Guide to Communication Options.* 3rd ed. Bethesda, MD: Woodbine House.

Sigafoos, J., Didden, R. & O'Reilly, M. (2003). Effects of speech output on maintenance of requesting and frequency of vocalizations in three children with developmental disabilities. *Augmentative and Alternative Communication 19* (1), 37-47.

Resource Guide

There are websites that serve as a portal to a vast amount of information. Since these websites are for organizations and government agencies concerned with technology, they are usually updated regularly. Many links to assistive technology/AAC websites can be found at:

- www.augcominc.com
- www.atia.org
- www.aacproducts.org
- www.assistivetech.net

Alliance for Technology Access

(415) 455-4575

www.ataccess.org

At the ATA website, you can find information on centers and vendors of assistive technology equipment, including AAC devices, and the services that they offer. You can find a complete list of all 41 centers affiliated with the Alliance for Technology Access organized by state. Some centers will analyze your child's computer needs and provide free or low-cost evaluations; others will lend computers and software. You are not limited to the centers within your state. The website also provides information on adapting curriculum using technology (AT in K-12), questions to ask to ensure that AT equipment meets your child's needs (mini-assessment), how to find qualified AT professionals, AT bibliography (including information on toys and computer software and hardware), and links to other helpful AT websites.

Alliance for Technology Industry Association

www.atia.org

This association has information on hardware, software, and communication devices. It also has information on companies that design and distribute AAC devices, and a section with links to other AAC websites.

Apple Computer Disability Resources

www.apple.com/accessibility

The website explains features specific to Apple computers that can make computer technology more accessible to people with disabilities and also provides links to other manufacturers' AT products.

Center for Applied Special Technology (CAST)

www.cast.org

The CAST website provides information on technology-based educational resources. The strategies are based on the principles of Universal Design for Learning (UDL). The information is helpful for adapting curriculum for children who have language and learning difficulties.

Closing the Gap

www.closingthegap.com

Closing the Gap is a resource center for technology information. It publishes a bimonthly newsletter and holds an annual conference. The website provides library resources, article summaries, and a list of upcoming conferences.

Communication Aid Manufacturers Association

www.cama.org

CAMA sponsors local and regional conferences and exhibits and demonstrations of communication aids. The website has a schedule of conferences.

Microsoft Accessible Technology Group

www.microsoft.com/enable

This website provides information on computer accessibility and assistive technology for people with disabilities. Some of the information is for adults in the workplace.

National Down Syndrome Congress

www.ndsccenter.org

Grace Williams, a professional who specializes in AAC for children with Down syndrome, has developed a current list of companies that provide AAC devices, with information about their products. Williams has also developed a bibliography of related articles and publications. To find the information, look up "parent resources," go to "In-depth resources," then choose "Augmentative Communication Resources."

RESNA

www.resna.org

The Rehabilitation Engineering and Assistive Technology Society of North America provides information on state Technology Assistance Projects which will provide hardware and software support. The Resna website provides a complete list of state centers that are funded under the Technology-Related Assistance for Individuals with Disabilities Act.

Trace Research and Development Center

www.trace.wisc.edu

This website provides information about assistive technology, including augmentative and alternative communication. Trace focuses on making hardware, software, and the Internet more accessible for people with disabilities.

United Cerebral Palsy

www.ucp.org

On the site, search for AAC. UCP has a special technology project that provides current information on legal, systems change, and funding issues. A booklet on selecting an AAC device for your child and handouts from AAC conferences can be downloaded.

The U.S. Society for Augmentative and Alternative Communication (USSAAC)

www.ussaac.org

Information and resources regarding augmentative communication, hardware, and software. The organization supports individuals who use AAC, their families, and the professionals who work with them. Website includes information on advocacy, AAC organizations, publications, listservs and blogs, and manufacturers and distributors of AAC equipment.

Canadians will find similar information through the International Society for Augmentative and Alternative Communication (ISAAC) at www.isaac-online.org.

DOWN SYNDROME

Canadian Down Syndrome Society
811 14th St. NW
Calgary, AL T2N 2A4
Canada
800-883-5608; 403-270-8500
www.cdss.ca

    The CDSS advocates for people with Down syndrome, provides information to families, and sponsors conferences. Several parent-friendly publications are available online, as well as online forums on a variety of topics. Visit the website for links to local affiliates all across Canada.

Down Syndrome Education International/Down Syndrome—USA
www.downsed.org

    Down Syndrome Education International is the expanded and reorganized organization and website founded by Sue Buckley (it was formerly known as the Down Syndrome Educational Trust).Extensive information on cognitive development, memory, reading, and communication is available on this website. Current and past research findings of Sue Buckley and colleagues are available. Publications include books, videos, and DVDs, and journal articles from Down Syndrome-Research and Practice are available.

Down Syndrome: Health Issues
www.ds-health.com

    An award winning website related to medical and developmental issues in children with Down syndrome developed by Dr. Len Leshin. Dr. Kumin's chapter on comprehensive speech and language intervention is on this website.

Down Syndrome Research Foundation
1409 Sperling Ave.
Burnaby, BC V5B 4J8
Canada
604-444-3773; 888-464-DSRF (in Canada only)
www.dsrf.org

    The DSRF conducts research with the goal of improving the quality of life for people with Down syndrome and their families. It also publishes the *Down Syndrome Quarterly* journal.

National Down Syndrome Congress (NDSC)
1370 Center Drive
Suite 102
Atlanta, GA 30324
800-232-NDSC (6372)
www.ndsccenter.org

    A national organization of parents and professionals dedicated to improving the lives of people with Down syndrome and their families. The NDSC provides free information on important issues affecting children with Down syndrome in English and Spanish. It also provides information and referral to local parent groups and comprehensive Down syndrome centers and holds an annual conference. See Dr. Kumin's resource guides for speech and language.

National Down Syndrome Society (NDSS)
666 Broadway
New York, NY 10012
800-221-4602
Web site: www.ndss.org

    A national organization that works to promote a better understanding of Down syndrome. Sponsors scientific and educational research into Down syndrome, provides online and print publications, sponsors "Buddy Walks" to raise money and promote Down syndrome awareness, and operates a website with extensive links.

DEVELOPMENTAL DISABILITIES

The Arc of the United States
1010 Wayne Avenue, Suite 650
Silver Spring, MD 20910
301-565-3842
www.thearc.org
The Arc is a national organization that advocates on behalf of people with developmental disabilities, including Down syndrome. Publications and an online Discussion Board are available from the national office, above.

National Dissemination Center for Children with Disabilities (NICHCY)
P.O. Box 1492
Washington, DC 20013-1492
800-695-0285; 202-884-8441 (fax)
www.nichcy.org
This organization has many publications on special education issues and other disability issues available. They can be downloaded free from the website or ordered for a nominal fee by phone or mail. Website information and some publications available in Spanish.

AUTISM

Autism Society of America
7910 Woodmont Avenue, Suite 300
Bethesda, MD 20814
800-328-8476; 301-657-0881
www.autism-society.org
The ASA is a national organization of parents and professionals that promotes a better understanding of autism spectrum disorders. It acts as an information clearinghouse about autism and services for people who have autism.

Autism Speaks
www.autismspeaks.org
The Autism Speaks website offers a wide variety of resources in English and Spanish, including parent information packets and an ASD Video Glossary which enables the viewer to see video clips of characteristics of children with autism spectrum disorders.

Down syndrome and Autistic Spectrum Listserv
http://groups.yahoo.com/groups/ds-autism
An online discussion group from families and professionals with an interest in the dual diagnosis of Down syndrome and autism.

SENSORY INTEGRATION

American Occupational Therapy Association
4720 Montgomery Lane
P.O. Box 31220
Bethesda, MD 20824-1220
301-652-2682
www.aota.org
The AOTA can help you locate an occupational therapist to work with your child on sensory processing.

Sensory Processing Disorder Foundation
www.spdfoundation.net
The foundation provides information, publications, and resources regarding sensory processing disorders for parents and professionals.

SPEECH AND LANGUAGE

Most states have associations for speech and language professionals. If you need information about how and where to find appropriate services in your state, you may contact your state professional association. State associations can provide resources, referrals, information, pamphlets, and possibly speakers for your parents' group. The address and phone number of your state speech and hearing association is usually available from directory assistance or by calling the American Speech-Language-Hearing Association (below). For example, ask for the "New Jersey Speech-Language-Hearing Association."

American Speech-Language-Hearing Association
2200 Research Blvd
Rockville, MD 20850
800-638-8255
www.asha.org

The ASHA is the national professional association for speech-language pathologists and audiologists. To locate certified speech-language pathologists or audiologists in your area, go to "Find a Professional" on the website. ASHA has a toll-free information line that can provide information and resources and help you find services in your area.

Apraxia- Kids
www.apraxia-kids.org

A comprehensive website on Childhood Apraxia of Speech which includes expert articles, research findings, a discussion list, and other pertinent information. It does not have information specifically on Apraxia in children with Down syndrome.

Better Hearing Institute
515 King St.., Suite 420
Alexandria, VA 22314
703-684-3391
www.betterhearing.org

A nonprofit organization that educates the public about hearing loss by providing general information about types of hearing losses and treatments. The website includes a "hearing loss simulator" that lets you hear what it is like to have a mild or moderate hearing loss. There are many links to resources, including some related to children and financial assistance.

National Cued Speech Association
23970 Hermitage Rd.
Cleveland, OH 44122
216-292-6213; 800-459-3529
www.cuedspeech.org

This organization advocates for the use of cued speech. A variety of fact sheets and other publications are available; the website offers contact information for cued speech instructors and links to resources.

SPECIAL EDUCATION/ DISABILITIES

ERIC Clearinghouse on Disabilities and Gifted Education (ERIC EC)
Council for Exceptional Children
1110 N. Glebe Rd.
Arlington, VA 22201-5704
800-328-0272
ericec@cec.sped.org
http://ericec.org

ERIC offers many fact sheets and digests on the education of children with disabilities. Many publications available in Spanish. Documents may be downloaded free of charge from the website. If you do not have Internet access, you may write or call for documents in print form. One copy of each document is available free of charge; additional copies of most publications cost $1.00 each. Website provides access to the ERIC database of publications on disabilities.

Office of Special Education Programs Website

www.ed.gov/offices/OSERS/OSEP

Fact sheets and other online publications about U.S. special education regulations and laws are available here.

Special Education Law

Wrightslaw website

www.wrightslaw.com

A great deal of information is available for parents interested in being their child's educational advocate. The website includes many informative articles on IEPs, inclusion, etc., and the option to subscribe to a free online newsletter.

LEARNING MATERIALS

Listed below is the contact information for the makers of software, DVDs, and other learning materials mentioned in this book. This is just a small sample of products available that can be helpful in working on communication skills with children with Down syndrome.

Autism Asperger Publishing Company

877-277-8254; 913-897-1004

www.asperger.net

Publishers of *Power Cards: Using Special Interests to Motivate Children and Youth with Asperger Syndrome.*

The Gray Center for Social Learning and Understanding

4123 Embassy Dr., SE

Kentwood, MI 49546

616-954-9749

www.thegraycenter.org

The official sources for books, videos, DVDs, and training on how to write Social Stories.

Innovative Therapists International

888-529-2879; 520-795-8544

www.talktools.net

This is the website to find oral-motor books, materials, whistles, horns, and straws to use with the Sarah Rosenfeld-Johnson oral-motor therapy program.

IntelliTools, Inc.

800-899-6687; 707-773-2000

www.intellitools.com

This company sells *IntelliKeys* (specially designed limited choice and adaptable multiple choice programmable keyboards); keyguards; and literacy products for struggling students.

Laureate Learning Systems

800-562-6801

www.laureatelearning.com

Laureate sells an extensive variety of well-designed language software for learners with special needs.

Mayer-Johnson Company

P.O. Box 1579

Solana Beach, CA 92075

800-588-4548; 858-550-0084

www.mayer-johnson.com

Mayer-Johnson sells a wide variety of AAC systems and tools, including *Picture Communication Symbols,* which can be photocopied or printed by computer with *Boardmaker* software (available in ten languages).

Model Me Kids

888-938-3240

www.modelmekids.com

Videos that demonstrate social skills made for children with developmental disabilities.

Pyramid Educational Products

5-C Garfield Way

Newark, DE 19713

888-255-6089; 302-894-9155

www.pyramidproducts.com

Pyramid makes and sells products for parents and teachers who are using PECS, the Picture Exchange Communication System.

Success Stories

800-704-7815

www.sandbox-learning.com

Personalized books to help children with disabilities learn social, safety, and communication skills.

Games for Speech and Language Skills

This section includes descriptions of some commercially available board games and card games that can be used to help your child learn and practice communication skills. This is just a small sample of the games available, and you can find many other worthwhile games by browsing in a toy store, checking online toy stores such as Educational Learning Games (www. educationallearninggames.com), or by asking friends and teachers for recommendations. Some of these games call for reading skills or other language skills that a younger child may not yet have acquired, but usually there are ways to adapt the rules to enable your child to play the game.

GAMES FOR PRACTICING A VARIETY OF LANGUAGE SKILLS

Apples to Apples (3 versions: Regular, Junior (ages 9+), and Kids' version (ages 7+) (Out of the Box)

Players take turns being the judge and put a card with an adjective in the middle of the table. The other players look at the cards in their hand and put down a noun that goes with the adjective. The judge then decides which card is the best match. (e.g., the adjective card might be *soft,* and players put down cards that say *Kittens, Big Bird, My Dad*.) While the judge is deciding which noun card makes the best match with the adjective card, the players can argue as to why their answer is the most appropriate or why someone else's isn't ("Kittens aren't soft! They bite and scratch!") A good game to play with players of varying abilities because there is no real right or wrong answer.

Balderdash (Mattel)

Each game card has questions about people, words, initials, movies, and laws. The player needs to make up an answer, and the other players guess whether this is the correct answer or whether she is bluffing. The player needs lots of expressive language to make up the answers. Since it is a game about bluffing, it can lead to family discussions about kids who mislead you in school, and about white lies and comments that can hurt. It also can lead to a discussion of nonverbal cues and facial expressions.

Battle in a Bucket (International Playthings)

To play, one person pulls a card out of a bucket, then tries to get other players to guess the word by either describing it, drawing it, or acting it out. A good game for nonreaders, as well as players who do not have much spoken expressive language yet.

Catch Phrase, Jr. (Hasbro)

Players divide up into two teams to play this game. An electronic device shows one team member a word. She then tries to get her partner to guess the word before time runs out by defining the word or giving examples without using the word itself. For instance, if you see the word *lightning,* you can say "Thunder and —" or "When there is a thunderstorm, you can see this in the sky." Because the game is timed, it might be frustrating to children who don't like to be rushed, but you could ignore the time limit for your child or children under a certain age to reduce the frustration.

Cranium (Cranium, Inc.)

Players work in teams. There are four card decks that require players to answer questions about fun facts, sketch or sculpt with clay, act out or hum something, and use language skills such as guessing definitions, filling in blanks, or spelling backwards. The game is fast paced and requires players to get up and move around in addition to using speech and language skills. *Cranium CADOO* is available for younger children or children who need questions that are more basic.

Cranium Whoonu (Cranium, Inc.)

This card game focuses on guessing the other players' favorite things (e.g., burgers or bubble gum, sand castles or snowmen). For practice in asking and answering "why" questions, the game can be adapted by asking players "Why? ("Because I like the beach.")

Green Alligators (Talicor-Aristoplay)

Green Alligators is a simple game where one person gives clues and the other tries to guess an object. This would be good for practicing convergent language skills.

Last Word (Buffalo Games)

This is a good game for working on phonics, memory, and divergent language. Players draw two cards—one with a beginning letter and one with the name of a category. For instance, a C and *vegetable* are drawn. All of the players begin calling out, naming vegetables that begin with C. The last player to give a word before the timer goes off wins that round and moves ahead a space on the board. (To make the game easier, just turn over the category card, and not the letter card, and allow players to name anything that fits in the category.)

Location Bingo Game (Learning Resources)

Each player is given a bingo card with pictures showing prepositions (on, under, etc.). A player spins the game spinner, which points to a preposition. Players who can find a picture matching that preposition on their card put a token on it. The winner is the first to fill in a row on their card.

Luck of the Draw (Gamewright)

This is a game similar to the classic *Pictionary*, but all players draw everything, instead of taking turns drawing. Players turn over a card that tells them what to draw (e.g., Shrek, an elf, apple pie). Then everyone has 45 seconds to draw it (you can allow more time if you want). You don't have to be a good artist to win, because after every drawing is completed, players draw a card that tells them to vote on which drawings meet certain criteria—e.g., "most embarrassing," "most complicated," "neatest," "had no idea what to draw," etc. A good game for learning vocabulary and practicing the superlative form of adjectives.

Password (Endless Games).

Players divide into two teams then try to get members of their own team to guess the target word by giving only one-word clues.

Pictionary Jr. (Hasbro).

The "junior" version of Pictionary is a good one for practicing vocabulary as well as categories. Players divide into teams, then take turns drawing pictures for teammates, trying to get them to guess the target word. The only spoken clue allowed is the category that the word falls under (e.g., animal, sport, person). Pictures are supposed to be drawn before the timer runs out, but you can extend the time or do without a time limit to reduce frustration. Also available in a DVD version which does not require drawing.

Pictureka (Hasbro)

Players draw cards showing their "mission" (pictures they must find), then race to be the first to find those pictures on a very intricate board. This game can be used to help children develop vocabulary if you name the unfamiliar pictures for your child. A good game for children who are nonverbal and/or nonreaders, this is also one where players who are visual learners can shine.

Proverbial Wisdom Junior (Talicor-Aristoplay)

This game requires players to sketch, act out, or define expressions such as "as wise as an owl." A good game for helping children practice understanding expressions.

Zingo (Think Fun)

Zingo comes with a device that dispenses picture cards one by one. Players match the picture cards with pictures on their boards. A good game to help with vocabulary and matching skills that is appropriate for children who are nonverbal and/or nonreaders.

GAMES FOR PRACTICING CATEGORIES

Animal Lotto (Galt America)

Any lotto game you can find is good for practicing categories. Generally, the games come with boards for one or more categories of objects, and cards that are drawn from a pile and then matched to the appropriate pictures on the board. The Galt Animal Lotto game requires players to decide whether pictures belong on the board for Pets, Farm Animals, Rainforest Animals, or African Animals.

I Spy in Common (Briarpatch)

This game has several variations, all involving looking at the pictures on cardboard tiles and figuring out what they have in common (e.g., they are animals, they are round, they are hot). No reading skills necessary to play.

Last Word. See listing above in section above.

Pictionary Jr. See listing in section above.

Scattergories (Parker Brothers)

To play this game, each player is given a list with 12 categories (e.g., heroes, vechicles, dairy products) and tries to write down one thing that fits the category. If you are following the rules, you roll a die first to see what letter all responses must begin with, but an easier adaptation is to skip this step and let players write down any word that fits the category. This is a good game for practicing categories. The skills can carry over into activities that involve staying on topic. Use the answers to discuss what is on topic, in the same catergory, and what is not.

GAMES FOR STORYTELLING/ SEQUENCING

Life Stories (Talicor)

This is a noncompetitive game designed to get family members talking to each other. Players take turns drawing a card and then doing what the card tells them to do: e.g., describe one of your best or worst teachers, tell about a time when you helped someone, tell one of the other players to imitate a snore.

The Storytelling Game (International Playthings)
Tell-a-Story (Ravensburger)

Both of these games involve putting picture cards in order and then telling a story about them. No reading required.

GAMES FOR CONVERSATION/ ANSWERING & ASKING QUESTIONS

Guess Who? (Milton Bradley)

Players each have an identical set of cards with character faces and plastic stand-up "frames" showing the same faces. They each choose one character to be their "mystery person" then try to guess the identity of their opponent's mystery person by asking yes and no questions. "Is it a man or a woman?" "Is he wearing a hat?" "Does he have brown hair?" Each time their opponent answers, they remove the stand-up frames that they can now eliminate. *Guess Where* is a similar game by Hasbro that involves asking questions to try figure out where the other player has placed various characters in a plastic play house.

Jewel of Truth (International Playthings)

This game includes a "fortune telling board" with a swinging jewel that indicates whose turn it is to tell a secret or express a like or dislike. Players try to predict what others will say. Again, there are no right or wrong answers.

Loaded Questions, Jr. (All Things Equal, Inc.)

Players draw cards and answer questions (in writing) about what they like and don't like and other players try to guess who answered what. If you guess right, you get to move ahead on the board. There are no right or wrong answers, making this a good family game for players at many levels.

Peanut Gallery (International Playthings)

This card game calls for players to express their opinions on a wide range of topics and try to persuade others to agree that they are right.

You Gotta Be Kidding (Zobmondo)

Players answer questions like "would you rather be covered in itchy scabs or have popcorn kernels stuck between every tooth" and predict how others will answer such questions. (An adult version of this game called Would You Rather? is also available.) Game can be adapted to practice asking and answering questions. When a player chooses, he can ask another player "Why?"

GAMES FOR SPEECH AND PHONOLOGY

Boggle Jr. (Parker Brothers)

The game comes with a set of letter cubes and picture cards with the words spelled out under the pictures. Children who are learning letters and letter sounds can match the letters on the cubes to the letters on the cards. Can be used for sound identifications and phonology awareness.

Last Word (Buffalo Games)

See description in first section. A game calling for both categorization and phonological skills.

Rhyming Fun-to-Know Puzzles (Learning Resources)

Players search for the two puzzle pieces that rhyme and fit them together. Can be played alone.

Rhyming Sounds Game (Brighter Starts)

Players match pictures on cards with the rhyming words on the board.

Scattergories (Parker Brothers)

If you play according to the rules, the game requires that players come up with words in a particular category that begin with a particular sound.

Voice Changer (Sakar)
Voice Scrambler (Wild Planet)

These are both voice recorders made for kids that allow you to change how your voice sounds after you have recorded it. A fun way to bring speech intelligibility into your child's awareness.

Appendices

Comprehensive Language Evaluations: A Longitudinal Plan

The comprehensive language evaluation is sensitive to differences in growth and development, and communication needs at different periods during childhood, adolescence, and young adulthood. Following is a longitudinal plan for language evaluation for children through young adults transitioning from school to the workplace:

I. Before the First Spoken Word

Hearing status and sensory integration status should be determined through reports from specialists. Feeding evaluation may be conducted separately or as part of the oral motor evaluation. These evaluations will document the child's sensory, motor, and hearing skills, which are skills that contribute to the ability to learn language from the environment around you. Usually, children with Down syndrome entering kindergarten will be speaking, but if they are not, there is a need to investigate how the child is communicating and whether he is using a language system such as sign language.

    I. Pre-language Period

        A. Pragmatics Skills for Communication (e.g., shaking head for no)

        B. Pre-Language Skills (e.g., turns head to find the source of a sound he hears)

        C. Use of/Need for a Transitional Communication System

            1. Total Communication (sign language)

            2. Communication Boards (picture boards)

            3. PECS (the Picture Exchange Communication System—communicating by showing a picture of what you want to say)

            4. Electronic Communication Systems (e.g., Chatbox)

II. One-Word to Three-Word Period

Hearing status, sensory integration status, play skills, and attending skills should be determined through reports from specialists. Impact on communication status should be confirmed through observation.

        A. Pragmatics Communication Skills (e.g., turn taking and short mini-conversations)

        B. Receptive Language Skills (follows instructions to go get his coat)

        C. Expressive Language Skills (can say his name and label items—e.g., "my bear")

        D. Semantic Skills (vocabulary)

        E. Morphosyntax Skills (grammar and word endings)

        F. Mean Length of Utterance (says one word at a time, then combines 2 words, progresses to 3 words)

        G. Emerging and Early Literacy Skills (likes to look at books with parent, progresses to early reading skills)

III. Three-Word Phrases to Sentences

        A. Pragmatics Communication Skills (e.g., introduces self—"Hi, I'm Daniel!")

        B. Receptive Language Skills (e.g., understands "who" questions and plot of story in a children's book)

        C. Expressive Language Skills (uses speech to express thoughts and feelings; can answer questions about a story)

        D. Semantics (increasing vocabulary)

        E. Syntax (grammar and word endings)

        F. Mean Length of Utterance (beginning with three-word phrases; progresses to sentences)

        G. Conversational and Discourse Skills (can have a back-and-forth conversation with two or more turns)

IV. Elementary School Years

    A. Receptive Language Skills
- 1. Comprehension (understands simple instructions, progressing to complex directions; comprehends a story)
- 2. Semantics (understands vocabulary for school subjects and for daily activities)
- 3. Morphosyntax (understands possessives, plurals, verb tenses)

    B. Expressive Language Skills
- 1. Semantics (uses more and more vocabulary words for school subjects and in daily living)
- 2. Morphosyntax (uses appropriate word endings for possessives and plurals; uses correct word order in sentences)
- 3. Mean Length of Utterance (uses longer sentences)

    C. Pragmatics Skills
- 1. Social Interactive Skills (greets teachers and peers appropriately)
- 2. Communication Activities of Daily Living (can comprehend others and speak in school and in the community)
- 3. Discourse Skills (can retell what happened at school or retell a story)
- 4. Requests (can make requests appropriately)
- 5. Clarification Strategies/Repairs (can provide more information when someone doesn't understand something he is talking about)

    D. Language and Literacy Skills
- 1. Phonological Awareness Skills (can identify initial sounds; make rhymes)
- 2. Whole Language Skills (can understand and talk about topics of interest in school learned through reading and other experiences)
- 3. Reading Comprehension (understands and can answer questions about what he reads)

    E. Curriculum-Based Language Skills
- 1. Subject Based (understands new vocabulary in school subjects)
- 2. Language of Instruction (can follow instructions such as "underline the correct answer")
- 3. Other Classroom-Based Language skills (includes behavior, test taking, and other areas)

V. Middle School and High School Years

    A. Receptive Language Skills
- 1. Comprehension (understands spoken instructions)
- 2. Semantics (understands the meaning of vocabulary words; is expanding understood vocabulary)
- 3. Morphosyntax (understands increasingly complex grammar; e.g., "Will's bike was broken. Now it is fixed")

    B. Expressive Language Skills
- 1. Semantics (uses vocabulary appropriately; is expanding spoken vocabulary)
- 2. Morphosyntax (uses grammatical markers such as verb tense appropriately; can construct sentences correctly)
- 3. Mean Length of Utterance (is expanding length of phrases and sentences used)

    C. Pragmatics Skills
- 1. Social Interactive Skills (uses appropriate greetings for peers, teachers, etc.)
- 2. Communication Activities of Daily Living (e.g., can give biographical information)
- 3. Discourse Skills (can give accurate facts sequenced correctly when telling a story)
- 4. Requests (uses appropriate phrases and questions to make requests)
- 5. Clarification Strategies/Repairs (can provide more information when someone doesn't understand something he is talking about)

D. Language and Literacy Skills (reading and comprehension skills continue to improve)
E. Curriculum-Based Language Skills
   1. Subject Based (understands new vocabulary in school subjects)
   2. Language of Instruction (can follow instructions such as "Give two reasons why the colonists were upset about the new tax on tea")
   3. Other Classroom-Based Language skills (includes behavior, test taking, and other areas)
F. Metalinguistic Skills (analyzing the rhythm and rhyme of a poem; using language to talk about language—e.g., giving an example of a metaphor)
G. Work- and Community-Related Language Skills (filling out forms; reading schedules and maps; asking for information, etc.)

Sample Diagnostic Language Evaluation (Completed at Speech-Language Center)

Identification

Daniel is an 8-year-old boy with Down syndrome who has been receiving therapy at the Speech and Language Center for the past 7 years for the remediation of speech and language difficulties secondary to Down syndrome.

Daniel currently attends second grade at his local elementary school where he receives speech therapy twice a week and occupational therapy once a week. The purpose of the language evaluation is to determine his level of receptive and expressive language and identify the areas of language that are challenging for him. The results of the evaluation will be used to plan an appropriate language treatment program.

Behavioral Observations

Daniel presents as a happy and friendly child. Separation from his father in the waiting room poses a small struggle. Daniel hides under the table and does not want to go in to the diagnostic testing room. However, once in the room, he actively engages with the clinician. His participation in the testing activities is inconsistent between enthusiastically participating and refusal of all activities. Daniel particularly enjoys story time. He shows no difficulty transitioning from one activity to the next, following a visual schedule board. A sentence strip is used with Daniel so he can let the clinician know which activity he would like to do next. After completion of each activity, Daniel places the appropriate picture in the "all done" folder. He attends best when seated in a large Rifton chair, positioned perpendicular to the mirror in order to minimize distractions during planned testing activities.

Level of Attention

According to Reynell's levels of attention, Daniel demonstrates level three attentional skills. His attention is singled-channeled in that he focuses only on the activity he is doing, while ignoring other visual and auditory stimuli. For example, Daniel cannot shift his full attention between the clinician and the task spontaneously. To gain his attention, the clinician has to call his name, ask him to look at her, and repeat the question or direction that was asked (e.g., "wh" questions during story time). When Daniel enjoys an activity he attends for 10-20 minutes. If he is not interested in the activity, he attends for approximately 5 minutes.

Levels of Play

According to Blackstone's levels of play, Daniel demonstrates simple symbolic play. He participates in simple sequences of activities (e.g., art projects, reading books) and stays on task for an extended period of time (on average, 15 minutes).

Assessment Results

Information regarding Daniel's receptive and expressive language skills and progress in therapy was obtained through formalized testing using the Clinical Evaluation of Language Fundamentals Preschool-Second Edition (CELF/P-2), parental observation reports, and informal assessment.

FORMAL TESTING   Clinical Evaluation of Language Fundamentals Preschool-Second Edition (CELF/P-2). The CELF/P-2 was administered to Daniel in order to evaluate his level of language processing. The CELF/P-2 explores the foundations of language form and content: word meanings, word and sentence structure, and recall of spoken language. It is a formalized test that measures receptive and expressive language abilities. Daniel's results are as follows:

**NOTE: Daniel's scores are based on a 6 year, 11 month age equivalent. This is the oldest age group for which the test is normed.

Receptive Subtest	Raw Score	Scaled Score	Percentile Rank	Age Equivalency
Sentence Structure	7	2	4	<3:0
Concepts and Following Directions	2	1	.1	<3:0
Word Classes	N/A	1	.1	<4:0
Basic Concepts	9	N/A	N/A	N/A
Receptive Language Index	N/A	N/A	<.1	N/A

Expressive Subtest	Raw Score	Scaled Score	Percentile Rank	Age Equivalency
Word Structure	2	1	.1	<3:0
Expressive Vocabulary	2	1	.1	<3:0
Recalling Sentences	0	1	.1	<3:0
Expressive Language Index	N/A	N/A	<.1	N/A

The CELF/P-2 is divided into two major subdivisions. The first measured Daniel's receptive language skills. The receptive portion of the test contains four basic subtests: basic concepts, sentence structure, word classes, and concepts and following directions. The CELF/P-2 defines emerging skills that were not demonstrated consistently throughout testing. It is noted that Daniel's overall receptive language scale placed him in the less than 1 percentile as compared to typically developing children of 6 years, 11 months.

BASIC CONCEPTS

According to the basic concepts subtest, Daniel demonstrated knowledge of the following concepts: number/quantity (e.g., empty, many, full), dimension/size (e.g., tall, long, large), and same/different (e.g., same, different). Each of these concepts was receptively identified following a verbal command given by the clinician (e.g., "Point to the glass that is empty"). Daniel demonstrated difficulty with the following concepts: direction/location/position (e.g., inside, bottom), sequence (e.g., first, last), and attribute (e.g., cold, slow, dry, hard).

SENTENCE STRUCTURE

The sentence structure subtest required Daniel to point to the appropriate pictured item (from a matrix of 3) in the stimulus manual that corresponded with the statement given by the clinician (e.g., "Point to the object that smells good"). Sentence structures that he understood included prepositional phrases (e.g., in the wagon, under the big tree), verb condition (e.g., is running, will find, can get), copula (e.g., is sleepy), and relative clause (e.g., who is sitting under the big tree). Daniel demonstrated difficulty understanding modification (e.g., big, spotted, first), infinitive (e.g., to bake, to go), negation (e.g., not), passive (e.g., is being followed, is being pushed), compound sentence (e.g., the first two children are in line, but the third child is still playing), indirect object (e.g., the cat), indirect request (e.g., shouldn't you wear your jacket), and subordinate clause (e.g., although she doesn't need it; before she ate the sandwich).

CONCEPTS AND FOLLOWING DIRECTIONS

The concepts and following directions subtest required Daniel to point to the appropriate pictured item that corresponded with the spoken statement (e.g., point to the tallest animal). He had to interpret, recall, and execute spoken directions while understanding the linguistic concepts during this subtest. Daniel demonstrated emerging comprehension of the concepts that included dimension/size (e.g., tallest, big/little), inclusion/exclusion (e.g., both, all, except), equality (e.g., match), temporal (e.g., when, after), location (e.g., next to, closest to), and condition (e.g., unless). Daniel demonstrated difficulty comprehending sequence concepts (e.g., first/last, second/third).

WORD CLASSES

The word classes subtest evaluated Daniel's ability to perceive relationships between words that are related by semantic class features and to express those relationships. Daniel selected two words that go together out of three or four words that were read aloud (e.g., for the word class of toys, pool/swimsuit). Daniel demonstrated emerging comprehension for home items (e.g., blanket/pillows), clothing (e.g., pants/coats), school items (e.g., crayon/pencil), food (e.g., milk/juice), parts of the body (e.g., foot/hand), and transportation (e.g., car/bus). When he was asked how the two selected words go together (e.g., how do key and door go together?), Daniel was unable to express the relationship between items in each category including toys, home items, clothing, school items, food, parts of the body, and transportation.

The expressive portion of the CELF/P-2 measured Daniel's expressive language abilities. It consists of three subtests: recalling sentences in context, expressive vocabulary, and word structure. It is noted that Daniel's overall expressive language score placed him in the 1st percentile as compared to typically developing children of 6 years, 11 months.

RECALLING SENTENCES

The recalling sentences subtest evaluated Daniel's ability to listen to spoken sentences of increasing length and complexity, and to repeat the sentences without changing words, meanings, inflections, and sentence structure. He was unable to recall the spoken sentences.

EXPRESSIVE VOCABULARY

The expressive vocabulary subtest required Daniel to label objects (e.g., picture of a calendar) and actions (e.g., wrapping). Daniel demonstrated skills in labeling geography/social studies items (e.g., flag). He had difficulty with verbs (e.g., riding, pouring), food (e.g., carrot), occupations (e.g., firefighter), music (e.g., piano), communication (e.g., newspaper), science (e.g., telescope), part/whole relationships (e.g., branch), math (e.g., calculator), and health care (e.g., wheelchair).

WORD STRUCTURE

The word structure subtest required Daniel to complete sentences using the correct form of a word (e.g., this boy is sitting). Daniel's strengths in this area include: progressive -ing (e.g., sleeping), and contractible copula (e.g., it is big). He demonstrated difficulty expressing prepositions (e.g., on the chair), regular plurals (e.g., horses), possessive nouns (e.g., king's), third person singular (e.g., sleeps), future tense (e.g., will slide), regular past tense (e.g., climbed), irregular past tense (e.g., blew), uncontractible copula/auxiliary (e.g., she is), objective pronouns (e.g., her), possessive pronouns (e.g., hers), subjective pronouns (e.g., he is), reflexive pronouns (e.g., herself), noun derivations (e.g., singer), and comparative and superlative (e.g., faster, fastest).

Single word receptive vocabulary was measured by the Peabody Picture Vocabulary Test (PPVT-IIIB) and was below average. Age equivalent receptive language score was at 3 years 6 months.

Single word expressive vocabulary was tested using the Expressive One-Word Picture Vocabulary Test. The examiner was unable to establish a basal level of six consecutive correct responses. Working backwards from the chronological age of 3-6 to 4-5, back to 2-0 to 2-11, it was not possible during this session for Daniel to provide eight consecutive correct responses. Although he could say many of the words, e.g., apple, bird, eyes, leaf, and tiger, he made errors on other words at the same age level, e.g., chickens, penguin, sofa, train, resulting in no score.

Knowledge of basic concepts was below average as measured by the Boehm Test of Basic Concepts (BTBC), a test which measures receptive language skills involved in following directions. The difficulties that Daniel experienced with test items would apply directly to skills that he needs for following directions in school (e.g., first, last, through, on the bottom of the page). The following errors were noted: Booklet 1: first, last; Booklet 2: right, third, fewest, pair.

This indicates that although Daniel has mastered many basic concepts, he has difficulty with application of concepts within functional directions.

AUDITORY SKILLS

Throughout the testing, Daniel demonstrated slow processing and frequently needed repetition and/or clarification of oral directions and information. He did not know how to ask for help, and became frustrated when he did not know what to do. Results of formal assessment of auditory processing skills revealed significantly below average performance.

The Goldman-Fristoe 2: Test of Articulation was used to evaluate Daniel's sound productions. It tests each individual speech sound in various positions at the word level. Daniel demonstrated difficulty with the following sounds:

$$/p/, /b/, /m/, /t/, /d/, /k/, /g/, /s/, /l/, \text{and } /r/$$

The sound errors indicate that Daniel is having difficulty with sounds involving lip compression, tongue tip elevation, and elevation of the back part of the tongue. These lip and tongue movements can be worked on in therapy sessions.

INFORMAL TESTING

Observations of Daniel in therapy sessions, and data describing his progress in therapy were used to determine Daniel's current strengths and difficulties in receptive and expressive language.

REPORTS FROM PARENTS AND TEACHERS

According to his mother, Daniel is very distractible and fidgety. It is hard to get his attention, and he is easily distracted by noises in the environment. He has tactile defensiveness. When he is uncomfortable, he will hide under the table. He has difficulty understanding and following directions. Daniel appears to hear you, but does not always remember what was said. He is reported to get frustrated when having difficulty expressing himself, and he sometimes runs away or hides.

According to the classroom teacher, organizational strategies that are provided for Daniel in the classroom include a visual activity schedule, a checklist on his desk for completing worksheets and heading his papers, and multiple verbal prompts. Daniel has difficulty with everyday routines, and at times he seems to forget what was just explained. He doesn't appear to know how to ask for help when he doesn't know what to do in class. Difficulties with attention, distractibility, focusing, work completion, math, and oral communication skills have been noted since Daniel has been in elementary school.

THERAPY OBSERVATION AND PROGRESS

1. Functional Vocabulary: Daniel consistently uses functional vocabulary throughout each session, particularly when transitioning between activities and during crafts. When an activity is finished, he moves the picture of the activity on his schedule board to the "all done" folder and simultaneously says "all done." During crafts, Daniel receives a verbal reminder (e.g., how do we ask?) from the clinician each time; currently Daniel requires an initial reminder, then he spontaneously asks for help or more of an item.

   a. Nouns: Nouns are targeted each session through therapy materials including books and games. Books Daniel has read include: *Hop to the Top* and *In my Box*. He learns many words from reading and games, as he loves reading and activities with manipulatives. Various nouns and categories have been targeted through books and bingo including: transportation (e.g., helicopter, boat, bus), clothing (e.g., boots raincoat, baseball hat), animals (e.g., monkey, cow, horse), and food (e.g., cookie, pancake, hot dog). The following are examples of nouns Daniel spontaneously uses during the sessions: hot dog, cookie, pancake, apple, cow, horse, monkey, hat, book, paint, and computer. He shows receptive understanding of all nouns while playing bingo (e.g., transportation, food, clothing, animals) and placing a chip on each noun given a matrix size of twelve).

   b. Size Concepts: Size concepts have not been directly addressed this semester due to time constraints. According to the CELF/P-2, Daniel showed receptive understanding of the following size concepts: tall, long, and large. He has difficulty with the following size concept: big/little. No expressive use of size concepts has been observed.

    c. Wh- Questions: Wh-question have been targeted using therapy materials such as the "wh" computer program and books. The clinician asks Daniel "who, what, and where" questions about the book being read. He is able to answer "who, what, and where" questions with 70% accuracy by pointing to the corresponding answer. While using a computer program, Daniel is presented with a "wh" question and he chooses the appropriate answer from a matrix of 3 pictures. He is able to correctly answer the questions with 50% accuracy. Daniel needs to be reminded to "keep hands on the table and listen" to increase attention. Expressively, he answers "what" questions 1-2 times per session (e.g., "what's that," "What's this?"). "When and why" questions have not been targeted.

    d. Plurals: Plurals have not been directly addressed this semester due to time constraints. During articulation drills and craft projects, Daniel shows receptive understanding of plurals. For example, when asked to point to the picture of cats (given a matrix of two), Daniel does so appropriately, or when asked to paint the snakes, Daniel is able to do so without hesitation.

    e. Modifiers: Modifiers are addressed informally when activities (e.g., crafts) are related. For example, during crafts, the clinician may say "paint the top animal blue" or given a choice of two chairs, the clinician asks Daniel to sit in the big, red chair. Daniel correctly responds with an action following the command. The following modifiers have been informally addressed throughout the semester: colors, numbers, and size. Expressively, use of color (e.g., black, blue, orange) modifiers has been observed at the single word level.

    f. Prepositions: The prepositions top and bottom have been addressed throughout the semester. While reading (e.g., The blue dot monster is on top of the page. Daniel, which dot monster is on top of the page?) and given 2-d pictures (e.g., crafts), he spontaneously demonstrates receptive understanding of top and bottom with 70% accuracy given a matrix of 3 to 5. No expressive use of prepositions has been observed. To increase Daniel's understanding of prepositions, use children's literature and photographs, books such as *My Up & Down & All Around Book,* during therapy sessions and home activities.

2. Intelligibility Related to Phonological Processes: Daniel's intelligibility continues to be judged as fair in context and poor out of context. This is due to his short utterances, articulation errors, and use of phonological processes including syllable reduction and cluster simplification. In imitation of the clinician, Daniel's precision and clarity of all phonemes increases. It should be noted that with the use of Visual Tactile cues, his production accuracy increases. The Visual Tactile cues that have been used throughout the semester include /p, b, m, t, d, k, g, h, s, w/.

    a. Syllable Reduction: Daniel demonstrates progress in improving his articulation of two-syllable words (e.g., pancake, monkey, baseball, holding). Practice is provided through two-syllable word drilling cards and two-syllable word bingo. At the beginning of the semester, Daniel was able to correctly produce two-syllable words with 30% accuracy. He now is able to produce two-syllable words with 50% accuracy. Daniel's accuracy increases with the use of a pacing board, Visual Tactile cues, and clinician modeling.

    b. Cluster Simplification: Daniel demonstrates progress in improving his articulation of cluster words (e.g., key/ski bed/bread). Practice is provided through cluster reduction drilling cards. He is presented with one cluster reduction pair at a time (e.g., key/ski). At the beginning of the semester, he was able to correctly produce the cluster word (e.g., bread) with 20% accuracy. Currently, he is able to produce the cluster word (e.g., bread) with 40% accuracy. Daniel is unable to produce the cluster reduction pairs (e.g., key/ski) spontaneously, requiring Visual Tactile cues and clinician modeling for increased accuracy.

3. Length of Utterance: Daniel continues to demonstrate the use of 2-3 word spontaneous and imitated utterances. With the use of a pacing board and imitation with expansion, Daniel demonstrates use of 3-4 word utterances. Parents report that he uses 1-3 word utterances at home, depending on the situation. He often answers questions with single words. The following is a sample of his spontaneous (s) and imitated (i) speech:

1-word:	2-word:
Paint (s)	All done (s)
Mouth (s)	What's this (s)
Computer (s)	More please (s)
No (s)	Glove please (s)
Apple (s)	No book (s)

3-word:	4-word:
More paint please (i)	I want glove please (i)
	Penguin is on top (i)

5-word:
    Now it's time for computer (s)

The following structures were observed in Daniel's spontaneous speech:
    Singular nouns (e.g., glue, book)
    Functional Vocabulary (e.g., please, more, want)
    Negatives (e.g., no)

The following structures were not consistently observed in Daniel's speech in therapy, or at home (as reported by his parents) and may be in need of remediation:
    Verbs (e.g., push, open)
    Modifiers (e.g., pink, black)
    Prepositions (e.g., in, on)
    Personal Pronouns (e.g., me, you, I)
    Possessive Pronouns (e.g., my, your)
    Wh- questions (e.g., who, why, where, what)

4. Following Oral Directions: Following directions is addressed when activities (e.g., transitions, crafts) lend themselves to following directions, i.e., in naturalistic settings. For example, the clinician may say "Daniel put the book away, sit in your big red chair, and place the picture in the 'all done' folder." He correctly responds with an action following the command of 2-3 step directions. While cooking, Daniel was able to correctly follow the four steps, given both oral and visual cues, as well as recall the steps by correctly placing the visuals in order. No expressive recall of directions has been observed from him.

5. Pragmatics: Informal evaluation in therapy sessions by the clinician and at home by Daniel's parents indicated the following function in the area of pragmatics:

   a. Eye Contact: Daniel does not spontaneously establish or maintain eye contact with the clinician during therapy sessions. With verbal prompts (e.g., "Daniel, look at my face please"), he establishes and maintains eye contact for approximately 1 minute. Joint attention continues to be established throughout the therapy sessions in the presence of a stimulus of high interest to him (e.g., books, painting). Referential gaze is established each session through activities that include books and art activities. Parents report that they need to call his name first to get his attention at home. After he hears his name, he looks at the person and he does maintain eye contact for a short period of time. He is able to look at a book, or an item of interest in the environment (trucks, an airplane flying overhead) for a longer period of time.

b. Greeting/Parting: Spontaneous greeting and parting has not been observed. Daniel greets the clinician from under the waiting room table each session, saying "hello" when prompted by his father. When parting, he demonstrates verbal parting (e.g., "bye") 50% of the time, even with clinician and parent prompting. Parents report that he says bye and hello when his dada leaves for work in the morning and comes home in the evening.

c. Requesting: Daniel demonstrates requesting by using an appropriate statement (e.g., "more please," "I want please"). With the use of a pacing board and imitation with expansion Daniel expands upon his request (e.g., "I need more glue, please"). He requires initial reminding the first time to request and then continues to spontaneously request.

d. Protesting: Daniel demonstrates protesting by repeating "no, no, no" and hiding under the table or chair.

e. Initiating: Daniel demonstrates initiation by rearranging his schedule board and choosing activities in which he wants to participate and in what order.

f. Turn Taking: Daniel appropriately takes turns with the clinician while playing games, including bingo. The clinician marks turns during games.

FAMILY PARTICIPATION   Both parents have observed each therapy session. Various activities (e.g., worksheets, books, bingo boards) have been sent home with him to facilitate reinforcement of speech and language skills. His parents work hard to encourage generalization of skills at home, as this is apparent from Daniel's progress.

Recommendations

It is recommended that Daniel continue to receive two 45-minute-therapy sessions per week at this center for the remediation of receptive and expressive language delays secondary to Down syndrome.

THERAPY GOALS   Based on formal and informal test results and input from Daniel's family and teachers, the following is the language therapy plan:

1. To increase Daniel's receptive and expressive vocabulary skills in the following areas:
    a. Functional Vocabulary (e.g., help, please, all done)
    b. Nouns (e.g., transportation, home/school items)
    c. Size Concepts (e.g., big, small)
    d. Wh- questions (e.g., who, what, when, where, why)
    e. Plurals (e.g., dogs, boys, cars)
    f. Modifiers (e.g., big, little)
    g. Prepositions (e.g., under, on top, behind)

2. To increase Daniel's ability to follow and recall 3-4 step directions with the use of picture and verbal cues in goal-oriented activities including the following targets:
    a. Sequence (e.g., first/last)
    b. Location (e.g., next to, closest to, top/bottom)
    c. Temporal (e.g., after, before)

3. To improve Daniel's pragmatic skills in the following areas:
    Eye contact
    Greeting/Parting

Requesting
Protesting
Initiating
Turn-taking

4. To increase Daniel's spontaneous length of utterance to a consistent 3-5 word level through the use of imitation with expansion, clinician modeling, and a pacing board. Targets include:

Pronouns + action + modifier + noun (e.g., I want blue marker)
Action + object + please (e.g., want book please)
Agent + action + object + please (e.g., I want paint please)
Agent + action + modifier + object + please (e.g., I want red paint please)
Pronouns (e.g., I, you, me) in phrases
Articles (e.g., the, a) in phrases
Prepositions (e.g., in, on) in phrases

5. To increase Daniel's precision of vocalizations for the following processes through the use of visual-tactile cues:

a. Syllable reduction
b. Cluster simplification

6. To provide parents with information regarding Daniel's speech and language development and to provide activities for speech and language activities and stimulation at home.

Sample School Speech and Language Evaluation

Speech and Language Programs
Department of Special Education
Office of Instruction & Program Development

Report of Speech/Language Triennial Reassessment

Student Name: Abby Baker
Age: 10-11
Grade: 5
Neighborhood Elementary School
Dominant Language: English
Reassessment Dates: 5/14/08, 5/15/08
Date of Report 5/30/08

Purpose of Assessment

The purpose of this reassessment is to determine if Abby continues to have a speech-language impairment and by reason thereof needs special education.

Reason for Referral

The recommendation for a speech-language reassessment was made at the IEP Team meeting held at the end of Abby's 4th grade year. Questions relevant to speech-language include: should there be any modifications or additions to the current related services? Does Abby continue to present with a speech and language disorder?

Background Information

MEDICAL/PHYSICAL

Hearing Status: Per parent report Abby passed a hearing screening this winter.

Abby has a diagnosis of Mosaic Down Syndrome. Medical history is remarkable for frequent ear infections. The ear infections have been managed with the placement of tubes in her ears. She has also had an adenoidectomy.

EDUCATIONAL PROGRAM

Disability Code: 08 (other health impairment)

Special Education Services: During the school year, Abby received 12 hours classroom instruction, 1 hour of speech, and consultative occupational therapy services.

Areas of Educational Concern: Math, Reading Comprehension, Writing, Personal Management, Organization, and Self-Advocacy

SPEECH-LANGUAGE PROGRAM

Type of Disorder and Severity: mild speech and language impairment

Areas of Need: Carryover for target phonemes. Improve vocal loudness. Improve pragmatic skills. Improve comprehension and use of vocabulary skills.

Speech-Language Intervention: Abby has received 1 hour of speech and language services a week since the last speech and language reassessment.

Progress on Speech-Language Goals and Objections: Abby continues to demonstrate a distortion of "r" and sometimes "s" when speaking. Her ability to produce "r" correctly at the word level fluctuates. Progress has been slow in this area due to ear infections this school year. Abby is able to use correct intonation in short phrases when given prompts. Although Abby easily states how to initiate conversation and identifies the characteristic of a friend, she demonstrates difficulty transferring these skills to peer interactions. Some vocabulary words from math and social studies were taught to Abby this past school year (e.g., liberty, independence, etc.). She demonstrated comprehension of the presented curriculum-based vocabulary by either choosing the correct definition, defining the word, or using it in a sentence.

Speech-Language Assessment Techniques and Analysis

<table>
<tr><td>

INFORMAL ASSESSMENT PROCEDURES

</td><td>

LANGUAGE SAMPLE

A spontaneous language sample was elicited to informally assess expressive language skills. A variety of tasks were utilized including social conversation and relating personal experiences. Abby was cooperative, friendly, and easily engaged in conversation. Abby demonstrated use of simple and compound sentences. Her sentence length and vocabulary skills were appropriate. She answered all "wh" questions correctly. Her use of grammar and syntax were appropriate. Articulation errors were noted such as distortion of "r" and occasional substitutions of "s" for "sh." Articulation errors reduced the clarity of her speech. Abby's speech was judged to be 90-95% intelligible. A student her age should be 100% intelligible when speaking. On several occasions Abby had to repeat words such as "Garfield" and "Shrek" before this examiner understood her. Her vocal quality is monotone when speaking.

</td></tr>
</table>

INFORMAL PROTOCOLS

Analogies 8/10

Inferences 6/7

Abby was able to answer inferential questions regarding a short orally presented passage with 85% accuracy when given moderate repetitions of the passage and extra time to think about her response.

STANDARDIZED ASSESSMENT PROCEDURES

For each test administered the following verifications were made:

- The test was selected and administered so as not to negatively discriminate on a racial or cultural basis.
- The test was provided and administered in the student's dominant language taking into consideration the impact of other languages on performance.
- The test was selected and administered so as best to ensure that when used with a student having impaired sensory, manual, or speaking skills, the test results accurately reflect the skills that the test purports to measure, rather than the student's impaired sensory, manual, or speaking skills, unless those skills are the factors being measured.
- The instrument is technically sound and provides relevant information.
- The test is validated for the specific purpose for which it was used.
- The test was administered by trained and knowledgeable personnel in accordance with any instructions provided by the producers of the test.

<table>
<tr><td>

THE RECEPTIVE ONE-WORD PICTURE VOCABULARY TEST (ROWPVT)

</td><td>

The student must select from four pictures the one that best represents a word spoken by the examiner to demonstrate understanding of single words.

Mean = 100, Standard Deviation = 15

Standard Score: 86

Confidence Band (90%) = 81-91

Interpretation/Comments: Compared to age expectations, single word receptive vocabulary is within expectancy range. Although test scores on the ROWPVT fell within the average range, Abby's standard score of 86 was a decrease in her receptive vocabulary compared to the score achieved 3 years previously. It should be noted that ROWPVT was one of the first standardized measures administered to Abby, and she required redirection during testing because she tried to check her answers. Her concern regarding her performance could explain the decline of her receptive vocabulary skills on the ROWPVT.

</td></tr>
<tr><td>

EXPRESSIVE ONE-WORD PICTURE VOCABULARY TEST REVISED (EOWPVT-R)

</td><td>

The student must name a picture of a thing, a category of things, or an action to show ability to express an idea with a single word.

Mean = 100, Standard Deviation = 15

Standard Score: 85

Confidence Band (90%) = 80-90

</td></tr>
</table>

Interpretation/Comments: Compared to age expectations, single word expressive vocabulary is within expectancy range. This is a slight decline from her previous speech and language reevaluation 3 years ago.

THE LISTENING
TEST

The Listening Test was administered to assess Abby's strengths and weaknesses in specific listening skill areas related to classroom listening situations. It is important to note that while this test measures areas related to classroom situations, it is administered in a one-to-one setting and, thus, does not represent the natural context of a classroom. The student is read a passage by the examiner and is required to answer questions pertaining to main ideas, details, concepts, reasoning, and story comprehension. There are no picture cues except for eight items on the Concepts Subtest. The test has a mean standard score of 100 and a standard deviation of 15. Abby earned the following scores:

Subtest	Standard Score
Main Idea	88
Details	79
Concepts	76
Reasoning	71
Story Comprehension	89
Total Test	77

Interpretation/comments: It was noted during testing that on several occasions Abby stated, "I forgot" and on one occasion she indicated, "I forgot the first part" after listening to an orally presented passage. Although repetition of the passage was not allowed, when a passage was repeated she was able to answer the question correctly. Strengths were noted in her ability to identify the main idea of a short passage read by the examiner. Another area of strength was her story comprehension. Story comprehension requires that a student use the following elements such as remembering details, main ideas, understanding concepts, and verbal reasoning, as well as attending and maintaining focus to the story. Although Abby did well with story comprehension, weaknesses were noted in her ability to listen for details and verbal reasoning skills. Abby also demonstrated difficulty on the subtest of classroom concepts. Allison was able to correctly complete the task with the exception of following directions on a map. Abby's total test score is statistically below average and indicates that she has weaknesses in her ability to listen for information when that information is presented solely in an auditory format.

CLINICAL
EVALUATION OF
LANGUAGE
FUNDAMENTALS III

This assessment compares receptive and expressive language skills. Receptive language subtests require that the student point to pictures and give oral responses to orally presented information to demonstrate skills in following oral directions, recognizing words which can be categorized, completing sentences with a word having the appropriate meaning questions about paragraph narratives. Expressive language subtests require the student to repeat sentences, formulate a sentence about a picture using a given word or set of words, and formulate a sentence from a scrambled set of words and phrases presented in writing and orally.

Subtest Mean = 10, Standard Deviation = 3

Composite and Test Mean = 100, Standard Deviation = 1 5

Subtest	Standard Score
Concepts and Directions	13
Word Classes	9
Semantic Relationships	11
* Listening to Paragraphs	9
RECEPTIVE LANGUAGE SCORE	106 Confidence Band (90%) = 98 to 114
Formulated Sentences	9
Recalling Sentences	6
Sentence Assembly	13

EXPRESSIVE LANGUAGE SCORE   96 Confidence Band (90 %) = 89 to 103

TOTAL LANGUAGE SCORE   101 Confidence Band (90%) = 95 to 107
Not included in calculation of receptive or total language scores.

Interpretation/Comments: Compared to age expectations, Abby's receptive and expressive language skills are within expectancy range. Strengths were noted in her ability to following multi-step directions containing concepts of inclusion/exclusion (e.g., all but), location (e.g., next to), sequence, condition (e.g., unless), and temporal concepts. It should be noted that she only missed two directions out of thirty on this subtest. Abby also demonstrated strength in her ability to rearrange given words to create semantically and syntactically correct sentences. Her success on the Sentence Assembly subtest suggests that Abby has good command of grammar and syntax. Her ability to establish relationships between words by part/whole, semantic class, synonym, and antonym while holding them in her memory fell within the average range. Furthermore, her ability to understand semantic relationships such as comparatives, spatial, temporal, sequential, and passive concepts also fell within the average range. In addition, Abby's ability to construct a semantically and syntactically correct sentence from a given word fell within the average range. Abby's ability to listen to an orally presented passage which included questions pertaining to main idea, detail, sequence, inference, and prediction also fell within the average range. The only questions that Abby demonstrated difficulty with were those related to detail, inference, and prediction. Weaknesses were noted in her ability to recall sentences of increasing length and complexity.

ARTICULATION ASSESSMENT

Observation and language sampling analysis indicated the continued presence of misarticulations. Standardized measures and informal measures were used to reassess speech intelligibility and articulation proficiency.

Goldman-Fristoe Test of Articulation was administered to assess Abby's articulation skills. Nondevelopmental errors included distortion of "r" and "s."

An examination of the oral peripheral mechanism indicated that Abby is able to perform movements for the production of speech sounds. Although Abby demonstrated mild difficulty elevating her tongue independently from her jaw, the structure and function is appropriate for speech production.

Summary

Abby was referred for a speech-language reassessment to answer diagnostic questions regarding should there be any modifications to current related services? Does she continue to present with a speech and language disorder? Analysis of assessment data in conjunction with the county public school's speech-language severity rating scale indicates that Abby continues to demonstrate a mild to moderate speech and language impairment with mild to moderate weaknesses in articulation skills and mild weaknesses in listening comprehension for details and reasoning tasks. Strengths exist in her comprehension of an orally presented passage, receptive single word vocabulary, expressive single word vocabulary, comprehension of concepts and directions and grammar, conversational skills, and fluency skills. Based on observations, this speech and language impairment negatively impacts educational progress in expressing ideas verbally in class and comprehending language.

Because the degree of educational impact is such that other educational resources cannot make adequate accommodations, it is recommended that the IEP team consider continued speech-language intervention to meet Abby's needs in the least restrictive environment.

Suggestions for Classroom Accommodations

The current pattern of strengths and weaknesses for this student indicates that the following instructional accommodations may be helpful:

- Demonstrate, model, and use gestures when giving directions or explaining content.
- Present information and directions orally and visually.
- Use visual aids to explain and model key points.
- Repeat what the student has said so that the student can judge its appropriateness and self-correct if necessary.
- Model correct production of the word.

Sample Language Treatment Progress Report (Completed at Speech-Language Center)

Beth is a 10 year, 2 month old girl with Down syndrome. She has been receiving therapy at this center since age two for the remediation of speech and language delays secondary to Down syndrome. She is currently enrolled in the 4th grade.

Beth presents as a friendly, interactive child who enjoys participating in activities at therapy, especially when they involve dolls or cooking. Beth's other favorite activities include arts and crafts projects and role play activities. She appears much more willing to participate in therapy when her dolls are involved in the activity.

Beth demonstrates a decrease in attention level when she is presented with a task that places a high level of demand on her. For example, she is not responsive when she is asked to choose her answer from a large set size of options (e.g., "find the picture that shows the worm beside the apple"). According to Reynell's levels of attention Beth displays an attention level of 6. This level recognizes the child as having fully integrated auditory, visual, and manipulatory channels. According to Blackstone's levels of play, she is functioning at the complex level of play. At this level, a child is able to relate several schemes in a sequence and includes dolls in the activities by giving them personalities and having them participate.

No formalized testing was administered at this time. Information regarding Beth's progress in therapy was obtained through clinical observation and parent observation in the home.

Goal 1. To improve receptive and expressive language skills in the areas of:
  a. Pronouns:
       Personal pronouns (I, we, he, she, they)
       Object pronouns (him, her)
       Possessive pronouns (his, hers)
  b. Concepts:
       Same/different
        Relational (in, out, on top of, beside, behind, etc.)
       Temporal (days of the week, months of the year)
       Order (first, second, third, fourth, fifth, etc.)
  c. Present Progressive Tense
       (to be + verb-ing)
  d. Past Tense (regular, irregular)

Progress—This goal has been targeted throughout most of the therapy sessions. During each task the clinician models and expands Beth's utterances, targeting correct use of pronouns, articles, days of the week, and months of the year.
  a. Pronouns: Beth's spontaneous language continues to reflect a limited use of pronouns. Pronouns and articles have been specifically targeted through cooking activities. Every session includes a cooking activity that specifically targets temporal concepts, pronouns, articles, nouns, and verbs. Every week Beth is given a sheet of paper that has eight pictures on it which describe the steps for completing the recipe. From these pictures, Beth tells the clinician what each step is ("First, we open the cookie dough"). At the beginning of the semester Beth's directions did not include the temporal concepts, pronouns, and articles ("open cookie dough"). With cues from the clinician and use of a visual aide (felt board with a color coded word system, red-temporal concepts {first, second, third...}, green-pronouns {I, We, them}, orange-articles {the, a}, yellow-nouns, blue-verbs), Beth is now consistently including pronouns in each step. This goal will continue to be targeted throughout therapy.

  b. Concepts: Order concepts (first, second, third) and cohesive terminology (then, next, after, that) have been targeted throughout the cooking activities along with pronouns. Beth sequences the steps of the recipe using these concepts by counting the number of pictures up to the picture she is currently working on (one, two, "third, we open the sauce"). Beth demonstrates the ability to sequence each step without the help of the clinician.

Temporal concepts (days of the week and months of the year) have been targeted through a variety of activities. Beth and the clinician made a train that included the days of the week in order from Sunday to Saturday. Beth demonstrates her ability to name the days of the week without difficulty. The days of the week will continue to be targeted in different ways other than strictly listing them in order (what day is before Monday, what is tomorrow, what day was yesterday, etc.). Months of the year have been targeted through books. Beth and the clinician made a calendar with each month representing a holiday or special birthdays. A book called *All Year Long* has also been used to help Beth sequence the months and match the pictures to the months that they represent. Beth is unable to list the months of the year in order but she has demonstrated the ability to recognize a few months that have specific meaning to her (November-her birthday, December-Christmas). These temporal concepts will continue to be targeted throughout therapy using several different activities such as a tape which will be sent home with Beth that contains a song on it called *Months of the Year.* Her ability to recognize same and different has been assessed and she showed no difficulty in this area.

c. and d. Verb Tense: This goal has not been specifically targeted this semester. Beth has not demonstrated the ability to use irregular past tense. For example, her sentence may say "Know how to cook these, before," rather than, "I made these before." Regular past tense and present progressive have not been used consistently and will continue to require remediation.

Goal 2. To increase length of utterance to a consistent 5 to 6 word level. Targeted structures will include:

Agent + action + article + object
"I am stirring the applesauce."
Agent + action + article + object + location
"I put the crayons into the box."

Time + agent + action + object
"First, I will sprinkle the cinnamon."

Progress—This goal has been targeted throughout the sessions during all cooking activities. In spontaneous conversation, Beth typically speaks in utterances of 3 to 6 words. She continues to demonstrate a limited use of personal pronouns, as well as errors in verb tense. However, through the use of the felt board (acting as a replacement for a pacing board) and clinician cuing, Beth has been able to expand her utterances and correct her errors.

Examples of Beth's spontaneous (S) and imitative (I) expressive language are as follows:

3 Words
I don't know. (S)
Where's the bag? (S)
I need "two." (S)
Have sodas then. (S)

4 Words
First, I need first. (S)
The piece of bread. (I)
Have a tea party. (I)
Help me here, ok. (S)

5 Words
First, we open the bag. (I)
When are open the cheese. (S)
I won't break the cheese. (S)

6 Words
One for mom, one for you. (S)
Know how to cook these, before. (S)
Yeah, looks like a silly duck. (S)

7 Words
I don't know, I can't find it. (S)

8 Words
Fifth, we put the cheese on the bread. (I)

9 Words
Second, we put the bread on the baking sheet. (I)

The following structures are present in Beth's utterances:

> Action + article + object + location + object
> "Put the bread in baking sheet."

> Time + agent + action + object
> "First, I need first."

The following structures are emerging in her language:

Present progressive	ing	(e.g., running)
Prepositions	in/on	
Regular plural	-s	(e.g., apples)
Possessive	's	(e.g., baby's)
Contractible copula		(That's a fly.)
Articles		(I won't break the cheese.)

The following structures are not used consistently and require remediation:

Regular past tense	(I learned that in 4th grade.)
Present progressive	(I am gluing the picture.)
Irregular past tense	(I made applesauce.)
Uncontractible copula	(Where is the bag?)

Goal 3. To improve Beth's ability to sequence and verbalize 5 to 6 step events of goal-oriented activities.

Progress—This goal has been targeted through goal-oriented cooking activities. As stated previously, visual cues (pictures for each step) are given to Beth to help her explain the steps of the recipe to the clinician. Beth's utterances have included a minimum of 3 words. However, with consistent cues from the clinician to include order concepts (first, second, third,) pronouns (I, we), and articles (the, a, and), Beth's length of utterance has increased to 5 to 8 words. She has been able to imitate the clinician's utterances with approximately 95% accuracy. After Beth and the clinician verbalize the step together, Beth places each word of the sentence on the felt board by herself and then repeats the sentence, including order concepts, pronouns, and articles. She is currently demonstrating the ability to view each picture and then start each sentence by herself (First, we…) without any cues from the clinician.

Goal 4. To improve pragmatic skills, specifically in the areas of requesting appropriate protesting, and eye-contact.

Progress—Beth spontaneously greets the clinician at the beginning of each session and typically remains verbally interactive throughout the session. She spontaneously establishes eye-contact and consistently maintains this eye-contact with the clinician. Beth has demonstrated topic initiating and topic maintenance skills, as she is able to maintain a topic over approximately 5 to 6 turns. She exhibits proper turn-taking skills by telling the clinician "No, you do it." Beth's requesting skills have improved. The clinician has had to provide her with prompts to elicit requests but she has demonstrated an increase in her ability to request items. For example, if when placing the words on the felt board, she can't find a word out of the set, she will reply by saying "Where's the sauce?" or "Where is it?" If she can't find the word she is looking for, Beth will point to one and then look at the clinician for a yes or no response. She will not verbally ask if that is the correct one. Beth continues to exhibit her dislike of a task by putting her head down, rolling her eyes, or by saying "Not this" or "That's weird."

Goal 5. To provide parents with information concerning speech and language development and techniques for stimulation in the home.

Progress—Beth's mother has been able to observe each session and can therefore implement at home the strategies and techniques demonstrated by the clinician. Materials from the cooking activities such as the picture cards with the sentences on them are sent home for Beth to review with her parents. A calendar has also been sent home so that Beth can continue to review the temporal concepts and increase carry-over.

RECOMMENDATIONS

It is recommended that Beth enroll in two 45-minute sessions of therapy per week for the remediation of speech and language difficulties secondary to Down syndrome. The therapy program at the Speech and Language Center will be coordinated with the school-based therapy program.

Comprehensive Language and Speech Treatment

The charts that follow outline areas that are often challenges for children with Down syndrome. Language and speech treatment should always be individualized. If your child has mastered a particular skill, it does not need to be addressed in therapy sessions.

Language Assessment and Treatment Planning in Early Elementary School

I. Receptive Language
   A. Comprehension
   B. Vocabulary and concept development

II. Auditory Memory
   A. Auditory processing
   B. Following complex directions
   C. Literacy

III. Expressive Language
   A. Semantics
   B. Expanding MLU
   C. Morphosyntax
   D. Answering questions
   E. Literacy/reading aloud

IV. School Language Skills
   A. Language of the curriculum
   B. Language of instruction
   C. Language of the hidden curriculum
   D. Language of testing
   E. Language of classroom routines

V. Pragmatics
   A. Requests
   B. Social interactive skills
   C. Conversational skills
   D. Narrative discourse

VI. Speech Areas (for more detailed information, see the form called *Evaluating Speech Intelligibility in School Age Children with Down Syndrome,* below)
   A. Articulation
   B. Phonology
   C. Oral motor skills
   D. Childhood Apraxia of Speech (if needed)
   E. Speech intelligibility

Language Assessment and Treatment Planning in Later Elementary School

I.   Receptive Language
    A. Comprehension
    B. Vocabulary and concept development
    C. Literacy

II. Auditory Memory
    A. Auditory processing
    B. *WH* questions (who, what, when, where, why)
    C. Following complex directions

III. Expressive Language
    A. Vocabulary
    B. Expanding MLU
    C. Morphosyntax
    D. Answering questions

IV. School Language Skills
    A. Language of the curriculum
    B. Language of instruction
    C. Language of the hidden curriculum
    D. Language of testing
    E. Language of classroom routines

V.   Pragmatics
    A. Requests
    B. Social interactive skills
    C. Conversational skills
    D. Narrative discourse
    E. Clarifications and repairs

VI. Speech Skills
    A. Articulation
    B. Phonology
    C. Oral motor skills
    D. Childhood Apraxia of Speech (if needed)
    E. Speech intelligibility

Language Assessment and Treatment Planning in Middle School

I.   Receptive Language
    A. Comprehension
    B. Vocabulary and concept development
    C. Literacy

II. Auditory Memory
    A. Auditory processing
    B. *Wh* questions (who, what, when, where, why)
    C. Following complex directions

III. Expressive Language
    A. Vocabulary
    B. Morphosyntax
    C. Answering questions
    D. Encoding/sentence formulation

IV. Pragmatics
    A. Requests
    B. Social interactive skills
    C. Conversational skills
    D. Narrative discourse
    E. Clarifications and repairs

V.   School Language Skills
    A. Language of the curriculum
    B. Language of instruction
    C. Language of the hidden curriculum
    D. Language of testing
    E. Language of classroom routines

VI. Speech Skills
    A. Articulation
    B. Phonology
    C. Oral motor skills
    D. Childhood Apraxia of Speech (if needed)
    E. Speech intelligibility

Evaluating Speech Intelligibility in School-Aged Children with Down Syndrome

This evaluation form can be used by the speech-language pathologist to ensure that he or she is looking at all the major issues that can affect speech intelligibility in children with Down syndrome. The parent survey following this form can be included as part of the speech intelligibility evaluation.

I. Anatomical Factors
- A. Lips
- B. Tongue
- C. Teeth/Occlusion
- D. Hard Palate
- E. Soft Palate
- F. Upper Jaw (maxilla)
- G. Lower Jaw (mandible)
- H. Oropharynx
- I. Nasopharynx
- J. Tonsils/Adenoids
- K. Larynx
- L. Ears

II. Physiological Factors
- A. Lip Posture/Movement
- B. Tongue Posture/Movement
- C. Palatal Movement
- D. Intra-Oral Air Pressure
- E. Velopharyngeal Closure
- F. Jaw Movement/Stability
- G. Trunk Stability
- H. Vocal Vibration
- I. Breath Control/Support
- J. Other
  - 1. Involuntary movements
  - 2. Drooling
  - 3. Tooth grinding (Bruxism)

III. Neurofunctional Level
- A. Neuromotor Component (Oral Motor)
- B. Childhood Verbal Apraxia (Motor Planning)
- C. Swallowing Pattern/Feeding Pattern
- D. Hearing

IV. Perceptual/Speech Symptoms
- A. Sound Errors
  - 1. Articulation
  - 2. Phonological Processes
- B. Voice
  - 1. Volume
  - 2. Pitch
  - 3. Voice Quality
- C. Resonance (Oral/Nasal Balance)
  - 1. Hyponasal
  - 2. Hypernasal

D. Rate
E. Fluency Pattern
  1. Repetitions
  2. Blocks
  3. Other Characteristics
F. Prosody (rhythm)

V. Pragmatic Language Factors
  A. Social Language Skills
  B. Conversational Skills
  C. Narrative Discourse Skills
  D. Other Language Factors

VI. Nonverbal Factors
  A. Eye Contact
  B. Gestures
  C. Facial Expressions
  D. Proxemics (distance)

VII. Language Message Factors
  A. Greetings
  B. Routine/Automatic Verbalizations
  C. Longer Verbalizations
  D. Complex Messages
  E. Other

VIII. External/Environmental Factors
  A. Visual
  B. Auditory
  C. Listener Variables
  D. Other

Copyright 2008 Libby Kumin, Ph.D., CCC-SLP

Down Syndrome Speech Intelligibility Parent Survey

Dr. Libby Kumin, Ph.D., CCC-SLP

This is a survey of the speech characteristics that parents observe in their child during the course of daily living. It can be used as part of the case history in a speech intelligibility evaluation. Parents can also fill it out and submit it to the IEP team, since IDEA requires that parents be allowed to provide information as part of the evaluation process. The SLP can use it to determine whether oral motor skills and Childhood Apraxia of Speech are affecting the child's speech.

Child's Name:_____   Today's Date:_____

Child's Birthdate: (Month/Day/Year) : _____

My child communicates by using (check all that apply):
- ❑ Speech
- ❑ Sign Language
- ❑ Pictures/Photos
- ❑ Communication Board
- ❑ High Tech Communication System
- ❑ Other: _____

My child began to speak at about (age):_____

On a scale of 1 to 10, where 1 is completely unintelligible and 10 is completely intelligible, how would you rate your child's speech? _____

Have you been told that your child has oral motor difficulties?   ❑ Yes   ❑ No

Have you been told that your child has apraxia or dyspraxia?   ❑ Yes   ❑ No

For each question, please check only ONE answer

	always	frequently	sometimes	never
1. People who know my child well have difficulty understanding his/her speech	❑	❑	❑	❑
2. People who first meet my child have difficulty understanding his/her speech	❑	❑	❑	❑
3. My child communicates primarily by using speech	❑	❑	❑	❑
4. When someone can't understand my child's speech, family members interpret for him or her	❑	❑	❑	❑

	always	frequently	sometimes	never
5. In infancy, my child made cooing sounds (single sounds)	❑	❑	❑	❑
6. In infancy, my child babbled strings of sounds	❑	❑	❑	❑
7. My child had difficulty sucking and swallowing liquids in infancy	❑	❑	❑	❑
8. My child had feeding difficulties when he/she started eating solid foods	❑	❑	❑	❑
9. My child currently has difficulties with swallowing liquids	❑	❑	❑	❑
10. My child currently has difficulties with feeding/ eating	❑	❑	❑	❑
11. My child had low tone in the muscles of the face (lips, tongue, cheeks) in infancy	❑	❑	❑	❑
12. My child currently has low tone in the muscles of the face (lips, tongue, cheeks)	❑	❑	❑	❑
13. My child was late (delayed) in beginning to speak	❑	❑	❑	❑
14. My child makes the same speech errors consistently	❑	❑	❑	❑
15. Sometimes, my child can say a word but at other times, my child has difficulty saying the same word	❑	❑	❑	❑
16. My child is understandable when he/she says single words, but has greater difficulty in conversation	❑	❑	❑	❑
17. My child uses a few sounds, but does not make many different sounds	❑	❑	❑	❑
18. My child can sing the words in songs more clearly than he/she can say them when speaking	❑	❑	❑	❑
19. My child shows very slow improvement in speech therapy	❑	❑	❑	❑

	always	frequently	sometimes	never
20. My child seems to be struggling so hard to say words and sounds	❏	❏	❏	❏
21. My child speaks rapidly	❏	❏	❏	❏
22. My child has fluency (stuttering-like) difficulties when speaking	❏	❏	❏	❏
23. My child has difficulty hearing	❏	❏	❏	❏
24. My child has more difficulty saying longer words than shorter words	❏	❏	❏	❏
25. My child has more difficulty speaking when he/she is using longer phrases or sentences	❏	❏	❏	❏
26. My child has difficulty saying some consonant sounds	❏	❏	❏	❏
27. My child has difficulty saying some vowel sounds	❏	❏	❏	❏
28. My child often reverses sounds in words (e.g., aminal for animal)	❏	❏	❏	❏
29. My child has difficulty with the rhythm of speech (speech sounds choppy, or sometimes slow and sometimes fast)	❏	❏	❏	❏
30. My child prolongs vowel sounds	❏	❏	❏	❏
31. My child leaves out sounds in words	❏	❏	❏	❏
32. My child leaves out syllables in words	❏	❏	❏	❏
33. My child's speech sounds hypernasal (as if it's coming through his/her nose)	❏	❏	❏	❏
34. My child talks less with people outside of the circle of friends and family	❏	❏	❏	❏
35. It is hard for my child to imitate a word that I say	❏	❏	❏	❏

	always	frequently	sometimes	never
36. My child's speech is easier to understand when he/she is saying familiar words	❏	❏	❏	❏
37. My child understands more than he/she can say	❏	❏	❏	❏
38. My child may unexpectedly say a word or phrase perfectly, but then he/she can't repeat it	❏	❏	❏	❏
39. My child has difficulty with grammar	❏	❏	❏	❏
40. My child is frustrated when people don't understand what he/she is saying	❏	❏	❏	❏

41. My child's voice sounds: __ breathy ____ hoarse ___ other _____

42. My child has difficulty saying his/her name   ❏ Yes   ❏ No

43. The sounds that are hard for my child to say are: *(check all that apply)*
    Consonants:

p	❏	b	❏	t	❏
d	❏	k	❏	g	❏
s	❏	z	❏	f	❏
v	❏				

    unvoiced th [thin, thick] ❏   voiced th [this, that] ❏

sh	❏	zh [Asia] ❏		ch	❏
j [judge] ❏		r	❏	y	❏

    Vowels:

a	❏	e	❏	i	❏
o	❏	u	❏		

Sample Diagnostic Speech Evaluation (Completed at a Speech & Language Center)

Identification

Bobby is the 6-year-old son of Robert and Joan Smith. Bobby was diagnosed at birth with Down Syndrome. He was seen for a diagnostic evaluation at the Speech and Language Center to determine the cause of his speech unintelligibility. He was accompanied by both parents at the evaluation.

Bobby currently attends kindergarten where he receives speech and language therapy, occupational therapy, and has an IEP in place.

Reason For Referral

Bobby was referred to the Speech and Language Center for a diagnostic evaluation due to parental concerns that his speech is unintelligible most of the time. It was reported in the case history that Bobby does well articulating single words and repeats individual words clearly when instructed. However, he has difficulty in phrasing, syntax, and intelligibility in a conversation. His parents were also concerned that Bobby may have childhood verbal apraxia.

Medical History

According to the case history completed by Bobby's parents, he was born following a 35 week pregnancy with normal delivery. He weighed 5 lb. 12 oz. His general health at birth included polycythemia, hyperbilirubinemia, and hypothyroidism, all of which resolved or were treated appropriately. He had moderate GERD within his first year, which was treated and resolved with growth.

It was reported in the case history that Bobby had a history of otorreah in his left ear, as well as the insertion of middle ear tubes bilaterally at 18 months and 4 years. He has experienced chronic ear infections, sinusitis, and pneumonia. Bobby's hearing was tested and was found to be in the range of borderline normal to very mild hearing loss. He has some vision difficulties and has been wearing glasses since the age of 3.

Developmental History

As reported in the case history. Bobby began sitting at 9 months of age, and walking at 18 months of age. He has toileted independently since the age of 4.5 years. His parents reported he eats and sleeps well. They are currently seeking more information and testing regarding a possible diagnosis of sleep apnea. Bobby is right handed.

Speech And Language History

According to case history information, parental report, and formalized test results, both Bobby's receptive and expressive language skills are delayed. According to results from the Preschool Language Scale 3 (PLS-3), as reported on the school Speech-Language Therapy report, his expressive language age equivalent is 1 year, 5 months. It was reported that this score does not reflect responses that were signed or understood by the examiner due to familiarity. It was reported that Bobby has a minimal vocabulary of about 20 words and 50 signs. His words are typically approximations for the initial consonant sound. Mother reported that Bobby will sometimes put signs together such as signing "more juice," as well as pairing word approximations with his signs.

According to results from the PLS-3 (IEP, 2004), Bobby's receptive language equivalent is 1 year, 7 months. According to the Communication report by the school's Speech-Language Pathologist, he demonstrated the following receptive language skills: following directions for participation, understanding intent of a message, and is able to recall information from a storybook.

Behavioral Observation

Bobby presented as an energetic, happy, and playful child who did not appear to have difficulty in separating from his parents. He engaged in play in the motor room with the clinicians (e.g., car, slide, and swing). Bobby was cooperative during the oral motor exam. It was reported that his social skills appear to be a relative strength for him, although he has developed better interaction skills with adults than with children. Previous behavior observations of Bobby by his parents and teachers indicated that although he is passive with peers at times, he is strong-willed when interacting with adults.

Level of Attention

According to Reynell's levels of Attention Bobby demonstrated level 3 attentional skills, which is characterized by single channeled attention, meaning Bobby did not attend to auditory and visual stimuli from different sources at the same time. He demonstrated the ability to shift full attention between the speaker (e.g., clinician, parent) and the task (e.g., game, activity) with the help of the speaker (e.g., prompt to "look" or said his name). He demonstrated this while drinking water from a cup. While he was drinking, the clinician asked him if he would like an cracker and he did not respond. When the clinician said his name first, and then asked the question, he looked at the clinician and responded appropriately.

Level of Play

According to Blackstone's Levels of Play, Bobby demonstrated representational play skills. He was aware of self pretending (e.g., riding in a "car") and stacked a tower out of blocks. He also took part in activities that involved his own body; for example he went down the slide, through a tunnel, and on the swing. It was reported on the Vineland Adaptive Behavior Scales (VABS), interview edition, that Bobby's parents indicated that he participates in at least one game/activity with others, plays make-believe, and shares toys without being told to.

Assessment Results

The following information concerning Bobby's present level of performance was obtained through formalized assessment using *The Apraxia Profile* and *The Clinical Assessment of Articulation and Phonology (CAAP),* informal assessment, using the Down Syndrome Childhood Verbal Apraxia survey, informal observations, and parental report during a one day, two hour diagnostic evaluation.

Parent Interview

Bobby was described as a child who was delayed in speaking, and who struggles to say words and sounds. Parent report indicated that he began to speak at 3 years of age. Parents rated Bobby's unintelligibility as a 5 on a 10 point scale, with 1 being completely unintelligible. Parent report stated he often reverses sounds and syllables, omits the sounds at the beginning or end of words, demonstrates difficulty imitating words, and struggles to say words or sounds. Bobby's parents explained that his speech is easier to understand when he is using familiar words (e.g., milk), although others often have a difficult time understanding what he is saying. Parents completed the Down Syndrome Childhood Verbal Apraxia survey. The results of the survey were reviewed and discussed in detail with them.

Parents described Bobby's primary method of communication as speech. Parent report indicated he is able to understand more than he can say. Bobby presents with low tone in the muscles of the face (lips, tongue, and cheeks). No difficulty with movements and coordination of the muscles in the facial area was described by his parents. He was able to suck and swallow liquids as an infant. He was described as a healthy eater who eats well-balanced meals.

The results of the parent interview and the Down Syndrome Childhood Verbal Apraxia survey indicate that Bobby displays a profile consistent with characteristics of childhood verbal apraxia. His speech production includes unintelligibility, inconsistencies, omission of initial consonants, and the inability to imitate.

Formal Assessment

The Clinical Assessment of Articulation and Phonology (CAAP) is a formal assessment used to assess a child's articulation and phonology at the preschool and school-aged levels. It does so at the singleton consonant level, multsyllabic level consonant cluster level, and at the sentence level. During the diagnostic evaluation, administration of the test was interrupted twice so as to allow Bobby to have a motor break.

PART I: SYLLABLE STRUCTURE PROCESSES

In assessing syllable structure processes, Bobby's verbal language skills were assessed according to the presence or absence of final consonant deletion, cluster reduction, and syllable reduction. Words from the consonant singleton were assessed and then scored according to the CAAP checklist. The results show no occurrence of postvocalic voicing in his speech.

Words taken from the cluster words list and the multisyllabic words list were assessed and then scored according to the CAAP checklist. The results show a 78% occurrence of cluster reduction in Bobby's speech. For example, in the word, "bridge," he omitted the initial /r/. In the words "clown" and "glove," Bobby omitted the initial /1/.

Words from the multisyllabic words list were assessed and then scored according to the CAAP checklist. The results show that Bobby has a 44% occurrence of syllable reduction. For example, in the word "computer" he omitted the middle syllable /pju/.

PART II: SUBSTITUTION PROCESSES

In assessing substitution processes, Bobby's verbal language skills were assessed according to the presence or absence of gliding, vocalization (i.e., a syllable or postvocalic liquid replaced by a vowel), fronting of velars or palatals, deaf frication, and stopping. Words taken from the consonant singletons list, the cluster words list, and the multisyllabic words list were assessed and then scored according to the CAAP checklist. The results show no occurrence of postvocalic voicing in his speech.

Words from the consonant singleton word list, the cluster words list, and the multisyllabic words list were assessed and scored according to the CAAP checklist. The results show a 40% occurrence of fronting in Bobby's speech. In the word "gate," he replaced a palatal phoneme with an alveolar (/d/ for /g/). The results show a 20% occurrence of stopping in Bobby's vocabulary. In words such as "jar" and "cheese," he replaced the initial /j/ with a /d/ and the initial /ch/ with a /t/.

PART III: ASSIMILATION PROCESSES

In assessing assimilation processes, Bobby's verbal language skills were tested according to the presence or absence of prevocalic voicing and postvocalic devoicing. Words from the consonant singleton word list, the cluster words list, and the multisyllabic words list were assessed and scored according to the CAAP checklist. The results show a 25% occurrence of prevocalic voicing. In words such as "pig" and "computer," Bobby replaced the initial voiceless /p/ with a voiced /b/.

PART IV: OVERALL

Overall, the results of the CAAP test given to Bobby give the following results:

1. A consonant inventory score of 37, giving him a standard score of 55. This places him in the 1 percentile rank with an age equivalency of 2.9.
2. A school-age sentences score of 63, giving him a standard score of 55. This places him in the 1 percentile rank with an age equivalency of 5.
3. The consonant inventory scores and school-age sentences scores validate the need for intervention.
4. Bobby's speech exhibits the presence of the following phonological processes more than or equal to 40% of the time: cluster reduction, syllable reduction, and fronting.

RESULTS OF THE APRAXIA PROFILE

The Apraxia Profile is an assessment tool for children that identifies and describes the apraxic component in speech. The information obtained from this tool assists in the determination of a child's level of functioning and the most appropriate place to begin intervention. This assessment is also beneficial in describing a child's specific motor sequencing errors.

PART I: ORAL MOTOR EXAM

A. **Automatic Oral Movements:** Bobby performed most of the automatic oral movements with ease. Minimal drooling was observed when he was leaning on the table and concentrating on various tasks. Food pocketing was not observed during the eating/swallowing task. Parental report indicated that Bobby displays drooling. He received a score of 5/5 on this section.

B. **Volitional Oral Movements-Nonverbal:** Although Bobby was able to perform all of the lip movements upon imitation, his lip retracting and rounding were not at their maximal potential. There was no asymmetry noted during this task. He received a score of 3 /4 on the nonverbal imitated lip movements. He exhibited groping behavior when sticking his tongue straight out and moving his tongue from side to side. He received a score of 2/3 for the nonverbal imitated tongue movements. His overall score for volitional oral movements-nonverbal was 5/7.

C. **Volitional Oral Movements-Verbal:** Bobby successfully imitated all of the verbal lip movements. He received a score of 5/5 on the imitated verbal lip movements. He imitated all of the verbal tongue movements except raising his tongue tip to his alveolar ridge for /t/ and touching the back of the tongue to his velum for /g/. Additionally, he did not maintain appropriate tongue posture for airflow on the /sh/, resulting in a distorted sound. Bobby earned a 2/5 for the verbal imitated tongue movements and an overall score of 7/10 on the volitional oral movements-verbal.

PART II: WORDS

A. **Word Repetition:** Bobby produced 50 words on imitation for this section. The words ranged from simple 1-syllable words (e.g., boy) to complex 5-syllable words (e.g., refrigerator). He produced 30% (15/50) of the words accurately. Bobby omitted phonemes from his speech. Omission errors found in his speech include syllable deletion and consonant cluster reduction. Bobby produced a wide range of phonemes but he had many misarticulations. The chart below summarizes the substitution and omission errors to Bobby's speech. As seen in the table, Bobby's errors were not consistent in all phonemic contexts.

Phoneme	Initial	Medial	Final	Blends
/p/				
/b/	/d/ and /h/			/br/ = /b/
/h/	/l/			
/d/			omitted	
/n/			omitted	
/f/	/b/	/p/		
/v/	/b/		omitted and /d/	
/j/	/th/			
/l/	/w/ and /b/	/d/		
/r/	/b/	omitted		
Th (voiceless)			omitted	
th		/d/		
/s/	omitted	/p/ and omitted	/t/	/sk/ = omitted
/z/		/th/ voiceless		
/sh/	/s/	omitted		
/t ch/	/th/ and /s/			
/d g/	omitted			
ing			omitted	

PART III: PHRASES AND SENTENCES

For this section, Bobby was asked to repeat 2 and 3 word sentences with the same prosody as the experimenter. Prosodic features included happy/sad, fast/slow, question/statement, and varying syllabic stress. Bobby repeated 6/20 sentences with the experimenter's prosody. His intelligibility decreased during this section. He often omitted small words, such as "the" or "and" within the phrase. Additionally, he would tend to only repeat back the last couple sounds or the last word out of the phrase. This may be related to sound production ability, hearing loss, or auditory memory difficulties.

PART IV: CONNECTED SPEECH SAMPLE

A connected speech sample was obtained as Bobby interacted with the experimenter during the testing session. His intelligibility significantly decreased during conversational speech. When the context was not known, his intelligibility was poor. When the context was known, his intelligibility was fair. He typically spoke in 1-2 word sentences. He had an MLU (mean length of utterance) of 1.28 morphemes per utterance. He was 52% intelligible during the connected speech sample. Bobby's intelligibility rating may be inflated due to his use of short utterances (the intelligible utterances were mostly one word responses). Additionally, 4 utterances consisted of counting numbers which could be a task that is repeated on a daily basis. He became highly unintelligible as his utterances expanded in length. Bobby's volume was soft for the speaking environment. His prosody appeared to be within normal limits.

PART V: APRAXIA CHARACTERISTICS CHECKLIST

This checklist consists of 49 characteristics typically seen in children with Childhood Apraxia of Speech. The first 10 characteristics are considered to be most significant to a diagnosis of apraxia. Bobby demonstrated 8/10 applicable characteristics of apraxia, yielding a score of 80%. He received a score of 55% on the entire checklist. These results indicate that approximately half of Bobby's intelligibility difficulties may be attributed to an apraxia component.

SUMMARY

Bobby presents with a moderate Childhood Apraxia of Speech evidenced by difficulty producing imitated nonverbal oral movements and decreased intelligibility as sentence length increases. In connected speech, his intelligibility is poor. Bobby's use of phonological processes also contributes to his unintelligibility. Although this test was designed to identify characteristics of apraxia, a dysarthric component in his speech was also noted.

Informal Assessment

Data collected during play activities was used. Bobby was observed playing with a basketball net, building blocks, on the swing, and on the slide.

RECEPTIVE

Bobby appeared to understand more than he could produce. During play activities, Bobby imitated the clinicians' actions such as throwing balls in the basketball net, building blocks on top of one another, and pushing a toy car. He followed 1 step directions given by the clinicians. For example, "Go down the slide" and "sit in the swing." He demonstrated an understanding of the concepts "hi" and "bye."

EXPRESSIVE

Bobby presented with multiple articulation errors during play. He omitted sounds or syllables (e.g., /Ing/ for "swing"). He did not distort vowel sounds. Many of his speech errors were inconsistent. He appeared to struggle when saying a single word or sound.

Intelligibility

Bobby's intelligibility was judged to be poor in both known and unknown contexts. His spontaneous length of utterance was observed as 1 word or syllable. Bobby demonstrated difficulty with rhythm, stress, and intonation in his voice. He used a few gestures and signs to assist the listener, while in the motor room, in inferring meaning when he was unintelligible. Bobby did not use connected speech; thus, his rate of speech was not measurable. According to parent report, he has demonstrated slow progress acquiring intelligible sounds in therapy.

Oral Motor Examination

Bobby's oral motor skills were informally assessed through an Oral-Facial Examination. Examination of oral-facial structures was completed with Bobby sitting in a chair across from the clinicians. Bobby demonstrated a slight open mouth posture at rest with tongue protrusion. He performed the following oral movements using his lips: puckering and blowing air. He was observed throughout the session opening and closing his jaw with ease. A slight clicking noise, as well as some teeth grinding, was observed. Intra-oral exam showed pink and white tissue, Class I occlusion, normal bite, and good dental hygiene. The vault and width of the hard palate was high and narrow. Appearance of the soft palate was symmetrical. Retraction for "ah" was equal. Closure at the velopharynx appeared complete. Palatine tonsils and uvula also appeared normal. Bobby demonstrated a tight lip seal with his bottom lip around the mouth of the bottle and his upper lip placed slightly on the edge. No leakage of the liquid was observed during bottle drinking.

Summary

Bobby is a 6-year-old boy with Down syndrome. He was seen at the Speech and Language Center to diagnose the cause of his speech intelligibility difficulties. Results from formal and informal assessment indicate Bobby displays a profile consistent with characteristics of Childhood Apraxia of Speech as well as speech containing phonological processing errors.

Diagnosis

The results of assessment indicate that Childhood Apraxia of Speech is affecting Bobby's speech, resulting in decreased speech intelligibility. Bobby has severe developmental receptive and expressive language difficulties secondary to Down syndrome. This delay has been documented in previous diagnostic evaluations, and documented in the IEP. The same difficulties were also observed at today's evaluation. However, speech was the focus of the present diagnostic evaluation. Bobby's oral motor abilities and CAS are affecting his speech intelligibility.

Recommendations

The following services and/or resources are recommended:

1. Speech-language pathology services are needed to address Childhood Apraxia of Speech which is negatively impacting on Bobby's speech intelligibility. A speech-language pathology treatment program should address:
    a. Intelligibility in multisyllabic words
    b. Intelligibility in longer phrases and sentences
    c. Phonological processes (i.e., cluster reduction, syllable reduction, and fronting (Velar and Palatal))
    d. Continued exercises to improve the strength and mobility of Bobby's articulators
2. Practice at home. Plans for a home-school communication program and a home practice program need to be included in the IEP. Consider the implementation of an apraxia treatment program, such as *Easy Does It for Apraxia: Preschool,* in Bobby's speech and language treatment program.

Resources that the speech-language pathologist and the family might find helpful are included below.

Resources

a. www.apraxia-kids.org by the Childhood Apraxia of Speech Association (The Bruce and Patricia Hendrix Foundation, 1997-2006)
b. *Easy Does It for Apraxia: Preschool* by Robin Strode & Catherine Chamberlain (Lingui Systems, 1994)
c. *Kaufman Speech Praxis Treatment Kit* by Nancy R. Kaufman, M.A., CCC-SLP (NSS-NRS, 1995)
d. *Becoming Verbal and Intelligible* by Kathleen E. Dauer, Sandra S. Irwin, and Sandra R. Schippits (Super Duper Publications)
e. *Oral Motor Activities for Young Children* by Elizabeth Mackie (LinguiSystems, 1996)

Speech Intelligibility Treatment Program Plan for Children with Down Syndrome

Name: _____   Date of Birth: _____

A comprehensive treatment plan for an individual with Down syndrome may include any of the following as needed.

    I. Exercise Programs
        A. Oral motor muscle strengthening
            1. Which structures and muscles? _____
            2. Strength
            3. Range of motion
            4. Graded movements
        B. Intervention for feeding problems
            1. Chewing
            2. Swallowing
        C. Intervention for tongue thrust/swallowing problems
            1. Lips
            2. Tongue
            3. Swallowing

    II. Muscle Programming and Coordination Level
        A. Intervention for Childhood Apraxia of Speech
            Program used: _____

    III. Speech Production Level
        A. Treatment for articulation
            1. Targeted sounds: _____
            2. Program used: _____
        B. Treatment for phonological processes
            1. Targeted processes: _____
            2. Program used: _____
        C. Treatment for volume and loudness
            1. Can child produce adequate volume?
            2. Is volume appropriate to the situation?
        D. Voice therapy
            1. Targeted difficulties
            2. Approaches used
        E. Treatment for resonance (oral/nasal balance)
            1. Hyponasality
            2. Hypernasality
            3. Approaches used: _____

F. Rate control
    1. Too fast
    2. Too slow
    3. Mixed
G. Treatment for prosody
    1. Monotone
    2. Other difficulties
    3. Approaches used
H. Fluency therapy
    1. Blocks
    2. Repetitions
    3. Describe dysfluencies
    4. Approaches used

IV. Pragmatic/Language Level
    A. Treatment for nonverbal factors
        1. Eye contact
        2. acial expressions
        3. Gestures
    B. Language skills that affect intelligibility
        1. Complexity of messages
    C. Conversational skills
        1. Insufficient turns
        2. Topicalization
        3. Conversation can't be understood
    D. Narrative discourse skills
        1. Includes pertinent facts
        2. Uses correct sequencing
        3. Goes off topic/irrelevant facts
        4. Length of story (too short or long)
V. Assistive Technology Needs
    A. Augmentative communication for classroom use
    B. Augmentative communication for general use
    C. Assistive listening devices

VI. Supports and Modifications Needed

VII. Referrals Needed
    A. Otolaryngologist (ENT)
    B. Audiologist
    C. Neurologist
    D. Psychologist
    E. Feeding specialist
    F. Other

Home-School Language Report

Child's Name: _____ Today's Date: _____

We are working on (check all that apply):
   ❏ Vocabulary   ❏ Morphosyntax   ❏ Following instructions
   ❏ Wh questions   ❏ Other (specify): _____

Therapy Targets This Week: _____

_____

_____

_____

Progress and Difficulties: _____

_____

_____

_____

Please work on the following at home: _____

_____

_____

_____

Home Practice Activities: _____

_____

_____

_____

Progress and Difficulties: _____

_____

_____

_____

Home-School Speech Report

Child's Name: _____ Today's Date: _____

We are working on (check all that apply):
- ❏ Articulation
- ❏ Oral motor skills
- ❏ Phonology
- ❏ Other (specify): _____

Therapy Targets This Week: _____
_____
_____
_____

Progress and Difficulties: _____
_____
_____
_____

Home Practice Activities: _____
_____
_____
_____

Progress and Difficulties: _____
_____
_____
_____

Index

Page numbers in italics indicate tables.

About the Author

Libby Kumin, Ph.D., CCC-SLP, is a professor in the Department of Speech-Language Pathology/Audiology at Loyola University in Maryland, where she founded the Down Syndrome Center for Excellence. She is the author of *EARLY COMMUNICATION SKILLS FOR CHILDREN WITH DOWN SYNDROME* and *CLASSROOM LANGUAGE SKILLS FOR CHILDREN WITH DOWN SYNDROME,* and the writer and producer of a DVD, *WHAT DID YOU SAY?*, all published by Woodbine House. A frequent speaker at professional and parent conferences across the country, Dr. Kumin works extensively with infants, toddlers, children, adolescents, and adults with Down syndrome and their families.